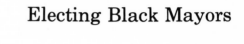

Electing Black Mayors

ELECTING
BLACK MAYORS

Political Action

in the Black Community

William E. Nelson, Jr., and Philip J. Meranto

Ohio State University Press: Columbus

Library of Congress Cataloging in Publication Data

Nelson, William E
  Electing Black mayors.
  Includes index.
  1. Afro-American mayors—Case studies. 2. Afro-Americans—Politics and
suffrage—Case studies. 3. Elections—Ohio—Cleveland. 4. Elections—Illinois
—East St. Louis. 5. Elections—Indiana—Gary.
I. Meranto, Philip J., joint author. II. Title.
JS395.N45   329'.023'730923   76-51347

Contents

Tables

Electing Black Mayors

Introduction

Future historians of American society will no doubt characterize the 1960s as a decade of unusual social change and dislocation. This characterization will be particularly striking if the past decade is contrasted with the 1950s, which was a decade largely devoted to celebrating the achievements and cohesiveness of America. If compared, it is apparent that the intensive turmoil and strife that emerged during the 1960s completely shattered the complacency and smugness of the 1950s. Those social commentators who maintained that America's most pressing problem in an age of non-ideological conflict was the management of affluence found their interpretations rudely undermined by the unprecedented conflict surrounding black liberation, women's liberation, the persistence of American poverty, the operation of American universities, the waging of the Vietnam War, and American foreign policy in general. The eruption of widespread civil disorder in black ghettos and on university campuses plus the outbreak of urban guerrilla terrorism made it abundantly clear that America is not a society that has reached consensus on the major issues of human life.

There are, of course, many complicated factors that have contributed to these developments. Included in virtually all explanations, however, is the spector of the world's most materially affluent nation utilizing its abundant resources to heap violence on a small country halfway around the earth and to send men to the moon while between one-fourth and one-fifth of its own people are condemned to a life of hopeless poverty. How and why the American political system produces such results is one of the most fundamental issues that has emerged in recent times.

Among the major contributing factors to the tension and conflict pervading contemporary American society has been the quest of black Americans, who constitute a large segment of the poverty stricken, to break the chains of economic, social, and political poverty. During the 1960s this quest was articulated through a revitalized civil rights movement that mobilized thousands of protest actions to secure "freedom now" for black Americans; however, by the mid-1960s, it became apparent to many civil rights activists that despite their efforts the goals of integration and equality remained extremely elusive for the overwhelming bulk of black people. As a result of this frustration and a growing understanding of power relationships in American society, a new dimension of black struggle emerged in the summer of 1966. During a civil rights march across Mississippi a young black leader of the Student Non-violent Coordinating Committee (SNCC), Stokely Carmichael, urged that blacks shift from an emphasis on civil rights to "black power." What Carmichael and other SNCC members meant by the concept of black power stimulated much controversial discussion and many interpretations among both blacks and whites. The term continues to carry a variety of interpretations; however, there are some fundamental aspects that have been widely accepted within black liberation circles. These aspects include: (1) the quest for a political organization that speaks directly for blacks and represents their needs and interests; (2) reconstruction of the black community and its identity, with an emphasis on racial pride and self-esteem; (3) the development of a sense of community and group cohesion; (4) the development of black organizations controlled by blacks, before any coalitions can be formed with whites; (5) black control for full participation in the decision-making processes of institutions that shape the lives of black people; (6) the need for whites to work in their own communities in order to fight the racism that exists there; and (7) the right to self-defense, due to the ineffectiveness of nonviolent tactics in situations where blacks are physically threatened.[1] An important ingredient of this concept holds that "where black people have a majority, they will attempt to use power to exercise control. That is what they seek: control."[2]

A year after the emergence of black power as a concept, the nation witnessed what many commentators and black citizens identified as prime examples of the notion: the election of blacks to the mayorship in two major cities of the urban North. In 1967 Richard G. Hatcher became the first black mayor of Gary, Indiana, and Carl B. Stokes became the first black mayor of Cleveland, Ohio. These black electoral victories carried a double meaning. On the one hand, they represented the end product of a major effort by blacks to gain control of the highest governmental office in a particular locale.[3] These victories also signaled, in the opinion of the authors, the beginnings of a new historical era in northern urban politics. We suggest that the history of the urban North can be broadly divided into three phases: (1) occupation of high municipal offices by white Anglo-Saxons; (2) the wresting away of this occupation during the 1930s by representatives of European ethnic groups; and (3) the initial ascendance of black officials in the late 1960s and the growth of black controlled offices throughout the 1970s and thereafter.

This study concentrates on analyzing the beginnings of the third phase. An effort is made to deal with several fundamental questions. First, given the harsh social, economic, and political obstacles blacks have faced in this country, how did they overcome these obstacles and successfully mobilize for victory in Gary and Cleveland? Second, how did the white communities in these cities react to the black thrust for the mayorship? Third, what happened when Hatcher and Stokes took office—were they able to solve the critical problems of the black community? Fourth, how does the election of black mayors relate to the general struggle for black liberation? Finally, we seek to shed light on the crucial question of the value and role of electoral politics in the process of black liberation.

To answer the questions raised above we engaged in extensive field research in Gary, Indiana, Cleveland, Ohio, and East Saint Louis, Illinois. Field research in Gary and Cleveland involved primarily the conducting of a series of oral interviews with select groups of citizens. The interviews were conducted between October 1968 and March 1969. Primary respondents were persons who had played active roles in the Hatcher and Stokes campaign organizations. These respondents were chosen in the following manner. One individual from each city who held an official position in the campaign organizations of the two black mayoral candidates was asked to supply an initial list of names of other persons who had played active roles in these organizations. Letters were sent to each of these individuals requesting an interview. Individuals who held formal positions in the campaign organizations were interviewed first. Each of these respondents, and each subsequent respondent, was asked during the interview to supply the names of others who had played active roles in the campaign organizations. Through this process of cross selection based on designations as "active participants" made by interview respondents a universe of forty-eight active campaign participants in Gary and forty active participants in Cleveland was obtained.[4] Interviews were conducted with forty-four Hatcher campaign workers in Gary and thirty-eight Stokes campaign workers in Cleveland. A special effort was made to contact all of the persons identified as active participants in Gary and Cleveland. Not a single person whom we were able to contact turned down our request for an interview. The four persons in Gary and two persons in Cleveland not interviewed—none of whom played crucial roles—could not be reached during the period in which interviews were conducted in the two cities.

Two additional sets of interviews were done in Gary and Cleveland. One of these involved interviews with the officers of prominent community organizations and other individuals singled out as being unusually knowledgable about civic and social activities in the two cities. Thirteen such persons were interviewed in Gary and twelve in Cleveland.

The other set of interviews involved conversations with members of the regular Democratic and Republican organizations in Gary and Cleveland. Following essentially the same procedure as that used to identify key actors in the Hatcher and Stokes campaigns, fourteen leading party figures in Gary and twelve in Cleveland were interviewed. Through these interviews, data were collected on subjects such as the development of party organizations in Gary and Cleveland, demographic changes in the black and white communities, the reaction of major party organizations to the growing electoral strength of the black community, and the reaction of party officials to the mobilization effort mounted in the black community in the 1967 mayoral campaign.

Formal interview schedules were used and each respondent in each set of interviews was asked approximately the same questions. Questions included in the interview schedule were mainly of the open-ended variety, permitting respondents full freedom to express opinions on issues raised. Separate interview schedules were used for campaign workers, community leaders, and party officials. A list of key questions was also composed for interviews with the black mayoral candidates in Gary and Cleveland.

All but four of the interviews conducted in Gary and Cleveland were recorded on tape. The length of the campaign-worker interview was approximately three hours, although several ran considerably longer. Interviews with community leaders and party officials ran an average of one hour. When all of the interviews were completed, long-hand transcriptions were made. Repeated checks on transcriptions were made in order to assure that the interview data used in the analysis were as accurate as possible.

Field research in East Saint Louis was conducted in the fall of 1967 and spring of 1968 by members of the Public Administration and Metropolitan Affairs Program, Southern Illinois University. One of the authors was a member of this research team. Interviews were conducted with key participants in campaign organizations established to work for candidates in the 1967 mayoral election as well as other individuals who had traditionally been actively involved in social and civic affairs.[5] Research in East Saint Louis also involved extensive examination of newspaper files, and the collection of historical and demographic data from public and private sources.

In order to treat questions relating to the election of black mayors, the study in this volume has been divided into three parts. Part one concentrates on illuminating problems blacks have traditionally faced in their efforts to mobilize for effective political action in the electoral process. Emphasis is on the social, economic, and political factors that make the surmounting of obstacles to effective political mobilization more difficult for blacks today than for European ethnics at an earlier period. As a means of illustrating the unique barriers to black political mobilization, an analysis of the 1967 mayoral election in East Saint Louis, Illinois, is included. The East Saint Louis case study is intended to show that obstacles to black mobilization continue to exist and affect the exercise of black political power even when blacks constitute a majority of the electorate.

Part two contains two extensive case studies of successful black political mobilization that eventuated in the election of black mayors in Cleveland, Ohio, and Gary, Indiana. Detailed accounts are included to illustrate how the black communities in both of these cities were mobilized to produce record-high voting turnouts and voting cohesion for black mayoral candidates.

Part three focuses on two concluding topics. First, what are the key variables in the black mobilization process? Under what conditions are blacks likely to secure control of high municipal offices and under what conditions are they likely to fail? The final two chapters discuss the impact and implications of successful mobilization efforts. Does the election of a black mayor make any significant differences in the life situation of the black masses? Is the electoral process capable of resolving the grievances of blacks in American society? If not, are there relevant alternative approaches?

We are deeply indebted to the numerous people in East Saint Louis, Gary, and Cleveland who granted us interviews concerning their understanding and experiences in the politics of those cities. Financial and administrative support for our research was provided by the Institute of Public Administration and Urban Affairs at Southern Illinois University, and the Institute of Government and Public Affairs and Department of Political Science at the University of Illinois. In addition, we are indebted to the following individuals for their assistance and support: Samuel R. Gove, Phillip Moneypenny, Joseph Piscotte, Seymour Mann, Elliot Rudwig, David Ranney, Jane Altes, Robert Mendelson, Curtina Moreland, James T. Jones, James Holland, and Emma and Milton Sutton. In addition, we are grateful for the extraordinary clerical assistance provided by Jean Baker, Yolanda Robinson, Faith Teitlebaum, and Penny Martin. We wish to dedicate this study to Della and Nicholas Fanon Nelson, and to Bruce Sidel, a special friend who gave his life in the struggle for human freedom.

1. See the position paper of SNCC, "The Basis of Black Power" that appeared in the *New York Times*, 5 August 1966; Charles V. Hamilton, "An Advocate of Black Power Defines It," *New York Times Magazine*, 14 April 1966; Stokely Carmichael and Charles V. Hamilton, *Black Power: The Politics of Liberation in America* (New York: Vintage, 1967).

2. Carmichael and Hamilton, *Black Power*, p. 46.

3. The extent to which the election of a black mayor constitutes control of a city is the central focus of our discussion in Part 3 of this study.

4. By "active" here, we mean individuals who had worked in both the primary and general campaign organizations on a continuous and formal basis. Our basic strategy was to interview committee chairmen and other campaign officials first, and then move on to interview other individuals identified to us through multiple designations as key campaign workers. Among the campaign workers interviewed in both cities were the black mayoral candidates.

5. In contrast to the research technique employed in Cleveland and Gary, no formal interview schedule was used in East Saint Louis.

PART I

Black Political Mobilization

1
Problems of Black Political Mobilization

INTRODUCTION

During recent years a number of calls have been made for black unity in order to maximize black power in politics. In sounding such appeals, frequent reference is made to the rise of other ethnic groups to positions of political and economic strength through cohesive political action. Consider, for example, the following excerpt from an editorial published in *Ebony* shortly before the 1968 presidential election.

> This year more than any other the Negro American should vote Black and should vote bloc. Taking a leaf from the political histories of the Irish, the Poles, the Italians and the WASPs, the black man should put aside the differences within the race and unite behind men who will look selfishly at the black man's interests. . . . A caucus of national leaders from Stokely Carmichael to Roy Wilkins should decide whom black people should support nationally. State and city caucuses should be held to endorse the "right man" in state and local elections. And once these candidates have been selected the Negro voter should religiously support them, even though at times it would be against his personal judgment. And the white man should have no reason to complain. After all he has been doing this for centuries.[1]

A similar pitch for the exertion of group power by blacks through united action was made in 1966 by a committee of black churchmen affiliated with the National Council of Churches. Note again the reference to the legacy of earlier groups in mobilizing for effective action.

> . . . America has asked its Negro citizen to fight for opportunity as *individuals*, whereas at certain points in our history what we have needed most has been opportunity for the *whole group*, not just for selected and approved Negroes. . . . We must not apologize for the existence of this form of group power, for we have been oppressed as a group and not as individuals. We will not find our way out of that oppression until both we and America accept the need for Negro Americans, as well as for Jews, Italians, Poles and white Anglo-Saxon Protestants, among others, to have and to wield group power.[2]

Among the chief proponents and architects of the ideology of black power are Stokely Carmichael and Charles V. Hamilton. They, too, place special emphasis on the experience of earlier groups in their call for black unity and power. They observe: "The black community was told time and again how *other* immigrants finally won *acceptance*: that is by following the Protestant Ethic of Work and Achievement. They worked hard, therefore, they achieved. We were not told that it was by building Irish Power, Italian Power, Polish Power or Jewish Power that these groups got themselves together and operated from positions of strength."[3] Given this situation, Carmichael and Hamilton call upon black people to recognize "the ethnic basis of American politics" and to "consolidate behind their own, so that they can bargain from a position of strength."[4]

These calls have immense relevance to the problems of black political mobilization, analyzed in this chapter. Their relevance derives primarily from two factors. One is that these appeals for black political unity indicate the growing awareness among black Americans of the value of their heavy concentration and segregation in the major northern urban centers and their ever-increasing sense of group consciousness, racial pride, and common fate as potential political resources in the quest for black power. The other factor is the assumption implicit in these appeals that the obstacles to black political mobilization today are essentially analogous to those faced by earlier groups and can be overcome by blacks "getting themselves together" in the same way other groups have closed ranks for effective political action in the past. The underlying assumptions of what we term here the "black analogy" will be subjected to close examination at later points in this chapter. Before such an examination can be made, however, it is necessary that we take a rather trenchant look at the political resources noted above. For it is these resources that give meaning and significance to the analysis of prospects for the emergence of blacks to power via the electoral process.

The concentration of blacks in the central cities of the North and West represents the end product of one of the most significant demographic changes occurring in the United States during this century. Blacks began moving from the rural South to the urban centers of the North and West in significant numbers during the decade immediately preceding World War I. The factors underlying this geographic shift are strikingly similar to those which stimulated the massive migration of Europeans to America during the nineteenth century. In this respect we might note that the delayed impact of the agricultural and industrial revolutions on the southern economy had the effect of displacing large numbers of black farm workers from their normal occupational pursuits.[5] Coterminous with these developments was a series of natural disasters, including boll-weevil plagues and floods during the five-year period between 1910 and 1915, that further weakened the southern one-crop economy and uprooted blacks from their southern moorings.[6]

The outbreak of World War I, coupled with the decline in immigration from Europe, created large numbers of unskilled jobs in northern industries. Blacks were vigorously recruited throughout the South to fill these positions in much the same way workers in Europe were recruited for American industry during the nineteenth century. Black newspapers, especially the *Chicago Defender*, significantly contributed to the effort of attracting blacks to the North. The *Defender* published news of job vacancies in northern industry and gave advice on procedures for securing these positions. It also stressed the liberal racial climate of the North, exhorting blacks to throw off the oppression of the South by moving North.[7]

Seeking a greater measure of freedom and worthwhile employment, blacks began moving from South to North in significant numbers around 1910. Although receding somewhat during the depression, emigration from the South was quickly revived by the northern industrial boom sparked by World War II. Since that time the stream of blacks from the South has received continuous stimulation from the increasing mechanization of agriculture and the relatively easy access by blacks to unskilled jobs in northern industries.[8] Like nineteenth-century European immigration, black immigration to the North has been spurred by a cumulative process. Letters back home by those who migrated first have tended to encourage the later immigration of friends and relatives who had remained behind.

The magnitude of the regional shift of blacks since 1910 is indicated in table 1. This phenomenon is further illuminated by census figures which show that whereas 91 percent of the black population lived in the South in 1910, this figure had dropped by 1966 to 55 percent.[9] As a result of this shift, the number of blacks residing in the North and West nearly quadrupled during the fifty-year period from 1910 to 1960.

TABLE 1

BLACK OUT-MIGRATION FROM THE SOUTH, 1910–1966

Period	Net Black Out-Migration from the South	Annual Average Rate
1910–1920	454,000	45,400
1920–1930	747,000	74,900
1930–1940	348,000	34,800
1940–1950	1,597,000	159,700
1950–1960	1,457,000	145,700
1960–1966	613,000	102,000

SOURCE: *Report of the National Advisory Commission on Civil Disorders* (New York: Bantam Books, 1968), p. 240.

It is significant to point out that the bulk of blacks who left the South settled in large urban centers rather than small towns and suburbs. Indeed, statistics show that blacks are more highly urbanized than whites. In 1960, about 70 percent of the black population as compared to 64 percent of the white population lived in metropolitan areas.[10] The differential between black and white residence in northern central cities is even greater. While the black central city population increased significantly between 1950 and 1960, the number of whites living in central cities during this same period decreased by 5.8 million.[11] Moreover, since 1960 the rate of white out-migration from the central cities has shown an even higher increase. Between 1960 and 1966 the white population of the central cities decreased by 4.9 million.[12] This dramatic out-migration of whites no doubt reflects in part an attempt by whites to flee the advancing black tide. It also probably reflects the increasing income of whites and the accompanying urge to secure all the trappings of middle-class life, including a home in the suburbs, a yard, better schools, and a two-car garage.[13]

Perhaps the most significant consequence of these trends is the fact that blacks are rapidly becoming a numerical majority in the largest and most important cities in the country. Blacks already make up more than 50 percent of the population in Washington, D.C., Newark, New Jersey, and Gary, Indiana. Estimates indicate that in 1968 seven of the nation's largest cities were more than 30 percent black. By 1970 blacks constituted 43 percent of the population in Detroit, 46 percent in Baltimore, 38 percent in Cleveland, 41 percent in Saint Louis, and 33 percent in Philadelphia.[14]

The significance of this growing black concentration in urban centers as a political resource is fairly self-evident. Politically, what the present statistics on black residence in central cities obviously mean is that blacks by virtue of their numbers are now in a better position than any other ethnic group to influence decisions and the outcome of elections in major municipalities. In fact, they presently stand in a better politically strategic position than any other ethnic group has stood before, except in isolated cases.[15] No other ethnic group has become so rapidly urbanized or has generally constituted as high a percentage of the population of major American cities as do the black Americans today. Where they are now in the majority, blacks have the opportunity to take over city administrations by electing members of their own group to major offices in city government. In those places where they are not a majority but are rapidly becoming one, the policy preferences of blacks can probably no longer be ignored. Furthermore, their percentage of the electorate practically guarantees that black neighborhoods will be essential campaign targets for every serious candidate and that party platforms will reflect the pressing needs and aspirations of a cross section of the black population. In sum, their concentration in major cities in the North has put within the reach of black Americans the capacity to overcome their historically powerless status and to operate in the political system from a position of greater strength. However, numbers and geopolitical concentration are not sufficient to accomplish the political mobilization process. Consequently, it is necessary to discuss the development of two additional political resources among blacks: group consciousness and racial pride.

The expanded development of black consciousness and racial pride during the decade of the 1960s enhanced the possibility of the development of black political activity in cities that would take advantage of the resource of black numerical strength. The surge toward black consciousness received its greatest stimulation from the series of mass-based protest movements mounted in behalf of civil rights during the 1950s and 1960s. The political assaults against southern segregation led by Dr. Martin Luther King stirred the emotions of blacks throughout the country; the success of the King movement was viewed not as just a triumph for those physically involved in the protest movement but as a solid victory for all blacks. For all strata of the black population, the southern protest movement represented an assertion of their human worth—an affirmation of their value as human beings and their determination to remove the yoke of racism whatever the cost. In the wake of clear signs that gains were being made through protest action by blacks in the South, the apathy and sense of hopelessness that had so long paralyzed the energies and emotions of the black masses—North and South—began a swift and decisive dissipation.[16]

The student sit-in demonstrations with their emphasis on confrontation through direct action, contributed significantly to the growth of political consciousness in the black community. Under the guidance of the leaders of the Student Non-violent Coordinating Committee (SNCC), protest activity began to be viewed as a power resource by which concessions could be obtained through the use of force rather than persuasion.[17] As concessions were made to student protestors and the symbols of southern white supremacy came tumbling down, blacks throughout America learned a lesson of enormous political importance: power when strategically applied can produce results in situations where all the efforts at persuasion in the world will have little, if any, effect. The success of the student sit-in movement in the South created among black Americans everywhere a keen sense of their power potentialities.

Northern blacks were especially influenced by the emphasis on power produced by the student protest movement. Consequently, when the protest movement swept North during the middle years of the 1960s, embracing the involvement of masses of the urban poor, the basic theme of the black rebellion shifted from "Freedom Now" to "Black Power". This new theme symbolized the growing group consciousness of blacks and their frustrations with the slow pace of their social and economic progress in the face of rising aspirations to enter the mainstream of American life. It represented a growing sense of community, of common situation, and common fate. It was a call for black control over social, economic, political, religious, and cultural institutions in the black community. And, fundamentally, it represented a recognition of the urgent need for black solidarity in politics—the necessity for blacks to "build political strength around the vote."[18] In this sense, black power denoted the use of ethnic or racial consciousness among blacks to build unity of action in the political process. It also prescribed independent black political action—the organization of cohesive voting blocs by blacks and their expeditious employment to elect public officials dedicated to the overall progress of the black community rather than to individual achievement. These various dimensions of black power —black pride, black unity, self-help, cohesive political action—have all played major roles in laying the attitudinal foundation essential for the political mobilization of blacks in city politics. The basic question, of course, is whether these attitudinal developments can be translated into political action.

THE ETHNIC ANALOGY

In assessing the potential political value of the key black resources of numerical concentration and racial consciousness, some analysts have attempted to draw an analogy between blacks and earlier white ethnic groups. From this perspective, blacks are seen simply as the most recent arrivals in a long list of ethnic groups that have flocked to the teaming cities of America. Accordingly, it is suggested that the most fundamental task facing black people is that of carving out their fair share of the social, economic, and political pie in the cities as had the Irish, Italians, Poles, and other ethnic groups before them.[19] Although recognizing that skin color is an added obstacle for blacks, this view holds that other ethnic groups were successful in achieving their goals through the building of internal group unity, hard

work, and the establishment of a broad network of political influence and that blacks will be able to achieve the same results
if they pursue a similar course of action. Thus, though race might
be a hindrance to black mobilization, it need not necessarily be
a greater an obstacle than for earlier ethnic groups. In the final
analysis, writes James Q. Wilson, resistance to black demands
for power and recognition is no different than "the general resistance put up by [for example] the Irish political leadership of
the big city to the demands for political recognition expressed
by Poles, Italians or Germans."[20] The logic of this view suggests,
in essence, that blacks will be able to overcome the political
barriers imposed by prejudice as easily as the European ethnics
who migrated to the cities in large numbers before them.

Implicit in the ethnic analogy is the assumption that America is
a democratic and pluralist society open to effective competition
by all groups who wish to use the political process as a lever to
social and economic progress. But this assumption does not take
into account the unique position of blacks in the American social
order—a fact that renders the ethnic analogy totally inappropriate
as a frame of reference for the analysis of black political developments in American cities. A number of recent studies have pointed
to a "mobilization of bias" in the political system that denies to
blacks sufficient access to resources to allow the black community
to effectively compete for important benefits.[21] Thus, whereas
the Irish, Italians, Poles, Jews, and other ethnic groups have been
able to mobilize resources within the political process, and to
make their collective weight felt on policymaking, no such opportunity for resource mobilization has been available to the black
community. Blacks have, in large measure, been systematically
locked out of the political process by institutional procedures
and mechanisms that foster white success at the expense of
less favored nonwhite groups.

The crucial difficulty with the ethnic analogy is that it ignores
or deemphasizes race as a fundamental factor in the distribution
and exercise of power in American politics.[22] That race does play
this crucially important role, however, is a truism too important
to be lightly brushed aside. In this regard, the point should be
underscored that European immigrants could improve their status
in America because they were white people operating in a white-
dominated political system that was relatively open to them and

responsive to their quest for important social, economic, and political benefits. By building community-based organizations and mobilizing the ethnic vote, they were able to compete with other interests for control over decision-making in city politics. Only during the era of reconstruction has black participation in American politics—because of racially oriented institutionalized barriers—approximated the experience of European ethnics. The Irish were able to move out of their segregated ghettoes into the comfortable surroundings of middle-class suburbia because they had the franchise, access to ward clubs, and incentives to compete for larger shares of political capital. And it is interesting to note that the Irish rise to power in New York City coincided with the post-reconstruction moves by whites to strip blacks of their voting rights in the South and to deny them entrance to important arenas of political influence in the North.

THE BLACK COMMUNITY AS INTERNAL COLONY

A more realistic and useful approach is one that sees black people not as just another ethnic group but as a group that occupies a unique position as an oppressed internal colony within the larger social, economic, and political system. Fundamental to this view is the historical fact that black people did not willingly migrate to this country as did other ethnics. They were forcibly removed from their African homeland, chained in the holds of ships, and sold as slave laborers in the southern economy. In contradiction to the national creed that all people are created equal and are endowed with certain unalienable rights, blacks were denied equal status, and their most basic human rights were flagrantly and violently disregarded. Indeed, the institution of slavery was such a blatant contradiction in a society that prided itself on principles of human dignity and freedom, that a vast ideological rationalization had to be constructed in order to justify the treatment of blacks. Basic to the ideology that emerged was the contention that black people were subhuman, and therefore not entitled to the rights and freedoms normally accorded to individuals in civilized society. In the minds of the slave master, the black slave was bereft of human qualities and was valuable only as a commodity to be brought, sold, and exploited.[23] Long after the Civil War era when formal slavery was destroyed, racist ideas, attitudes, and patterns of behavior were continued, taking various forms ranging from Jim Crow laws to physical brutality by the Ku Klux Klan in the South and mob violence in the North, to the use of I.Q. tests to maintain segregation in education throughout the country. Over the years racism has penetrated the deepest levels of American society. Ingrained organically in American culture, and permeating every facet of the nation's life, racism shapes the attitudinal predispositions of Americans more powerfully than any other single force.[24] Today the notion of *white superiority*—black *inferiority* has become so pervasive that the "normal" operation of every major institution produces and perpetuates racist results.[25]

There is no denying the fact that nineteenth-century immigrants from Europe faced numerous obstacles in constructing a decent life for themselves.[26] However, they could always take comfort in the knowledge that no matter how severe or desperate their socioeconomic situation, there was always one group that permanently occupied a position below them—black people. The factor of the superior group position of white ethnics over blacks has driven an enduring wedge between the two groups. Although there have been some instances when white people have joined together with blacks in a common struggle to improve their mutually degrading situation, the more usual relationship has been one in which whites of various backgrounds have united against black efforts for progress and liberation. The historical and contemporary evidence shows that even economically marginal whites, only a half a step above the poverty level, have generally mobilized against poor blacks—with whom they have a great deal in common economically—rather than join with them in a common struggle against the wealthy elites who have continuously exploited both groups.[27] The assault of white working-class Irish people on black school children in Boston is only the most recent example of this phenomenon. Consequently, black people experience a double source of oppression in this society—oppression based on their class position as the bottom sector of the working class, and the unique oppression of racism practiced against them by white Americans—including many white ethnic members of their same working class. To ignore this reality and view black people as just another ethnic group seeking its niche within the American socioeconomic system is to close one's eyes to the basic realities of American society.

One of the main results of this situation is that black communities exist as subsystems of the larger white society. That is, most of the land, housing, business, institutions, media outlets, health facilities, education centers, welfare agencies, political organizations, and police forces within black communities are controlled by white people and white institutions outside of the community. This outside control places black communities and their residents in a position of subordination and exploitation to the whole of white America. Economically, blacks are used by profit-seeking multinational corporations and middle-sized businesses (which make up the economic base of major cities) as a source of cheap labor—last to be hired, first to be fired or layed off. As the profits accummulated under the wage system are reinvested in advanced technology, unskilled and semiskilled jobs are eliminated, and blacks are increasingly viewed as "obsolete labor"—that is, no longer needed for profit-making.[28] However, the black community is still viewed as a potential market for the gluttonous consumption that is urged upon all Americans. Despite considerable talk during the Nixon years of black capitalism (which boiled down to black ownership of small businesses), little in the way of meaningful economic development in the black community has taken place. The great bulk of the job sources and the nature of economic activity continue to be controlled by white monopolies, a fact that substantially reduces the possibilities of black control over the economy of the black community.[29]

Socially, blacks are confronted with the fact that schools are controlled by a predominantly white middle class that imposes its standards and values on black children. Efforts by blacks to replace middle-class whites as administrators and teachers in black schools have often produced vociferous and virulent resistence in the white community.[30] Primarily because of strong white political opposition, community control of schools remains one of the most illusive items on the black agenda.

Blacks are also the continuing victims of social segregation. When blacks move to the city, they are typically forced to settle in areas with the worst housing, worst public facilities, and the most expensive food prices and credit loans. Isolated in the ghetto, blacks are extremely vulnerable to manipulation by powerful white forces external to the black community. The major television systems, movies, radio programs, and newspapers which bombard the black community, are controlled by wealthy whites and perpetuate white middle-class standards and values. Having no control over information in the black community or in the larger society, blacks often find themselves accused by whites who do of being the originators and major perpetrators of social problems in America. Indeed, in recent years some white intellectuals have built careers and gained national reputations by arguing that the structure of the black family and black life-style, rather than the socioeconomic characteristics of U.S. capitalism, are the primary factors that underly the oppressed condition of blacks in America.[31]

Politically, blacks have either been shut out of political decision-making and administrative processes through repression, deception, and discrimination, or victims of various so-called reforms that make it extremely difficult for blacks who truly represent the needs of the black community to get elected.[32] In cities where political machines continue to exist (such as Chicago, East Saint Louis, and Gary) the black community operates as submachine that is subordinate to the white machine, and black politicians are generally "bought off" for far less in rewards than the community contributes in voter support to keep the white-controlled machine in power.[33] This relationship of the black community to the political machine is in marked contrast to the role played by machine politics in the political life of European ethnics during their rise to power in American society. For European ethnics, the political machine was one of the primary institutions that helped to promote their social, economic, and political integration into the wider political community. In its vigorous pursuit of the European immigrant vote, the machine served the latent functions of inducting the immigrant into the political culture, stimulating his political consciousness, and socializing him into new political roles.[34] These latent political functions of the machine lay at the heart of the process of ethnic political mobilization and the rise of formerly powerless ethnic groups to positions of improved power in American society. Over time, immigrants were absorbed into meaningful positions within the structure of the machine, and given an opportunity to compete for power and influence with the Yankees who had previously dominated the electoral process.[35] Ultimately, European ethnic groups (especially the Irish and the Italians) were able to parlay their strategic positions within the structure of the machine into party nominations to major elective offices and appointments to key positions within city bureaucracies.[36]

In contrast, the leaders of contemporary political machines have been quite unwilling to share power with the black community. Blacks are rarely given important posts within the machines themselves, and even more rarely appointed beyond the token level to key positions in city government or slated as candidates for major city and county offices. Because of the critical state of the black economy in the cities, machine leaders have been able to count upon solid support from the black community without providing much in return beyond welfare handouts and low-level patronage positions to a few select black politicians. Lacking an independent base of power, leaders of the black submachine must accommodate themselves to the exploitative relationship of the white machine to the black community or face banishment into political obscurity. The unavailability of the machine as an instrument of power for blacks vividly illuminates the posture of the black community as an internal colony devoid of control over vital social, economic, and political resources.

Contemporary political and governmental reforms have contributed significantly to the maintenance of the colonial relationship between the black community and the larger society. For example, the switch from ward-based partisan electoral systems to nonpartisan at-large electoral systems by a number of cities means that black candidates must be able to attract significant white as well as black support—and they must do so without benefit of party label. In many cases, it is impossible for black candidates to get more than marginal white support, regardless of their qualifications or their political posture. In others, they can obtain considerable white support only by assuming political positions likely to alienate potential black supporters. Thus, at-large arrangements arbitrarily dilute the political impact of black numerical concentration, and render nearly impossible the election of black candidates who are commited to the advancement of the interests of the black community. Similar results are also produced by the consolidation of central cities into regional or "metropolitan" governmental units. Whatever else its assets might be, metropolitan government has the distinct liability of offsetting the political importance of heavy black concentrations in major urban centers

by shifting the boundaries of local government to the county or
regional level where elected officials (mainly white) will be responsive to a dominant political coalition made up of suburban and
inner-city whites.[37] Unquestionably, many proponents of metropolitan government are more concerned about maintaining white
control over the central city—in the face of declining white resi-
dency in the central city—than finding rational and efficient solutions to the problem of urban governance. For these individuals,
metropolitan government is no more than a convenient mechanism
for institutionalizing and perpetuating white domination over
political and governmental activity in the black community.

When black people have rebelled against their social, economic,
and political domination by white colonials, they have often faced
the armed might of local and extralocal police forces. As the black
thrust for liberation gained new momentum during the 1960s and
1970s, virtually every black leader was either killed, jailed, or
harassed by the police. No white ethnic group has encountered
the pervasive and severe repression that has been heaped upon
black militants. The racial makeup of almost any jail or prison in
the country is a testimony to the racist impact of the socioeconomic system, the double standard of legal "justice" under
the system, and political repression of militants.

It is important to understand that these socioeconomic arrangements not only repress the individual and community development
of blacks, but simultaneously grant material and psychological
benefits and privileges to whites.[38] White superiority and black
inferiority within this system exist in dialectical relationship to
one another. That is, the early plantation owners, industrialists,
and bankers could never have made the money they did if blacks
had not been held captives as slaves for two hundred years, and,
once freed, pushed to the bottom of the urban working class—a
position they still occupy. Although at a much lower level of material benefit, it is also true that white production and professional workers would not be able to have the jobs, wages, consumption levels, and various other benefits they derive from the
American economy if blacks were not contained below them and
if U.S. multinational corporations and the U.S. military were not
successful in reaping super profits from Third World people in
Asia, Africa, and Latin America. Most working-class white people have overcome many obstacles to obtain the marginal bene-

fits they have under American capitalism; yet their efforts to overcome these obstacles have been generally expressed in a framework in which their own economic advancement and security are placed above the injustices perpetrated against blacks and people of color throughout the world. Basically, they have internalized the economic and political ideology of the society as a whole and therefore have tended to view blacks as their enemies rather than potential allies in a common struggle that would improve the lives of all working-class Americans.

In short, powerful white businessmen and politicians have continuously secured great benefits out of the colonial relationship that exists between white and black societies in America. In their quest to develop the country and its cities so as to expand their own benefits, the powerful have used black people as expendable objects within the development process and have created a social system that has successfully socialized large numbers of white working class people to accept and support the racism inherent in the system. This alliance between both powerful and relatively powerless whites against the black masses invalidates the notion that black people are just another ethnic group attempting to join the "great American melting pot," and is the main means by which black people are subjugated as a national minority within the confines of this society.

IMPLICATIONS FOR BLACK POLITICAL MOBILIZATION

The position of the black community as an internal colony of white society has a number of important implications for black political mobilization. Control over black life by whites has had the effect of stifling the development of resources necessary for political mobilization in the black community. As we have seen, demographic shifts in the urban population since World War II have invested black communities with the important political resources of numbers and concentration. The point must be made, however, that the factors of large numbers and urban concentration are only potential resources at the command of ethnic groups seeking to advance in American society via the process of politics. Numbers and concentration do not automatically translate into political influence. These resources, if they are to be translated into political influence commensurate with their magnitude, must be supplemented by at least four other political resources:

1. *Group cohesion*—a feeling among people that they are in a common situation and face a common fate.

2. *Leadership*—individuals from the group who gain support for their suggestions as to how the group may improve its common fate.

3. *Political consciousness*—the realization by the group and its leadership that their common fate can be influenced by group political action.

4. *Organization*—the building of political organization to achieve group goals.

In order for a group to wield political power, it is not enough that it be concentrated in large numbers in a limited geopolitical area. Political power (the ability to influence the allocation of governmental resources), in so far as it flows from electoral action, is achieved only if numbers are augmented by group cohesion, leadership, political consciousness, and organization. Within this context the political mobilization process means the utilization of these resources to achieve group political goals.[39] The fundamental point to be noted is that when a group manifests potential strength in numbers and high concentration, it does not automatically manifest the latter four resources. These supporting resources develop only after the group has surmounted certain barriers to its effective emergence in the political process. They also develop over considerable periods of time, if at all, and often at uneven rates. Indeed, some groups may never mobilize themselves for political action because, for a variety of reasons, they are unable to muster the latter four resources. Political mobilization only results when all of the mentioned resources converge at a particular point in time.

Racism has been a pivotal stumbling block to the development of supporting resources for political mobilization in the black community. One manifestation of racism that has served as a formidable obstacle to black political mobilization has been the system of social control that has effectively locked blacks out of the arena of influence and competition in which important public policies are made. Professor Michael Parenti has described the operation of this system in Newark, New Jersey. He found that despite constant protests by blacks against the exorbitant rent they paid for substandard housing, and in behalf of the installation of a traffic light at an extraordinarily dangerous corner, the black community received little in the way of positive action from city officials[40] Essentially, their aspirations and needs never entered into the relevant sectors of the political process where serious grievances were heard and positive corrective action taken. Their position conformed perfectly with William Gamson's heuristic model of stable unrepresentation in which some groups are described as occupying a status outside the arena of decision-making on a more or less permanent basis.[41] The condition of stable unrepresentation that characterizes the political posture of the black community has lead to the development of a high sense of cyncism and futility by blacks regarding the responsiveness and legitimacy of the political process. Alienated from the political system, blacks have lacked the motivational incentives necessary for the development of group solidarity, effective organizations and selfless leadership.

Black victimization in the American social and economic system has also greatly hampered the process of political mobilization in the black community. Faced with problems of unemployment, underemployment, on the job discrimination, and deteriorated physical environments, many blacks consider involvement in political activity a luxury they can ill afford. These persons are so caught up in the sheer struggle to survive that political matters generally cannot stir their interest; and even if they did, they would have little time to devote to them.

Most critically, the political mobilization of working-class blacks is rendered difficult by their lack of a sense of political efficacy (a feeling of competency to affect the course of political events and decisions). The lower-class status of the black community has meant that in comparison with "better off" Americans the communications networks of black citizens are poor. They are less likely to belong to community organizations with direct, continuing interest in politics, read newspapers or consult other public media, have informal group associations that stimulate their interest in politics, or have educational skills enabling them to cope with complex political issues.[42] They are, so to speak, on the periphery rather than the center of society and are less likely to receive political messages that can be translated into concrete political terms. Relatively uninformed about political matters, they are also less likely to feel they can affect the outcome of elections or the making of public policy. "Quite understandably," writes Lester Milbrath, "a person who knows more about the political world is more likely to feel that he can do something to manipulate it. In addition, he sees others in his social milieu take political action with the obvious expectation they will get result."[43] Pushed to the bottom of the economic order, and insulated from arenas of influence in American politics, low-income blacks are likely to view government as remote and unresponsive and to feel themselves powerless to derive significant payoffs from their political participation.[44] They are, in the phrase of Penn Kimball, disconnected from the political system and are therefore among the most difficult of all Americans to mobilize for effective political action.[45]

The position of the black community as an economic colony of white America has stifled the process of black political mobilization in other ways. Money is a key resource in politics. However, because of the dire economic situation of blacks in America, it is a resource sorely lacking in the black community. Only a tiny fraction of the Black population has sufficient capital to help subsidize the cost of high-powered political campaigns—campaigns that rely more and more on the mass media, a costly political instrument. Most black entrepreneurs are small businessmen with little capital to invest in matters not directly related to their business interests. Furthermore, many black professionals prosperous enough to underwite such ventures have tended to be apolitical. Those willing to invest in political activities have often been shackled by nonpolitical policies adhered to by the institutions for which they work. The paucity of economic resources capable of being diverted to effective political use constitutes a powerful constraint on black political power.

The colonial experience of black America has produced intracommunal rivalry and tension that has tended to mitigate against the development of viable organizational structures and unified group activity required for effective political mobilization. This situation stems, in part, from the fact that political influence within the internal environment of the black community is aggregated through a variety of institutions organized around the needs of leaders and constituents who seek to maximize their impact on community decision-making. To be effective, each of these institutions must keep in its possession a minimum amount of organizational resources that can be employed in pursuit of social, economic, and political objectives. Professor Matthew Holden has identified these resources as: (1) technical bureaucratic skills; (2) money; (3) internal attention; and (4) external recognition.[46] Competition over these resources, which are constantly in short supply in the black community, constitutes a prime motivational force for factional disputes that tear black communities apart. Adopting the ageless strategy of divide and conquer, white political leaders sagaciously manipulate badly needed organizational resources in ways intended to intensify rivalry and competition between black political factions. In an atmosphere charged with suspicion spawned by competition over scarce resources, collective or community decision-making becomes a virtual impossibility. Prominent black organizations whose political stakes lie in different directions find themselves adversaries rather than allies in the political arena, despite their expressed desire for unity and sincere commitment to black liberation.

Competition over organizational resources does not take place in a vaccum; generally underlying such disputes are deep-seated ideological differences concerning ends and means of black political action. Ideological beliefs in the black community are broad, varied, and diffuse, running the gamut from extremely conservative to extremely militant.

Given the mosaic of ideological positions and approaches in the black community, it is hardly surprising that unity is difficult to obtain, and conflict and competition represent the more normal conditions of black life. Disparities in ideological outlooks result in internal feuding and jealousies that render the mounting of unified political movements extremely difficult. Thus, an aspiring black politician may find that the greatest resistance to his political success will emerge not from the white community but from the black community among forces with whom he is in sharp philosophical and political disagreement. Black conflict of this sort grows out of the fact that the ideological distance between two black factions is sometimes far greater than the distance between these factions and political activists in the white community. Sharing a community of interests with compatible whites, black leaders are sometimes prone to prefer whites to blacks as

partners in political alliances.[47] Passionate calls for black unity
have rarely contravened the pragmatic calculation by black leaders of where their best interests reside at any particular point in
time.

Social-class tensions have been a further source of factional disputes in the black community. Such disputes have resonated both
within and between classes. The most virulent tension, historically,
has flashed between low-income and middle-income blacks. This
tension has generally centered around the rejection of middle-class
black leadership by lower-class blacks on the grounds that middle-
class leaders have been "out for themselves" and accepted the multiple rewards of white society at the expense of their low-income
black brothers.

Distrust of black leadership has been a pervasive phenomenon
in the black community and has served to substantially retard the
development of an effective black political-leadership structure.
Black political leaders are frequently accused of selling out the
black community for the sake of obtaining highly valued benefits
for themselves. This charge undoubtedly is rooted, in large measure, in the widespread practice of black political leaders coming to
the fore as handpicked choices of dominate white forces. Many
blacks view such persons as illegitimate and harbor a deep suspicion that they are working in the interest of their white patrons
rather than that of the black community. The difficulty with such
labeling is that it is often applied indiscriminantly and does not
distinguish between black politicians who are deeply committed to
using their political positions to advance the social, economic, and
political welfare of the black community and those that are not.[48]

CONCLUSION

In this chapter we have attempted to establish the proposition
that blacks face more formidable obstacles to their mobilization in
the electoral process than those faced by earlier white ethnic groups.
Unlike European ethnics who have, over time, gained access to instruments of power in the American political system, blacks have
been excluded from meaningful participation in the electoral process and denied entrance into the arenas of vital decision-making
on a continuous basis. This condition of stable unrepresentation in
the political process is one component of a more comprehensive
system of racial oppression that has relegated the black community

to the position of an internal colony of white society. The glaring disparities in access to the instruments of power between white ethnics and blacks makes an analogy between the political mobilization of white ethnics and blacks both invalid and inappropriate.

Black leaders seeking to mobilize the black community for effective political action must, of necessity, come to grips with a range of important factors that help to establish and perpetuate the colonial relationship of the black community to the larger society. Invidious racist practices that result in widespread black poverty, unemployment and underemployment, psychological stress and low self-esteem, and an inadequate sense of political efficacy, are formidable barriers to political participation that cannot be overcome, in the contemporary context, through ordinary means. Similarly, the absence of black control over community resources and institutions means that the mechanisms for power—so crucial to the rise of other ethnic groups—tend to be permanently beyond the effective management of black leaders seeking to advance the political interest of blacks via the electoral process. More likely than not, they will find community-based civic groups, churches, financial and commercial institutions, and political organizations controlled by outsiders and used as impediments to the effective mobilization of the black community for independent political action. Thus, black political mobilization, perforce, involves more than an effort to assimilate into the ongoing political structure; it involves an attack against the entire panoply of colonial relationships that serve to repress the emergence of a politics of liberation in the black community. For this reason, the issue of black political mobilization provides for the black politician a host of demands and challenges never faced by the white ethnic politicians who led the effort to mobilize European ethnics for effective political action at an earlier time.

In light of the obstacles to effective black political emergence examined in this chapter, two crucial questions arise: (1) can blacks overcome these obstacles and mobilize successfully in the electoral process; and (2) if so, what are the ingredients of the mobilization effort that must be undertaken. To shed penetrating light on these questions, case studies of black political action in three cities are presented. In the final chapter in this section, a case study of the 1967 mayoral election in East Saint Louis, Illinois, is presented to illustrate in graphic terms the multitude of problems blacks have traditionally encountered in their efforts to mobilize effectively. Part two contains six chapters that analyze the sociopolitical environments of Cleveland, Ohio, and Gary, Indiana, and offer case studies of the 1967 mayoral campaigns in these cities. The stress in these chapters is on the identification of factors that contribute to the success of mobilization efforts in the black community.

1. "Vote Black, Vote Bloc!", *Ebony*, September 1968, p. 136.

2. Quoted in Stokely Carmichael and Charles V. Hamilton, *Black Power: The Politics of Liberation in America* (New York: Vintage, 1967), p. 49.

3. Quoted in ibid., p. 51.

4. Ibid., p. 47.

5. Philip M. Hauser, "Demographic Factors in the Integration of the Negro," in *The Negro American*, ed. Talcott Parsons and Kenneth B. Clark (Boston: Beacon Press, 1966), p. 74.

6. Benjamin E. Mays, "The Development of the Idea of God in Contemporary Negro Literature" (Ph.D. diss., University of Chicago, 1938), p. 2; St. Clair Drake and Horace Cayton, *Black Metropolis*, 2 vols. (Chicago: Harper & Row, 1962), 1:58.

7. Charles Silberman, *Crisis in Black and White* (New York: Vintage Books, 1964), p. 26.

8. *Report of the National Advisory Commission on Civil Disorders* (New York: Bantam Books, 1968), pp. 239-40.

9. See Thomas R. Dye, *Politics in States and Communities* (Englewood Cliffs, N.J.: Prentice-Hall, 1969), p. 352.

10. *Report of the National Advisory Commission*, p. 243.

11. Ibid., pp. 243-46.

12. Ibid., p. 246.

13. Silberman, *Crisis in Black and White*, p. 32.

14. U.S. Bureau of the Census, *Census of Population and Housing: 1970*, PHC (1), 19, 58, 181, 159, and 45.

15. Silberman, *Crisis in Black and White*, p. 194.

16. Lerone Bennett, Jr., *Confrontation: Black and White* (Baltimore: Penquin Books, 1968), pp. 199-204.

17. Lewis M. Killian, *The Impossible Revolution?: Black Power and the American Dream* (New York: Random House, 1968), p. 73.

18. David Danzig, "The Defense of Black Power," *Commentary* 42 (July-December 1966): 41.

19. The classic statement of this position is presented in Nathan Glazer and Daniel P. Moynihan, *Beyond the Melting Pot*, 2d. ed. (Cambridge, Mass.: M.I.T. Press, 1970). Variations on this theme have also been developed in other works, among them Oscar Handlin, *The Newcomers* (Garden City, N.Y.: Doubleday and Co., 1962); Edward Banfield and James Q. Wilson, *City Politics* (New York: Vintage Books, 1966); and James Q. Wilson, *Negro Politics: The Search for Leadership* (New York: The Free Press, 1960).

20. James Q. Wilson, *Negro Politics*, p. 24.

21. See Peter Bachrach and Morton S. Baratz, *Power and Poverty: Theory and Practice* (New York: Oxford University Press, 1970); also see Michael Parenti, "Power and Pluralism: A View from the Bottom" in *Political Power and the Urban Crisis*, ed. Alan Shank, 2d ed. (Boston: Holbrook Press, 1973); and Jewell Bellush and Steven M. David, eds., *Race and Politics in New York City* (New York: Praeger Publishers, 1971).

22. Raymond S. Franklin and Solomon Resnik, *The Political Economy of Racism* (New York: Holt, Rinehart and Winston, 1973), pp. 132–56.

23. The psychological foundations of this process of dehumanization are cogently examined in Joel Kovel, *White Racism: A Psychohistory* (New York: Vintage Books, 1970), pp. 18–20.

24. William H. Grier and Price M. Cobbs, *Black Rage* (New York: Bantam Books, 1968), p. 25.

25. Harold M. Baron, "The Web of Urban Racism," in *Institutional Racism in America*, ed. Louis L. Knowles and Kenneth Prewitt (Englewood Cliffs, N.J.: Prentice-Hall, Inc., 1969), pp. 142–43.

26. The best descriptive account of European immigrant experience is in Oscar Handlin, *The Uprooted* (New York: Grosset and Dunlap Publishers, 1951).

27. See, for example, the illuminating discussion of economic and political relations between black and white workers in James Boggs, *Racism and the Class Struggle* (New York: Monthly Review Press, 1970), pp. 10–16.

28. Samuel F. Yette, *The Choice: The Issue of Black Survival in America* (New York: G. P. Putnam Sons, 1971); Sidney Willhelm, *Who Needs the Negro?* (Garden City, N.Y.: Doubleday and Co., 1971).

29. William K. Tabb, *The Political Economy of the Black Ghetto* (New York: W. W. Norton, 1970).

30. The classic case of white resistance to black demands for increased control over the administration of education in the black community is the heated school controversy arising in the Ocean Hill-Brownsville area of New York City in 1968. For a thorough examination of issues, actors, and events surrounding this dispute, see Marilyn Gittell, "Education: The Decentralization-Community Control Controversy," in *Race and Politics in New York City*, ed. Jewell Bellush and Stephen M. David (New York: Praeger Publishers, 1971).

31. The most famous proponent of this view is Daniel P. Moynihan. Moynihan's analysis is subject to critical examination by a number of first-rate scholars in Lee Rainwater and W. L. Yancey, eds., *The Moynihan Report and the Politics of Controversy* (Cambridge, Mass.: M.I.T. Press, 1967); Moynihan's strategy of blaming the victims of racism for their plight, of course, is not new. For an insightful examination of this phenomenon, see William Ryan, *Blaming the Victims* (New York: Vintage Books, 1971).

32. Harold Baron, "Black Powerlessness in Chicago," in *Black Politics: The Inevitability of Conflict*, ed. Edward S. Greenberg, Neal Milner, and David J. Olson (New York: Holt, Rinehart and Winston, 1971).

33. See James Q. Wilson, *Negro Politics: The Search for Leadership*, for a penetrating analysis of this pattern of black-white political relations.

34. Elmer E. Cornwell, Jr., "Bosses, Machines and Ethnic Groups," in *American Ethnic Politics*, ed. Lawrence H. Fuchs (New York: Harper and Row, 1968), pp. 202–7.

35. Elmer E. Cornwell, Jr., "Party Absorption of Ethnic Groups," *Social Forces* 38 (March 1960): 205–10.

36. Robert Dahl, *Who Governs?: Democracy and Power in an American City* (New Haven, Ct.: Yale University Press, 1961), pp. 32-51.

37. Francis Fox Piven and Richard A. Cloward, "Black Control of Cities," in *Black Politics: The Inevitability of Conflict,* ed. Edward S. Greenberg, Neal Milner, and David J. Olson (New York: Holt, Rinehart and Winston, 1971), pp. 118-19.

38. Robert Blauner, "Internal Colonialism and Ghetto Revolt," in *Black Liberation Politics: A Reader,* ed. Edward Greer (Boston: Allyn and Bacon, Inc., 1971), p. 363.

39. Hubert M. Blalock, Jr., *Toward A Theory of Minority-Group Relations* (New York: John Wiley and Sons, 1967). Blalock contends that minority mobilization is a multiplicative function of the strength of group goals and the perceived probability of achieving these goals. He argues that both the perception of goal strength and the probability of achieving group goals are based on the possession and effective utilization of resources that affect the group's ability to compete for favorable benefits in society.

40. Parenti, "Power and Pluralism: A View from the Bottom," pp. 246-55.

41. William A. Gamson, "Stable Unrepresentation in American Society," in *Black Politics: The Inevitability of Conflict,* ed. Edward S. Greenberg, Neal Milner, and David J. Olson (New York: Holt, Rinehart and Winston, 1971).

42. Robert Lane, *Political Life: Why and How People Get Involved in Politics* (New York: The Free Press, 1959), pp. 220-34.

43. Lester Milbrath, *Political Participation* (Chicago: Rand McNally, 1965), p. 57.

44. In this context, Parenti writes of the attitude of poor blacks in Newark: "If I were to offer any one explanation for non-participation it would be the profound and widespread belief of so many ghetto residents that there exists no means of taking effective action against long-standing grievances, and that investments of scarce time, energy and money, and perhaps most of all, hope serve for nought except to aggrevate one's sense of affliction and impotence" (Parenti, "Power and Pluralism: A View from the Bottom," p. 258).

45. See Penn Kimball, *The Disconnected* (New York: Columbia University Press, 1972).

46. Matthew Holden, *The Politics of the Black "Nation"* (New York: Chandler Publishing Co., 1973), pp. 9-16.

47. The best treatment of this subject is Mack H. Jones, "A Frame of Reference for Black Politics," in *Black Political Life in the United States,* ed. Lenneal J. Henderson, Jr. (San Francisco: Chandler Publishing Co., 1972).

48. It has sometimes been the case that blacks have been reluctant to support black politicians not because they believed they were sell outs but because they believed they simply were not qualified to hold positions of public trust. This attitude is often expressed in the form of demands by blacks that their leaders be better qualified than their white counterparts. Apparently, many blacks have so internalized the white definition of their inferiority that they feel their leaders must be men of extraordinary ability to hold positions normally controlled by whites. A defeated black mayoral candidate in Memphis in 1967 hit at the crux of this problem when he commented bitterly after the election on his failure to generate a high level of support in the black community that he thought most blacks still believed that the white man's ice was colder.

2

The Defeat of an All-Black Ticket
in East Saint Louis

INTRODUCTION

East Saint Louis, Illinois, is one of the northern cities that provides a setting in which a successful black mobilization process could theoretically result in black control of the local governmental system. Except for Washington, D.C., which traditionally has lacked local government, East Saint Louis (ESL) was one of the largest northern cities in 1967 to have a black majority in both population and registered voters. This majority resulted from an absolute loss of white population and a gain of black population in ESL between 1950 and 1967. In the former year 54,725 whites resided in ESL; by 1960 this number had decreased to 45,309, a decline of 17 percent. In contrast, the black population was 27,570 in 1950 and increased to 36,403 in 1960, which meant that blacks constituted 45 percent of the total 81,712 inhabitants in 1960. Estimates made in 1967 indicated that the total population had increased to 83,890 and that the black proportion of the total population had increased to about 60 percent. In terms of registered voters, blacks constituted close to 50 percent of all voters in 1960 and about 58 percent by 1967.[1]

The social and economic characteristics of ESL blacks are similar to those of blacks in other central cities and in some respects are worse. For example, in 1964, about 33 percent of black males in the labor force were unemployed; the median family income for blacks was $2,509; a full 52 percent of employed blacks earned less than $3,000 per year; the median school year completed for adults was 8.1; and only 32 percent of the blacks lived in sound housing units. In short, a large segment of the black community in ESL lived in poverty-stricken circumstances.[2]

Until the 1964 establishment of the federal antipoverty program, virtually no public action was being conducted in the community to improve the circumstances of the black population. Neither the city government, the business community, nor the labor unions had made any notable efforts to widen the opportunity structure or eliminate the oppressive conditions of ESL blacks. The few advances that had been achieved in recent years occurred during the summer of 1963. Stimulated by the action of the national civil rights movement, a group of blacks boycotted and picketed several businesses in the city until blacks were hired; the group also conducted sit-ins against the banks for alleged employment and loan discrimination. On the whole, however, the ESL black community did not generate a sustained local civil rights movement nor did it operate as an organized, cohesive, demand-making force in the city. Some black spokesmen accused their people of being grossly apathetic compared with the civil rights activity of blacks in other cities.

During the spring of 1967 a group of young black politicians, who publicly pledged themselves to improve the depressing conditions of ESL blacks, attempted to rally the black community behind them by challenging the incumbent officials in the city election for mayor and council.[3] Since this election took place in a city with a majority of black voters and pitted an all-black ticket against four white incumbents and a hand-picked black incumbent, it provides a good opportunity to explore the difficulties encountered in attempting to mobilize the black masses for independent electoral action.

THE EAST SAINT LOUIS MAYORAL ELECTION OF 1967

The black ticket was headed by the mayoral candidate, Elmo Bush, a director of adult and vocational education in East Saint Louis. No neophyte to East Saint Louis politics, Bush had accumulated an unusual mixture of both formal and practical political experience. In addition to earning a master's degree in political science at the University of Illinois, he had served as a Democratic precinct committeeman in ESL for seven years, a county supervisor for three years, and had accepted a political appointment in the state capital to work in the Motor Vehicle Department. The other members of the Bush ticket included A. Wendell Wheadon, a part-time law student and civil-service engineer employed by the Illinois Division of Highways; William "Bill" Ray, an elementary school teacher and Democratic precinct committeeman; and Joe Lewis, a past president of the Metropolitan Republican Club, a black Republican organization in ESL.

The incumbent ticket was led by Mayor Alvin G. Fields, who was first elected to the office in 1951. Fields had run unopposed and won three consecutive terms since that year and was widely regarded as an important Democratic politician in the state of Illinois and certainly the top politician in the ESL area. Included on his ticket were three other long-time public officials: police commissioner, Russell Beebe; finance commissioner, Dan Foley; building commissioner, Robert Keeley; and fire commissioner, Ester Saverson, the only black on the incumbent slate and the only incumbent in his first term of office.

Saverson, who was chairman of the black Democratic organization in ESL (the Paramount Committeemen's Club), was added to the Fields ticket in 1963 when one of the former commissioners passed away. He was considered by many of his fellow blacks as the most influential black politician in the city because of his closeness to Mayor Fields, but a man who was so subservient and loyal to Fields that he was unwilling (or unable) to exert much independent pressure on behalf of his people.[4]

According to Saverson, however, others overestimated what a black politician could accomplish for the black community in a strongly white-controlled city and political organization. He emphasized the point that he had been elected to an office that would have been out of reach without white organizational support and therefore he had to operate within that framework. Recalling his feelings on this issue prior to his election in 1963, he stated:

I wanted to become commissioner, but I didn't push it. After all, what could I do to push it? If the city machine didn't support me, I couldn't get elected, could I? Fields is my friend and has been for over thirty years. He told me around 1956 that the first time there was a vacancy I would be the one considered. I couldn't have won without the Fields machine, and no Negro can win now without the

machine. . . . Do you know that I got 3,000 white votes and I would
have lost if those 3,000 white votes had gone to my opponent?

It was that sort of black dependency that the Bush campaign
hoped to eliminate. On 4 December 1966, Bush held his first press
conference and formally announced his candidacy. At that time he
accused the city council of reacting to progress rather than making progress; claimed that city hall had politically dominated the
school system, which had resulted in bad and unequal education;
contended that the city government was part of a corrupt political
machine that dominated Saint Clair County; and attacked the city
council for failing to provide improvements in urban renewal and
for filling key office positions with incompetent personnel. He
also stated that he did not expect to receive the backing of the
twenty-nine black Democratic committeemen because he realized
that most of them depended on the political machine for their
livelihoods through jobs with the city, county, Levee Board,
and school board. He was particularly critical of the city administration's personnel practices and singled out the director of the
Urban Renewal Program as a prime example of "the haphazard,
backslapping manner in which responsible offices are filled by
irresponsible parties, whose only qualification for office is loyalty
to the machine." Asked whether this criticism also applied to Commissioner Ester Saverson, Bush replied: "Where has Saverson
been during all of the years of mismanagement, what has been
his position on the issues of lagging urban renewal and incompetent city officials?"[5]

During the second week of January 1967 both Mayor Fields and
his challenger Elmo Bush went through the traditional ritual of
presenting their campaign platforms to the citizens of East Saint
Louis. The Fields platform attempted to denote a city on the move.
It called for the initial implementation of a $750 million redevelop-
ment plan, the erection of 1,000 new housing units per year, the
securing of state and federal funds to develop the river front, the
goal of having East Saint Louis declared a Model City, additional
efforts to establish an industrial park, and the securing of more
federal funds to continue the local war on poverty. The platform
also pledged racial equality in hiring and promoting practices,
the enactment of a civil service measure for city employees, the
adoption of a code of ethics for the city council, the development

of a scientific code enforcement program, the establishment of neighborhood councils to assist the police department, and several other measures that would supposedly keep the city on the offensive.

According to the Bush platform the city administration was viewed in exactly opposite terms—as a do-nothing administration. The platform was prefaced by a statement asserting that East Saint Louis needed a change from the "unscrupulous and domineering political machine which has eliminated all opposition . . . [and] has run our city for its own good—politics as usual—without regard to the needs of our people, our neighborhoods, our schools, our children or our senior citizens." Among other things, the platform pledged to eliminate the political domination of city hall over the schools, to develop the abandoned urban-renewal land lying waste in the heart of the city, to erase the city's critical need for low- and middle-income housing, to strengthen the city's depressed financial status, to support a strong ordinance on air pollution, to enact measures that would aid the victims of unemployment, and, interestingly enough, to work to change the commission form of government to the aldermanic plan, which would eliminate the jobs the commissioner candidates were running for. In fact, this last item was pushed by the Bush ticket as one of the key campaign issues in an effort to gain some white support.[6]

During the same period that the platforms were announced, it was revealed that A. Wendell Wheadon, the civil engineer on Bush's slate, was fired from his job with the Illinois Division of Highways because he refused to withdraw as a candidate in the election. Citing the Hatch Act, which prohibits certain public employees from becoming involved in partisan political activity, a spokesman for the state agency said that "Wheadon was fired because he declined to end participation in political activity."[7] Bush, however, argued that the firing of Wheadon was strictly a political move ordered by Mayor Fields. He noted that Fields was the vice-chairman of the Democratic state central committee and that the director of the state agency involved was politically appointed. Both Bush and Wheadon pointed out that the Hatch Act bars partisan activity and that the city election was conducted on a nonpartisan basis; thus the law was not applicable. The same point was made in an editorial that appeared in the city's daily newspaper, the *Metro-East Journal*. The editorial called for a public hearing on the matter, as well as the issuing of a statement by state officials that made it clear that the prohibition against political activity applied to everyone "and not just to a highway engineer who happens to run against the East St. Louis city hall organization."[8]

During the week of 22 January the incumbent city council ticket received the endorsement of three black political organizations. The Metropolitan Republican Precinct Committeemen Organization voted unanimously to back the incumbents and the Paramount Democratic Precinct Committeemen Organization, headed by Chairman Ester Saverson, also passed a resolution backing the Fields slate. Bill Ray, running mate of Elmo Bush, cast the lone dissenting vote. Support was also extended to the ticket by the Paramount Democratic Women.

These announcements were made with little fanfare and created little public comment since it had been assumed by many in the community, including the members of the Bush ticket, that these black organizations would come out for Fields since their members were politicians who were indebted to the city hall organization. However, the announcement made a week later that the Baptist Ministerial Alliance, a black religious organization, had voted to endorse the Fields slate, evoked a much more critical reaction in the black community. Although it eventually became known that the Baptist ministers had privately split over the issue, a number of outspoken blacks expressed dismay that the leading religious spokesmen of the black community had turned their backs on the Bush ticket and had gone on record for the Fields slate. The strongest reaction came from Eugene Redmond in a column in the *East Saint Louis Monitor*, pointing out that at least five of the ministers who endorsed the Fields ticket held city jobs and that one was on city, county, and state payrolls. Redmond denounced the members of the Black Ministerial Alliance as the kind of spiritual leaders that shamed all blacks, and whose primary political function was that of helping to keep black people in their place.[9]

As the primary election of 14 February approached, most of the excitement of the campaign had centered around the firing of Wheadon and the action of the Baptist ministers. The only substantive issue that gained unusual attention concerned the form of government in East Saint Louis. Citing the conclusions of a 1963 report issued by Southern Illinois University dealing with the government of East Saint Louis, Bush argued that the commission form of government was obsolete and should be replaced by an aldermanic structure to effectuate a more equitable representation of the city's neighborhoods. In an apparent effort to gain some white backing for his all-black slate, Bush implied that he was not attempting to head an effort that would result in black domination of the city by stating: "In view of the city's biracial structure, I don't see any other system which would provide the people with fair representation. The aldermanic form of government allows for representation in the City Council. Under the present system, you can have either an all-Negro or all-white council since all commissions are elected citywide." Mayor Fields took the opposite position by presenting the "good government" argument that the ward system encouraged parochialism whereas the commission form allowed representatives to take a citywide view in determining decisions. He also stated that the quality of officials was much more important than the structure of government. If officials were good the government would be good.

The primary election was conducted on 14 February 1967 and the entire Fields ticket was nominated by a substantial margin; all the incumbents received at least 60 percent of the citywide vote with Fields leading the ticket by gathering 67 percent of the total votes cast (see table 2). Bush also led his slate by collecting 33 percent of the vote and all but one of his running mates, Ray Willis, were nominated, although they ran about three to one behind the members of the Fields ticket. Relatively speaking, Bush did somewhat better than the rest of his slate since Fields collected 10,499 votes to his 5,154, a margin of about two to one. Jack Houston, a white independent candidate for commissioner, obtained 3,115 votes and ran ahead of three members of Bush's slate, thus knocking Willis out of the election.

An analysis of the primary vote by precincts shows that 5,796 votes or 36 percent of the total were cast in the twenty-two predominately white precincts. In these precincts the white candidates on the Fields ticket gathered an overwhelming proportion of the votes, ranging from a high by Fields of 5,128 or 88 percent to a low by Keeley of 4,459 or 77 percent (see table 3). The lone black on the Fields ticket, Ester Saverson, received only 2,987 votes

TABLE 2

EAST SAINT LOUIS PRIMARY ELECTION, 1967

(Total Votes Cast—15,653)

	Total Votes	Percentage of Total Votes
Fields ticket:		
Fields	10,499	67
Beebe................	10,055	64
Foley	10,367	66
Keeley	9,338	60
Saverson.............	9,367	60
Bush ticket:		
Bush	5,154	33
Lewis................	2,842	18
Ray	2,949	19
Wheadon	3,803	24
Willis................	2,728	17
Independent candidates:		
Brewer	1,616	10
Houston	3,115	20

SOURCE: Computed from Board of Election statistics and population projections of the Metropolitan Affairs Program of Southern Illinois University, Edwardsville campus.

TABLE 3

EAST SAINT LOUIS PRIMARY ELECTION, 1967:
BY BLACK AND WHITE PRECINCTS

	WHITE PRECINCTS (N—22) (Total Votes—5,796)		BLACK PRECINCTS (N—29) (Total Votes—9,857)	
	Total Votes Received	Percentage of Votes Cast in White Precincts	Total Votes Received	Percentage of Votes Cast in Black Precincts
Fields ticket:				
Fields...................	5,128	88	5,371	54
Beebe..................	4,952	85	5,103	52
Foley	5,006	86	5,361	54
Keeley	4,459	77	4,879	49
Saverson	2,987	52	6,380	65
Bush ticket:				
Bush	668	12	4,486	46
Lewis..................	293	5	2,549	26
Ray....................	339	6	2,610	26
Wheadon	485	8	3,318	34
Willis..................	310	5	2,418	25
Independent candidate:				
Brewer.................	498	9	1,118	11
Houston	2,330	40	785	8

SOURCE: Computed from Board of Election statistics and population projections of the Metropolitan Affairs Program of Southern Illinois University, Edwardsville campus.

in the white precincts but these votes were enough to give him a majority, and they represented a total that was more than four times what any member of the Bush ticket was able to achieve in the white precincts. In fact, Bush led his running mates in these twenty-two districts with a scant 668 votes or 12 percent of the total votes.

In the twenty-nine black precincts 9,857 votes were cast, which constituted 64 percent of the total votes. As might be expected, Saverson led the Fields ticket by receiving 6,380 votes or 65 percent of the total. The mayor obtained 54 percent of the black vote; his running mate Keeley was the only member of the ticket who did not receive a majority of the black vote, although he did obtain 49 percent. None of the candidates on the Bush ticket received a majority of the votes cast in the black districts. Bush came the closest to a majority by gathering 46 percent of the vote and Wheadon followed with 34 percent. The other members of his ticket, however, were able to attract only about one-fourth of the votes cast in black-populated precincts.

To summarize, then, the primary election resulted in a substantial victory for the incumbents. All of them were able to attract at least 60 percent of the citywide vote. With the exception of Saverson, they won overwhelmingly in the city's white districts and with the exception of Keeley, they were able to fashion majorities in the black districts. The Bush ticket, in contrast, was not nearly as successful. The candidates were overwhelmed in the white neighborhoods and were unable to achieve at least a majority in the black neighborhoods.

Ordinarily these results would be considered a landslide; but in the context of East Saint Louis politics where, for example, the mayor had run unopposed for three consecutive terms, the showing by Bush was viewed by some political observers as somewhat of a victory. One veteran politician was quoted as saying, "I wouldn't have given Bush more than 3,000 under any circumstances. I guess the machine is in trouble."

Bush did not choose to interpret the primary results pessimistically, particularly in the white neighborhoods. While admitting that his men had expected to lose heavily in the north end of the city (where white voters were concentrated), he stressed the point that "we did receive votes in all-white neighborhoods, and it's very gratifying to me that so many white residents of the city considered the issues in the election." He continued by stating, "We have to get some communication with the white voters. If I have an opportunity to talk with them, I think I can persuade them we deserve their votes."[10]

Bush's emphasis on extending more lines of communication into the white neighborhoods was based on the obvious fact that it was virtually impossible for him to win the election unless a larger proportion of white voters backed him. He felt that he had a reasonable chance to reverse the 900-vote margin that separated him and Fields in the black precincts. Therefore, he was confronted with the dual tasks of obtaining at least one-third of the white votes and of gaining a substantial margin in the black precincts, which had cast 64 percent of the primary votes. That he and his running mates might do both was possible, but the odds were clearly against them.

The Bush slate was given an opportunity to gain greater exposure to white voters through the invitation of the local NAACP to hold public town meetings for all the candidates in both the north and south sections of the city. The members of the Bush ticket announced immediately that they would attend both meetings. However, when the invitation was extended by the NAACP to the incumbents at a city council meeting, Mayor Fields stated that he could not promise to appear. "I'll have to check my schedule before I can tell you if I will come to your meeting. I'm working night and day right now carrying out my duties as mayor of this city." Mrs. Mildred L. Sammons, president of the local branch of the NAACP, responded to the mayor by saying, "I don't think, your Honor, that you have any duties to the citizens of this city that are more important than meeting the voters and informing them about your programs . . . giving time to your citizens is part of your job."[11]

Despite the urgings by Mrs. Sammons, none of the members of the Fields ticket appeared at any public meetings during the entire election campaign. The Bush ticket and Houston, in contrast, appeared at several question-and-answer sessions in both the white and black sections of the city. At these meetings, which were generally attended by small crowds (less than 100), the candidates expounded on and reiterated what they considered to be the many failures of the city administration and then presented their proposals for dealing with the past shortcomings. Although the meetings did give the challengers some publicity through newspaper coverage, it is doubtful that many votes were gained since attendance was meager and was made up, to a considerable extent, by many of the same people. In fact, some of Bush's advisors felt that the time devoted to the meetings would have been better spent on door-to-door campaigning. Certainly such a suggestion was persuasive. When questioned on this point, Bush stated that he decided that such an approach in the white community was simply too risky. "The one thing I didn't need was an incident in the white neighborhoods. That's all that had to happen was for me to go to some white's house and have them start something that might have gotten out of hand, and I wouldn't have gotten any white votes." Due to this possibility, Bush and his running mates were put at a disadvantage of not being able to do the kind of grass-roots campaigning that has proven valuable in many local elections.

A series of articles appearing in the *Metro-East Journal* disclosed another serious disadvantage that confronted the Bush ticket. The *Journal* charged that wholesale vote fraud occurred in the 14 February East Saint Louis primary. Citing specific precincts and names of voters, election judges and committeemen, the paper demonstrated that as many as fifty illegal votes were cast in each of several black precincts by individuals voting for deceased persons or voting for voters who had moved out of the precincts but had not had their names removed from the register. It was also noted that such action could not occur unless the election judges, who were hired through the efforts of their precinct committeemen, cooperated with the committeemen. For example, the paper reported specific instances of election judges allowing committeemen to enter the voting booth with healthy voters.

The members of the East Saint Louis Board of Election Commissioners, Clifford Easton, Alvin G. Fields, Jr., and Mead E. Dowling, responded to these accusations by promising to investigate any irregularities. In a formal statement the commissioners also argued that many of the voting cases that may have appeared fraudulent were clerical errors. "It should be noted that a clerical mistake made by a judge of election at the precinct polls on election day should not be confused with violations of the Election Code. The board supports its judges of election, although from time to time, clerical errors are committed and precise election procedure is not followed."[12]

The *Journal* replied to the commissioners' statement in a strong editorial that called for a vigorous investigation of illegal voting practices and the resignation of the mayor's son from the board, neither of which occurred before the final election.

Both the mayor and Bush condemned the apparent illegal voting that had occurred. The mayor pointed out that although the number of votes involved would not have made any difference in the outcome of the primary, he felt that one fraudulent vote was one too many. He noted that many of the irregularities occurred in one area of the city and suggested that the mobile population in that area was probably a contributor. As to the question of his son being on the Board of Election, the mayor maintained that he did not see any conflict of interest. Bush stated that the voting disclosures were symptomatic of "the disease" that had gripped the election process in East Saint Louis and argued that voting fraud "is part of the political pattern in the city that has contributed to voter apathy over the years." He called for a complete canvass of every precinct and the immediate resignation of Alvin G. Fields, Jr., from the Board of Election. Bush also emphasized the linkage between the city hall-controlled political machine and the election judges. "In East St. Louis the precinct committeeman names the election judges in his precinct. They serve as long as he wants them to and the $25.00 they get paid is a lot of money to many of them."[13] Bush contended that an honest election was impossible as long as the precinct committeemen was boss at the polling place.

As the final election day of 4 April approached, the chances of an upset seemed to slip away. The Bush ticket did not attract large, enthusiastic crowds in any of the city's neighborhoods, and their reception in the white sections of town was particularly meager and cool. Moreover, and more importantly, the all-black slate did not gain the overt support of any of the leading, nonpolitical blacks or black organizations in the city. Bush and his running mates had hoped that as the election approached, more and more black people would publicly support them and create a bandwagon effect. However, the anticipation that the black community and whites who were dissatisfied with the city hall administration would rally together around the anti-Fields ticket was not realized, for reasons discussed below.

Two days before the election, Elmo Bush shared a rally platform with Stokely Carmichael, chairman of SNCC, who drew a crowd of over one thousand people into East Saint Louis's Lincoln High School auditorium. Bush made a plea to the crowd for electoral support and noted that "some people told me not to come here today. They told me it would cost me votes, that the white people wouldn't vote for me. Well, I see white people in this audience. The people who won't vote for me because of Mr. Carmichael won't anyway—they didn't in the primary." Carmichael delivered a blistering speech against white America and strongly endorsed Bush for mayor.

Although the 1967 mayoralty election provided ESL blacks with a unique opportunity to gain governmental control of the city, and thus make ESL the first city in the nation an example of black control, few residents of the community were surprised by the election results. Despite strenuous efforts by Bush and his running mates to mobilize the black community behind their candidates, the incumbent ticket won a landslide victory. Fields received over 70 percent of the citywide vote, and his running mates collected between 60 and 69 percent of the vote (see table 4). A

TABLE 4

East Saint Louis Mayoralty Election, 1967

(Total Votes Cast—20,212)

	Total Votes	Percentage of Total Votes
Fields ticket:		
Fields	14,430	71
Beebe...............	13,703	68
Foley	14,025	69
Keeley	12,417	61
Saverson.............	12,036	60
Bush ticket:		
Bush	5,782	29
Lewis...............	4,074	20
Ray	4,021	20
Wheadon	5,157	26
Independent candidate:		
Houston	6,292	31

Source: Board of Election statistics.

breakdown of the vote by the racial composition of precincts shows that Fields received 88 percent of the votes cast in predominantly white precincts whereas Bush was able to capture only 12 percent of such votes. The other members of the Fields ticket, with the exception of Saverson, gathered at least 75 percent of the white votes. Although Saverson did much better in the white neighborhoods than any of the blacks on the Bush slate, the white independent, Houston, did outpoll him by almost 1,000 votes in the twenty-two white precincts, thus contributing to the speculation rumored around the city that some of the white precinct committeemen were not pushing Saverson along with the rest of the incumbent ticket because of his race. In the black precincts, where 59 percent of all votes were cast, Fields obtained 60 percent of the black vote while Bush received only 40 percent. Fields's running mates also gained majorities in the black precincts with Saverson leading by gathering 69 percent of the vote (see table 5). In summary, not only did the black challengers fare poorly in the white precincts, but they failed to attract even half of the votes cast by the city's black majority.

TABLE 5

EAST SAINT LOUIS MAYORALTY ELECTION, 1967:
BY BLACK AND WHITE PRECINCTS

	WHITE PRECINCTS (Total Votes—8,243)		BLACK PRECINCTS (Total Votes—11,969)	
	Total Votes Received in White Precincts	Percentage of Votes Cast in White Precincts	Total Votes Received in Black Precincts	Percentage of Votes Cast in Black Precincts
Fields ticket:				
Fields	7,264	88	7,166	60
Beebe...............	6,939	84	6,764	57
Foley	7,005	85	7,020	59
Keeley	6,204	75	6,213	52
Saverson............	3,798	46	8,238	69
Bush ticket:				
Bush	979	12	4,803	40
Lewis...............	769	9	3,305	28
Ray	746	9	3,275	27
Wheadon	975	12	4,182	35
Independent:				
Houston	4,606	56	1,686	14

SOURCE: Computed from Board of Election statistics and population projections of the Metropolitan Affairs Program of Southern Illinois University, Edwardsville campus.

AN ANALYSIS OF THE ELECTION RESULTS

In view of the most recent phases of the "Black Revolution" in American society, the basic question that emerges from the results of the 1967 East Saint Louis mayoralty election concerns the failure of the black majority to capture political power when they clearly had the numbers to do so. What went wrong with the simple equation that states a majority of black voters equals the election of black candidates? Why were the black candidates unable to mobilize the black community behind them?

There were several factors that obstructed the transformation of numbers into political control in East Saint Louis. These factors included the existence of a powerful, white-controlled political machine in the city, a considerable amount of internal conflict and mistrust of politicians within the black community, the failure of a majority of registered black voters to participate in the election, and the low level of white support for black candidates. The discussion below illustrates how each of these conditions contributed to the defeat of the black candidates.

The Persistence of a Political Machine

Our discussion of the 1967 mayoralty election hinted at the fact that ESL was one of the few American cities that continued at that time to be governed by a political machine. The machine style of government (with its emphasis on the exchange of material rewards for political support devoid of ideology), which was common in many cities during the period between the Civil War and the Second World War but has since disappeared in most cities, continued to operate in ESL for a variety of historical and contemporary reasons.[14]

The persistence of the machine may be explained in part by the historical role played by the city within the larger Saint Louis metropolitan area. Since at least the turn of the century, ESL has had a reputation as the "sin city" of the area, controlled by corrupt and graft-ridden politicians. In his analysis of the 1917 ESL race riot, Elliott Rudwick observed that:

> During the years before the race riot (1917), East St. Louis had a national reputation as a wide-open, wild and woolly gambling town. For convenience of patrons, politicians and the police, activities were centralized in the valley, a congested district of saloons, gambling parlors, and houses of prostitution.[15]

Apparently this reputation had the dual impact of attracting a wide assortment of undesirable characters to ESL and of discouraging upright individuals from residing in the community. Consequently, the composition of the population promoted the existence and operation of a less than honest city government, which in turn allowed the conditions that contributed to the city's bad reputation to continue. These developments meant that the existence and action of political reform type individuals, which were common in many cities during that period, were unusually scarce in ESL. The more affluent businessmen and professionals who earned a living in ESL and who were potential reform supporters did not reside in the city. Further, it was common knowledge that a considerable number of managers and businessmen tolerated the operation of the political system because it was beneficial to their financial interests in a variety of manners, particularly in terms of the low taxes they paid relative to the value of their property.[16] In short, the widespread reputation of the city did not attract reform-oriented individuals as settlers, and segments of the population both in and around the community developed an interest in maintaining the existing governmental system.

Another characteristic of East Saint Louis's historical development that has contributed to the endurance of machine politics is the early and continuous influx of a highly dependent type population. The restrictive immigration laws of the 1920s combined with the federal welfare programs enacted during the New Deal period and the general economic affluence of the society eventually reduced the number of city dwellers interested in the rewards of the old-time machines as they operated in most cities. As a consequence of these developments, many machine organizations declined because they lacked the necessary clientele base. The major influx of southern blacks into the cities came after many of the machines had already declined or after the internal immigrants could be effectively assimilated into the organization and therefore fill the vacuum left by the earlier ethnic groups. This was not the pattern in ESL. Being situated as the closest northern city that was a terminal point for major railroads, ESL had experienced a relatively heavy immigration of southern blacks for over a half a century. For the past thirty-five years, blacks have constituted a larger proportion of the population in ESL than they have in any other major northern city except Washington, D.C. In 1940, for example, approximately 25 percent of the population of East Saint Louis was black, whereas the black proportion of the population in other cities at that time was as follows: New York—6

percent; Chicago—8 percent; Philadelphia—13 percent; Detroit—
9 percent; Cleveland—10 percent; Pittsburgh—9 percent; Buffalo
—3 percent.[17] Consequently, the machine in ESL did not sustain
a shrinking clientele base in the sense that other city machines
did. The early and steady arrival of a large number of dependent
blacks provided the organization with a continuous flow of needy
individuals who were quite willing to exchange votes for assistance.

The ESL political system not only experienced an uninterrupted supply of dependent people who desired tangible political
rewards, but the system was also very adept at furnishing the
necessary inducements. The fact that the city operated without a
general civil service law until 1967 meant that many city jobs
could be utilized for patronage purposes. The organization's control of Saint Clair County, including the Levee District, produced
additional sources of patronage; and even the city's independent
school district was a significant source of patronage, both in
jobs and contracts, for the political organization. Ties between
city hall, organized crime, and local labor unions have been documented by several studies.[18] Machine intervention with the police
department and welfare department was common; and, of course,
the five-dollar vote and protection for illicit business operations
had been the norm for many years.

The distribution of these favors in a manner that supported the
organization was facilitated by the centralization of power.
Although there had been periods of intrasystem conflict for the
boss position, by 1959 Mayor Alvin Fields had solidified his position so that there was little question among observers that he
"called the shots." As noted earlier, he ran unopposed until challenged in the 1967 election. Although ESL was formally governed
under the commission system of government, it was clear that
nothing of significance occurred without the backing or tolerance
of Mayor Fields.[19] The fact that Fields had this amount of power
was functional for the persistence of the machine in another way.
It made the organizational accommodations to changing situations easier to accomplish than if power were dispersed. For
example, when it became expedient to allocate additional patronage to some of the black politicians and to include a black candidate on the machine's slate in 1963 to solidify the support of the
growing black population, the mayor possessed the necessary in-

fluence to make these decisions without causing serious internal conflict within the organization. Some of his fellow white politicians may have disagreed with his action, but none of them were willing to outwardly oppose him.

The machine was also very skillful in strengthening its viability by playing the white community against the black community and vice versa. In this respect, the memory of the East Saint Louis race riot of 1917, which took the lives of nine whites and thirty-nine blacks, is a crucial fact. According to a long-time participant-observer of ESL politics, fear among whites and blacks that such an episode would be repeated gave the macine a significant lever in dealing with and controlling the political behavior of both races. He states that:

> For decades the machine has told the Negro that the whites don't want change and that there could be another race riot if Negroes pressed too hard. The machine for years presented itself to Negroes as [their] protector, who would see that no new riot occurred. And the machine has presented itself to whites as the institution which would see that the Negroes didn't make trouble. The Negroes have been kept in poverty, thus making it easier to control them.

Finally, the ESL machine continued to function because, even if there had been some potential white reformers residing in the community, they and most of the affluent whites had left the central city as the black population became a majority. Of the whites who remained in the city, many were linked to the machine in some manner and therefore were not about to contribute to its decline. Likewise, although some blacks would have liked to have seen the machine demolished, many blacks in ESL, as the following section illustrates, supported its continuation because of the rewards they had been able to derive from it.

The Machine and the Black Community

As noted earlier, a large segment of the blacks in ESL can be classified in the poverty-stricken category. The population has all of the characteristics of a highly dependent one that has lacked the means for combating the so-called poverty cycle. In every sense of the concept, the black community of ESL exists as an economic colony of white society. Until the establishment of the

Saint Clair County Economic Opportunities Commission under the federal antipoverty program, the political machine was virtually the only instrument of assistance available to blacks. As a result, blacks with a wide variety of needs turned to the machine for help, which they generally received, and they therefore reciprocated with political support. Some blacks (generally middle class) viewed this heavy reliance on the machine for aid in a paradoxical manner. On the one hand, they recognized that the machine provided many lower-income blacks with the necessities of life when other institutions did not. However, on the other hand, they were distressed by the fact that along with machine assistance went subordination to the white machine leaders and the reality that it was not wise for black politicians to buck the machine in an effort to gain greater amenities for the general black community. According to one long-time black resident of ESL:

> We are at the brute level, the pure level of existence, so politics means money, a job, or placement on relief. The politicians have exploited us and our fears, so Negroes do as they are told. . . . The machine has the power to stop progress by threatening people with loss of jobs. [It] can get almost every family in East St. Louis. Somebody [in the family] has a job.

Within this context, the development of independent black leadership was extremely difficult. Potential leaders were constantly bought off by the machine and were encouraged to think of political participation only as a stepping stone for personal ambition, not as a means for group improvement. In exchange for political jobs and other favors, potential leaders had traditionally become controlled. They were placed in positions of apparent influence, such as precinct committeemen or city inspectors; but due to their subordination to white organization leaders they were unable to use their positions for the advancement of the black masses. The emphasis was on what the machine could do for them individually and what they could do for the machine, not on what could be done to help alleviate the problems of average black citizens.

This inability of blacks to wield independent influence in the city was intensified by the fact that the machine was operated on a bipartisan basis. Machine leaders saw to it that the organization overarched both political parties (the city is only nominally nonpartisan) and included members from both parties. Prior to the election of Mayor Alvin Fields in 1951, for example, Dan McGlynn was the boss of both Republicans and Democrats and could dictate a political slate for both parties. After Fields's election, Republican influence sharply declined, but Fields still worked closely with them and controlled both Republican and Democratic committeemen. This arrangement worked to the disadvantage of black politicians who pointed out that their rewards for political work would have no doubt been far greater if competition among whites for their support had existed. However, with the exception of a few instances, the white politicians displayed enough cohesion to prevent the blacks in ESL from having the opportunity to play the swing role by delivering votes to the side that would promise the most to the black community. As one black politician commented: "We don't have whites in East St. Louis who will take the initiative to oppose the Fields machine and form an independent political machine, consequently we don't have any place else to go." This virtually undisputed control by the Fields machine forced black politicians, if they desired any favors from the political system, to be subordinate to the white leaders of the organization.

Although ESL black politicians often used such terms as "graft ridden," "corruption," "bloated contracts and patronage" to describe the political system ruled by the whites, they readily admitted that their subsystem was largely a reflection of the white system. Patronage was their major concern and the thing that bothered many of them was that they lacked sufficient bargaining power to capture a proportionate share of the prizes. White leaders constantly reminded them that they would have even less if the machine did not work on their behalf. This point is well illustrated by the fact that prior to 1963 when black political leaders asked to have a black commissioner candidate on the Mayor's ticket, they were told "no Negro can get elected—if the organization came out for a Negro, the North End [the white community] wouldn't support the organization candidates." Given this stance, no black was able to achieve high public office in a city with a nearly black majority. When the mayor decided, however, that it was appropriate to include a black candidate for commissioner on the organization ticket, he tapped Saverson. With the organization's backing Saverson, as we noted earlier, was able to gain

3,000 white votes in the 1963 election, which assured him of victory —a feat he could not have accomplished on his own.

Despite the fact that some blacks personally profited through machine efforts, many black civic leaders in ESL believed that the machine had not appropriately repaid the general black community for the electoral support provided by blacks. They particularly condemned black politicians for placing their personal goals and the goals of the Fields machine above those of the black community. The politicians were accused of being fearful of doing anything for their people that would cause displeasure among the white leaders and thus endanger their personal privileges.

> They fear that the machine will get back but they don't know where to expect the revenge. It is not necessarily a political job they'll lose—there are other privileges they get, such as free gas from the city or the privilege of getting their girl friends on ADC.

Not only were black politicians and some of their constituents indebted to the machine, but also the machine took considerable pains to gain the favor of nonpolitical black leaders. There was general agreement among the black respondents, for example, that the leadership within the East Saint Louis NAACP had been closely tied to the machine and had therefore largely ignored discrimination in public accommodations, labor unions, and city hall. NAACP leaders were described as being bought off by petty favors extended by Mayor Fields and other white politicians. To illustrate the point one respondent recounted the following episode.

> You know after a meeting of the Coordinating Council, Randolph, X [NAACP president], and I were walking to our cars and we chatted briefly. I said that X had better hurry on because he had to phone Fields and tell him what we were doing. I told X that he shouldn't rush so, though, and he might want to wait until tomorrow morning to call Fields, but knowing him I knew he couldn't delay one more minute. Then Randolph asked X why he had to tell Fields everything. X denied it and said that it was unfair that he had this reputation—he was simply friendly to Fields who had been kind to him. X then told us how he had built his house on Fourth Street, some years ago, and had very little money. One day two men brought bathroom fixtures and the next day they came back to install them. When X asked where they came from the plumbers said that Alvin Fields had sent them. X said he went to see Fields and told the mayor:

"Thanks for sending the men, but I wish you had told me before you did it because I don't have much money and. . . . " Fields told him that he didn't owe anything and that it was a gift. X told Randolph and me this story to show how kind Fields was. Randolph, after listening to this tale then said to X, "So, the mayor bought you for a shithouse!"

The support of ESL ministers was cultivated by the machine in a similar manner. Through contributing money to church causes, appointing selected ministers to certain "prestigious" public committees, and providing some ministers with jobs, among other things, the machine successfully gained the backing of the Baptist Ministerial Alliance, the most influential back religious organization in the city. The long-time president of this organization, generally referred to as "Dean" of ESL Baptist ministers, the Reverend X, was viewed as a supporter of the Fields organization. "Fields made a pawn out of him . . . whatever Fields wants, X will do." He was accused by some respondents of using the pulpit to endorse machine candidates. One parishioner stated: "Oh, X was sneaky. I remember going to his church years ago and he'd stand in his pulpit before an election and say 'I've given the subject careful thought and I think I'm going bo support those in office now. I'm not going to name names, but you know who I mean.' " Other respondents pointed out that the backing of the machine by Reverend X and other black ministers was usually more indirect. Rather than actively working for the machine, they were urged "not to work against the politicians—certainly not to get involved in any crusades for better government."

The entrenchment of the machine within the black comunity in 1967 is further indicated by the fact that Clyde Jordon, the black publisher and editor of the major black newspaper in ESL, wrote a lengthy editorial the week before election day endorsing Fields. Jordon's statement is particularly interesting because it articulates the dilemma that confronted many East Saint Louis blacks as they weighed the value of their linkage to the machine against an opportunity to strike a blow for their race. Observing that Elmo Bush was his close personal friend and former business partner, an outstanding black leader, and a highly qualified mayoral candidate, Jordon stated that he would nevertheless vote for Mayor Fields "because I work as his administrative aide and believe in the age-old philosophy of loyalty. He has been my friend and done so much for me that I would be less than a man to do otherwise. I think my friend Elmo Bush understands this better than anyone else."[20]

The fact that a close friend like Jordon, who had often written editorials that demanded equal rights and greater political representation for blacks, was unwilling to support Bush because of his indebtedness to the machine is illustrative of the great difficulty Bush and his running mates encountered in gaining support from both so-called black leaders and rank-and-file blacks.

In summary, then, the existence of a machine style of government, the tight control of the organization by Mayor Fields for over fifteen years, and the machine's strength in the black community gave the members of the Fields ticket an impressive array of political resources that simply could not be matched by the members of the Bush slate. The organization's distribution of jobs, contracts, money, protection from the law, and numerous other favors to a countless number of blacks meant that a substantial segment of the ESL black population had concrete stakes in the organization's continued control of the city government. Due to the machine's ability and willingness to exchange these rewards for votes, the principal potential advantage of the black challengers, the number of black voters in the city, was seriously diluted. The implicit appeal that blacks should vote for blacks could not overcome the past and promised rewards doled out by the machine to the large number of dependent blacks. The challengers did not have comparable tangible rewards to lure voters away from the incumbents, nor could they match the manpower of the machine's organization in either the white or black sections of the city. As one participant in the Bush campaign put it: "The machine had everything going for them, not only money, but time and people. Policemen, firemen, inspectors, practically all the city employees were out working for them. They were all over the place at all times of the day and night. How the hell can you beat that?"

Internal Conflict in the Black Community

Another factor that contributed to the defeat of the all-black ticket in ESL is, in a sense, an outgrowth of the historical relationship of the black community to the white-controlled political machine. The general subordinate status of blacks as a minority within the general society and the reinforcement of this subordination within the political system seems to have fostered a considerable amount of distrust and jealousy between the black electorate and black politicians, and among the political leaders themselves.[21] Given a situation where whites have had a virtual monopoly over amenities, and the only blacks able to share in these amenities have been those willing to come to terms with whites, it is understandable that many blacks are suspicious of any black leader who claims to place group interests above his own personal interests. Based on past experiences, many ESL blacks developed the notion that there is no such thing as a sincerely independent black leader; devious motives were always thought to be lurking in the background. Few blacks were willing to go out on a limb to support a declared independent because, as the following quotation illustrates, they could not be certain he was truly on their side.

> These would-be leaders make trouble because they know that if they act as if they're going to fight the machine, the machine will call them in to give them a job or a better job . . . and after that you don't hear from them. People have been sold down the river so often. . . . Who is going to lead, which Negro, none of them is sincere?

That not a single black institutional leader or organization endorsed Bush and his ticket can be attributed in part to the fear of machine reprisal, but perhaps just as importantly to the widespread uneasy suspicion that Bush would sell out sometime before the election campaign was over and leave many public supporters holding the bag.[22] Since Bush and two of his running mates carried the stigma of having been members of the Fields organization in the past and having been involved in some political maneuvering, it was difficult for them to convince potential supporters that such a development would not occur. Consequently, many blacks were extremely reluctant to openly support Bush for fear that they would be "hustled." In order to protect themselves in both directions, however, some blacks (such as bar owners) secretly slipped Bush a modest sum of money to help finance his campaign but they provided no public support.

Other segments of the black community also found reasons for not supporting Bush and his ticket. Some of the small number of militant blacks in the community distrusted him because they believed that during the 1963 demonstrations in East Saint Louis he at first had led them and urged them on but then backed off. The more conservative church-going blacks disapproved of him because of his reputation as a playboy, a ladies' man, a drinker, and so on. Others simply mistrusted him because of his political background. As one black respondent put it: "I don't trust the *man*, but I don't trust the *boy* either."

Not only did some of the black electorate mistrust the black candidates, thus weakening their chances of gaining solid support in the black precincts, but other black politicians refused to support them. The fact that the black politicians were members of the Fields organization was, of course, important, but the high degree of jealousy and mistrust among the black politicians themselves was also relevant. A history of competing with one another to gain greater favors from the white leaders meant that any black politician who seemed to be moving ahead of the pack would be resented by the others. This was particularly the case with Bush who had the reputation as a climber because he was able to by-pass many of the black committeemen when he was part of the organization, and he was consequently disliked by some of them for that reason.

> He is the biggest farce in the world and he is a friend of mine. He is loud, everything is "I" and "me." He tries to push himself. He is an educated fanatic, who looks down his nose at non-degree people. The committeemen resent him and dislike his education. They didn't want him to have the Springfield job but he had to get it because of the rule that committeemen have first crack at jobs . . . and none of them was qualified to take that Springfield job—only Bush was.

In this respect, the black politicians in ESL not only faced the prospect of losing their jobs and whatever influence they may have had in the political arena by backing Bush and his mates, but their own prestige and status within the black political sub-system would also have been threatened by a Bush victory.

The chances of the Bush ticket attaining a victory were further eroded by the development of dissension among the black candidates over the use of campaign funds and advertisements. Some of the members of his slate felt that Bush was not using the limited contributions he received to elect the entire ticket, but only for his own election. Obviously, this kind of internal bickering among the candidates could only reinforce the distrust and suspicions of the black electorate.

Given these factors, it is not surprising that only 49 percent of the registered black voters bothered to participate in the election. The fact that an all-black ticket headed by Bush was on the ballot did not stimulate a greater black-voters turnout over earlier mayoralty elections (the black turnout in 1963 was 52 percent and in 1959 it was 37 percent). It appears that this relatively low turnout resulted from the fact that the Bush slate did not have the necessary resources in terms of time, money, and manpower to build a grass-roots movement that would produce a solid black vote and overcome the strength of the Fields machine in the black community. The lack of such resources, however, must be traced, in part, to the mistrust and fear of a sell out that lingered in the minds of many black voters.

The combination, then, of the indebtedness of many blacks to the Fields organization, the considerable degree of distrust of black politicians throughout the black community, and the failure of over one-half of the registered black voters to vote when given an opportunity to back an all-black slate, clearly indicates that the numerical majority of blacks in ESL constituted only a potential political resource for the independent black candidates. Their failure to unite the black community behind them in a common assault to gain command of the government is illustrative of the difficulty that confronts blacks seeking political power. The task of mobilizing the black community to produce a bloc vote for black candidates is, to say the least, not easily accomplished.

Inability to Attract Substantial Support

The weak showing of the black candidates in the white neighborhoods of the city constitutes a final factor underpinning the defeat of the Bush ticket. If the black candidates were unable to gain the support of a large proportion of the black community, why were they unable to attract a larger number of white voters? The answers to this inquiry duplicate, to some extent, what has already been said. First, a long history of strained race relations in ESL meant that there were many whites in the city who simply would not vote for a black man. Although it is difficult to isolate and assess the extent of such feelings, it is worth noting that even with the endorsement of the Fields organization Saverson received less than a majority of white votes and trailed the lowest vote-getting white candidates on the incumbent ticket by some 30 percent of the white vote. Second, many whites, as was the case with numerous blacks, were indebted to the Fields organization and consequently partially repaid their debt to the organization by supporting the incumbents in the election. Concerning those whites who may have been predisposed to campaign and vote against the machine, they could not be sure that Bush and his running mates were sincere, for the same kinds of reasons that blacks mistrusted politicians formerly tied to the machine. The pat question often posed was: "Why should whites support corrupt black politicians against corrupt white politicians?"

CONCLUSION

In 1967 the black community in East Saint Louis was enmeshed in a web of social, economic, and political relations corresponding closely to the model of internal colonialism discussed in chapter one. For years major decisions affecting the lives of black citizens had been controlled from the outside by white power-brokers who sought to exploit the resources and potential power of the black community for their own purposes. Entering ESL at the bottom of the economic ladder, blacks were not afforded the opportunity to compete with whites for jobs, government contracts and subsidies, and other forms of economic benefits essential to the elevation of minority groups into the mainstream of American society. In sheer desperation, blacks turned to the only agency prepared to effectively respond to their urgent need for social and economic assistance—the political machine.

White leaders of the ESL machine courted the black vote through assistance and promises of assistance. Over time, their control over political matters in the black community became so complete that black leaders were compelled to compromise the interests of their constituents for the sake of cultivating and maintaining the minimum level of machine support necessary for the perpetuation of a public career. Co-optation of black leadership led inexorably to the subordination of the entire black community to the commanding influence of the political machine in the ESL political system. In those rare instances where black politicians sought to challenge the machine for support in the black community, they found themselves confronted with an inpenetrable wall of opposition constructed by both blacks and whites caught up in the pervasive network of machine politics.

The colonized position of the black community was clearly manifested in the failure of an all-black slate in 1967 to win the city election, despite the existence in the city of a black electoral majority. Black politicians running independent of the ESL machine found black voters unwilling to sacrifice the material benefits they had customarily received from the mchine in order to elect to public office blacks committed to the social and economic improvement of the community as a whole. Given the dependent political position of the black community in the political system, efforts to mobilize the community to translate black potential power into black control were doomed to failure.

This case study of East Saint Louis illuminates some of the critical obstacles facing blacks in their quest for political power. Specifically, this discussion demonstrates that though the concentration of blacks in central cities and the current emphasis on racial solidarity may increase the possibilities of greater political influence, they are not sufficient to insure the development of cohesive black political action leading to the election of black candidates to high public office. In this context, it should be stressed that a number of factors associated with the phenomenon of internal colonialism act as intervening variables between the naked numerical strength and growing racial awareness of blacks and the translation of these resources into concrete political power. Among the most important of these variables is white control over the electoral decisions of blacks, a factor that serves to hamper the mobilization of the black vote as an effective independent force in the electoral process.

Part two of this volume provides evidence that obstacles to black political mobilization are not necessarily insuperable. Chapters in part two focus on the cities of Cleveland, Ohio, and Gary, Indiana. In-depth case studies of the 1967 mayoral elections in Cleveland and Gary are undertaken for the purpose of identifying the factors that enabled black politicians in those cities to overcome a range of obstacles and successfully mobilize the black community for independent political action.

1. These estimates are based on field research conducted by the Public Administration and Metropolitan Affairs Program, Southewn Illinois University, Edwardsville Campus.

2. A compilation of the socioeconomic characteristics of bbacks in ESL may be found in Robert Mendelson, *Why East St. Louis Needs to Be a Demonstration City* (Edwardsville: Public Administration and Metropolitan Affairs Program, Southern Illinois University, 1967).

3. East Saint Louis is governed under the commission form of government. Under this system the voters vote for a mayor and four commissioners, all of whom exercise both executive and legislative responsibilities. Each of the commissioners, including the mayor, is the chief executive for one of the city's departments, and the commission collectively makes policy.

4. Speculating on the reasons underpinning Saverson's behavior, one black politician suggested: "Maybe it is a thirty-year devotion which Saverson has built up—I mean a real emotional kind of devotion with Fields and some of the whites Saverson has dealt with. He thinks white men have done so much for him personally that he just can't see himself turning against them in order to really exert the pressure necessary to improve the lot of Negroes here. He would really be turning against himself. He has been admitted into a clique of whites who have dominated politics in East Saint Louis. He is part of the system we are trying now to destroy." This quotation and following unattributed quotations are derived from interviews conducted by members of the Public Administration and Metropolitan Affairs staff of Southern Illinois University, Edwardsville in connection with a larger study of black leadership in East Saint Louis. The authors would like to express appreciation for the permission to use these quotations and other relevant data from this study.

5. *Metro-East Journal*, 4 December 1966. All quotations from various editions of the *Metro-East Journal* are reprinted by permission of the publisher.

6. Ibid., 17 January 1967

7. Ibid.

8. Ibid., 22 January 1967.

9. *East St. Louis Monitor*, 26 January 1967. All quotations from various editions of the *East St. Louis Monitor* are reprinted by permission of the publisher.

10. *Metro-East Journal*, 28 February 1967.

11. Ibid., 8 March 1967.

12. Ibid., 22 March 1967.

13. Ibid., 27 March 1967.

14. Although the machine style has declined in most cities, aspects of machine-like organizations continue in such cities as Chicago, Philadelphia, Pittsburgh, Albany, and Gary; Edward C. Banfield and James Q. Wilson, *City Politics*, pp. 115-27.

15. Elliott Rudwick, *Race Riot at East St. Louis* (Carbondale: Southern Illinois University Press, 1964), p. 197.

16. Ibid., p. 220.

17. U.S. Bureau of Census, *Census of Population: 1940*.

18. G. Louis Heath, "Corrupt East St. Louis: Laboratory for Black Revolution," *The Progressive*, October 1970, pp. 24-27.

19. Fields's control over ESL politics remained firm until 1971 when he was defeated by James Williams, a black reform candidate who had no previous ties

64 / Electing Black Mayors

to the machine. Since 1971, the white machine has confined its activities mainly to county politics, leaving the struggle for control over city politics to competing sets of black politicians. In 1975 a city faction led by William Mason, superintendent of ESL public schools, defeated Williams in his bid for a second term as mayor.

20. *East St. Louis Monitor*, 24 March 1967.

21. The same phenomenon has been noted by Harry Scoble in his study, *Negro Politics in Los Angeles: The Quest for Power* (Los Angeles: Institute of Government and Public Affairs, University of California, 1967) in which he states that among blacks in Los Angeles there is an "ambivalence toward and distrust of all black leadership: an *almost* paranoid fear of a 'sell-out' " (p. 15).

22. Bush was very much aware of this obstacle and recognized the importance of finishing what he had started. In his campaign speeches Bush stressed the significance of his remaining in the race regardless of the outcome for the development of pride and political awareness by blacks in East Saint Louis. Bush believed that as a result of his running, little black children could look forward with hope "knowing that at least one Negro actually ran for mayor of East St. Louis and did not sell-out." *East St. Louis Monitor*, 24 March 1967.

PART II
Cleveland and Gary:
The Ingredients of Successful Mobilization

3
Cleveland: The Economic, Social, and Political Setting

INTRODUCTION

Throughout their history as citizens of the United States, blacks have been isolated from the levers of power in American politics. Despite extensive black involvement in American electoral politics dating back to the reconstruction era of the nineteenth century, at no point have blacks exercised sufficient control over the electoral process to demand that the priorities of governmental decision-making shift in a fundamental way toward issues and problems affecting the black community. As we have seen in chapters one and two, the influence of the black community in the electoral process has been diluted by a welter of institutional barriers that discourage black registration and stifle the organization of the black vote as an independent force.[1] Lacking sufficient economic, technical, bureaucratic, and organizational resources to overcome these institutional barriers, blacks have generally been locked out of public and private arenas where important policy issues are debated and resolved. If E. E. Schattschneider is correct in his assumption that some issues are organized into politics while others are organized out, it is clear that issues relating to the social and economic interests of the black community have been among those most often "organized out."[2]

The election of black mayors in Cleveland and Gary in 1967 provided the first important contemporary sign that the historic pattern of black powerlessness in the political process might be fundamentally changing. Carl Stokes and Richard Hatcher were not, of course, the first blacks in modern times to hold high public office. They were preceded in office by a number of black congressmen, among them William Dawson, Adam Clayton Powell, Charles Diggs, Robert Nix, and Augustus Hawkins. However, their elections as the first black mayors of major American cities were uniquely significant for two reasons. First, they represented the coming to power of blacks in northern urban politics. Prior to 1967, European ethnics, exercising tight control over local party organizations, had successfully blocked the ascension of blacks to high local offices. In 1957 it would have been as irrational for a black person to aspire for the mayorship of a major northern city, as it is for a black person to aspire for the presidency today. Black political-career prospects in local politics ended with a seat on the city council. To move beyond the council to the mayorship, or a top county post, was unthinkable. Second, the black victories in Cleveland and Gary in 1967 were achieved on the strength of the mass mobilization of the black vote for independent political action. In these elections, black voters appeared to turn their backs on white-controlled political organizations in order to vote for politically independent black candidates dedicated to expanding black control over broad sectors of local government. Thus, coming on the heels of massive urban uprisings by the black under class, and a spectacular growth in black political consciousness generally, these elections appeared to represent the opening events in a campaign of black revolt against domestic colonialism through the electoral process.

   This chapter begins our analysis of the 1967 campaigns and elections in Cleveland and Gary. The principal focus of this analysis will be on the factors that enabled blacks in Cleveland and Gary to overcome obstacles to the successful mobilization of blacks for independent action in the political process. Since it is impossible to understand contemporary events without an adequate comprehension of prior developments, we cast our analysis in the context of the political history of the two cities, particularly those aspects of that history pertaining to changes and continuities in black-white political relations. The central emphasis, however, is on the 1967 primary and general campaigns and elections. In the following four chapters on the campaigns and elections in both cities, we attempt to analyze the dynamics of political organization in the black community. This discussion enables us to at once take a trenchant look at the array of factors that impede the mobilization of the black vote, as well as the social, economic, psychological, and organizational factors essential to the successful surmounting of such obstacles.

Much of the material in the chapters on the 1967 elections will relate to the issue of strategies and techniques for activating and organizing the black vote. Although the examples used will be drawn from Cleveland and Gary, we are convinced that they are applicable to many communities where blacks are searching for the keys to a successful mobilization effort. We have therefore attempted to make our analysis of the Cleveland and Gary experience both detailed and lucid, with the hope that the facts and interpretations presented will be of great practical value to community leaders actively involved in the process of power transformation.

CLEVELAND: HISTORICAL BACKGROUND

The development of Cleveland began in 1796 when a surveying party for the Connecticut Land Company arrived at the juncture where the Cuyahoga River empties into Lake Erie. The surveying team, under the direction of Moses Cleaveland, proceeded to survey the entire Western Reserve of Connecticut and lay out a capital town. Both of these tasks were accomplished by late 1797.[3]

During the early years the settlement grew slowly. By 1815 only about 150 people had survived the frontier hardships of travel, land clearance, food production, war, and disease. The population increased to 1,075 during the next decade and a half as the community shifted from a frontier settlement to one that had the appearance and characteristics of a small New England village. Growth was stimulated by improved transportation facilities, the emergence of steam craft on Lake Erie, harbor improvements, and, most importantly, the completion of the Erie Canal in 1825 and the opening of the Ohio Canal in 1827, which linked Cleveland to Akron and eventually to the Ohio River. Traffic on both canals and Lake Erie throughout the 1830s and 40s transformed Cleveland into a flourishing mercantile center. By mid-century the population had spurted to 17,034 as "every stage, every canalboat and ship which entered port added to the population of the thriving community."[4]

During the second half of the nineteenth century Cleveland

emerged as an important and booming industrial center. Situated between the Marquette iron-ore range in upper Michigan and the coal of southern Ohio and Pennsylvania, the city was ideally located for the numerous industries interested in providing iron and steel for the Civil War and postwar market. Throughout this same period, the growth of industrial activity was supplemented and stimulated by the extension of railroads to Cleveland. The first railroad line reached the expanding community in 1851, and within a decade Cleveland "became the terminus of lines from the south and an important way station on the level lakeshore route to the west."[5] Cleveland's industrial growth was also spurred by the oil magnate John D. Rockefeller and his associates who decided that the city was ideally located for oil refining. Thus, by the 1880s Cleveland was a thriving industrial and railroad center, which became known as the oil capital of the world.

The combination of post–Civil War industrial development and transportation expansion transformed Cleveland into a classic boom town. Between 1860 and 1890 the population increased 600 percent to a total of 261,351 residents, thus making Cleveland the tenth largest city in the nation.

An extremely important component of Cleveland's economic growth and rapid population growth consisted of European immigrants who were attracted by the wide variety of economic opportunities associated with Cleveland's industrialization. An account of the 1890s reads:

> Into the industrial districts the immigrants swarmed with their large families, eager to work for small but alluring wages. Labor laws and factory protective devices were few. Factories and still more factories rose around downtown Cleveland, southwest to Newburgh and along the lakeshore, blanketing the congested areas with soot and smoke. As workers crowded together in old dwellings and tenements, housing facilities became wholly inadequate, and unhealthful living conditions developed. The more fortunate families escaped to the suburbs and the country, but the poor hurried into their places in the blighted sections. Here they struggled to keep body and soul together in communities where even trees had died.[6]

By the turn of the century representatives of virtually every nationality group in the world resided in Cleveland, and one out of every three Clevelanders were foreign born. The combination of that third of the population and those inhabitants who had at least one foreign-born parent constituted about 75 percent of the city's population in 1900.[7] This large, cosmopolitan segment of the population obviously had a significant impact on the social, economic, and political life of the community.

Each nationality group tended to congregate within certain neighborhoods throughout the city. Within these neighborhoods, immigrant institutions such as churches, schools, newspapers, political and civic organizations, social clubs, coffee houses, and food specialty stores and restaurants fortified a culture and life-style distinctively European in character. Ethnic festivals and celebrations, which often featured parades composed of individuals in homeland costumes, also contributed to the European flavor of the city.

Economically, the immigrant groups supplied the great bulk of the city's labor force. Their abundance furnished the cheap labor that was a necessary ingredient of the tremendous economic expansion experienced by Cleveland's industrial firms. In addition, some members of each group became small businessmen who tended to specialize in products and services for their own nationality group, although there were also instances in which their clientele was citywide in scope.

Their great numbers made the immigrants an important political resource. This fact, of course, was not ignored by the political leaders in the city. Since the trains that carried immigrants into the city were almost never on time, it was difficult for friends and relatives to meet the newcomers. Consequently, their places were often taken by agents of various ward politicians. The following description illustrates how the new arrivals were initiated into the local political system and linked to it within the neighborhood wards.

The political boss of the foreign wards in Cleveland was the same type to be found in most American cities. He was either a naturalized citizen or native born of the first generation, a resident of the ward he ruled, spoke the mother tongue, and of common race and religion with the people he controlled. The new arrival was gathered into the fold at the railway station and through further services was made to feel his obligation to the ward boss. Among these services were boarding houses and hotels to which the stranger was guided, aid in getting a job, small loans, and saloons and eating houses which served as clubs. Within the community, donations to charity, contributions for the celebration of various local and racial holidays, bail and legal

aid for the immigrant in court, acting as mediator in domestic and
community disputes, and supporting all projects for church and
community welfare added to the [ward leader's] influence and
power within the ward.[8]

Around the turn of the century, then, Cleveland, like many
other American cities at that time, was governed by a machine
style of politics that relied heavily on the immigrant vote to keep
the bosses in office. Being unfamiliar with the American political
system and extremely grateful for the services extended to them
by the political machine, most of the immigrants were more than
willing to trade their votes for the favors received. Indeed, this
exchange was based in many instances on a personal relationship
that was completely devoid of political ideology. The newcomers
generally voted for the candidates endorsed by their ethnic leaders because they were personally indebted to the leaders and
trusted them as friends, not because they weighed the political
posture of the various politicians.

OVERVIEW OF THE POLITICAL SYSTEM

A possible exception to this pattern, at least at the mayoralty
level, occurred between 1901 and 1909 when Tom Johnson served
as mayor. Prior to his mayorship, Johnson was a street-railroad
magnate who had made a fortune by the usual corrupt methods
that were characteristic of the period and machine-style government. However, during a railroad trip Johnson read the work of
socialist Henry George, who argued that although the nation
was prospering the masses of people were becoming increasingly
impoverished. George identified the private ownership of land
as the main root of injustice and called for a "single tax" on increased land value that was not derived from the labor of the
owner. Johnson found George's arguments so convincing that he
joined the progressive reform movement, won four successive terms as mayor of Cleveland on antibusiness platforms, battled for municipal ownership of utilities and the single tax, and
became one of the most famous mayors in the nation. During his
reign reformers from all over the country visited Cleveland to exchange information with Johnson and learn his methods of operation.

The Republican machine in Cleveland finally beat the Democrat Johnson in 1910. Under the direction of Maurice Maschke, the son of German Jewish immigrants, the party selected Herman Baehr, a candidate with German ancestry, to run against Johnson. As one of the largest ethnic groups in the city, the Germans had solidly backed Johnson in previous elections; but in 1910 Baehr carried the German wards, which proved to be the difference.[9] From that time until the early 1930s, with the exception of the years 1912–15 when Democrat Newton Baker was mayor, the Republican party machinery, directed by Maschke, controlled city hall and elected a string of Republican mayors.

Republican domination of city hall included the years 1923–31, during which time Cleveland became the largest city in the nation to adopt the city-manager plan. The plan was approved by the voters after a crime commission exposed numerous city hall scandals in the early 1920s. The political bosses, however, did not allow the new form of government to curtail their influence. Maschke and Burr Gongwer, the Democratic leader, agreed to join forces by having their respective councilmen, who numbered twenty-one of the twenty-five members on the city council, vote for the same city-manager candidate. As part of the same deal, Maschke was given control over 60 percent of the available patronage jobs and Gongwer the remaining 40 percent.[10] This arrangement continued until the Republicans achieved majority control of the city council in 1929. However, in that same year a new series of city hall scandals were uncovered, and several Republican councilmen were indicted for their involvement in shady city-land deals. As a consequence, during the following two years the city-manager plan was voted out and the fifteen-year Republican hold on city hall was broken in 1932 by the mayoral victory of Democrat Ray T. Miller. Miller was propelled into the political limelight of the time as the county prosecutor who had successfully handled the graft cases and exposed Republican corruption.

Despite the Roosevelt victory at the national level (Cleveland delivered a large Democratic majority for him) and additional Republican scandals that led to indictments against Maschke, the Democrats were able to control city hall for only two years. In 1934, Harry Davis, the Republican mayor between 1915 and 1919, defeated Miller, who was hampered by internal splits within the Democratic ranks.[11] Davis, however, also encountered discordance within his party, and two years later he was defeated in the Republican primary by Harold Burton.

Burton proceeded to defeat Miller, who was once again the Democratic candidate, and became known as the first of a succession of what has been termed the "independent-newspaper mayors" of Cleveland. With strong newspaper backing, Burton played down the importance of party affiliation by conducting his campaign out of an independent headquarters and a Republican headquarters. During his tenure in office the local newspapers began to supersede the political parties as the dominant political influence in selecting and electing Cleveland mayors. According to a political reporter with the *Cleveland Press* since 1932,

> Eagle-eyed criticism was the newspaper rule for Miller and Davis, but Burton became sort of a sacred cow. During his first term, every action he took won him praise. He played a cagey game. His ear was always cocked toward the editors' offices. He kept in constant touch with the three editors, and carried his problems to their door steps. . . . Reporters found that stories they uncovered about him often had already been divulged to the "front office" by the mayor and were being held subject to his release. He was a terrific worker, both at City Hall and on the stump, and often would climb the steps of newspaper offices at night delivering himself statements he had written out in longhand.[12]

Burton served three successive terms and was elected to the United States Senate while still in his third term. Edward Blythin, his law director, filled his unexpired term and sought the mayorship in the election of 1941. Blythin's Democratic opponent was Frank J. Lausche, a well-known judge and son of immigrant Slovenian parents. The *Cleveland Press* vigorously backed Lausche, who garnered a solid vote from the various ethnic wards (precincts populated by European immigrants) and became one of the first ethnic mayors of a major American city.

Lausche's triumph represented the beginning of a new political era in Cleveland's history. Prior to his election the political system was generally dominated by Republican WASPs. Ethnic voters and politicians were important influences, particularly at the ward level; but up until that time, despite their large numbers, the southern and eastern European ethnics never had a representative in the highest political spot—the mayorship. Thus Lausche's ascendance to the mayor's seat signaled at least the symbolic conclusion of Republican WASP control and symbolized for many of the ethnic voters a vicarious achievement of acceptance into the American political system. "For the first time, one of their boys had made it to the top." From that time on, each of the succeeding mayors was in some sense a representative of the ethnic voters. Lausche's successor was Thomas Burke, an Irish Roman Catholic, who served from 1945 to 1951. He was followed by Anthony Celebrezze, an Italian-American who won five straight mayoralty elections (1953–61) before he joined the Kennedy administration as Commissioner of Health, Education, and Welfare. Celebrezze was succeeded in 1962 by his law director Ralph Locher, a Lithuanian, who serve as mayor until 1967.

Each of these Democratic, ethnic mayors was sustained by heavy support among ethnic voters and the newspapers, particularly the *Cleveland Press* headed by Louis B. Seltzer. The relationship established between the mayor's office and the newspapers during the Burton administration became even stronger throughout the next four decades. The prevailing political lore of the city maintained that "if you don't have the backing of the *Press*, you can't win." Seltzer as editor of the *Cleveland Press* gained the informal title of "Mr. Cleveland," and in political circles the universal opinion was that he personally selected who would be mayor and then utilized the full resources of the newspaper to promote the candidate among the ethnic voters and successfully elect him. Why the *Press* was able to exert such influence is partially explained by the following observation:

> Here was the situation. The Hannas, the Rockefellers, the Boltens, the owners of the mills, the coal mines, and the railroads—the people who built Cleveland and brought these people over here to work looked to the *Plain Dealer*. It was their paqer, the Vales were their people. Francis Bolten, who served twenty-two years in Congress and whose husband was there twenty years before was for many years the principal owner of the *Plain Dealer*. It was the Establishment paper. Now as the mill workers and ethnic community grew, Louie Seltzer saw that his audience was not going to live in Pepper Pike or the other suburbs, but that he was going to appeal to the ethnic community. So the *Press* was written in simple language with a reasonable amount of pictures. It was specifically directed toward these communities and did a first-class job of gaining their loyalties. For example, he would sponsor a Slovenian Day in Rockefeller Park, and his carriers would get out and sell in those neighborhoods. The ethnic community was Seltzer's prime audience.[13]

In addition, Seltzer employed a special "ethnic affairs" reporter named Dominic Andrika, who not only covered ethnic events in Cleveland but also spent about six months each year touring Europe to visit the relatives of Clevelanders and report news about the hometowns of various immigrant citizens. Consequently, although the *Press* was an American newspaper, it provided a direct linkage for many hyphenated Americans to the old country and therefore: "Whatever the *Press* said politically was gospel to these people—it was like the bible." Within this context, it is understandable that the front-page, banner editorials endorsing a particular candidate for mayor and numerous favorable news stories about him generally resulted in impressive electoral majorities within the ethnic wards.

As the political influence of the *Cleveland Press* increased, the ability of the political parties to control city hall diminished. Emulating the posture first assumed by Burton, each of the successive mayors emphasized their independence from the party. Their newspaper endorsement was generally accompanied by a mayoralty campaign platform that was antiparty and antibossism in content. The objective of this political posture was to project an image of honesty and independence that contrasted with the historical party image of corruption and bossism. Thus, although all of the mayors since Burton were Democrats, "they were newspaper candidates first who happened to be Democrats, they were not selected by the party leaders." The usual pattern was one in which the *Press* would select a candidate, the Democratic party an opposing one, the newspaper candidate would receive strong media backing and would win, and the party would then support the incumbent mayor when he ran a second time. In each instance it was clear to all political observers that the party came to the man, rather than the man to the party and that the key political resource was the endorsement by the *Press*.

This situation had the obvious effect of splitting the Democratic party organization into at least two factions, one centering around the mayor and the other around county and state offices and, to some extent, city council positions. Whereas the *Press* was particularly successful at selecting and electing Cleveland mayors, the Democratic party was generally quite successful at electing its candidates to the other local offices and state offices. However, despite its greater degree of success at these other levels, the fact that the party was unable to control the mayorship clearly weakened its position within the city's political system. Without centralized party control over city-hall patronage, it was difficult for the party to exert its influence at the ward level. As a result, each councilman tended to develop his personal political organization, and his ward was operated more as an individual fiefdom than an integral part of a well-oiled, citywide party organization. This is not to say that the Democratic party organization was not important at the ward level—it was in the sense that its endorsement helped a candidate; but the party lacked the potency to command ward-level politics and city council decision-making. In contrast to Chicago, for example, where the party organization is highly integrated and power-centralized, the Cleveland Democratic party was not united and thus power was highly decentralized.

During this period the Republican party in Cleveland experienced a greater decline in influence than did the Democratic party. Republican councilmen never constituted a majority on the council, and no Republican mayoralty candidate ever received more than 43 percent of the vote. Indeed, on three occasions the Republican party did not even bother to slate a mayoralty candidate, and numerous other offices went uncontested to the Democrats. In many instances, winning the Democratic primary (and it was on that occasion that the party organization was most influential) was tantamount to winning on general election day. In sum, the Democratic organization was hampered by factionalism, but the Republican organization was even weaker.

The regime of mayors beginning with Lausche produced a city administration that was characterized by party independence, honesty, low taxes, low service levels, and, in the words of a long-time observer, "a caretaker type government that never really appreciated the tremendous changes taking place in the city and never moved to really respond to them." Although some commentators criticized the city government for the above-mentioned characteristics, it was a government that largely reflected the nature of its primary constituency. As noted earlier, the bulk of the population was composed of European immigrants and their offsprings. For the most part, these were working-class people who opposed high taxes and were not particularly convinced that the city government should become involved in a wide range of costly activities. They appeared to be quite satisfied with a government that provided traditional municipal services in a modest and honest manner. Whether this type of government was appropriate for the times is a subjective question not easily answered. It is apparent, however, that after World War II Cleveland did experience significant changes that the city government found extremely difficult to cope with. Indeed, the changes were of such magnitude they eventually led to the end of the regime ushered in by Lausche.

POSTWAR CHANGES

Similar to many other northeastern and midwestern cities, Cleveland experienced a dramatic population transformation in the post-World War II period. Table 6 illustrates the most significant aspect of this shift—the decrease in white inhabitants and increase in black residents. Between 1930 and 1965 almost 300,000 whites left the city while the black population increased by 204,000; thus by the latter date one out of every three Clevelanders was black. This simultaneous shift began in the 1930s but was most pronounced during the 1950s when the white population decreased by 142,000 and the black population increased by 103,000.

TABLE 6

WHITE POPULATION DECREASE AND BLACK POPULATION
INCREASE IN CLEVELAND, 1930–1965

Year	Total (000)	White (000)	Percentage Change	Black (000)	Percentage of Total
1930	900	828	+ 8.6	72	8.0
1940	878	793	− 4.2	85	9.7
1950	915	765	− 3.5	148	16.2
1960	876	623	−18.6	251	28.7
1965	811	523	−14.7	276	34.0

SOURCE: U. S., Bureau of the Census, *U. S. Census of Population: 1960* and *Current Population Reports: Special Census of Cleveland, Ohio, 1965.*

Two basic population trends contributed to this pattern. On the one hand, the white decline was largely due to the migration of whites into the surrounding suburbs. As was the case in other cities, the more affluent, well-educated whites selected suburbia as a more pleasant residential setting for raising their families.[14] This preference left Cleveland with an unusually small, white-collar, middle class. Indeed, among the twenty-one cities with populations over 500,000, Cleveland ranks last in percentage of white-collar workers. Another indication of the middle-class exodus to the suburbs is the generally accepted figure that the Jewish population of Cleveland is 500, compared to 85,000 for the surrounding suburbs.[15] Most of the whites left behind in the core city could not afford the move to suburbia or they were so attached to their working-class, ethnic neighborhoods that they were reluctant to leave. Complementing this suburbanization of the more affluent whites was the in-migration of southern blacks. The multitude of industrial jobs in Cleveland and the active recruiting in southern communities by several Cleveland firms resulted in the fact that in 1960 nearly 50 percent of all of the blacks in Cleveland were southern born, giving Cleveland a higher proportion of black migrants from the South than any other northern city with a large black population.[16]

Approximating the experience of the immigrant groups before them, the masses of the new black arrivals found that they were confined to the bottom rung of Cleveland's socioeconomic ladder and that they faced pervasive discrimination. In the area of housing, for example, the black newcomers found it virtually impossible to buy or rent homes in Cleveland suburbs, although many whites with similar incomes were successful.[17] Not only were blacks restricted to the core city, but within the city they were pressed into an overcrowded area of Cleveland's East Side. As a result of this process Cleveland began to resemble two cities: one that was largely populated by blacks and located on the east side of the Cuyahoga River (which runs through the middle of Cleveland) and the other that was largely populated by white ethnic Americans and located on the west side of the Cuyahoga River. That housing discrimination was practiced against blacks is indicated by the fact that none were able to rent housing in the forty-nine census tracts on the West Side that had median rents comparable to the black neighborhoods. Their confinement to the overcrowded section of the East Side resulted in 9,000 black families living in substandard units, 13,100 living in overcrowded units, and 23,400 families paying more than a quarter of their income for rent.[18]

Black workers confronted similar difficulties in their search for employment. Their unemployment rate in 1965 was 8.9 percent compared to 2.4 percent for white workers. In some sections of the black ghetto, the unemployment rate for young black males (fourteen to twenty-five) ranged from 23 percent to 38 percent.[19] Among the blacks that were employed, most were confined to the most menial and low-paying jobs. This was not only the case in private industry but also in public employment. The city of Cleveland, for example, had a work force that consisted of 28.6 percent black employees; but one-half of them worked as laborers for the Division of Streets.[20] Despite federal compliance laws requiring equal employment opportunities, the membership of most unions that worked on federal construction projects in the Cleveland area contained virtually no blacks. In 1966, for instance, the ironworkers had 1,786 members and no blacks; the pipefitters 1,319 members and 1 black; the electricians 1,258 members and 2 blacks; the plumbers 1,482 members and 3 blacks; and the sheet metal workers 1,077 members and 45 blacks.[21] In this regard, the U.S. Commission on Civil Rights concluded that the Bureau of Apprenticeship and Training, U.S. Department of Labor, had failed to meet its responsibility for insuring nondiscrimination in federally registered apprenticeship and training programs in Cleveland.[22]

One obvious consequence of this dismal employment situation was that the average black family earned $2,500 less than the average white family: $4,768 compared to $7,350. Further, 28 percent of black families contrasted to 9 percent of white families earned less than $3,000 (in the 1960s, an often-used poverty index). These income figures indicate that a majority of blacks in Cleveland were living in poverty or the close fringes of poverty in 1960.

Those blacks who were forced into the welfare assistance program found no relief from poverty there. The Cuyahoga County Welfare Department (the welfare agency in the Cleveland area) established in 1960 that an Aid to Dependent Children family of four required $200.95 per month to maintain a "decent" living level. Yet the Welfare Department provided only $170.81 a month in 1960 (only 70 percent of its own minimum standard); and despite the cost of living increase of 11 percent by 1966, the agency provided 81 cents *less* to ADC recipients.[23] Since any earnings from work were subtracted from the monthly welfare check even when earnings and welfare assistance together added up to less than 100 percent of the minimum standard, the welfare recipients could not realistically undertake full- or part-time work to overcome their poverty existence. Needy children of an employed

father who earned less than the standard were ineligible for supplementary aid. The children would become elgible for assistance
only if the father left home and the welfare department was satisfied that there was "no man in the house." Individuals on
welfare not only received less than the minimum standard (a
standard that was 20 percent less than the federal government's
poverty level) but were also made to suffer numerous indignities
and inconveniences in order to receive their assistance. Eligibil-
ity, for example, was established through a personally embar-
rassing process and was continuously challenged. Welfare recipients, most of whom received their checks on the same day, had
difficulty cashing their checks at Cleveland banks; had to wait
in long lines at the two food-stamp distribution centers; and then
were restricted in their purchases with food stamps—for example,
they could not use the stamps to purchase soap and cleaning
supplies. Thus, the welfare system in Cleveland, rather than operating to assist blacks out of poverty, more often than not condemned them to a life of poverty.

Some salient characteristics of the Cleveland school system suggest that it was making little progress toward insuing that the
younger generation of blacks would fare any better in the community than their parents. Despite onsiderable research showing the detrimental impact of segregated education on black students, the Cleveland school system, by adhering to a neighborhood school-attendance policy, maintained highly segregated
schools. In 1965, for instance, about 91 percent of elementary
students attended schools that were 95 to 100 percent white or
black. Further, although black teachers constituted 43 percent of
the staff, over 80 percent of them taught in all-black schools.[24]
A study of the school system in 1956 found a marked difference
in the academic performance of black and white students in Cleveland. This study reported that black students consistently scored
lower on standardized achievement tests, and suggested that the
gap between black and white performance tended to grow wider
at each successive stage in the educational process.[25] In comparing the annual student dropout rate between black and white
students, the same report found that the dropout rate in predominantly black schools was more than double what it was in white
schools, 14.6 percent to 6.5 percent. In addition, it was found that
among the thirty-two school districts in the Cleveland metropoli-

tan area, the city system ranked twenty-eighth in per pupil expenditures and had the highest teaqher-pupil ratio. Consequently, many of the black students who did graduate from Cleveland schools found that the quality of education provided did not prepare them adequately for either the labor market or higher education.

In addition to the problems faced in the above mentioned areas of life, many blacks found the Cleveland police department to be anything but a friendly and helpful agency. The prevailing attitude among most ghetto residents was that the police were prejudiced, discourteous, unwarrantedly brutal towards blacks, permitted prostitution and gambling to flourish in black neighborhoods, and discriminated in their treatment of white and black citizens.[26] These beliefs were well justified, given the experiences of numerous blacks with the police department. A statistical study of police practices, for example, strongly supported the pervasive feeling among blacks that the police responded more slowly to their calls for help than they did to calls for assistance in white neighborhoods. The investigator found that in every crime category the police responded more slowly to calls in black neighborhoods than white neighborhoods and that in some categories, such as robbery, it took the police almost four times as long to respond to calls in black areas. After considerable testimony and investigation, the U.S. Civil Rights Commission concluded that black residents in Cleveland were "often arrested without a warrant, without probable cause, and without an offense being committed in the presence of the police officer, and are detained for as long as 72 hours under a nonexistent charge known as 'investigation' which makes them ineligible for bond."[27] Many persons arrested in this manner were denied the right to make a telephone call to an attorney or their family—a violation of state law. It was found that such unlawfully detained persons were not charged with a violation of law, but that before being released they were required to sign a waiver. This waiver was a police department form on which the signer pleaded guilty to a charge, usually that of being a "suspicious person," and waived his right to sue the city for unlawful arrest and detention. If a citizen chose to complain about such practices, the complaints were handled by the district commander of the officer against whom the charge was filed. The Commission also discovered that Cleveland had no central complaint system; no policy that complaints be funneled to the Chief of Police; and no written or publicized procedure for review of complaints.

One black citizen testified before the Civil Rights Commission that he and a friend were arrested for no apparent cause, taken to the fourth floor of a police station, and beaten by several policemen. While being beaten his friend was told to bark like a dog: "Hill wouldn't, at first, so I could hear them punching on him harder and harder and pretty soon he started to bark and he said, 'That is right, you bark like a black dog.' "[28]

Prior to the emergence of the civil rights movement in the early 1960s, blacks found that they had little political leverage to alter the oppressive conditions they lived under. It is true that as each ward shifted in composition from white to black another black councilman would eventually be elected to the city council; however, this process did not result in any basic redress o$ black grievances. If any fundamental race policy was placed before the council, the blacks (who held only ten of the thirty-three seats) were decisively outnumbered and outvoted by the white councilmen. Further, the black councilmen, except for one or two of them, rarely pushed race issues at the council meetings. Reflective of the highly decentralized political system of the city, black councilmen "never worked together to push or block legislation. Each one was concerned only with his own image, his own ward organization, his own petty patronage, his own hustle—they never got together to help the entire black community. . . . The average black would support a politician they thought would help them individually, but concerning collective Negro political power—it was never seriously considered by them because it was never practiced by the so-called leaders." Consequently, although Cleveland did not have a machine-type political system as was the case in East Saint Louis, black politics was still characterized by an emphasis on individual advancement and benefit, notbgroup progress. Virtually all of the black politicians were primarily interested in what tangible rewards they and their close associates could secure from the system, not what they could do collectively to improve the living conditions of average blacks. Black councilmen were described by one respondent in the following manner:

> The major black politicians were all councilmen, except Stokes, and each of them had his own principality. They were divided and only had support within their limited areas. Few of the Negro councilmen

were any different from the county political people who were basically concerned with control and their own personal betterment. They were not concerned with community issues or the improvement of their neighborhoods. Frequently, in Council, these black politicians supported special interests who were after liquor permits, or housing and zoning exceptions and variations which were opposed by the bulk of the people in the neighborhood.

Little wonder, then, that many blacks felt that the Cleveland political system "offered them no real alternatives—the Republicans were out of the question but white and black Democrats weren't much better from the black man's point of view. A lot were naturally cynical about politics."

RACIAL POLARIZATION

The depth of the black plight was apparently unknown or simply ignored by most white Clevelanders until the early 1960s. This lack of awareness or concern resulted from several factors. First, as was noted earlier, the city was highly segregated, thus blacks and whites had few contacts with one another. Second, at a symbolic level individual blacks seemed to be doing quite well in Cleveland. This success of highly visible blacks cultivated the notion among many whites (who had themselves, together with members of their immediate families, experienced numerous hardships in industrial Cleveland) that blacks as the newest immigrants were progressing from the depths as did the other ethnic groups before them. The prevailing image among whites was that Cleveland was a good town for blacks. The observations of a white, life-time resident of Cleveland illustrates the point and indicates how the myth was first shattered:

Cleveland prided itself on quote, "good relations," even as late as the 1960s. The head of steam that Cleveland built up in the 1920s and 1930s as a good city for Negroes lulled many people into a sense of false pride. Cleveland had Negro judges, Negro councilmen and Negroes working in milk delivery trucks and things like that long before many other cities. . . . Larry Doby was the first Negro to play baseball in the American League, and he played here in Cleveland. The Cleveland Browns was the first major professional football team to have Negroes. Paul Brown went out and actively recruited Bill Willis and Marion Motely. So the fact that Cleveland had Negroes in sports and had Negro judges and councilmen created an image of good relationships. . . . And earlier Cleveland never had a concentrated ghetto as such. Negroes were spread, in clusters nevertheless mind you, but they were spread in various parts of the city —Glenville, Mount Pleasant, Fairfax, places like that in the central area. However, with the rapid exodus of whites from the city in the late 1950s and the increasing number of Negroes coming into the city and the development of a black belt and overcrowding of the schools, things started to come to a head. All of a sudden, the presumed good relations turned sour—arising out of the school crisis. [Before then] the NAACP was the major civil rights group in town and it made a quiet, low-key effort to redress long-standing grievances. The thing that got the civil rights movement in active gear in this town were the newer groups, groups like CORE. It was CORE that precipitated the show down with the school board. They were much more militant and began to define the problem in terms of housing, jobs, and schools. This took the discussion from the level of the successful individuals to the problems of the masses—it got down to the nitty-gritty. And when you got down to that level and the Negro community let it be known that it wasn't content to have judges and football players and baseball players—that there was more at stake and brought this to the attention of the white community, then there was a hardening of feelings. Then it became a frontal attack and this got the backs up of the great middle body of white people who felt threatened and who were angered. . . . So about 1963-1964 a change came about in race relations here from passive, low-key complaints to militant confrontation; and for the first time in my memory, there was open hostility between the races.

Cleveland, then, like many other northern cities had experienced fairly placid race relations prior to the early 1960s. To be sure, the appalling living conditions of blacks were there, and the festering grievances of the black community boiled below the surface; but for the most part that is where things remained, below the surface. The legalistic, diplomatic, behind-the-scenes negotiation approach of the major civil rights organization, the NAACP, tended to keep the visibility of black distress low and contributed to the conventional assumption among whites that conditions were not exceptionally bad among blacks. This deceiving serenity was eventually shattered in Cleveland as a result of a new phase in the civil rights movement that emerged in the South during the late 1950s and early 1960s. The southern emphasis on taking to the streets and involving masses of people in direct action became the model for northern activity, and was soon being practiced in the streets in Cleveland.

Although it is difficult to pinpoint with any certainty when the new civil rights thrust began in Cleveland, the forming of the local chapter of the Congress of Racial Equality (CORE) in 1962 is a logical date. As in other northern cities, CORE, with its stress on militant, direct-action tactics, became the major competitor of the NAACP and pushed the traditional organization into assuming a more militant posture. By early 1963 the Cleveland NAACP found that its leadership was being challenged by the newly formed CORE chapter and some fifty other civil rights groups in the community. Consequently, in part to insure its own survival, the NAACP attempted to bring about some unity among the groups, and, by the summer of 1963, it was instrumental in forging a new coalition of civil rights organizations entitled the United Freedom Movement (UFM). The new coalition had a membership that included "inner-city ministers, leaders of the Jewish community, traditional Negro leaders, and some of Cleveland's new breed of angry young black men."[29]

The UFM's first action was directed against the contractors and unions who were involved in building the city's Convention Center. In July 1963 the UFM proclaimed that it would picket the center unless 3 black electricians and 2 black plumbers were hired to work on the project.[30] This first threat stimulated a series of negotiations but failed to produce any satisfactory results, because the electricians had only 2 blacks among 1,400 members, the plumbers no blacks among 1,300 members, and neither union was about to admit blacks immediately. Consequently, the UFM announced that it would place 1,000 pickets at all entrances to the center project and would attempt to have all public funds withdrawn from the apprenticeship-training programs of all discriminating unions. After this second threat, the electrical union agreed to accept 2 black apprentices on the project, and the plumbers consented to accept 2 black journeymen.

The compromise agreement did not end the conflict, however, because when the 2 black plumbers showed up for work 11 union plumbers, who considered the blacks "house plumbers" walked off the job and were followed by 45 pipe fitters and asbestos workers. Thereafter, the plumber's union voted to declare a "holiday" beginning Monday, 29 July. On that day, no union plumbers showed up for work at the center, and 700 other plumbers stayed home. This action produced a series of lengthy negotiations that finally resulted in a settlement on 4 August 1963. The agreement was a mixed victory for UFM; black journeymen would be accepted into the union, but not until they passed the standard examination administered by the plumber's union.

Immediately after the employment controversy was settled the UFM turned its attention to the Cleveland school system. The rapid influx of blacks into Cleveland and their concentration into already overcrowded East Side neighborhoods placed a great enrollment strain on the neighborhood schools. Consequently, by 1960 many black students, particularly those in the Hazeldell area, were attending half-day sessions, and other black students were crammed into greatly overcrowded schools. Various civil rights organizations and parent groups petitioned the Board of Education to provide more schools in the area and to bus children currently in the overcrowded schools to under-utilized schools. Finally, in October 1961 the board responded to these requests by authorizing the superintendent of schools to prepare a transportation plan. The plan was submitted and approved the following month.

Soon after, black students were being bused to vacant classrooms in predominantly white schools on the fringes of the East Side. The board made it clear that the bussing was only a temporary arrangement and would be eliminated when new facilities were constructed in the overcrowded neighborhoods. The board policy also called for the black students not to be integrated into the classrooms of the receiving schools, rather they were transported as "administrative units" with the teacher accompanying each class. Thus, black and white students attended separate classes. Further, the bussed students were not permitted to use certain facilities in the receiving schools. At Murray Hill School, for example, bussed students were not permitted to use the school swimming pool.[31]

In August 1963, the UFM presented the school board with a list of demands relating to discrimination in the schools, one of which called for the immediate integration of transported classes into the receiving schools. When the school board failed to meet a 23 September deadline, the UFM responded by picketing the board headquarters. Five days later the board held a public meeting at which it pledged to take steps toward the "fullest possible integration consistent with sound educational practice" in the receiving schools and to create a citizen's committee to encourage true integration in the schools.[32] The policy statement was accepted, not without internal disagreement, by UFM; the matter appeared to be resolved.

In January 1964, however, the UFM leadership announced that in their estimation the board was not fulfilling the agreement. Subsequent meetings between the UFM and the board produced only frustration; whereupon the UFM decided to picket the receiving schools. On the first day of picketing the demonstrators were met by angry groups of whites, who at one school forced the demonstrators off the sidewalks into the path of passing automobiles. The following day produced an even more dangerous and intensive confrontation. The demonstrators planned to picket at Murray Hill School, in the heart of Cleveland's "Little Italy," but a crowd of enraged whites had already surrounded the school before they arrived. It became obvious that picketing might produce bloodshed, so the demonstrators did not march on the school. The angry whites, however, moved to a busy intersection and began to attack blacks driving by in their automobiles. During this action the Cleveland police simply stood between the demonstrators and the whites, making no arrests, "despite the fact that for an entire day the Murray Hill mob roamed the streets beating Negroes, newsmen, anyone who enraged them, and throwing rocks and bottles at passing automobiles."[33] The response from city hall was not particularly encouraging; Mayor Ralph Locher maintained that the school conflict was outside his jurisdiction.

The struggle was escalated further on 3 February 1964, when the UFM staged a sit-in at the Board of Education building and were forcibly removed by the police. Matters were temporarily resolved, however, the next day when the board publicly announced that it would take immediate steps to integrate the bussed students.

Two months later the controversy was reopened once again when the UFM directed its protest against the construction of new schools within the black areas of the East Side. They maintained that constructing schools in those areas would only resegregate schools, not desegregate them. Consequently, the UFM joined the Hazeldell Parents Association, a group of Glenville residents, in picketing one of the school construction sites. In their efforts to stop construction, some of the demonstrators placed themselves into construction pits and in front of construction equipment. Whereas bloodshed was averted in Murray Hill, it was not avoided on this occasion. In the confusion of the demonstrations, the Reverend Bruce Klunder, a white minister who had helped to organize the local chapter of CORE, was run over by a bulldozer and killed. Police attempted to end the demonstration by dragging demonstrators away from the construction site; but as word of Klunder's death spread, violence erupted throughout the area. "Bands of angry Negroes roamed the streets, looted stores, and battled police late into the night."[34]

Following the death of Reverend Klunder, the UFM was blocked by a court injunction against further interference with school construction. The UFM reacted by calling for a school boycott, and on 20 April about 85 percent of the black students stayed home. Although the boycott was successful in demonstrating an unprecedented display of unity in the black community, this action and the other demonstrations were unable to reverse the increasing segregation of Cleveland schools. In the final analysis, the protests did not alter the board's building plans or the board's commitment to neighborhood schools. Consequently, the school system was more highly segregated in 1965 than it had been in 1963.

If there were any lingering doubts among blacks as to where the white-controlled city government stood on their grievances, additional proof was provided in May 1965. Testifying before an Ohio state legislative committee on the question of the state's death penalty, the Cleveland police chief, Richard R. Wagner, argued that it should be retained. His rationale was: "In Cleveland . . . we have people saying they intend to overthrow the government of the United States and incidentally, shoot all the Caucasians. One of these groups is RAM [Revolutionary Action Movement]." This statement was widely interpreted in the black community to mean that the death penalty should be retained as an instrument for keeping black militants in line. Consequently, the UFM leadership requested a meeting with Mayor Locher to discuss the police chief's statement. Although they called Locher, wrote letters to him, and sent telegrams, they received no reply. Therefore, five of the leaders (a black attorney, three ministers, and the local director of CORE) began a "wait-in" at Locher's office. Each day they asked for an appointment, it was refused, and they sat there throughout the day. Richard Gunn, the black attorney, recounts the incident: "We didn't have any signs, and we weren't singing; we just sat there quietly. On the third day we decided not to go home at five o'clock, when City Hall closed. At five-twenty we were arrested and taken to jail."[35]

The mayor's refusal to meet the delegation and his order to jail them, particularly the ministers, was interpreted as a stinging insult to the black community. From that time on "Ralph Locher's name became dirt among blacks. That incident became a symbol of the badly deteriorated relations between the mayor and the black community of Cleveland." The incident also signified beyond doubt the growing hostility and polarization of the races in Cleveland. Just how intense the racial division had become was made abundantly clear by the 1965 mayoralty election.

THE 1965 MAYORALTY ELECTION: VICTORY IN DEFEAT

Recruiting a Black Candidate

Early in 1965 it was obvious to many Cleveland citizens, including two politically active black women, Geraldine Williams and Jean Capers, that Mayor Locher would seek reelection and probably win again in the coming fall election, and that the black community would be subjected to another two years of Locher rule. Both women were officers in the Nonpartisan Voters League, a biracial organization that was formed in February 1964 to study Cleveland's government and determine how blacks could play a greater role in it. They decided that the population shift in Cleveland had advanced to the point where it was conceivable that a black could be elected mayor. Once that determination was made they went over a list of prominent black political figures searching for "a man whose name was not unknown, that could command a vote, that had demonstrated vote-getting power in the past." The man they selected was Carl B. Stokes, a representative in the Ohio state legislature.

Stokes had a variety of characteristics that made him a particularly appealing choice. He had grown up in Cleveland's black ghetto and had experienced firsthand all of the hardships it entailed. He was a high school dropout who had returned from the army to finish high school and then proceeded to earn a college degree and a law school degree. In 1958 he was appointed to Cleveland's law department as an assistant police prosecutor, a position he held until 1962. In the latter year he was elected to the Ohio House of Representatives, thus becoming the first black Democrat to serve in the Ohio legislature. He was reelected to his legislative seat in 1964.

Besides being "a very personable, young black man who was knowledgeable about politics," Stokes was considered as an especially good prospect by the two women because he had been elected to the legislature both times by running at-large in Cuyahoga County. This meant that he was acceptable to both white and black voters, a factor that would be of considerable importance in the forthcoming mayoralty election, since blacks constituted only 40 percent of Cleveland's voters. In contrast to the other leading black politicians in Cleveland, Stokes was the only well-known one with a record of biracial support. The ten black councilmen had been elected from solidly black wards; there were no black congressmen because the congressional districts were gerrymandered to include a majority of white voters; and although black judges were elected with white support, they generally had low political visibility. Further, Stokes was one of the few black politicians who had gained support from the entire black community. Unlike the black councilmen who generally had strength only in their own wards, Stokes had been elected twice to the legislature with solid support from black voters in all neighborhoods. Consequently, the league members decided that if they were going to propose a black to be mayor of Cleveland, Stokes was about the only black politician with characteristics that gave them a reasonable chance of gaining wide public support for their choice.

After settling upon Stokes as the best prospective candidate, the two women journeyed to the state capital and proposed to Stokes that he seek the mayorship. According to one of them "he laughed and thought the idea was ludicrous." The conversation centered upon what it would take to convince Stokes to run. One of the women suggested that they return to Cleveland and initiate a draft movement, independent of any involvement by Stokes himself, to see how much popular support they could generate for him. Stokes agreed to the plan but made no commitment one way or the other. Whereupon, the two women returned to Cleveland and proceeded to collect the signatures of about 25,000 citizens (approximately 12 percent of whom were white) who pledged to support Stokes if he ran. With this mandate in hand, Stokes officially announced on 13 May 1965 that he would run for mayor as an independent candidate.[36]

The mandate represented by the draft petitions was, of course, an important factor in persuading Stokes to run; however, there were other compelling considerations that contributed to his final decision. Stokes, like the women from the league, was also very conscious of the fact that the shifting population composition of Cleveland had resulted in blacks constituting about 40 percent of the electorate, which made them the largest single ethnic group in the community. Further, there were good reasons to believe that he could obtain a solid bloc vote from the black community. The national civil rights movement and the local movement created a climate that was highly favorable for Stokes's candidacy. Local civil rights activity had the double effect of creating a higher level of race consciousness and unity within the black community and of exposing, in a dramatic fashion, the racism of white city officials. This was particularly the case with Locher, who had received solid support from the black community in his victories of 1961 and 1963. His posture on race issues between 1963 and 1965 made it certain that few blacks would vote for him again; thus those votes were up for grabs, and Stokes would clearly be the logical heir. Further, Stokes believed that this new awareness and discontent within the black community could be transformed into massive political action because this had already been demonstrated at least twice. The school boycott was one instance; and in early 1965 the black community, at the urging of UFM, voted in mass against a new tax levy for the school district, on the grounds that it was too small and would be an illusion of progress if passed. These two events suggested to Stokes and his close advisors that the black community was beginning to close ranks as it had never done before in the face of white oppression and was taking the first steps toward independent group political action. Finally, there was the high probability that the white vote would be split among three white candidates, which would make it feasible for Stokes to be elected with less than a majority of the vote. This possiblity existed as a result of the fact that Ralph McAllister, chairman of the Cleveland Board of Education, had declared himself as an independent candidate for mayor before Stokes made his own announcement. McAllister had gained considerable popularity in the white community for his hard line during the school crisis and therefore was considered a strong contender for the conservative white vote. At the time Stokes announced, the Republicans had yet to slate a candidate. However, given Locher's declining popularity and the emerging racial split within the Democratic ranks, it was likely that they would field a major candidate and they did. A short time after Stokes entered the race, Republican Ralph Perk, the county auditor and the first Republican to win a countywide office in nearly thirty years, also announced. As a second generation Czech-Bohemian, Perk hoped to combine his white ethnic appeal and economy-in-government program into a winning combination against the fractionalized Democrats.

With three white candidates slated to be in the general election and the greater than usual strength of the Democratic party in the primary elections, it was evident to Stokes and his supporters that his chances for victory would be measurably improved if he skipped the Democratic primary and ran as an independent in the general election. Therefore, Stokes, a life-long Democrat, decided upon the independent route as the most feasible one to the mayor's office. This decision meant that it would be necessary to collect at least 16,223 signatures on a petition to get Stokes's name on the 2 November ballot. As a means for demonstrating the seriousness of his campaign and the strength of his support, Stokes publicly stated that he would collect 32,000 signatures, twice the required number, and file on 20 June, his thirty-eighth birthday, which was ten days before the deadline. A close aide describes the tremendous push made so that Stokes could fulfill his public pledge:

> We counted them [petition signatures] on Friday night the 17th and found that we had only about 10,000 signatures; so we were far short, but we had the weekend to go. Well the word went out and I have never seen a sight like it before. They came in by little children bringing in batches that their parents had sent along, they came in by taxi, by car, by bicycle, and on foot to his law office on East 55th and Woodlawn. They just poured in, people were riding herd on their cars and calling in to find out where more were to be picked up and going to collect them. . . . Finally, on Sunday night we counted them twice, and we had over 30,000 signatures.

Campaign Strategy and Execution

Stokes filed on his birthday and began almost immediately to implement a campaign strategy that would hopefully result in victory. The overall strategy was based on the thesis that Stokes could win in a four-way race if he (1) could produce a solid bloc vote within the black community and (2) earned the votes of "fair-minded" whites. Recent events in the black community mentioned earlier suggested that his chances of securing a substantial black vote were very good indeed but that the number of fair-minded white voters was unknown. This meant that in terms of emphasis, Stokes would have to devote most of his time and energy to solidifying the black vote; however, at the same time, he would have to conduct a campaign that did not write off the white community. Indeed, he felt that it was absolutely essential that he present himself as a candidate for all the people and not as one who represented any special interest groups. Above all else, Stokes was determined to sell the idea that he was the best qualified candidate to reverse the retrogressive deterioration the city had experienced and that both blacks and whites would bene-fit if he were elected. Stokes harbored no easy illusions about how important the race issue would be in the campaign, but he hoped to rise above it by projecting himself, to members of both races, as better qualified to be mayor than any of the other candidates.

In viewing the black community, the Stokes supporters were encouraged by two sets of election statistics. First, voter registration in the heavily black wards had increased from 88,497 to 103,123 (a gain of 14,626 voters) between 1963 and 1965. This increase was primarily due to a vigorous voter registration drive conducted by the Democratic party during the 1964 presidential campaign. The political posture of the Republican presidential candidate, Barry Goldwater, was particularly offensive to black citizens; consequently, most of the registration drive money and energy had been expended in black neighborhoods. As a result, the increase in registered voters was greater in black wards than it was in white wards; and, therefore, although blacks constituted only 34 percent of the 1965 population, they composed about 40 percent of all registered voters. Thus, ironically, the 1964 Democratic party registration drive assisted the Stokes cause. The other set of encouraging election statistics emerged from the 1965 Demo-cratic primary. Although Stokes had decided to pass up the primary, Mark McElroy, the county recorder, challenged Locher and almost beat him (McElroy received 45 percent of the vote and Locher 52 percent). In 1963 Locher had run unopposed and had received over 80 percent of the vote in the ten black wards, but in the 1965 primary his poor showing in those same wards (he gathered only 25 percent of the vote) almost gave the primary victory to McElroy. The 1965 primary results demonstrated, in quantifiable terms, the sharp decline of Locher's support in the black community and also indicated once again that the black community was beginning to function in a politically cohesive fashion against its enemies. Furthermore, the primary results clearly suggested that Stokes would have a potential monopoly on black voters. Certainly the blacks were not going to vote for Locher nor McAllister, who they perceived to be a hardened racist, nor in all probability would they vote for Perk, the white ethnic Republican. The objective for the Stokes supporters, then, was to turn this potential situation into a real monopoly of black votes for Stokes. In order to do so, they had to accomplish two tasks: (1) persuade black voters to go to the polls on election day and (2) convince them to vote for Stokes.

As has already been indicated, the general racial situation in Cleveland, the inept behavior of white officials, the general politi-cal climate in the black community, the personal characteristics of Stokes, and the unattractiveness of the white candidates all favored the achievement of the twin goals. However, the trans-formation of these somewhat intangible factors into maximum voter strength on election day required a key ingredient of any successful electoral campaign—organization. That is, there is the essential need for a structure that has a decision-making apparatus and a division of labor that utilizes material and people in a ra-tional fashion to accomplish the numerous tasks that emerge in a political campaign. Somehow voters must be personally contacted before and on election day; literature must be written, printed, and distributed; money collected and spent; meetings set up and attended; speeches written and delivered; transportation and information must be provided for the voters; and the polls checked on election day. Putting together such an organization in a short period of time is obviously not an easy job, nor in some cases possible. Consequently, an alternative is to utilize an already existing organization that is capable of fulfilling these essential functions.

The only existing structures within the black community that did have such capabilities were the political organizations of the ten black city councilmen. It was conceivable that the Stokes campaign organization could have as its core the existing ward organizations instead of attempting to duplicate them. It was conceivable, but highly unlikely, since none of the major black politicians were willing to openly support Stokes in his bid for the mayorship. There were those "such as Leo Jackson who had fought for civil rights for ten years and was viewed as *the* Negro spokesman," who felt they were better qualified than Stokes to be the mayor if there was to be a black mayor. Most of the others, however, simply "did not think he was a good risk . . . ; they decided to do the safe thing which was to stick with the party." After all, the limited power that they did wield flowed from their positions within the Democratic party organization; why jeopardize it on what would probably be a losing cause?

Without access to or the support of the existing political structures within the black community, the Stokes supporters proceeded to build their own campaign organization or, put more accurately, "a quasi-organization grew like Topsy, with no planning and virtually no central direction." Stokes and his close associates made contacts with their personal friends, whether they had past political experience or not (most of them did not), and tried to persuade them to join the campaign. The many who did, in turn, recruited their friends and, they, their friends. One worker described the development of Stokes's organization in the following manner:

> It was a real grass-roots campaign in the true sense of the word. As each person was called in by Mr. Stokes himself or someone close to him, they stuck and brought in others. In fact, the thing mushroomed to such an extent that a couple of months before November there was complete chaos in the campaign. No one knew who was doing what because so many inexperienced people were involved.

What the Stokes campaign organization lacked in terms of rational structure and coordination was supplanted, however, by the raw zeal, enthusiasm, and inventiveness of the workers. In contrast to workers in most political campaigns, none of them received money or expected personal gain for their efforts. Indeed, as was the case with the Hatcher volunteers in Gary, it cost people money to work for Stokes. The campaign took on a "crusade-like quality," which stimulated the volunteers to work long and grueling hours with unbelievable spirit. Reflecting on the character of the campaign organization, one of the principal workers described it as:

> . . . a free-wheeling campaign. Everybody was trying to figure out what we were doing and hell we didn't even know what we were doing ourselves. It was a real free-flowing, free-wheeling movement. Everybody sacrificed and worked their fingers to the bone and *spent* money, you know, to get this guy into office. Everybody's ideas were taken into consideration and given some merit. A guy would come in with an idea—sounds good, can *you* do it? Put it into effect, let's see what happens. It was a great campaign.

In summary, Stokes's bid for the mayorship in 1965 was not supported by a well-oiled campaign organization, but it was bolstered by a dedicated and energetic group of volunteers who were, with a few exceptions, political amateurs. These political amateurs were recruited from both races. However, most of the key workers in the 1965 Stokes campaign organization were whites, although several blacks were in top decision-making positions. The large number of whites in the organization did not mean that Stokes lacked black support, it simply reflected the fact that whites had more time to devote to the campaign than the average black. What attracted these people to the Stokes campaign varied, of course, from individual to individual; yet there were two principal motivating factors that were identified by most respondents. Some workers (particularly the white suburban liberals) were attracted primarily, but by no means exclusively, by the image of Stokes as a governmental reformer who had the qualities to reverse the physical and social decline of Cleveland. They viewed the Stokes effort as essentially a "good government" campaign, which would reverse the decline of Cleveland and inaugurate a new era that was more responsive to the dramatic social changes that were occurring in the community. Others were stimulated to join, again not exclusively, by the fact that Stokes was a black candidate who symbolized many of the goals of the civil rights movement. In their view, electoral politics was an extension of the movement; a shortcut to the civil rights goals of housing, education, welfare, and so forth. If Stokes were victorious, they would be helping to achieve those ends, and they also would be making political history by electing the first black mayor of a major American city.

In their attempt to rally the black community behind Stokes, his campaign workers discovered that the most intractable obstacle they encountered was the pervasive attitude among numerous blacks that a black man could not be elected mayor of the city. Supporting their general cynicism regarding the possibilities of a black occupying the highest position in city government was the fact that in 1955 a black man named Alexander Martin had run for mayor in the Democratic primary and was overwhelmingly defeated. Despite the various changes that had taken place within the black community during the decade since Martin ran, there were many blacks who continued to maintain that no black man, regardless of his qualifications, could be elected mayor. This notion was, of course, prevalent among black politicians and, according to campaign workers, more widespread among middle-class blacks than others.

To counteract this skepticism, the campaign workers emphasized the statistics of the situation. They continuously drove home the point that blacks constituted about 40 percent of all registered voters. Therefore, if they voted as a bloc for Stokes, if he received "the vote of fair-minded white citizens who want the best qualified candidate for mayor," and if the three white candidates split the remaining white vote, Stokes could win. The pitch made to black doubters went something like the following:

> Many thought he didn't have a chance; but when you started to spout statistics to them about what could happen if they really turned out and voted, because they usually were apathetic and sat home and didn't vote at all, then they started to listen. . . . Look, nobody ever before had broken down for them the ethnic pockets in Cleveland and how in a four-man race those ethnic pockets would work to their advantage—if they would vote as a solid bloc. . . . We tried to show them that electing Stokes would be a milestone in black history. We urged them to get rid of their personal hang-ups, if they had some, and view Stokes as a symbol to prove that we can do something as a people.

Stokes and his workers were aided in selling this argument to the black public by the local civil rights organizations, the *Call and Post* (the black newspaper), various black social organizations, a young student's group, and, perhaps most importantly, several of the leading black ministers. Concerning the support of the black ministers, one of the workers exclaimed, "we were able to get to the ministers because at that particular time Martin Luther King was organizing them for his nonviolent movement. So we were able to touch the ministers and get them interested in politics for the first time." The combination of this support, the enthusiasm of Stokes's workers, and the general political circumstances of the time, as we shall see, did result in an unprecedented turnout and cohesive vote for Stokes in the black community. However, before discussing the election results in the black community, it is necessary to review the campaign the Stokes organization made for white votes.

As we noted earlier, Stokes had decided that although the black community was his major constituency, it was essential to conduct a campaign that appealed to the entire electorate of Cleveland. If he could gain support of some white voters his chances of victory would be improved; and, just as important, if he did win with whites as part of his electoral coalition, it would certainly make the task of governance somewhat easier. There was no question, then, about the need to gain white support; however, the means for doing so was a confounding question.

In approaching the white community, Stokes was confronted with the difficulty of cutting through the traditional prejudice of white ethnics plus the intensified negativism that had resulted from the national and local civil rights movement (relative to this latter point, it is also important to note that the Watts racial disorder occurred in August 1965). He fully understood that although he benefited from the increased black consciousness and unity induced by the civil rights movement, he also was hindered by its negative impact on whites. Whereas his candidacy symbolized for many blacks their quest for racial justice, it also symbolized for many whites all that they feared and resented about the new black thrust.

Stokes and some of his supporters were convinced that if he could get exposure in the white community he would overcome this obstacle and win some whites over to his cause. It was believed that if whites met Stokes personally, they would see that he was not a "black extremist" to be feared but "an intelligent, dynamic individual who had the qualifications to be mayor of all the people." The resources available for reaching the white community, however, were meager. Although he was a life-long Democrat, the fact that he had chosen to run as an independent gave the West Side ward leaders a good excuse to bar him from appearing at the all-important ward meetings. Thus, he was cut off from one of the most crucial instruments for reaching white voters. A small group of Stokes workers did pass out some literature, make some phone calls, and set up some meetings on the West Side, but only a small minority of the voters was reached. According to one of the West Side workers: "The response was very negative, people wondered why we were asking them to vote for him —they were really antagonistic."

Not only did Stokes have little opportunity to personally talk to white voters but the lack of money (the entire campaign was run on $44,000) severely restricted the utilization of television, radio, and newspaper advertisements as a means of reaching whites. The campaign organization simply did not have access to the amount of money required to launch any kind of public relations campaign that would project a positive image of Stokes into the white community. The two Cleveland newspapers did little to aid Stokes in surmounting this barrier; both endorsed Locher and gave Stokes only minimum coverage until the very end of the campaign. Stokes did, however, receive wide media coverage on the occasions when he made major joint appearances with the other mayoralty candidates. During such opportunities, Stokes presented a wide-ranging program to improve the quality of life in Cleveland and made special appeals to allay the racial fears of whites. Note, for example, the following exerpt from one of his principal speeches:

Now, as one running for mayor of Cleveland who happens to be a Negro—I want to make this one thing clear. I do not run as a Negro, but as a Clevelander thinking of the best interests of all Clevelanders. My election would not mean "Negro takeover," a "black" cabinet or the establishment of a subsidiary office of the civil rights movement in City Hall. I would be a fair and just mayor. Problems would be dealt with according to their severity—not their black,

white or yellow political impact. Prospective employees of the City
of Cleveland would be judged solely on their merits.
I would be a full-time mayor. Before a Watts, Los Angeles, devel-
ops in Cleveland, I would be on the scene—not in my locked office,
not leaving by the back door, and not just saying, "I will not tolerate
the disrespect for law and order."
I want no Negro to vote for me simply because I am a Negro; and
I would hope that no white person votes against me simply because
I am a Negro.[37]

For the most part, however, the Stokes campaign, as the election results indicate, did not penetrate the white community of Cleveland. The bulk of his white support came from white liberals who
lived in the surrounding suburbs, particularly the members of
Americans for Democratic Action. These whites occupied important positions within the Stokes campaign organization and
worked hard for his election, but they were unable to vote for him
on election day.

Despite the obstacles faced by Stokes in both the black and
white communities, his campaign gained sufficient momentum to
alarm all three of his white opponents. Consequently, each of
them employed a late campaign technique aimed at defeating
Stokes. All of them conducted a whispering campaign among
white voters that a vote for the other two white candidates was
a wasted vote and would result in electing "that Nigger mayor."
They argued that Stokes would win unless a majority of the white
community united behind one white candidate just as the blacks
were uniting behind Stokes. Naturally, each of the white candidates maintained that he was the person white voters should back.
The election results suggest that this strategy worked best for the
incumbent, Locher, who had the support of both major newspapers, the Democratic party, the labor unions, and the downtown
business establishment. Given this broad institutional support,
most white voters evidently decided that if they wanted to defeat
Stokes they had best vote for Locher.

Election Results and Lessons Learned

Election night proved to be a tantalizing event. After much see-
sawing back and forth, Locher finally emerged on top, edging out
Stokes by the wafer-thin margin of 2,458 votes. Given the closeness of the results, Stokes filed for a recount, which officially

determined that Locher had received 36.7 percent of the vote, Stokes 35.8 percent, Perk 17.1 percent, and McAllister 9.5 percent (see table 7). Thus, Locher's final edge over Stokes was 2,142 votes, a difference of less than one percent.

TABLE 7

CLEVELAND MAYORALTY ELECTION, 1965

Candidate	Vote	Percentage of Vote
Locher	87,858	36.7
Stokes	85,716	35.8
Perk	41,045	17.1
McAllister	22,650	9.5
Total	237,269	99.1

SOURCE: Board of Election voting returns.

An analysis of the election returns by the racial characteristics of the wards shows that, as expected, Stokes gained a solid vote (85.4 percent) from the black community, where he received the overwhelming proportion of his total vote, and only 3 percent of the vote in predominately white wards. In the eight wards that contained a mixed racial composition, Stokes received a vote that was very close (about a 4 percent variance) to the percentage of blacks in the ward. Thus, the election results almost exactly reflected the racial divisions within the city; about 95 percent of the white voters voted for one of the three white candidates and about 85 percent of the blacks pulled the lever for Stokes.

With a few minor, but crucial, exceptions, then, the analysis and projections set forth by the Stokes workers were realized (see table 8). He was able to achieve a substantial bloc vote in the black community; however, about 15 percent of the black voters

TABLE 8

CLEVELAND MAYORALTY ELECTION, 1965: BY RACE

	Black Wards	White Wards	Mixed Wards	City Totals
Registered voters..........	103,123	159,419	75,261	337,803
Percentage turnout........	72.1	69.7	71.7	70.9
Stokes votes	63,550	3,300	18,866	85,716
Percentage for Stokes	85.4	3.0	35.0	35.8

SOURCE: Computed from Special Census of 1965 and Board of Election voting returns.

still marked their ballot for one of the white candidates. The white office-seekers did split up the white vote but not nearly as evenly as the Stokes people had hoped they would. Even the weakest of past Republican mayoralty candidates, for example, had never attained less than 25 percent of the vote, yet Perk was able to gather only 17 percent—an all-time low. The proportion of white votes for Stokes was also a disappointment. He and his workers realized that he would capture only a small portion of the white vote but the approximately 3 percent he did receive was even lower than they anticipated.

Despite these drawbacks and his loss at the polls, the Stokes campaign was in several respects a victory in defeat. His campaign produced a record-high turnout of black voters for a municipal election. Never before in the history of Cleveland had so many blacks journeyed to the polls and voted so cohesively for a mayoralty candidate. Just to take one example, in the 1963 mayor's election only 57 percent of registered black voters voted, whereas in 1965 72 percent of them went to the polls. The fact that this record black turnout came extremely close to putting Stokes in the mayor's seat "was viewed in the black community as an elating moral victory and one that meant that the black community would have to be seriously contended with in all future elections, particularly the 1967 mayoralty election." Stokes's narrow miss not only stirred his backers, it also made a deep impression on the "doubting Thomases" in the black community who had failed to support him on the grounds that the "time is not ripe," "he doesn't have a chance—why back a loser," or "he will polarize the community." If Stokes ran again in 1967, and it was obvious that he would, these people would be hard pressed not to fall in behind him.

A concrete manifestation of the inspiring effect the near-win had on the black community was the amount of money and the manner in which it was raised to finance the vote recount. At the conclusion of the campaign the Stokes organization was at least $4,000 in debt and needed an additional $11,000 to pay for the recount. Although the organization had experienced great difficulty in raising money during the regular campaign, it found that money poured in from all corners after the word went out about the financial situation. The words of an individual on the finance committee captures the spirit of the occurrence:

> The recount in 1965 was an experience that I'll never live through again, and I don't think anybody else ever will because it was as exciting as anything that happened. People just started to bring money in from all over. Bars would put up big containers—in fact, these containers were all through the neighborhoods, in the bars, stores, barber shops, everywhere. . . . People were walking up and down the streets collecting nickels and dimes and bringing it all into the office. It was really exciting, and it was a very moving thing.

Indeed, the effort to finance the recount was so successful that enough money was raised to pay for it and also to liquidate the campaign debts that had accumulated.

As we have already noted, Stokes made very little headway into the white community during the 1965 election campaign. It is obvious that the average white voter was not persuaded by his approach; however, during the course of his campaign Stokes did make a positive impression on some members of an influential group within the white community—the downtown business establishment. Although Stokes was largely unknown to the business community in 1965, by the end of the campaign he, in the words of a member of the establishment,

> . . . emerged as a fellow who was clearly a cut above the kind of candidate for public office that we've had in Cleveland for a number of years. He was an attractive, imaginative, and even inspiring person, and you couldn't help but hear him speak out on the issues. He was very well informed on a whole range of issues, not just civil rights, but matters of taxes, revenues, city development, and what have you. He spoke out on the issues and did his homework well. So he was not simply a handsome black candidate for office, but a knowledgeable and better informed candidate than most men who have run for public office in this community.

By the time this assessment of Stokes had begun to circulate through business circles it was too late to have any impact; the downtown establishment, although not particularly satisfied with Locher, supported him as the "safe" candidate. But Stokes's 1965 performance laid the groundwork for the considerable business community support that he would enjoy in the 1967 mayoralty campaign.

Another positive outcome of the 1965 campaign was the development of a core of Stokes supporters who had gained invaluable experience and had learned some important lessons that would be very useful in the next election. One of the fundamental lessons learned was that enthusiasm was a necessary but not sufficient ingredient to produce victory. The high spirit and zeal of people had to be channeled into specific, coordinated campaign tasks; and this required a more structured organization than the Stokes forces possessed in 1965. In the future, considerable stress would be placed upon developing an organization that could fruitfully utilize scores of volunteers in a rational fashion. If accomplished, this would be instrumental in obtaining an even greater black voting bloc.

It was also learned that reaching white voters was an extremely difficult chore, certainly far more difficult than Stokes had expected. Given the past and anticipated resistance of the Democratic party organization and West Side ethnic organizations to appearances by Stokes at their meetings, it was clear that any future effort would require that Stokes rely heavily on the mass media to present himself to white voters. This approach would necessitate much more money than was available in 1965 and some professional public relations expertise that could project to white voters a persuasive mass-media campaign. Consequently, if success was to be achieved in the future, it could not be financed on a shoestring as was the case with the 1965 campaign.

Finally, the Stokes supporters learned the very hard lesson that if they did not want victory stolen from them, they needed challengers and election judges in every precinct. In studying the election returns, they discovered, for example, that in some precincts every single registered voter voted (none were sick, out of town, working overtime, or simply staying home), and not one voted for Stokes. In addition, on election night two ballot bags (paper ballots are used in most precincts) from two black wards disappeared and were never accounted for. Assuming that Stokes received a similar proportion of the vote in the uncounted black neighborhoods that he did in other black precincts, it is possible that his total vote was higher than Locher's. Indeed, many of the Stokes supporters were convinced that he did win the 1965 election and that it was stolen from him by those who controlled the election machinery. The next time they would have to be much better prepared to cope with fraud at the polls.

In summary, although the 1965 endeavor to elect Stokes did not succeed, it firmly established that the black community in Cleveland could be mobilized behind him, and it developed valuable electoral political experience and insights among his supporters. Two years hence, most of them would have another opportunity to use their newly acquired experience.

1. For an incisive analysis of these institutional barriers, see Penn Kimball, *The Disconnected* (New York: Columbia University Press, 1972).

2. See E. E. Schattschneider, *The Semi-Sovereign People* (New York: Holt, Rinehart and Winston, 1960).

3. The early history of Cleveland is described in William Ganson Rose, *Cleveland: The Making of a City* (Cleveland: World Publishing, 1950), and Edmund H. Chapman, *Cleveland: Village to Metropolis* (Cleveland: Western Reserve Historical Society and Press of Western Reserve University, 1964).

4. Chapman, *Cleveland: Village to Metropolis*, p. 38.

5. Ibid., p. 98.

6. Rose, *Cleveland: The Making of a City*, p. 500.

7. For an account of immigrants in Cleveland history, see the series of articles by Wellington G. Fordyce in the *Ohio Archaeological and Historical Quarterly*: "Immigrant Colonies in Cleveland" (1936), pp. 320-40; "Nationality Groups in Cleveland Politics" (1937), pp. 109-27; "Immigrant Institutions in Cleveland" (1938), pp. 87-103; and "Attempts to Preserve National Cultures in Cleveland" (1940), pp. 128-49.

8. Fordyce, "Nationality Groups in Cleveland Politics," p. 110.

9. Ibid., p. 111.

10. Richard L. Maher, "Cleveland: Study in Political Paradoxes," in *Our Fair City*, ed. Robert S. Allen (New York: Vanguard Press, 1947), pp. 131-40.

11. Ibid., pp. 138-39.

12. Ibid., p. 140.

13. This quotation and following unattributed quotations are derived from interviews conducted in Cleveland by the authors.

14. For a discussion of the factors spurring suburbanization, see: Richard Dewey, "Peripheral Expansion in Milwaukee County," *American Journal of Sociology*, May 1948, pp. 417-22; Robert C. Wood, *Suburbia: Its People and Their Politics* (Boston: Houghton Mifflin, 1958); William Dobriner, ed., *The Suburban Community* (New York: G. P. Putnam's Sons, 1958); Edgar M. Hoover and Raymond Vernon, *Anatomy of a Metropolis* (Garden City, N.Y.: Doubleday, 1962); Raymond Vernon, *The Myth and Reality of Our Urban Problems* (Cambridge, Mass.: Joint Center for Urban Studies, M.I.T.-Harvard, 1962); and York Willbern, *The Withering Away of the City* (Tuscaloosa, Al.: University of Alabama Press, 1964).

15. "U.S. Letter: Cleveland," *New Yorker*, October 1967, p. 212.

16. *Hearing Before the U.S. Commission on Civil Rights: Cleveland, Ohio* (Washington, D.C.: Government Printing Office, 1966), p. 646.

17. Ibid., p. 651. Only 400 black families with incomes under $6,000 were able to rent in the suburbs compared with 28,000 such white families.

18. Ibid.

19. Ibid., p. 390.

20. Cleveland Subcommittee, U.S. Commission on Civil Rights, *Cleveland's Unfinished Business in Its Inner City* (Cleveland, 1966), p. 25.

21. *Hearing Before Commission on Civil Rights*, p. 444.

22. *Cleveland's Unfinished Business*, p. 25.

23. Ibid., p. 40.

24. *Hearing Before Commission on Civil Rights*, p. 751.

25. Ibid., p. 755.

26. *Cleveland's Unfinished Business*, p. 30.

27. Ibid.

28. *Hearing Before Commission on Civil Rights*, p. 545.

29. Louis Masotti and Jerome R. Corsi, *Shoot-Out in Cleveland* (New York: Bantam Books, 1969), p. 6.

30. An account of this dispute is provided in Ray Marshall, *The Negro and Organized Labor* (New York: John Wiley, 1965), chap. 6.

31. *Hearing Before Commission on Civil Rights*, p. 757.

32. Masotti and Corsi, *Shoot-Out in Cleveland*, p. 7.

33. Ibid., pp. 8-9.

34. Ibid., p. 10.

35. Quoted in John Skow, "Can Cleveland Escape Burning?" *Saturday Evening Post*, 29 July 1967, p. 42.

36. *Cleveland Plain Dealer*, 14 May 1965. All quotations from various editions of the *Cleveland Plain Dealer* are reprinted by permission of the publisher.

37. Carl Stokes, speech before Cleveland City Club, 22 October 1965; from an unpublished typescript in the files of the Stokes campaign organization. Used by permission.

4

Cleveland: The 1967 Primary Election

THE EXPLOSIVE INTERLUDE: 1965-1967

On the evening of his defeat in 1965 Carl Stokes announced that he would run again in 1967 unless Congressman Charles A. Vanik decided to seek the mayorship. In the event that Vanik did run, Stokes indicated that he would support him and implied that he would pursue Vanik's seat in Congress.[1] Despite this consideration for what Vanik would do, most of the core Stokes supporters were convinced that he would seek the mayor's seat again in 1967, and they acted upon that premise. They decided to form an informal group called "Stokes's Folks," which would meet from time to time before the next election and discuss what they had learned in 1965 and what they would do differently in 1967.

Any question about whether Stokes would or would not run again was essentially resolved by a series of events that made the political climate increasingly ripe for a second Stokes effort. In April 1966, for instance, the U.S. Commission on Civil Rights conducted its first hearings on ghetto life in a northern city and laid bare the desperate conditions of blacks in Cleveland. "For six days radio and T.V. covered the hearings and exposed for all to hear and see the boiling grievances of black Clevelanders. . . . I am convinced until that time most whites still did not know how rotten things were."[2]

Three months later, during the sweltering heat of a July evening, the cry of black anguish was raised to a pitch that could not be ignored. The white manager of a bar at Seventy-nineth Street and Hough Avenue put a sign on the front door that read: "No Water for Niggers." As a crowd of enraged blacks began to gather in front of the bar, the manager and another white man strutted on the sidewalk with a shotgun and a pistol.[3] Several wagonloads of police arrived and began to disperse the crowd by shoving and pushing people down Hough Avenue. Either a sniper's bullet or a cherry bomb exploded in the tense atmosphere, and within seconds the police were shooting out streetlights and into buildings (a women calling for her children was killed). The crowd threw bottles and bricks, began to break store windows, and sniper shots rang through the air. For a full week massive civil disorder—burning, looting, vandalism, sniping, police shooting, and National Guard occupation—raged in Cleveland's black ghetto. When the violence finally subsided on 24 July, four blacks had been killed, hundreds of people injured, and blocks of buildings gutted. If there were any lingering questions about racial polarization in the city, they vanished. Cleveland had joined Harlem, Watts, Detroit and scores of other cities that already had experienced or soon would experience racial rebellions in the "hot summers" of 1965 through 1968.

On 9 August, the grand jury of Cuyahoga County issued its investigatory report on the civil disorders. The jury blamed the riot on "a relatively small group of trained and disciplined professionals at this business . . . aided and abetted, wittingly or otherwise, by misguided people of all ages and colors, many of whom are avowed believers in violence and extremism, and some of whom also are either members of or officers in the Communist Party." Mayor Locher endorsed the conclusion and congratulated the grand jury for having "the guts to fix the approximate cause which had been hinted at for a long time, that subversive and Communist elements in our community were behind the rioting."[4]

The people of Hough, however, strongly disagreed with the conclusions of the all-white grand jury (headed by Louis Seltzer) and the mayor. Their biracial review panel conducted their own investigation into the events and judged that "the underlying causes of the rioting are to be found in the social conditions that exist in the ghetto areas of Cleveland." In reference to the influence of Communist agitators, their report stated: "We would believe that an individual living in such poverty as exists in Hough needs no one to tell him just how deplorable his living conditions are."[5] This position was bolstered by the United States attorney general and the FBI, which maintained that there was no masterminded plot or communist influence on the riots.[6] However, appearing before a congressional hearing, Mayor Locher argued: "I would disagree with the statements of the Attorney General, and I would wholeheartedly agree with the conclusions made by the grand jury report."

Locher's refusal to admit that decaying social conditions and the lack of governmental response were responsible for the violence, and his insistence that a small group of extremists were at fault, encouraged an increasing "billy-club mentality" in city administration-black community relations.[7] He and his law director, Bronis J. Klementowicz, made numerous public statements that a stronger police department and filling of jails were appropriate means for quelling agitation. Police officers were publicly urged by the mayor's office and white city council members to "get tough" with the "hoodlums." Among other things, the police force was expanded, and each night a special police helicopter, armed with a Thompson submachine gun, hovered over the ghetto and scanned the ground with a searchlight. In the early summer of 1967, Locher even went so far as to brand Martin Luther King, Jr., an extremist when King arrived in Cleveland to preach nonviolence to black high school students. Locher refused to meet with King and repeatedly refused to meet with other black leaders. Needless to say, these actions merely intensified the already pervasive anti-Locher sentiment in the ghetto and no doubt increased the growing cohesion among blacks. As each event unfolded and was added to the impact of earlier ones, it became virtually impossible for any blacks to defend the city administration. The black community became more and more united against what was perceived by all but a small handful of blacks as the common enemy.

The ineptness of the Locher administration in dealing with racial strife not only alienated the black community, it also generated considerable discontent within the white business community. Racial violence and acute conflict had marred the reputation of Cleveland and was "making it more and more difficult to attract new businesses, new employees, and conduct business along usual lines." City hall suffered additional loss of support in business circles in January 1967, when the then secretary of Housing and Urban Development Robert C. Weaver, took the unprecedented step of curtailing all urban renewal funds to Cleveland and withdrew $10 million already committed for the second stage of downtown commercial renewal. The secretary's decision was based on the fact that Cleveland had failed to complete a single urban-renewal project in eleven years and that it had more vacant land under urban renewal than any other city in the nation. Weaver warned that unless substantial progress was made by July, all funds would be cut off for the administration of on-going projects.

Further lack of administrative leadership and competency was exhibited by city hall in May 1967. All of the major cities in the nation were competing for a portion of the $900 million available under the new federal model-cities program. Under the new program, money would be distributed only to those cities which indicated in their application that they had the ability to launch innovative social and physical programs to improve the quality of life for their deprived citizens. Cleveland filed its application on the last possible day, it lacked details, and it did not have the required approval of the city council. The mayor attached a note to the document indicating that he would attempt to have the application more fully completed by the end of the month. When the cities were selected, few individuals were surprised that Cleveland was not among those chosen.

By early summer 1967, the national media began to focus on Cleveland as the classic example of urban malaise. News magazines such as the *Saturday Evening Post, The Nation, Time,* and *Newsweek* all carried stories highly critical of the Locher administration and the consequent decline of the community. Some Clevelanders began to circulate the suggestion that the city's slogan be changed from "The Best Location in the Nation" to "The Mistake on the Lake." Among the businessmen who traveled extensively, some "were becoming ashamed to admit that they lived in Cleveland." Even the local press, which had backed Locher in 1965, began to levy unrelenting criticism against city hall. The atmosphere became so antagonistic that Locher refused to talk with out-of-town reporters, reduced press conferences to a minimum, and erected an icy wall between himself and the local media.

This was the political climate that prevailed in Cleveland as the time approached for the 1967 mayoralty election. The extent to which this climate promoted or impeded the political fortunes of the leading candidates was the fundamental question endlessly discussed and debated in political circles. Although various political camps had radically different interpretations of who was gaining and who was losing as a result of the developments, they all agreed that the situation had become increasingly complex and that this complexity created a fluid circumstance. Few things were certain other than the consensus that several candidates would be testing the political winds when the primary election approached.

THE CANDIDATES

Among the potential candidates there was, of course, the incumbent Locher. Given his near complete loss of support among blacks, segments of the business community, and elements of the local mass media, it is understandable that some leading Democratic officials attempted to ease Locher out of the running. Albert Porter, the Democratic county chairman, promised Locher a federal judgeship, for example, if he would agree to step down. Locher, however, despite his eroding political base, indicated that he would not be pushed aside and would run on the integrity of his administration. "My reelection campaign," he announced, "will be based on the record of this administration. This administration has served all of the people with fairness. I pride myself on being honest. Throughout my career, there has been no price tag on honesty in government."[8]

In his quest to gain the endorsement of the Democratic party for the 3 October primary election, Locher faced stiff competition from James Stanton, president of the city council. Stanton had become council president by defeating Jack Russell, a longtime powerful figure in Cleveland politics, and his triumph established him as one of the brightest young stars on the local political horizon. Indeed, he seriously considered running for mayor in 1965 but eventually concluded that the time was not ripe. There were strong indications that Porter and other leading Democratic officials favored Stanton over Locher (Stanton petitions were being circulated by party workers and it was rumored that in a closed party meeting, ten of the seventeen vice-chairmen preferred Stanton as the party nominee).[9] Stanton, however, found himself in a difficult predicament. If Locher refused to bow out, his entrance into the primary race along with Frank Celeste (another announced candidate) would no doubt persuade Stokes to also enter the Democratic primary instead of running as an independent. Such a lineup would clearly give Stokes the advantage; consequently, Stanton would run only if Locher or Celeste were convinced to drop out—he did not want to be the man to insure a Stokes victory.

Frank Celeste, like Locher, however, was not about to step aside for Stanton or anyone else. A sixty-year-old man, Celeste had spent eight years as the mayor of Lakewood, a Cleveland suburb, and had earned a highly favorable reputation for his executive ability. His reputation was particularly attractive to a group of Cleveland businessmen who had become deeply disenchanted with Locher's inability to handle the mounting problems of Cleveland but who were not ready to support a black, even one as impressive as Stokes, for mayor of the city. This group, including Louis Seltzer who had retired as editor of the *Cleveland Press*, convinced Celeste to move into Cleveland and run for mayor. In order to persuade Celeste to do so, they promised to raise $100,000 for his campaign, attempt to get both newspapers to endorse him, and try to convince the Democratic party to select him as its nominee in the primary. Celeste agreed to run and the effort to deliver on the support package was mounted. According to a respondent who was intimately involved in attempting to secure the party endorsement for Celeste, the business group had decided to take a leaf out of the Duquane Club in Pittsburgh, which supports Democratic mayors for the city but are still Republicans, and back Republican candidates for offices at higher levels. In line with this strategy, the business group made an offer to officials of the Democratic party to supply $100,000 to finance the Celeste campaign and two newspaper endorsements if the party endorsed the candidacy of Frank Celeste. Although some party leaders who knew of the offer were inclined to accept it, the deal ultimately fell through when it was vetoed by James Carney who favored going with Locher for one more term and then supporting Stanton two years hence.

The veto by Carney (who was reported to be the most power-ful behind-the-scenes figure in the Democratic party) was known by only a few, thus causing much speculation and jock-eying concerning who the party would endorse during the first week of August.

The candidate with the slimmest possibility of gaining the Democratic endorsement was Carl Stokes. It was inconceivable that the party would select a black man, particularly one who had run as an independent in 1965 and had endorsed selective Republicans in 1966, to carry the banner. Stokes would, however, play an important role in the Democratic primary. If he decided to run as an independent, as he had in 1965, the primary would be wide open, but his entry into it would undoubtedly shrink the number of white candidates. Which of these two courses Stokes intended to take was a closely guarded secret that was not to be revealed until filing day, 5 July. In order to give himself com-plete flexibility on the matter, Stokes collected two completely different sets of petitions; thus he would be able to go either way when it came time to file.

Most respondents were of the opinion that Stokes preferred to run as an independent again because he was hopeful that at least two, and perhaps more, white candidates (a Democrat and a Republican) would be in the race and consequently split the white vote. Two factors, however, mitigated against the inde-pendent route for Stokes. First, there were the urgings of high national Democratic officials that Stokes run as a party mem-ber. If he won under the party label it would help his administra-tion in obtaining special federal assistance, and it certainly would be beneficial if he had higher political ambitions. Second, the Republican candidate, Seth Taft, after studying a commissioned public opinion poll conducted in May 1967, concluded that he would do worse in a three-man than in a two-man race. There-fore, he explicitly informed Stokes that if Stokes ran as an inde-pendent he would withdraw rather than be an instrument for fragmenting the white vote. Taft made this announcement pub-licly and reinforced it through a private meeting with Louis Stokes, the brother of the candidate.[10] Stokes concluded that Taft was not bluffing and decided to enter the Democratic pri-mary where his chances of victory appeared to be greater than they would in a head-on general election against one white

Democrat who would no doubt draw the overwhelming proportion of white Republican votes.

Consequently, Stokes appeared at the Board of Elections in the late afternoon of 5 July 1967 and filed in the Democratic party primary. Fortunately for the Stokes campaign, two aides of James Stanton appeared earlier that afternoon to file his nominating petitions and were informed that they lacked a master petition (a notorized statement that the candidate was a faithful party member). The shaken Stanton backers found their master petition in the bottom of a wastepaper basket, and a Stokes supporter who happened to observe the incident hurriedly relayed the news back to the Stokes headquarters. A master petition was quickly filled out there, and Stokes proceeded to file a few hours later without a hitch.[11]

Stokes's entry into the Democratic primary convinced Common Pleas Judge Frank D. Celebrezze, who showed up at the Board of Elections with the intent to file, that it was not even worth the effort. His entry also stimulated a strong movement among the Stanton supporters to persuade Locher and Celeste to drop out. The movement failed, however, and two days after filing Stanton withdrew with the explanatory statement: "I simply have to agree with Mr. Stokes that he and Mr. Locher are the two major candidates and I cannot win the race."[12] Thus, the field was reduced to three men (Locher, Celeste, and Stokes) and on 1 August the Democratic party, as expected, endorsed Locher as their candidate at a meeting in which party chairman Porter refused to allow Stokes to present his case.[13]

Temporarily out of the limelight was the fourth candidate, Republican Seth Taft. When Stokes filed as a Democrat, Taft (the grandson of former President William Howard Taft and nephew of former United States senator from Ohio, Robert Taft) moved into the city of Cleveland from the affluent suburb of Pepper Pike and filed as the Republican candidate for mayor. He would encounter considerable difficulty in attracting public attention during the Democratic primary, but once it was over he would be in the center of an intense campaign.

THE STOKES PRIMARY STRATEGY AND ORGANIZATION

The Stokes primary-campaign strategy was straightforward. He had to, on the one hand, retain and add to the 1965 black vote and, on the other hand, substantially expand the slight white vote he had received.

Voter statistics once again determined the strategy concerning the black community. Blacks constituted roughly 40 percent of the electorate. The 1965 election results proved that the black community was undoubtedly Stokes's stronghold, thus "it was necessary to aim for total turnout" among blacks, so that they would make up a larger proportion of the final vote than they were of the electorate. There was no question in the minds of the Stokes workers that blacks would vote for Stokes, the issue was getting them to the polls. This meant that every conceivable effort must be made to contact each black voter about the election, especially the traditional nonvoter. The operating assumption within the Stokes camp, according to a key worker, was:

> . . . we knew we were going to get the black vote, the game plan was to get it out. The guy who was most alienated, who stayed at home, was most inclined to vote for Stokes, if we could get him to the polls. Consequently, a great effort was made to get every eligible black voter into those voting booths.

Compounding the usual difficulties associated with such a task was the fact that Stokes was running in a primary election. Many blacks had traditionally resisted voting in primary elections "because it lets people know your politics, which isn't too good for people who live on the margin." Therefore, the Stokes workers had to devise a special approach for overcoming this historical reluctance, one that would result in an unprecedented primary election turnout among black voters.

The other dimension of the primary strategy was based on the notion that it was essential for Stokes to do much better among white voters than he had in 1965. Improving on his proportion of the white vote would be no easy accomplishment; the violence that had erupted during the intervening years had heightened antiblack feelings among whites, and there was one less white candidate in the 1967 campaign. Nevertheless, Stokes knew that he needed a larger white vote, and he set out to capture it.

Fundamentally, Stokes had to reassure white voters, particularly in view of the Hough riot, that he would be a mayor of all the people and that he was not a black power advocate. It was of the utmost importance that he calm the fears of whites who felt that his candidacy represented a black takeover of Cleveland.[14] Therefore, his strategy called for as many personal appearances before white groups as could be scheduled. He hoped that through personal meetings he would be able to demonstrate to the whites present (and hopefully their friends) that there was no need to fear him and that he was the best qualified candidate to turn the city around from its doldrums. During these meetings and when appealing to whites through the mass media, Stokes planned to stress three basic themes. He would attack the ineptness of the Locher administration and its failure to resolve the increasing problems of the city. The attack would not focus on Locher personally because "Locher was really a honest kind of fumbler, a nice guy, who people liked—but he just couldn't administer the city. Stokes therefore criticized the Locher administration through some of the people in it, like Klementowicz, instead of Locher personally." Supplementing this criticism, Stokes would attempt to project himself as a candidate with a firm grasp on understanding and knowing how to alleviate the community's pressing problems. He would strive to strengthen the image, which began to emerge toward the end of the 1965 campaign, that he was not only qualified to be mayor but indeed *better* prepared than the average candidate of the recent past. An important dimension of this image was the implied notion that Stokes was the one man who could fashion a reconciliation between the races in Cleveland; he was the one person who could keep the lid on and prevent another Hough-like uprising. In short, Stokes hoped to assure whites that they had as much as any other group to gain through his election; his goal was to resolve the major difficulties confronting the entire city, and he would not do so at the expense of one group over another.

In order to execute this dual strategy, the Stokes campaign organization was divided into two basic groups. The group that occupied the apex of the command structure and utilized most of its time in dealing with the white electorate consisted of Stokes, his campaign manager, Dr. Kenneth Clement, and a public relations expert, Al Ostrow. All basic policy decisions concerning the Stokes campaign were made by these three men. In addition, Clement (a well-known black physician, who had run Stokes's 1965 campaign) was given the responsibility of being the liaison man between the Stokes organization and the white establish-

ment in Cleveland. His primary function was to channel establishment people who were disenchanted with Locher into the Stokes
corner and to persuade them to contribute money to support a
public relations campaign among white voters. Clement was an
individual "who had many IOUs among the white power structure types and he cashed them all in 1967." Ostrow, who was
a public relations consultant for Locher in the 1965 campaign,
was charged with developing Stokes's general campaign approach, particularly as it related to the white community.[15]
It was his task to develop and then project an image of Stokes
that would favorably impress white voters. Although stress was
placed on having Stokes personally appear before white audiences, it was Ostrow who was highly influential in determining
the sort of pitch Stokes would make to white gatherings and the
kind of Stokes message that would flow from the mass media.

The other key group within the Stokes campaign organization
was headed by Geraldine Williams and Kenneth McGhee. Although these individuals were theoretically under the command
of the central triumvirate, they had virtually complete freedom
to perform their functions of directing and coordinating the street-
level campaign in the black community. More specifically, they
were responsible for building enthusiasm for Stokes in the black
community and tending to all of the detailed tasks—raising
money, registering voters, preparing voter lists, producing and
distributing literature, setting up phone committees, canvassing precincts, getting people to the polls, checking the vote
count, and so on—that would transform enthusiasm into concrete
votes on election day. While the triumvirate tended to concentrate on cultivating white money and voters, the street-level
people used all of their time and energy in attempting to produce
a huge black vote for Stokes. Since many of the key individuals
involved in this latter effort had worked in the 1965 campaign
and had learned some lessons, their 1967 work was accomplished
in a more coordinated and organizationally skillful manner than
was the case in 1965. This time, when people wandered into the
campaign headquarters volunteering their services, the organization had the capacity to channel them into useful tasks. Indeed,
at the height of the campaign the street-level organization had
some five thousand volunteers working without bumping into
each other or duplicating work. Once again, this component of

the organization was composed almost entirely of amateur volunteers who were attracted to the Stokes campaign because of its reformist and civil rights–black power image.

A similar, but much more limited, street-level organization also operated on the West Side. This group, however, was essentially confined to passing out literature and arranging for Stokes to speak before white groups. The hostile political atmosphere in the white neighborhoods severely restricted any door-to-door canvassing or other kinds of grass-roots campaigning. It was this hostile circumstance, in fact, that made it necessary for Stokes to raise a considerable amount of money so that he could purchase the required mass media time and space for reaching into white homes.

MOBILIZING THE BLACK COMMUNITY

The effort by the street-level organization to mobilize the black community behind Stokes was promoted by several factors. Most important among these factors was the near Stokes victory in 1965. As we noted earlier, the 1965 loss was viewed as a moral victory by blacks; "it proved that the black community could get itself together and with a little more push put one of its own people in the mayor's chair." According to one of the few black politicians who backed Stokes during both campaigns, the closeness of the 1965 election

. . . gave both the mayor and the people a deep desire to make 1967 different than 1965 through intensive voter registration and campaigning. It completely disarmed those people who said it couldn't be done. They felt guilty after the 1965 election and were some of the first to come around in 1967.

In addition to stimulating confidence and overcoming the "doubting Thomas" obstacle, Stokes's 1965 performance clearly established him as the leading black politician in the city. The fact that he had placed himself out on a limb in 1965 and almost won, while virtually every other black politician hung back, gave him an undisputed claim on being *the* mayoralty candidate from the black community. None of the other black politicians were in a position to challenge Stokes; consequently, it was unlikely that another black candidate would enter the race and seriously split the black vote. In fact, there is reason to believe that any other black politician who did so would have encountered considerable ostracism in the black community. This was a very important factor because it provided the black community with a single goal —to elect Carl Stokes—whereas the white community would be seriously split over what to do in the election.

The mobilization attempt was also advanced by the events discussed earlier. Although there was no consensus on the desirability of the Hough riot among blacks, the reaction to it on the part of white officials contributed to the growing coehsion within the black community. Locher's insistence that the cause of the disorder was a handful of extremists, not ghetto living conditions, the get-tough behavior of his officials, and his rude treatment of Martin Luther King gave blacks all the more reason to back Stokes as a means for ousting Locher. These actions, added to Locher's earlier civil rights posture, created a political climate that was highly conducive to uniting the entire black community behind Stokes. The objective of the street-level people was to take advantage of this political climate and convert it into electoral action.

In approaching black voters, the Stokes campaign workers emphasized three themes. First, at every opportunity they stressed that the near-victory of 1965 could be transformed into a victory if each eligible black registered and voted for Stokes. To highlight the importance of every single vote, they pointed out that Stokes would have won in 1965 if he received two additional votes per precinct. Second, they also argued that the 1967 mayoralty election offered every black a unique opportunity to take part in making black history and to elect a man who would do something about black grievances. In the words of a black campaigner:

> We sold blackness. We tried to convince people that this was their opportunity to vote for a brother and make him mayor of the city. This was their opportunity to make black history by electing the first black mayor of any city in the country. The only important and overriding issue was the blackness of the candidate and his interest in the black community. If he won, it would give black people their first opportunity to have some pride in this city.

Finally, it was reiterated over and over that the one chance to vote for Stokes was on 3 October. None of the campaign literature or messages indicated that 3 October was only the primary election date and that if Stokes won on that occasion people would have to vote for him again on 7 November to elect him mayor. The decision to underplay 3 October as only the first of two voting occasions was based on the notion held by one of the chief organizers that "most black folks don't believe in voting in primaries. That's when they usually stay home. So we simply did not mention that 3 October would be followed by another election day, because we knew we had to win then or else there wasn't going to be a 7 November for us." This strategy made good sense in terms of past primary turnouts and the past thirty years of electoral history, which showed that the winner of the Democratic primary always won the general election.

A necessary prerequisite to winning the Democratic primary was to have every eligible black adult registered to vote; consequently, one of the first jobs undertaken by the street-level organization was to launch a drive to accomplish that objective. This was a formidable chore for several reasons, including the fact that the number of registered black voters had *decreased* since 1965 due to the Ohio law which holds that a person who does not vote within a two-year period is automatically removed from the voter registration lists. The Stokes workers knew that a list of such dropped persons was made available to the Locher camp; however, they encountered considerable difficulty in procuring a list to work from. Further, the Board of Elections scheduled only one in-ward registration day. That is, with the exception of one day, a person desiring to register would have to journey to the central office in downtown Cleveland to do so. According to a Stokes worker: "Having only one evening neighborhood registration time is particularly hard on black people because many black people work day and night. If they happened to work the night of the neighborhood registration day, they wouldn't be able to register at all because the central office closes before they get off work." The Stokes organization had no success in convincing the Board of Elections to stay open longer hours. Additional difficulties were encountered by black voters who were registered but who had moved since the last election. According to the chairman of the registration committee: "If a person had moved we could give them a change of address card and they could send it in to the Board. If you were lucky the Board would send it back telling you where to vote, but they weren't very good at it. Most of the people we knew never got their cards back."

In attempting to surmount these obstacles, the Stokes workers organized a door-to-door registration drive. Each black ward was assigned a captain (except in one or two wards where the black councilman put his precinct committeemen to work on registration) who generally divided the ward into smaller units and assembled a group of workers to systematically canvass each block. Each worker had a large folder that was printed on the outside in bold type: "Register STOKES, Vote Primary—Vote STOKES." This folder, along with a "Stokes" button, proved extremely useful to the worker in making initial contact with people. "You see, many blacks don't like to answer the door, for a whole variety of reasons. But when they saw we were working for Stokes, most of them welcomed us." Included with the folder was a pad that the workers used to record the name, address, and telephone number of nonregistered adults. If a person was not registered and could not go to the Board of Elections at that time (baby-sitters and car pools generally accompanied the Stokes workers), the worker would arrange a date and time for transporting the person to the registration office. One copy of this information would be given to the nonregistered voter and another copy would be turned in at the ward headquarters to the individual coordinating the car pool. This individual was responsible for following up on the arrangements and seeing to it that those who made a commitment to register were delivered to the Board of Elections at the prearranged time.

If a person was already registered (and when they became registered), they were given a bright orange sticker that read: "We're Registered, STOKES, Vote Primary, Vote STOKES." It was intended that these stickers be "put in house windows to instill some pride and show how many people in the neighborhood were registered to vote. But we found that these stickers showed up all over the place—on cars, kids' bikes, billboards, poles, everywhere —and they helped create a kind of bandwagon effect for registering." This bandwagon effect, according to a seasoned black politician, attracted many apolitical people into the Stokes movement:

> For the first time since I've been in politics, the black ministers united and stayed united. They preached registration and set up car pools out of their churches. Surprisingly enough, a lot of people who had not participated in politics before—they never even voted because they were not interested—would admit "No I'm not registered, I want to though, where do I go?" It became the thing to do.

Indeed, the registration drive gained sufficient thrust in the black community to stimulate Ahmed Evans, the leading black nationalist in Cleveland, to register. Although the black nationalists in Cleveland, in the opinion of one ward captain, "felt that politically there was no way for black people to function in this society, Evans made public his registration and set the example for most nationalist organizations. It had a great impact; it was one of the mayor's [Stokes's] major coups. It influenced many black youths, who couldn't vote, to work in the Stokes campaign."

The voter registration drive conducted by the Stokes campaign organization was supplemented by a CORE drive and a Southern Christian Leadership Conference drive. However, in the opinion of the Stokes workers, the registration effort by the two civil rights organizations was not as systematic nor as effective as their own. In fact, they felt that the two groups, to some extent, might have endangered Stokes's election chances. This hazard was explained by a Stokes ward captain in the following manner:

> SCLC hurt us at one time. They came here with a voter registration drive which was going on at the same time as ours and CORE's. . . . Just prior to the primary they came out with a statement saying that they had registered so many thousands of black people, which is what we didn't want because we were afraid that if the white community found out that we were registering people at that great numbers they would begin to organize too. . . . Stokes didn't want this kind of publicity with SCLC or King because it threatened his image of being a mayor of all the people, and it would scare the white community.

Considering the fact that approximately 30 percent of the black registered voters did not vote in the 1965 election and thus were dropped from the registration list, the 1967 registration drives were quite successful in building the number of eligible black voters back up to the high 1965 level. The effort did, however, fall about 3,000 persons short of the 1965 figure in the predominantly black wards. This meant that if the Stokes organization was going to achieve a higher number of black votes than they did in their losing struggle of 1965, they would have to increase the proportion of voter turnout in the black community. Since the 1965 turnout occurred in a general election and it constituted a historic high, it was clear that it would be no easy accomplishment to surpass the 1965 turnout in a primary election.

The existence of an organizational structure with experience and skill to produce maximum voter turnout would have been extremely useful to the Stokes camp. Once again, however, the Stokes workers were denied access to the one structure in the black community that approximated this function. With the exception of a few black councilmen, most of the other black ward leaders decided not to support Stokes in the primary; consequently, their precinct organizations were not available to assist the Stokes campaigners. Indeed, in order to gain access to the voters in Ward 10, the Stokes people organized a successful protest march against the ward officials who refused to provide Stokes with a forum.[16] As a result of such resistance, however, the Stokes people devised their own organizational structure to insure that voters were fully informed about the Stokes campaign and that they poured into the polls on election day.

The organizational structure that was eventually constructed to perform these functions was the brainchild of Marvin Chernoff, an individual who had no prior political experience and who first became involved in the Stokes campaign by stuffing envelopes. Chernoff proposed that the way to duplicate, and indeed improve upon, the precinct committeemen structure was to organize block supervisors throughout the black community. These block supervisors acted as "the direct link between the Stokes campaign organization and the voters on their block. They specialized in two activities: voter education and, most importantly, voter turnout on election day."

The block supervisors were recruited and organized about eight weeks before the primary in the following manner. First, the workers took a crisscross directory, which lists people by their street address and phone number, and cut it up into streets and geographic areas. Then they took ward maps and matched the street numbers to specific wards. This was followed by identifying the areas populated by blacks, a tedious undertaking in transitional neighborhoods. Finally, each of the black areas was divided into a "block," a term used to identify thirty to forty houses, and the names of the persons living in the block were listed.

Once the lists were compiled, a campaign worker would call the first person listed, state that he was calling for Carl Stokes, stress the importance of his election to the mayorship, note his need for campaign workers to help him win, and invite the person called to accept the responsibility of being the block supervisor in his or her neighborhood. The exact duties of the block supervisor were explained; it was also emphasized that the supervisor would be the *personal* representative of the Stokes organization in that particular neighborhood. Seldom did a caller have to contact more than two or three people on a list before someone accepted the job, a revealing indication of the high enthusiasm for Stokes in the black community.

After individuals agreed to be block supervisors they were sent personal letters telling them what they would be doing and that they would be receiving further information and materials at a later date. Enclosed with the letter was a list of the house numbers in their block and a test to find out if they were real workers. They were asked to collect the names and addresses of all the registered voters (this occurred after the registration drive) on their block and return that information to the Stokes headquarters. The response to this first assignment was, in the words of one of the organizers, "enormous, about 80 percent of them did the job and supplied us with the list of voters." Those who did not complete the assignment were replaced by calling down the original list.

Approximately 2,050 volunteers were recruited into the Stokes organization through this process. In order to make communications with such a large number of people manageable, a ward structure was constructed that had one ward leader, four or five ward captains under him, and thirty to forty block supervisors reporting to each of the ward captains. Once this structure became operative, the Stokes camp had what many believed to be a stronger, more responsive and more respectable precinct committeemen organization. From the point of view of the Stokes organization this ward structure was, in effect, a bureaucratic structure that made possible a continuous up and down flow of information. Further, it was projected that even if the structure was only 35 to 40 percent effective, the Stokes organization would still have eight hundred people working in their own neighborhoods among people they knew.

As the primary campaign proceeded, constant contact was maintained with the block supervisors as a means for preparing them to fulfill their ultimate objective of producing a record voter turnout on election day. On the weekend before the election they received a package containing a badge, election day instructions, and doorknob stickers. The badge, which included the supervisor's name and the statement "Official Block Supervisor—Stokes for Mayor Committee," identified the supervisor as an official representative of the Stokes organization and was viewed by headquarters personnel as "a way to give psychological support and a feeling of involvement to the supervisors." The instructions called for them to canvass their block the day before the election to remind people once more how vital it was that they vote the next day. Further, in order to counteract the tendency for people to come home from work and not go out again to vote, the supervisors were provided with door knob stickers which were to be placed on each door in their block on election day morning. These stickers read: "Stop! Have You Voted Today? Do It Now at [polling place was inserted]. Vote Carl B. Stokes X." According to one of the principal organizers, it was "very important that the supervisors inserted where people should vote because they [the Board of Elections] changed a lot of voting places immediately before the election." The supervisors were also involved, of course, in canvassing, phoning, and arranging car pools on election day.

Virtually every respondent viewed the block supervisor structure as a tremendous success; indeed, most considered it as the very foundation of the street-level organization. In addition to the widespread eagerness within the black community to assist Stokes, the supervisor concept had some unique characteristics that contributed to its success.

> First, they did not have to devote huge chunks of time. It was a small enough task so that they could do it without becoming full-time campaign workers. Second, by involving people in their own neighborhoods we got them over the psychological block of having to knock on unfamiliar doors. People with no past experience are reluctant to canvass, but by having them do it among their own neighbors it's possible to overcome their hesitation. Also, we had the feeling that there were a lot of people out in the community who wanted to help but didn't know how to go about it because they had never done any political work before. Well the block supervisor thing was perfect for getting those people involved in the campaign, for giving them a concrete way to help.

The fact that the Stokes camp could establish such a large, successful structure in a very short period of time illustrates several characteristics of the Stokes organization: the almost unbelievable excitement generated by the organization, its ability to attract volunteers with organizational skill who were willing to work long hours, its flexibility in allowing political amateurs to organize and execute good ideas, and its capacity to rationally utilize the energy of rank-and-file blacks who were eager to become involved in the Stokes struggle. As we shall see, this was not the only example of these characteristics.

During the same period that some of the Stokes workers were spending virtually all of their time organizing block supervisors, other workers were involved in additional mobilizing activities. Individuals on the finance committee, for example, were engaged in sending out fund-raising letters, making personal solicitations, selling buttons, placing cans in business establishments, and doing everything legal to raise money.

One program, entitled "Thins for Stokes," was particularly effective in both raising funds and involving women from all levels of the black community. It was initiated by one woman who convinced one hundred women to contribute a dollar each and to recruit ten of their women friends to contribute a dollar who, in turn, also got an additional ten women each to do likewise. By utilizing this approach, the women were able to raise approximately $24,000 in about two weeks. This was viewed as an important mobilizing effort within the black community because "it was the kind of activity that gave everyone—from people on welfare to white-collar workers—an opportunity to participate. . . . It also meant that there were over twenty thousand people who were going to vote on election day if they had to turn heaven and hell upside down because in addition to everything else they had an investment in Stokes."

Money to help finance the Stokes campaign was also raised by numerous middle-class black organizations, which held cocktail parties, teas, luncheons, and so forth. "The doctor's organization raised about $5,000 at a cocktail party, the real estate men did likewise, and the lawyers and dentists did their own thing. These groups really raised large sums of money. In fact, they did so well that unlike 1965 we didn't have to have any chicken dinners where you only make one dollar for every ten you spend." In the opinion of one of the individuals responsible for finances, "the money raised in the black community was one of the largest self-help programs of a political nature that a black community in America ever got involved in." He estimated that the black community contributed about forty-five percent of the total one-half million dollars raised to finance the Stokes campaign.

The amount of money collected within the black community is a telling reflection of the widespread support that existed for Stokes. His candidacy clearly generated a bandwagon momentum that attracted virtually every segment and organization in the black community (except most black politicians) into his corner. The words of a black councilman who campaigned for Stokes captures the crusadelike atmosphere that prevailed. When asked if he had encountered any difficulty in persuading blacks to support or work for Stokes, he responded:

No, it was just the reverse, instead of problems there was enthusiasm. It was a very easy thing to do because people were walking in off the streets wanting to know what could they do. "Just what can I do in the campaign, how can I be useful? What can I do to help my man?" You see, Stokes was a symbol. He was a symbol at that time for black progress. You would see old people walking to the polls and perhaps they never voted a day in their lives. They considered politics a white man's business. We could have councilmen and judges, but they never dreamed that the day would come when a black man would be mayor of the town. This was a symbol, just like a flower bursting to bloom. And everybody wanted to be part of it and do his little bit as far as pushing this man on. Even myself as a professional politician, I felt a certain degree of pride and enthusiasm and I wasn't going to let this year pass by without giving all that I had. If he failed it would be because I short-changed him, and I think this was the attitude of the *total* community.

The constant preoccupation of the Stokes forces was how to insure that this bounding spirit would produce a maximum number of black votes on election day. Everything would be for naught unless they achieved an unprecedented turnout. The block-supervisor structure was erected to accomplish precisely that objective, but the Stokes organization did not rely on that alone; two additional election day programs were established in the quest to get every eligible black voter to the polls and to obtain an honest vote count.

The additional program, which focused on turning out voters, was based on identifying precincts that appeared to be lagging on election day and then saturating them with canvassing college students. Plans for executing such a process were laid out weeks before election day. Identifying which precincts to concentrate on was accomplished in the following manner. Workers at the campaign headquarters were supplied with a sheet of paper for each precinct in the black community. Included on each sheet was a precinct identification number, the number of registered voters in the precinct, and spaces to write in the number of voters that had voted in the particular precinct by 10 A.M., 12 noon, and 4 P.M. The latter information was supplied by Stokes workers who "at the assigned time went to a polling place, checked the ballot stub number [which indicated the number of people who had voted], wrote it down on their copies of the sheet, and went on to another polling place to repeat the operation." When the worker completed his run he telephoned the results into headquarters where the ballot stub numbers were entered on the appropriate sheet. If, upon inspection, the stub number indicated that a precinct was lagging behind what had been previously projected as an acceptable percentage turnout for that time of day, two actions were initiated. The block supervisors were notified that their precinct was not turning out at a high enough level and that they should "hit it again." Additionally, a call was made to an in-ward church where about four hundred college students were stationed. A group of the students would be deployed into the lagging precinct where they canvassed each house.

They would knock on every door and tell the people that Stokes was doing poorly in their neighborhood and that, in fact, he might lose because of their poor showing. They were to get those people to the polls and if they had already voted they were encouraged to contact their neighborhoods. And the kids did everything to get them out— they babysat, took them to waiting cars, reminded them where to vote, cajoled them, begged them, everything.

After the students completed covering a precinct in their storm-like manner, they returned to the church and waited for the next assignment, which usually came in a few minutes. This process was repeated throughout the day and ultimately about 40 to 45 percent of the precincts in the black community were canvassed on election day through this program.

The students were recruited and organized to operate in this fashion by Bill Hunter, a young white college student who spent the six weeks before primary election day visiting over thirty college campuses in Ohio. On each of the campuses he attempted "to make the students who showed up at a well-publicized meeting feel that it was the most important thing in their lives—at that moment—to become involved in the Stokes struggle. This would give them a tangible opportunity to work on one of the problems—the race issue—that many of them were concerned about." Hunter found this approach to be extremely successful in persuading the students to join the Stokes campaign. The students were not only anxious to participate, but their election day work was both impressive and highly valuable. As one Stokes worker put it:

> We knew where we were weak, where we needed the work, and where the kids would be most valuable. . . . When the areas were identified they went in and blanketed the area. And what a great and marvelous job they did. The whole campaign was exciting, but they added that much more excitement and feeling of motion—you just can't capture it with words.

The 1965 election experience taught the Stokes workers that a block supervisor and college student program that turned black voters out could not guarantee that their votes would be honestly counted in the final tally. During the 1965 campaign the Board of Elections, for example, shifted polling places in many black areas just prior to election day and installed voting machines in places where people had never used machines before. Further, as we noted earlier, two ballot bags from black wards disappeared and were never accounted for. This latter incident occurred because, in part, the Stokes organization did not have enough workers to cover all of the polling places in the black community, thus they were "forced to trust a lot of people in 1965 that couldn't be trusted and we paid dearly for it. Our objective in 1967 was to cover *every* polling place and to have someone there when they counted the votes." The extensive organizational effort that was made to reach that objective is described by the woman who was responsible for that portion of the campaign work.

> I decided that it was absolutely necessary that we have a witness and challenger at every polling place on election day and that they be identified as Stokes people so that they would know that we were on the spot. We knew we would have a lot of trouble with people who

were registered in one party and who wanted to cross over party lines to vote for another candidate. We had a great deal of this with Mr. Locher, a lot of Republicans tried to vote for him. Our people were instructed to challenge them even though we legally couldn't stop them from switching parties. Our challengers also stopped six major check-off lists in six West Side wards. They were so effective that Mr. Stanton had to go out himself and collect the check-offs [a list of voters who had not voted by 2 P.M. and who would be called by Democratic party workers and encouraged to vote]. We also had challengers in black wards and where black people voted in white areas—specifically, Murray Hill. We put John Wooten of the Cleveland Browns there to be sure that black voters were not intimidated like they had been in the past. We had other black football players in some black wards, like Ward 11 where we think votes were stolen in 1965. . . . It is very simple to invalidate paper ballots (anyone can do it) so we gave fifteen instruction sessions to over three thousand people on all the ways there are to cheat. Additionally, we had a pool of lawyers with two-way radios who went to polling places where challengers were having trouble. These twenty-five lawyers were in roaming cars and they handled about two thousand complaints on election day. Finally, when the polls closed at 6:30 P.M., we had the vote checked and called in to our headquarters by our people, and we had 98 percent coverage by 9 P.M.

The effectiveness of this operation is suggested by the fact that only 15 people out of 3,200 did not show up to man their assigned place on primary day; and among those who did, 2,100 returned questionnaires describing what occurred in their polling place. This intelligence was used to strengthen the ability of the Stokes organization to cope with the upcoming general election. According to the worker quoted above, these procedures were highly effective in dealing with the innumerable problems that arose, and in her estimation "as honest a vote as can be expected was achieved."

APPEALING TO THE WHITE COMMUNITY

At the same time that the street-level organization was concentrating on mobilizing and delivering the black vote, the other main branch of the Stokes organization was focusing on appealing to the white community. This latter dimension of the campaign organization was itself divided into two operations, one dealing with the white business establishment and the other with rank-and-file white voters.

In approaching the business community, emphasis was placed

upon the numerous failings of the Locher administration, how these shortcomings undermined Cleveland's business climate, and why Stokes was the one candidate that could revitalize the city's health. Stokes's campaign manager, Dr. Kenneth Clement, as we noted earlier, played an important role in cultivating support for Stokes in business circles. There were other individuals, however, who also performed this function. A respondent, for example, who identified himself as the only "real" WASP in the Stokes camp described how he exposed Stokes to the power structure:

> This town is run by a group of forty or fifty who make all the major decisions. They are the presidents of the utilities and banks, the major law firms, the major architects and doctors. I exposed them to Carl early in the campaign, in September. I invited them to dinner and planned a three-way debate, but the mayor refused to attend. We had a guest list like you've never seen, every major corporation president, every major civic leader and so forth. I got about 90 percent of them to attend. Some of these people were supporting Frank Celeste, but they quickly dropped their financial support for him and in some cases actively brought out their financial support for Carl. . . . That particular night Celeste was such a poor speaker and uninformed and made such a poor showing that the unanimous reaction was "Gee this guy Carl Stokes is quite something." Carl performed just beautifully, the guy simply has great appeal.

Another respondent related how Stokes was able to gain access to and support from traditional Republican strongholds.

> At a cocktail party for Seth Taft I bumped into [X]. [X] is a rock-ribbed Republican who happens to play tennis and ski with the old, old social, monied group in Cleveland. Not the managerial men, but the people who really have it socked away. Well [X] came up to me at that party and said "Hey, you know I would like to meet Carl Stokes." And I said, "You just made a date." I got hold of Carl and we set up a lunch. Well [X] got excited about the whole campaign, and he ended up getting these people to contribute money and give small luncheons with other industrialists being invited. The people doing the inviting had never done this sort of thing before. Maybe in the inner-circles of the Republican party they had, but it never happened for a black Democrat. . . . Don't ask me what motivated them but I think some felt that Carl Stokes represented some kind of "responsible" black leadership and that unless the community accepted him things would get even worse.

Stokes's ability to secure backing from the white establishment was further enhanced on 3 September when the *Plain Dealer*, in a front-page editorial, endorsed him for mayor. Given the traditional clientele of the *Plain Dealer* and the fact that the editor, Thomas Vale, was himself a member of the WASP establishment, the Stokes endorsement represented sort of a seal of approval. It was a statement to the community by the editor that this man had the qualifications to be mayor. The endorsement not only aided Stokes's capacity to raise money from white businessmen, it also had, according to a Stokes campaigner, "a tremendous psychological impact on the campaign workers. They knew it was a crucial breakthrough, and it stimulated them to work that much harder; you could almost feel the momentum grow."

In summary, Stokes was very successful in his quest to acquire support from Cleveland's business world. Large sums of money were donated to the campaign, plus lawyers and other professionals were recruited to assist in the struggle. This element of support was a welcomed addition to the Stokes camp, one that was totally absent from the 1965 effort.

In contrast to this favorable reception, the Stokes forces confronted considerable resistance and hostility in their attempt to approach ordinary white voters. The prevailing political environment that the Stokes workers were operating in is suggested by the account of a worker who had conducted interviews for a national polling concern among white Clevelanders after the Hough riot of 1966.

> The level of hostility in the cosmos [ethnic] wards was tremendous, just unbelievable. . . . There's great resentment and absolutely no desire to be interested or understand. It is strictly "we've worked all our lives, we've got our own homes, we're hard workers, and we resent that our tax money goes to support those niggers." And that's exactly the attitude and the only word I can use because I heard it over and over again. . . . By the time we got about three-fourths of the way through the questionnaire they would usually turn on me and suggest that I was a "nigger lover." It was painful, absolutely painful. The hostility was just unbelievable.[17]

Given this situation, it is not surprising that the white workers who directed Stokes's West Side headquarters encountered a multitude of obstacles: some of the workers were physically attacked for passing out literature; windows at the campaign headquarters were broken several times, once by a molotov cocktail; and gun shots were fired at a guard. It was exceedingly difficult to recruit anywhere near the large number of people who volun-

teered to work in the black community; indeed, only forty workers were involved on the West Side in contrast to over four
thousand on the East Side. According to one of the workers, the
entire West Side operation was conducted in a climate of fear.
"We were constantly harassed—threatening phone calls, signs
ripped off our cars, people spitting and screaming at you, and
everywhere you looked there were Locher signs." There was no
way of predicting how many votes Stokes would amass in the
white community because "people wouldn't talk about it, it was a
secret. Those who did vote for him did it without anyone knowing—they were fearful too."

It was decided within the Stokes camp that the most effective
way to combat these barriers was to give Stokes as much personal exposure to white audiences as possible. Consequently,
great emphasis was placed upon arranging meetings of any sort
that would provide Stokes with opportunities to personally present himself and his case for being elected mayor. Stokes was once
again barred by the Democratic party leadership from addressing
regular ward meetings; therefore, his workers relied heavily on
individuals and some church groups to sponsor these gatherings.[18]
It is likely that such meetings attracted a mixture of individuals.
That is, those who had already decided to vote for Stokes, those
who were undecided, and those who were against him. In the
opinion of persons who observed Stokes in action, the group
mixture appeared to have little impact on the eventual outcome
of the meeting—Stokes invariably gave a polished and winning performance. An individual who attended virtually every West Side
meeting explained:

> He has a terrific amount of political charisma. . . . Many people
> told us that personal exposure was the thing that convinced them.
> They would emphasize to us "get him over here to meet more people
> because he can't help but gain their support if they meet him and see
> him and talk with him." We heard this all the time. . . . In many of
> the meetings you could feel him winning people over as the meeting
> progressed. You could just feel the audience warming up to him and
> see that they were impressed by him.

Stokes, of course, was aware of this effect and believed that the
size of his white vote was likely to determine success or failure;
consequently, he spent an inordinate amount of time attending

meetings of all sizes on the West Side. In fact, some of the East Side workers felt that he was spending too much time on the West Side, thus neglecting and, in a sense, taking the black community for granted. On the other hand, West Side workers felt that he should spend even more time in the white community since it appeared that only he was capable of reaching the voters. This dilemma was never fully resolved to the satisfaction of either group; however, Stokes did conserve some time by gaining additional exposure in the white community through utilization of the mass media. During the closing weeks of the primary campaign Stokes received considerable television, radio, and newspaper exposure, through both news coverage and paid advertisements. The money raised through contacts with the business community was, of course, instrumental in making this type of exposure possible—such resources were dearly lacking in 1965. On all of these occasions Stokes continued to reiterate the double theme that he would be mayor of all the people and that he had the competence to pull the city out of the depths it had plunged to under the Locher administration.

As the above account has suggested, the Stokes campaign organization, considering its amateur and volunteer character, was well organized and coordinated. The organization did suffer, however, one serious split concerning approaches to white voters. After the East Side workers had completed recruiting block supervisors over the telephone, some of the workers felt that the freed callers should be used to conduct a telephone canvass of West Side homes. Other East Side workers and most of the West Side volunteers were opposed to the plan on the grounds that it would only antagonize white voters even more and perhaps stimulate some who were going to stay home to go out and vote against Stokes. This debate raged back and forth just prior to the primary election and was finally resolved against the plan, but not until it had split the top echelon of the street-level organization.

In their quest for white votes the Stokes workers also paid special attention to the Latin American segment of the white community. Historically, the eight thousand Latin Americans in Cleveland played a political role very similar to blacks; they voted heavily Democratic but received no special recognition nor encouragement from party leaders. In fact, because of their small numbers their political rewards were even more meager than the token payoffs distributed to blacks. With this in mind and the realization that the election could well be decided by a slim margin and that the Latin American community had experienced oppressions similar to those of blacks, a Stokes worker was assigned the task of stimulating support among Latin American voters.

This was accomplished by requesting a long-time resident of the Latin American community to form a political club that would concentrate on registering Spanish-speaking voters and organizing them to vote for Stokes and other candidates who promised to aid the community. According to the chairman of this club, it was not an easy task to get people registered because:

> . . . The people have been suffering for so long that they say that everyone who is running says the same thing, but when they get in office they never do a thing about our problems. They got their minds already made up that anyone who gets in office will do the same as the past one.

Despite this barrier, the club was able to get over six hundred new people registered, thus increasing the total Latin American registered voters to about two thousand, and to produce a solid vote for Stokes. The approach used to achieve this result stressed that Stokes "was from a minority group and he knows how much people have suffered. He would understand better and help us." The Stokes candidacy, because of his background, was viewed as representing for many of these voters "the first time that they had a real choice at the polls."[19]

THE LOCHER AND CELESTE CAMPAIGNS

The Locher campaign organization, in sharp contrast to the Stokes group, was not able to generate widespread enthusiasm for Locher nor was it sufficiently organized to match the performance of the Stokes camp. This condition emanated from several factors, not the least being that the Locher administration was constantly on the defensive throughout the entire campaign. Numerous mass media reports had depicted, for over a year, the various shortcomings of the Locher administration and had characterized it as one that was simply incapable of dealing with the complex problems that plagued Cleveland. All three of the challenging candidates (Stokes, Celeste, and Taft) picked up on these criticisms and added some of their own, the effect being that the Locher administration was the target of criticism from every angle.

It was true that, despite this negative image, Locher did receive the Democratic party endorsement. However, in assessing the importance of that endorsement, several factors should be considered. First, it was extended reluctantly; the party hierarchy had favored Stanton and had tempted Locher with a federal judgeship to step aside. When he refused to retire and Stanton dropped out of the race, the party went along with Locher but certainly with no great enthusiasm. Second, it must be remembered that the party lacked a history of electing mayors. Since the late 1930s, whenever the newspapers and the Democratic party had opposing candidates (which was often), the newspapers invariably won and their candidate invariably ran on a platform that included antiparty bossism. Consequently, the party had never been able to muster enough strength to defeat the newspaper-endorsed candidate. This historical pattern became particularly important in 1967 because the *Plain Dealer* endorsed Stokes and the *Cleveland Press* (the "political bible" of the ethnic wards) advised its readers to vote for anyone *but* Locher. When the newspapers abandoned Locher, the morale of his forces sank even lower; an atmosphere of pessimism pervaded his followers.

The lack of newspaper support not only weakened the morale of Locher's backers, it forced him to rely on a party organization that had declined over the years in its capability to deliver votes. This decline is reflected in the fact that at the time of the campaign there were over 200 vacancies among the 2,156 precinct committeemen positions, and many of the precinct people "were old, tired workers who didn't beat the bushes." Such a condition would never have existed at an earlier time, but the reduction of patronage and the spread of general economic prosperity, among other developments, undercut the attractiveness of precinct work.

The deterioration of grass-roots party work was also reflected, as noted earlier, by the ability of Locher and his predecessors to build their own personal organizations and defeat the party organization candidates. The success of the mayor's organization, however, was greatly aided by newspaper support. Therefore, the combination of the mayor's organization without newspaper support and an eroded party organization placed Locher in a vulnerable situation. His workers were confronted with doing a lot of things that they didn't know how to do because they hadn't been forced to do them in so long. Since the first election of men like Lausche and Celebrezze they had become soft.

Within this context, Locher conducted a highly traditional campaign. He made the rounds of the numerous ethnic organizations and hammered away at the theme that Ralph Locher had integrity and honesty; no one could accuse him of betraying the public's trust. He defended his administration as a solid and frugal one. In the words of one of his workers: "Just change the times and dates and it was the same old thing." He went lightly on the race issue, although he did attack Stokes for attempting to raise funds outside of Cleveland. In sum, the Locher campaign simply never caught on fire; the zeal and enthusiasm that characterized the Stokes effort was lacking.

Perhaps as a venture to spur enthusiasm into the lagging Locher campaign, the Democratic party mailed two intensely racist newsletters to white voters in the closing weeks of the campaign. One of the newsletters stated: "Will Dr. Martin Luther King actually be the mayor of Cleveland if Carl Stokes is elected Tuesday? This would give the noted racist control of his first city in the United States." This ploy, however, apparently backfired since it did not appreciably strengthen the Locher effort, but it did stimulate the Stokes people to work even harder. In addition, several respondents were of the opinion that the high-handed tactics of the party hierarchy may have pushed some fence-sitting whites into the Stokes column.

Mayoral-candidate Frank Celeste encountered even more difficulties than Locher in his effort to obtain the mayorship. Celeste had hoped to come across to the voters as the one experienced candidate who could succeed, who could make the city work. He argued that the election of Stokes would be replacing a sure loser —Locher—with an untried executive. He was a third option, a tried, experienced executive who had already proven he could be a successful mayor. Celeste had, however, no campaign strategy or organization for communicating this message to the electorate. Indicative of his organizational strength, for example, is the fact that he had to pay three councilmen to utilize their organizations to collect signatures for his filing petitions. According to one of his close advisors, "there never was a clear strategy for mustering votes—he simply hopped from one place to another announcing that he was running for mayor."

As an outsider to Cleveland politics, Celeste was not familiar with the inner workings of the political system nor did he have a political base within the city from which to launch his bid. If he had any potential political strength it was within the Italian community. His ethnic background, however, did not stir any growing support among Italians, perhaps because Celeste "had left the Catholic Church when he was young, he didn't live in the Italian community and wasn't well known there, and his name wasn't a popular Italian name—many people probably didn't even know that he was Italian."

Celeste did receive the financial support promised to him by the business group that convinced him to run; they did not, however, deliver the party nomination or newspaper endorsements. This failure in combination with Celeste's nonexistent political base reduced his chances of winning the election to near zero. Indeed, as it became obvious that the election had boiled down to a duel between Locher and Stokes, great pressure was exerted on Celeste to drop out of the race. A public opinion poll released two weeks before the election showed that Stokes was leading Locher by three percentage points (47.7 to 44.3) and that Celeste would capture about 8 percent of the vote, with the overwhelming proportion of his support coming from white voters.[20] Consequently, his critics accused Celeste of merely staying in the race to split the white vote and hand the election to Stokes. At one point he was supposedly offered a considerable amount of money to get out, but Celeste insisted on finishing what he had started.

THE PRIMARY RESULTS

As it turned out the fact that Celeste refused to drop out did not affect the final outcome of the primary election. When the votes were counted Stokes had beaten Locher by over 18,000 votes and Celeste had accumulated only 8,509 votes (see table 9).

TABLE 9

Cleveland Democratic Primary Election, 1967

Candidate	Votes	Percent
Stokes	110,769	52.3
Locher	92,321	43.7
Celeste	8,509	4.0
Total	211,599	100.0

Source: Board of Election voting returns.

Thus, even if Celeste had withdrawn from the race and all of those who had voted for him would have voted for Locher, Stokes still would have won by about 10,000 votes.

Stokes's surprisingly wide victory over Locher resulted from several factors. Most important was the fact that although voter registration in black wards was down from 1965, the black voter turnout (which amounted to 73 percent of all eligible black voters) surpassed the record-high 1965 percentage, and Stokes received a significantly greater proportion of the black vote than he had in 1965 (96 percent compared to 85 percent). In other words, an all-time high proportion of black voters went to the polls and voted with unprecedented cohesion for Stokes, thus providing him with about 7,000 more votes in the black community than he had received in 1965. These results clearly mirror the tremendous mobilizing effort that was accomplished in the black community. Complementing this enormous black voting bloc were two developments within the white wards. First, the white turnout of 58 percent was considerably below the 73 percent turnout among blacks. Whereas only 2 percentage points separated the turnout among the races in 1965, the difference in 1967 was 15 percent. Second, not only did a large proportion of whites fail to go to the polls, but among those who did over 15 percent voted for Stokes, which was considerably higher than the 3 percent who did in 1965. Stokes also increased his total number of votes and percentage of the vote in mixed wards (which probably reflects the in-migration of more blacks). In summary, his victory resulted from the ability of his organization to produce a historic turnout and number of votes in the black community (particularly for a primary), the considerable inroads he made among white voters, and the inability of the Locher campaign to stimulate a turnout among white voters

TABLE 10

CLEVELAND DEMOCRATIC PRIMARY ELECTION, 1967: BY RACE

	Black wards	White wards	Mixed wards	City totals
Registered voters	99,885	152,737	73,421	326,043
Percentage turnout.......	73.4	58.0	66.9	64.7
Stokes votes.............	70,575	13,495	26,699	110,769
Percentage for Stokes	96.2	15.2	54.4	52.3

SOURCE: Computed from Special Census of 1965 and Board of Election voting returns.

that approached the record display of the blacks (see table 10). As one of Stokes's aides put it: "We got our people to the polls and Locher didn't, it's as simple and complex as that."

1. *Cleveland Press*, 3 November 1965, p. 1. All quotations from various editions of the *Cleveland Press* are reprinted by permission of the publisher.

2. This quotation and following unattributed quotations are derived from interviews conducted in Cleveland by the authors.

3. Louis H. Masotti and Jerome R. Corsi, *Shoot-Out in Cleveland* (New York: Bantam Books, 1969), pp. 12–13.

4. Quoted in ibid., p. 14.

5. Ibid.

6. This was also the conclusion of the President's National Advisory Commission on Civil Disorders. See *Report of the President's National Advisory Commission on Civil Disorders* (New York: Bantam Books, 1968), p. 9.

7. See Roldo S. Bartimole and Murray Gruber, "Cleveland: Recipe for Violence," *The Nation*, 26 June 1967, pp. 814–17.

8. *Cleveland Plain Dealer*, 14 June 1967.

9. *Cleveland Press*, 20 May 1967.

10. At a press conference two days before the filing date, Taft stated: "I will not run if a major candidate declares as an independent. Splintered elections, where there are three or more candidates, result in what we now have—indecisive government with a mayor elected by only one-third of the vote." *Cleveland Press*, 3 July 1967.

11. This incident serves to illuminate again, the disadvantaged position of blacks in the political process. Because they have not been actively involved in elections as candidates or as election officials, blacks are often not familiar with legal requirements and are disqualified as voters and candidates because they have not satisfied legal technicalities. In the case of the master petition episode, it was good fortune, not expertise, that saved Stokes from being disqualified as a mayoral candidate. From this experience, members of the Stokes organization learned that they would have to become knowledgable about every aspect of the law pertinent to elections if they were to become an effective competitive force in the electoral process.

12. *Cleveland Plain Dealer*, 8 July 1967.

13. Ibid., 3 August 1967.

14. See, for example, the text of his speech that appeared in the *Call and Post*, 8 July 1967. The theme of the speech was that he would "serve all the people without fear, favor, or unfair special consideration."

15. Several respondents indicated that the $25,000 it cost to employ Ostrow was donated to the Stokes campaign by Cyrus Eaton, a Cleveland millionaire.

16. *Call and Post*, 9 September 1967.

17. On this point it is important to note that numerous civil disorders occurred throughout the summer of 1967 in such cities as Detroit, Newark, Toledo, New York, and Durham.

18. In August, Stokes received a letter from the party chairman Porter informing him that permission to speak at party meetings was a privilege not a right. Porter stated that Stokes's record did not reflect regularity of party service since he had run as an independent in 1965, and "failed to comply with the rules of the party." For that reason, Porter indicated that Stokes would not be accorded the privilege of speaking at party meetings. *Cleveland Press*, 9 August 1967.

19. A *Plain Dealer* public opinion poll showed that a large majority of Puerto Ricans were planning to vote for Stokes for the kinds of reasons noted above. *Cleveland Plain Dealer*, 17 September 1967.

20. *Cleveland Plain Dealer*, 17 September 1967.

5

Cleveland: The 1967 General Election

THE GENERAL ELECTION CAMPAIGN STRATEGY

The Stokes downtown headquarters was, of course, the scene of a jubilant celebration the evening of the primary election. The polls had closed at 6:30 P.M.; and by 9:15 P.M. Carl Stokes, relying on the results called in by his workers, proclaimed victory, even though the Board of Elections and NBC computers placed Ralph Locher considerably ahead. At 10:35 P.M. Locher, after being advised by his campaign manager Bronis Klementowicz that he could not win, conceded the election and journeyed with his wife to Stokes's headquarters to personally congratulate the victor. When asked by a reporter if he would support Stokes in the general election, Locher responded, "Traditionally, the party has always supported the victor in a primary election." When queried further as to whether that meant he would specifically support Stokes, Locher replied, "Yes, I will."[1]

In his victory statement, Stokes gratefully thanked all who had worked so diligently for his election. He pledged to wage a vigorous campaign against his opponent, Seth Taft, and if he were successful, to make Cleveland, Ohio, "a model city of the United States." Stokes seized the opportunity to begin his general campaign immediately by stating to his followers and the television audience that they had vindicated his faith in American democracy. He alluded to the notion that his triumph over Locher and

Frank Celeste was in the American political tradition of poor boy makes good. This was a conscious appeal on the part of Stokes to conjure up, in the minds of white voters in particular, the image that his journey was no different than that of the recent Cleveland mayors who had preceded him. If their elections had reassured their ethnic countrymen that there was substance to the American dream of an open opportunity structure for those individuals with industry and perseverance, then his primary victory was simply the most recent example of that respected principle. His success reaffirmed the faith in individualism and the notion that the American political system had room for all ethnic groups.

By striking these familiar chords, Stokes was already putting into operation an important component of his general campaign strategy. The primary election results had made it abundantly clear that the black community was solidly behind Stokes. Consequently, the general election strategy was simply to improve upon his highly impressive showing in the black wards by sharpening up even further the basic appeals and tactics utilized during the primary. On the other hand, he was still confronted with the problem of appealing to the overwhelming majority of whites who had voted for his opponents. This majority, combined with the city's Republican voters, could constitute a voting bloc capable of defeating him in the general election. His basic task was to prevent white Democrats from crossing party lines to vote for his Republican opponent, Seth Taft. In an effort to head off widespread desertion from the party ranks, Stokes planned to employ a strategy which stressed that: (1) he had won the Democratic primary handily and therefore had earned the support of all lifetime Democrats; (2) his commitment was to be mayor of all the people (not a black power advocate); and (3) his background, in contrast to his opponent's, better qualified him to be mayor of Cleveland.

The personal characteristics of Stokes's competitor, Seth Taft, made the latter aspect of the general strategy relatively easy to execute. Taft was a Republican in a city where there were approximately four Democrats to each Republican. He was a wealthy suburbanite who had attended the right schools, had the right acquaintances, had joined the right Cleveland law firm, and had moved into the city from the exclusive suburb of Pepper Pike to seek the mayorship. His uncle, the late Robert Taft, was cosponsor of the antilabor Taft-Hartley law, thus his name was anything but revered among the numerous union members in Cleveland. He was not well known to the voters, although he had worked on numerous civic projects (including an effort to install metropolitan government in the Cleveland area), and he had never held any kind of public office. In the words of one respondent:

> Taft, in essence, represented the white Protestant establishment that Frank Lausche had beaten many years ago. He symbolized all that the cosmos voters were against. He had all the handicaps; yet in the final analysis he was white and Stokes was black, and that eventually proved to be more important than anything else.[2]

Stokes could not attack Taft as he had attacked Locher and his administration for the problems plaguing Cleveland, but he did plan to emphasize Taft's above-mentioned shortcomings at every opportunity, particularly concerning his lack of contact and experience with the grave social problems of the city. Over and over again, Stokes would underscore that he possessed firsthand knowledge and daily contact with city problems whereas Taft had spent most of his life far removed from them. As in the primary, a major thrust of the Stokes's strategy toward white voters was to convince them that by any objective standards, he was clearly more qualified to be mayor than his opponent.

Given the characteristics of the two candidates and the exposure Stokes had commanded during the primary, it was not surprising that a September 1967 public opinion poll showed that if Stokes did win the primary, he would emerge with a considerable lead over Taft for the mayorship. The results of that poll indicated that Stokes would receive 46 percent of the general election vote compared to only 19 percent for Taft with 20 percent of the voters undecided and 14 percent claiming that they would not vote for either candidate. A subsequent poll, conducted about a week after the October primary, showed Stokes acquiring 47 percent of the vote and Taft increasing his proportion to 31 percent; but 18 percent of the voters were still undecided and 4 percent planned not to vote.[3] This latter poll indicated that Taft's growing strength flowed from support among those who had voted for Celeste or Locher in the primary. The crucial "swing vote" of undecideds and nonvoters was described as "white Democrats who probably have a strong dislike for both Negroes and Republicans and therefore are under very strong cross-pressures which could easily keep them from voting. If they do vote they would probably go for Taft by a wide margin."[4]

From Stokes's perspective it would have been obviously desirable if these cross-pressured voters decided to vote for him. Indeed, the basic thrust of his general strategy was geared precisely toward attracting these voters to his cause. Short of doing so, his bid for the mayor's seat would be enhanced if such voters remained at home on election day. Conversely, Taft could not win the election unless he was able to encourage the cross-pressured voters to vote and vote for him. His dilemma was how to accomplish this task without resorting to a racist campaign, which he had meticulously avoided during the primary and had vowed not to do during the general campaign or election. In fact, Stokes's victory in the primary took the Taft camp completely off guard, since their operating assumption was that Locher would win the primary and that they would inherit the Stokes vote. According to one of Taft's campaign strategists,

> Our whole campaign was geared to do one thing—defeat Ralph Locher. When Stokes won, the whole campaign had to be scrapped, all of the literature, the thinking, the approach. Our strategy against Locher was to get the black vote and the white liberal vote but when Stokes won he got them and we got stuck with Locher's vote.

Despite this unexpected development, the Taft strategy called for a continuance of the campaign waged during the primary. That is, Taft maintained that the resolution of racial strife and the social problems underpinning it constituted the most pressing problem confronting the city and would require the greatest amount of attention on the part of the new mayor. Although Taft was in a sense forced to accept former Locher supporters as his basic constituency, he decided not to inflame their uglier side but instead to project himself as a candidate committed to reconciling, not polarizing, the races. As we shall see, this strategy, for the most part, was pursued by the Taft camp until about fifteen days before the election.

REMOBILIZING THE BLACK COMMUNITY

One of the unanticipated outcomes of Stokes's primary victory was the serious letdown experienced by both the Stokes organization and the black community as a whole. The Stokes supporters had worked themselves up to such a high emotional pitch in their quest to defeat Locher that his defeat gave them considerable self-satisfaction and complacency. Since the winner of the Democratic primary invariably won the general election, there was the strong temptation among many of Stokes's backers to assume that he would beat Taft without much difficulty. This tendency was compounded by the presumption among some workers that the Democratic party would throw its weight behind Stokes. The condition of the Stokes street-level organization immediately after the primary was described by a worker responsible for several black wards as follows:

> For the first two weeks after the primary we didn't do anything. At first we felt that we were going to get support from the Democratic party. However, when we found out that they weren't going to do anything we went back to tighten up our block supervisor and ward captain situation. We notified them that they would have to perform one more time for us. The biggest problem was going back and selling the black community the idea that they had to go out and vote for Carl again. Since he won the primary, many people thought he was already mayor. That may seem silly, but remember we sold October 3 as the one chance to vote for Carl.

The above quotation is not included to imply that the Stokes street-level organization collapsed during the general campaign, for the opposite is closer to reality. The organization did experience a notable lull, and the zealousness that characterized the primary was for a time dampened; however, improvements in the functioning of the organization eventually occurred. For example, the block supervisor structure sustained less than a 10 percent turnover between the primary and the general elections. Consequently, the vast majority of the block supervisors knew virtually every voter in their area, had already contacted each of them several times, and had learned how to turn them out for the general election—and they did just that. Likewise, the participation of college students on election day was improved upon. The coordinator of that operation was able to identify those universities that turned out for elections and those that needed more pumping; he established more in-ward headquarters from which students could be deployed; he recruited assistant in-ward leaders to increase the efficiency of the deployment procedures; and he was able to have more people in motion on general election day than on primary election day. In sum, he felt that his component of the general campaign was a much more sophisticated operation because of the experience accumulated during the primary. The primary experience was also very valuable for the workers attempting to decide which precincts the college students should canvass. Whereas their estimates as to which precincts were lagging on primary day were based on educated guesses, the data collected during the primary provided them with empirical grounds for deciding where to deploy the student workers during the general election. The coordinator for polling-place witnesses and challengers also utilized information gathered during the primary to polish her operation. Soon after the primary was over she sent out 3,500 questionnaires to her workers asking them to detail as exactly as possible what occurred in their polling place during the primary. Based on the information culled from the 2,100 completed returns, those workers were able to identify the trouble spots and prepare themselves for doing an even better job on the general election day. That information also helped them to decide which workers needed to be replaced, which needed re-instruction, and where to reinforce the less solid segments of the work force. Since a little over 80 percent of the people who worked on that aspect of the campaign during the primary also worked in the general, most of the time and energy was devoted to refining a fundamentally sound procedure.

When asked to compare the functioning of the street-level organization in the primary and the general campaign, one respondent summarized the difference by noting that:

> We were much more sophisticated in the general election. We shaped everything up off the primary. Everything was much more efficient. We shaped up the witnesses and challengers, the block supervisors, the college out-lets, and the in-ward organization. The grass-roots campaign was really sharpened up as soon as we got moving again, although it took some time for us to get off dead center.

Thus, once the narcotic affect of winning the primary was overcome and it became clear that little help would be forthcoming from the Democratic party, the Stokes grass-roots organization moved into high gear again and, in the estimation of most respondents, functioned in a more well-oiled fashion than it had throughout the primary. The message disseminated throughout the black community by the organization stressed that Stokes had not been elected mayor yet and that he needed another enormous voter turnout on 7 November, the day of the general election. In the words of one campaigner in the black community, "We emphasized over and over again that we had to do it one more time for Carl. We had come this far, let's not blow it, let's go all the way." Despite the early lull in the general campaign, this message apparently did get across to the black masses, and they did provide Stokes with another huge voting bloc. His almost fatal difficulties emerged not from any inability to remobilize the black community, but from the tidelike wave of white Democrats crossing party lines to vote for his Republic opponent. How and why this phenomenon occurred is discussed below.

THE RACE ISSUE EXPLODES

While the street-level organization was engaged in remobilizing the black community to turn out for the general election, the other components of the Stokes organization were concentrating on building further Stokes support among the white population. Individuals, for example, who were charged with cultivating Stokes support within the white business establishment continued to solicit funds, endorsements, and the lending of professional assistance to the Stokes campaign organization. As noted earlier, considerable success was achieved in these efforts during the primary. However, once Locher was knocked out of contention there was a temptation within these circles to waver on strongly supporting Stokes in the general election. The basis of this development was explained in the following manner by a Stokes worker who shared responsibility for that aspect of the campaign.

A good number of these people were Republicans or friends of Seth Taft, so they wanted to support him or they couldn't make a choice between Taft and Stokes. They liked them both, they felt that they were both equal in ability and that they would both do a fine job. One of the most difficult things to deal with was the feeling among these people after Locher's defeat that "Oh, well Cleveland can't lose now either way, can it?" The prevalent feeling in these circles was that it was a toss-up as to which man was best qualified for the job. People felt that at last we have two good candidates for mayor and the town can't really lose no matter who's elected. So we had to combat all of this during the general.

Although this sort of difficulty did arise, and did cause some concern among his workers, Stokes's support within the establishment did not seriously erode during the general campaign. Obviously, Taft received considerable backing from traditional Republican strongholds within the business world, but Stokes did not become the victim of widespread defection to Taft's camp. In general, the business establishment was split into strong Taft supporters, and those who were either neutral or backed both candidates.

Indicative of Stokes's continued promotion among powerful elements within the white community was the posture of both newspapers that he be selected over Taft for the mayorship. Why Stokes remained the continued choice is summarized by the endorsing editorial of the *Plain Dealer*. In its endorsement the *Plain Dealer* stressed the fact that Stokes was a skilled professional politician who had grown up in Cleveland, was intimately aware of the city's problems, and was actively involved in efforts to find solutions to them. The editorial suggested that Taft, on the other hand, was a pleasant amateur and an outsider who had to move into Cleveland from Pepper Pike (a Cleveland suburb) to run for mayor. Fears by whites that, if elected, Stokes would limit his concerns to the black community were, according to the editorial, unjustified because in his campaign Stokes had appealed to "Clevelanders as a whole and has made clear that if elected he would serve all his fellow Clevelanders fairly."[5]

A problem for Stokes that was far more serious than his relationship to the white establishment consisted of his relationship to the thousands of white Democrats who voted for Locher or Celeste in the primary. A major effort to keep such voters within the Democratic fold was launched a week after the primary voting. All of the leading Democrats in the Cleveland area were invited to attend a Democratic unity rally sponsored by the Stokes for Mayor Committee, the Cleveland AFL-CIO, the Teamsters District Council, and the Democratic party. Virtually every well-known Democrat, including Senator Stephen M. Young, Congressmen Charles A. Vanik and Michael Feighan, former governor Michael V. DiSalle, and county chairman Albert Porter (whose resignation Stokes had called for during the primary) attended the mass meeting along with over two thousand of the party faithful. If the rhetoric of the speeches was denotative of support for

Stokes's candidacy, there was no question that the party was prepared to back him vigorously. The praises grew stronger and stronger as each speaker took his turn at the rostrum; by the end of the evening it appeared that the Democratic party was one big, happy family united behind Stokes and ready to do battle with its traditional Republican enemy.

As is often the case, however, once the enthusiasm of the moment fades, the nature of political reality reappears. In this case the nature of political reality was that the ordinary white voters in Cleveland's ethnic neighborhoods were not enthusiastic about Stokes; indeed, they were opposed to him, and the Democratic party representatives in their wards were not about to become engaged in a strong endeavor to change their inclinations. It soon became clear to the Stokes camp that the "big get-together was simply paper stuff—they went through the motions but there was no real commitment to elect Carl." According to some respondents, the fact that the party did not become involved in the Stokes struggle was a fortunate development:

> The difference between the primary and the general was we didn't know how to relate to the party. In the primary they were clearly the enemy. In the general we didn't know where they would fit in. You see, we were anxious to see if they would come in and disrupt our organization, try to take over the organization, join and help the organization, or stay away and be aloof. As it turned out they didn't fit in at all. They stayed aloof, and I think that was a healthy thing because it would have been more disruptive to try and work with them than to continue to function as we were already doing.

Although the local Democratic party organization did not follow through on its pledge to support Stokes in the general election (Stokes did receive considerable encouragement and some financial support from the national Democratic hierarchy), he did obtain some assistance from organized labor. The local AFL-CIO contributed a modest sum to his campaign chest, plus the local Teamsters conducted a telephone and mailing campaign, and they contributed money. Of the two labor organizations, the Teamsters were by far the more supportive and willing to engage in an earnest attempt to elect Stokes.

For the most part, however, Stokes discovered that winning the Democratic primary did not increase significantly his access to the political organizations on the West Side. He still encountered considerable difficulty in gaining admittance to ward club meetings and other functions. In fact, some councilmen, rather than face the dilemma of informally barring Stokes, simply did not hold meetings during the campaign. Consequently, Stokes was once again compelled to rely heavily on church organizations, civic groups, sympathetic West Side residents willing to sponsor home meetings, and the mass media as avenues for delivering his campaign pitch to white voters. Winning the primary did increase the number of invitations to appear on the West Side, and Stokes took advantage of as many as possible by appearing at several functions each day. In terms of emphasis, the great bulk of his campaign time (even more so than in the primary) was spent on the West Side, thus causing some grumbling within his organization that he was taking the black community for granted. This policy decision, however, was based on the judgement that the street-level organization was superbly equipped to turn out black voters with minimum involvement on the part of Stokes, whereas only his personal touch was capable of reaching and converting white voters. Assuming the validity of this proposition and given the fact that white voters constituted approximately two-thirds of the electorate, it is understandable that Stokes allocated his time and energy as he did.

Stokes's quest to garner white support was given a strong psychological boost on 14 October. On that day the influential ethnic daily newspaper *Szabadsag* (which is Hungarian for "liberty") ran a front-page editorial endorsing Carl Stokes for mayor. The reasoning of the editorial was in concert with Stokes's desire to portray himself as the most recent example of ethnic acceptance and achievement in Cleveland. Noting that Cleveland was the first major city in which ethnic groups scored significant breakthroughs to high administrative and judicial posts, and the first city to elect a man of ethnic background, Frank J. Lausche, to the position of mayor, the editorial stressed that the citizens of Cleveland had an opportunity to elect a black man, Carl B. Stokes, mayor and thereby demonstrate to the free world that they had none of the very prejudices that forced them or their parents to emigrate to America. The editorial also analyzed Stokes's qualifications, and promising potential to supply the dynamic leadership that Cleveland needed to regain its lost place in the front ranks of progressive American cities.[6] The Stokes camp was so impressed by the editorial that they had it reprinted as a full-page ad in both the *Press* and the *Plain Dealer*, so that all Clevelanders, particularly those in the ethnic wards, would be exposed to its message. For a short time, then, a growing optimism began to circulate throughout the Stokes organization; perhaps securing the support of white ethnic voters was not as formidable as it appeared. This brief encouragement, however, was dramatically shattered in less than a week's time.

Throughout the primary Taft had repeatedly set forth challenges to debate the winner (he assumed it would be the lackluster Locher, not the polished debater Stokes). Shortly after his victory, against the wishes of some advisors who thought it was a mistake to provide Taft with exposure, Stokes agreed to two debates plus the traditional City Club debate, which usually took place on the weekend before general election day. The ground rules stipulated that Taft could select an East Side location (he choose Alexander Hamilton Junior High School) and Stokes a West Side location (he selected John Marshall High School). The format included a twenty-minute period for each candidate to discuss the issues of his choice, a five-minute rebuttal period, and an open question period for the audience. Louis Seltzer, retired editor of the *Cleveland Press*, agreed to act as moderator for the programs, which were to be taped for a television showing later in the evening of each debate.

The first debate was conducted on 17 October at Alexander Hamilton Junior High and in Taft's own words, it was a "disaster" for him. Stokes simply demolished him with barbs, witticisms, attacks on his "carpetbagging," and his inexperience in dealing with city problems. The results dealt a near-death blow to the morale of the Taft people. "It was as if a funeral was taking place in our headquarters the next day," Taft remarked.[7] If his election chances seemed to be an outside bet before the debate, it appeared that they were now reduced to near zero.

This was the consensus in the Stokes headquarters also, which was of course elated by the outcome. Taft was even less effective than they had suspected. Indeed, Stokes had done so well against Taft that some of his supporters began to caution him about overpowering his opponent. This counsel was based on the following reasoning as explained by one of Stokes's key workers.

In the general election he had to fight off over-confidence. We urged him to alter his campaign style because Carl Stokes's campaign style traditionally has been to show up his opponent, to ridicule him—in a humorous way. And to establish his clear superiority in terms of facts and speaking style. But in the general election, all of a sudden he had to change this because it became apparent now that each time he appeared to be demonstratively better than his opponent someone would label him as an "uppity nigger." He almost had to carry his opponent, he couldn't appear to be too good, too superior.

In the primary he had to show the voters how much better qualified he was than Ralph Locher to be mayor and he would do it at every turn. But in the general he had to guard against over-kill because by this time the white voters knew he could beat a white man in a two-man race, and he had to be careful not to make Taft the beneficiary of the sympathy vote against an "uppity nigger."

On the occasion of the second debate, held at John Marshall High School on 19 October, the worst fears of Stokes's supporters concerned about overkill and making Taft a sentimental underdog materialized. Taft led off the debate before an audience that was openly friendly toward him, but his talk was no more effective than the first one. In an effort to counter Stokes's accusation that he was a carpetbagger, Taft charged Stokes with bringing outside influence into the campaign through his attempt to raise money outside the city. He made specific reference to a Hollywood fund-raising party planned by Sammy Davis, Jr. (perhaps a subtle bit of implied racism, since it was well known that the black actor had a white wife).

Stokes took the rostrum admist polite applause but a smattering of boos. He was also booed when he attacked Taft for living in a seven-bedroom mansion in Pepper Pike. Undeterred by the visible hostility of the crowd, Stokes then launched into a section of his prepared speech, which undoubtedly proved to be the turning point of the entire campaign. He said:

> I am going to be brutally frank with you—brutally frank with Seth Taft. The personal analysis of Seth Taft—and the analysis of all competent political experts—is that Seth Taft may win the November 7th election for only one reason. That reason is that his skin happens to be white.[8]

The school auditorium was instantly filled with boos and jeers that lasted for several minutes as Stokes attempted to continue and explain what he meant. He continued over the murmuring by stating: "On this question, which I could have avoided so easily but brought out in the open for you to see, Seth Taft has pretended to bypass the so-called black-white issue. . . . But in practically every public utterance he has made during his campaign, he so subtly points out that, and I quote, 'Carl Stokes has more experience at being a Negro, but Seth Taft has more experience at being a white man.' "[9]

The level of noise increased and Stokes, in a flash of uncustomary anger, snapped at the crowd: "Just be quiet for a moment." Once again he was drowned out by boos and catcalls to which he responded: "If you don't agree with me, that's what ballot boxes are for." In a final effort to recover, Stokes stated: "Seth Taft is not a racist; Seth Taft is not a bigot. But he does not believe that the people of Cleveland can rise above the issue. He believes that any white candidate could beat Carl Stokes in the election. How do I know this is true? Because Seth Taft told me." Stokes attempted to describe a private conversation he had with Taft but it was too late; the audience was in no mood for the explanation, and Stokes finally sat down.

Taft had been alternately shaking his head in disbelief and reviewing a file that was prepared for him in the event that Stokes ever raised the race issue. He never thought he would get an opportunity to use the material; this was clearly the moment, and Taft played it perfectly.

> Well, well, well! It seems the race issue is with us. I was charged at Carl Stokes's campaign opener of bringing up the race issue. It now appears that if I say something on the subject, it is racism. If Carl Stokes says something it is fair play.

He held up a full-page newspaper ad and read from it.

> "Don't vote for a Negro: Vote for a Man!" he says in his ads. I agree with that. After the primary, the theme changed to "Let's Do Cleveland Proud." What has Cleveland done that makes it so proud? Nominated a Negro for mayor. Now it is "Do something proud by electing one."
>   It is impossible to ignore this issue, but I have not brought it out once in the debates. I had no intention of bringing it up. The reverse is true. If Carl Stokes talks about it, nobody else can.[10]

In less than an hour the entire character of the campaign had changed dramatically. The self-confident and sure-footed Stokes was for the first time visibly shaken. The promising momentum of what seemed to be a successful campaign was suddenly halted by Stokes himself, who apparently did what Taft was unable to accomplish—build a fire of enthusiasm under the white electorate. Almost instantaneously, Taft, who had been conducting a lethargic and defensive campaign, took the offensive against the stunned Stokes camp.

The following day the Stokes headquarters was reminiscent of the Taft headquarters after the first debate. A feeling of disbelief and gloom permeated the entire atmosphere. According to one campaigner: "Practically everyone felt that he had blown the whole thing. We couldn't believe it, we just couldn't believe it. I just wanted to cry." Stokes called a meeting of the entire staff. He admitted that perhaps a mistake had been made but reminded his workers that they had experienced nothing but success in the campaign thus far and that what many considered a setback did not make or break a campaign. He argued that the manner in which they responded to the crisis would determine the outcome; if they became disheartened it would produce defeat, if it stimulated them to work even harder, it would produce victory.

The decision to raise the race issue was made by Stokes and his public relations manager, Ostrow; it was evidently based on two considerations. First, it was maintained that "Taft was taking both the high road and low road." Although he had publicly stated that he would not pursue a racist strategy (and most of the evidence suggest that this was a sincere pledge on Taft's part), the top decision-makers in the Stokes camp felt that he was constantly making remarks with subtle but effective racial overtones. In addition, and perhaps without his knowledge, many of his campaign workers were using a racist pitch on their door-to-door campaigning and producing racist literature. It was felt that Taft might win the election with these tactics without the issue ever being explicitly raised. Consequently, it was decided that Stokes needed to point out that racism was the only factor that could defeat him. Indeed, Stokes had often and skillfully expounded this very view in scores of smaller meetings he attended on the West Side. At those meetings, however, he was speaking to essentially friendly audiences, which was not the case in the John Marshall debate. There, the audience evidently interpreted Stokes as saying anyone who planned to vote for Taft, which included many of them, was a racist. They did not take kindly to the accusation, nor in all likelihood did the bulk of the white television audience.

It is clear that the John Marshall debate was the turning point of the general election and that it did not help Stokes's cause in the white community. However, the decision to raise the race issue was not based exclusively on the campaign in the white community; there was another consideration related to developments among the black electorate. As we noted earlier, a lull beset the Stokes organization and the black community after the primary victory. Ostrow apparently decided that one way to combat this complacency and remobilize people was to raise the specter that Stokes was in danger of losing because of the subtle and underground racist campaign being conducted against him. It was hoped that the exposure of this danger would sufficiently anger and regenerate the determination in the black community to do everything possible to elect Stokes.

It is impossible to determine, on balance, whether the Stokes cause experienced a net gain or loss as a result of the John Marshall debate, but it is obvious that the last fifteen days of the general election campaign were quite different than the preceding days. After the debate, the Taft headquarters, for example, was flooded with inquiries from people seeking to help in the campaign. In assessing the impact of the debate on his campaign, Taft remarked:

> The next day everything was great and everybody went back to work a lot happier than they had been a couple of days before. And it clearly helped just in terms of morale, people were willing to go out and work a lot harder when it seemed suddenly that their man could take it. So it did make a tremendous difference. . . . By the end of the campaign we had 4,000 people out working and a significant number of them would not have been out working if we did not have the success of that debate.

In Taft's estimation, the debate was a breakthrough success because it allowed him to point out how Stokes was utilizing the race issue while at the same time denying it to him. He believed that Stokes's basic technique in dealing with white voters was to "shame them into saying, 'If I don't vote for Stokes I am a bigot.' . . . At the same time he was saying if Taft brings up race he is playing a racist campaign—so he had it going both ways. That was the thrust of his 'Do Cleveland Proud' slogan which meant nothing more than saying you have done yourself proud by voting for a black man. . . . He was using two inconsistent arguments, and I finally had a chance to point out the inconsistency."

Race, of course, had always been the fundamental, although perhaps submerged, question of the campaign; but once this inconsistency was publicly placed on the table, it dominated all other issues. Soon after the debate Taft, for example, allowed a letter to be sent to 45,000 members of various nationality groups. It encouraged the ethnic voters to "protect our way of life and to protect Cleveland, the citadel of nationalities in America." It maintained that "Taft and Taft alone can give Cleveland back to the law-abiding citizenry" and made reference to "false charges of police brutality."

There is no question but that Taft picked up tremendous momentum on the West Side after the debate at John Marshall. In the words of one of the principal volunteers in Stokes's West Side office: "It was all Taft on the West Side for that last few weeks in the general. There were parades, spotlights, searchlights, offices everywhere and the fanaticism of his workers." Asked what the Stokes workers did to counteract the growing strength of Taft, he responded:

> We tried to talk to people, reason with people, tried to make them give the man a chance. We tried to remind them that they were Democrats. . . . We did the best we could in talking to people, but you can't talk to someone who is not there and the Stokes voters were not there, they didn't want to be seen or heard because they were afraid—it was real fear.

When questioned why the West Side workers were unable to duplicate the block supervisor structure that was constructed on the East Side, this respondent explained:

> When you're downtown and on the East Side it is easy to say "you've got to do this, you've got to get out there and do that." But when you're over here and see what's happening, like a guy gets beaten up and almost dies, things get thrown through the window, the place almost gets burned down a couple of times, people threaten you and slash your tires and no one will even talk to you, you wonder where in hell you're going to get block supervisors. It just wasn't possible. . . . There were only 40 of us actively involved in the Stokes campaign, and we had to beg for help. The precinct committeemen

wouldn't even talk to us. We got most of our help from younger kids who got all kinds of hell from their parents who felt threatened by the whole thing.

This same respondent felt that the West Side Stokes volunteers confronted considerably more harassment during the general campaign than they did in the primary. They also found it extremely difficult to combat the emergence of so-called independent Democratic organizations and the unwillingness of councilmen to cooperate in pushing Stokes's candidacy. They discovered that white councilmen were giving lip service to supporting Stokes but in reality were doing nothing to actually promote his election. Most simply claimed that they had little or no influence over the voters in their wards. Whether the councilmen could have changed any minds if they had wanted to remains an open question, given the general outlook of white voters as described below.

If you listen to the people talk like I did you would have to conclude that they just didn't understand Stokes's position at all. They saw his blackness and that's it. The thought that if he was going to be elected there was going to be a black police chief, a black safety director, all black members of the cabinet, and that they were going to take over city hall and keep it. . . . You can't imagine how the people were threatened, really threatened.

In essence, the West Side Stokes volunteers found that despite all of his assurances to the contrary, it was extremely difficult to dispel the widespread notion among white voters that Stokes would be a black mayor if he were elected instead of a mayor for all citizens. Thus, although Stokes fought vigorously to undermine such an image, in the minds of thousands of white voters he was the personification of black power. Therefore, it is not surprising that the following anonymous leaflet was widely distributed in some white neighborhoods just prior to election day.

STOKES IS BLACK POWER
VOTE RIGHT—VOTE WHITE

You can rest assured that if Stokes is elected mayor of Cleveland you will get Negroes for neighbors and your children will have niggers for playmates. . . .

Fellow white Americans—This is not an election between the Republicans versus Democrats—this is a war between the niggers and the whites. All of the niggers and nigger lovers are voting for Stokes. Don't be a Judas to your own race. If the niggers win, it will be taken as a signal in Washington by Johnson to raise your taxes and spend more and more on the nigger and less and less on the white man and his children. If the nigger Stokes wins, it won't be safe for your women and children to walk the streets. Don't let the kikes from Shaker Heights and Cleveland Heights and the niggers run your city.

Get out and vote-vote-vote-for Taft![11]

THE GENERAL ELECTION RESULTS

The debate at John Marshall and its aftermath had such a devastating effect on the Stokes campaign that he agreed to engage in an extra debate with Taft. Billed as the great rubber match between the two candidates, it proved to be nothing more than a ritualistic performance in which Taft took the offensive by attacking Stokes with personal barbs; but Stokes ignored them and discussed his program for improving Cleveland in an extremely detailed fashion. According to an astute observer of the Cleveland political scene, the third debate "solved nothing, [it] gave neither candidate the edge and was, in fact, rather boring to sit through."[12] However, this same observer did note a significant change in Stokes's strategy: "He was trying to appear more humble, trying to assume a quiet, defensive position in contrast to the bold, attacking manner he had exhibited in the earlier debates."

The results of a *Plain Dealer* poll, released on 2 November, suggested that it may have been too late for Stokes to effectively alter his approach, for apparently the damage had already been accomplished. It showed that the substantial difference (16 percentage points) separating the two candidates in the middle of October had vanished. If the poll was accurate, the election had boiled down to a virtual dead heat, with Stokes receiving 50.1 percent of the vote compared to 49.9 percent for Taft.[13] In the final analysis, this slim difference resulted from the fact that Stokes was unable to prevent traditional white Democratic voters from crossing party lines to support and vote for his opponent. Testimony to this desertion is provided by a Stokes aide who was given the responsibility of visibly surveying the West Side on election day to see how things were going. He recalls:

I went out on election day to the West Side of town and except for the area of the near West Side which has a Spanish population, you didn't even see a Stokes poster. I can remember being outside the polling places on election day. The precinct workers were out in front and there were independents for Taft, Democrats for Taft, and supporters of the incumbent councilmen but there was nobody passing out Stokes literature—nobody.

Further testimony to the widespread disaffection of Democrats into the Republican column was provided as the voting results began to emerge on election evening. During that night the atmosphere in the Stokes headquarters was much different than it had been on primary night. On the earlier occasion there had been a considerable amount of confidence and certainty among the Stokes workers: they had gotten the returns quickly and efficiently from their poll watchers; they analyzed the results, projected them, and were sure of victory. They were even bold enough to advise Stokes to announce victory when he was losing according to the calculations of all other commentators. This confidence and boldness was not characteristic of the general election evening. The polls closed at 6:30 P.M. and by 8 P.M. Taft had accumulated a 10,000-vote lead. Taft maintained a lead for the next six hours, during which time numerous misprojections, mistakes, and rumors had Stokes losing or conceding the election. The same crew of Stokes workers who had so professionally and accurately projected the primary vote "were completely off base during the general—we had him losing all the way." By 2 A.M. there was talk of making a victory statement in the Taft headquarters and talk of a recount among the Stokes people. At approximately 3 A.M., however, Stokes took a slim lead for the first time in the entire evening, and from that point on he remained in front. By 4:45 A.M. it was official Carl B. Stokes was elected mayor of Cleveland by a margin of 1,698 votes (see tables 11 and 12—a recount reduced the margin to 1,679).

SUMMARY

When requested to explain why Stokes was able to successfully mobilize the black community and thus become the first black mayor of Cleveland, one respondent paused for a considerable time and then answered: "I'll give it to you in a nutshell. It was the right time, the right man, and the right kind of organization." Assessing the utility of this formulation requires, of course, additional comment. The Stokes campaign occurred at the right time in the sense that the black community in Cleveland had

TABLE 11

CLEVELAND MAYORALTY ELECTION, 1967

Candidate	Total vote	Percentage of vote
Stokes.................	129,396	50.3
Taft....................	127,717	49.7

SOURCE: Board of Election voting returns.

TABLE 12

CLEVELAND MAYORALTY ELECTION, 1967: BY RACE

	Black wards	White wards	Mixed wards	Total wards
Registered voters..........	99,885	152,737	73,421	326,043
Percentage turnout........	79.7	78.5	66.9	78.9
Stokes vote	75,586	23,158	30,872	129,616
Percentage for Stokes	95.0	19.3	54.1	50.5

SOURCE: Computed from Special Census of 1965 and Board of Election voting returns.

undergone a series of experiences that heightened group consciousness, cohesion, and a sense of growing group power. The national civil rights movement obviously contributed to these developments, but local civil rights activity appears to have been even more significant. Not only did local actions encourage thousands of blacks to participate in demonstrations, marches, rallies, and boycotts, the actions exposed beyond question to the black community the racist nature of white officials, particularly Mayor Locher. As the blacks pushed harder and harder to achieve their civil rights goals, the Locher administration became increasingly resistant and repressive. Instead of recognizing the legitimacy of black grievances and making at least symbolic efforts to alleviate them (thus undermining or coopting the movement), city hall took exactly the opposite tactic. It attributed the racial conflicts in Cleveland to a small number of troublemakers and responded to the problem with a get-tough program.

As a consequence, Mayor Locher, who had received overwhelming black support in the election of 1963, discovered that his standing in the black community plunged to near zero. Indeed, Locher and his administration became the common enemy that did much to build cohesion among blacks. Each attack on Martin Luther King, local black ministers, civil rights leaders, and black militants welded the black community closer and closer together. It became increasingly apparent to blacks that in order to protect themselves and improve their situation it was necessary to engage in united group action. There is no question that there continued to be numerous factions within the black community. However, for the first time in the history of Cleveland the black community began to display to itself and others that it was capable of achieving political unity. The 1964 school boycott, the vote on the school bond issue, the 1965 primary vote against Locher, and the 1965 general election vote for Stokes all provided examples that the black community was "getting itself together."

It is conceivable, of course, that this new sense of group consciousness and cohesion could have been directed toward supporting another white politician for the mayorship, but for obvious reasons it was not. The most obvious of these reasons was the pervasive notion among black citizens that blacks could assume leadership posts comparable to individuals from other ethnic groups. Indeed, an editorial in the *Call and Post* made the solid point that black voters had been instrumental in electing an Irishman, a Slovenian, an Italian, and a Lithuanian to the mayorship, and thus could rightfully back a member of their own ethnic background.[14] As the editorial went on to point out, this was particularly the case when the black candidate, Carl Stokes, was excellently qualified for the position. There could be little question that Stokes was highly qualified; he was intelligent, well informed, politically experienced, a witty and charismatic public speaker, and confident of his own ability to handle the job. He generated an enthusiasm that is difficult to capture with words. However, it is not an exaggeration to note that many blacks viewed him as a champion—indeed, a savior of the black struggle in Cleveland. As far as can be determined, no sizeable number of blacks expressed reservations concerning Stokes's commitment to the black community. The issues of sell-out to the white power structure and individual advancement at the expense of group progress were simply never raised because rank-and-file blacks had every reason to trust Stokes. An index to this trust was the support Stokes received from the militant black nationalists who were highly skeptical of electoral politics in general. Thus, Stokes was the right man in the sense that the black community could trust him and feel proud of him because of his oustanding qualifications. He was a living example of the "black is beautiful" theme that was circulating throughout the black community, and, in fact, his campaign provided an opportunity to translate that slogan into practice.

These characteristics were clearly instrumental in stimulating the development of Stokes's campaign organization. Without them it is doubtful that the organization would have been capable of attracting hundreds of volunteers who were willing to work long and grueling hours to help elect Stokes. But Stokes did possess the right characteristics and as a result his people not only worked those hours, they worked with a zeal, a creativity, and an enthusiasm that did take on the aura of a crusade. Consequently, the entire black community became like a giant tidal wave that was intent on placing Stokes in the mayor's seat. The campaign organization was responsible for stimulating the tidal wave and at the same time direct its energy toward necessary organizational tasks. The level of success is reflected in the results; the black community went to the polls in unprecedented numbers, they voted for Stokes, and the votes were counted in an honest fashion—essentially as a result of organizational work.

In short, then, Stokes was able to mobilize the black community behind his candidacy because of recent political developments in Cleveland, his own personal characteristics, and the hard work of his campaign organization. A similar set of circumstances resulted in the election of Richard Hatcher to the mayorship in Gary, Indiana. The details of that story are contained in the following three chapters.

1. *Cleveland Plain Dealer*, 4 October 1967, p. 1.

2. This quotation and the following unattributed quotations are derived from interviews conducted in Cleveland by the authors.

3. These polls were commissions by Taft and conducted by the Market Opinion Research Company of Cleveland, Ohio. The authors would like to thank Mr.

William Silverman, an associate of the Market Opinion Research Company, for making manuscript copies of these polls available to us.

4. Ibid. There is considerable social science support for the notion that cross-pressured voters will not vote. See Lester W. Milbrath, *Political Participation* (Chicago: Rand McNally, 1965), p. 98.

5. *Cleveland Plain Dealer*, 22 October 1967.

6. *Szabadsag*, 14 October 1967.

7. Quoted in James M. Naughton, "The Making of a Mayor," *Cleveland Plain Dealer Sunday Magazine*, 10 December 1967. Reprinted by permission.

8. Quoted in ibid.

9. Ibid.

10. Ibid.

11. Reprinted in Kenneth G. Winberg, *Black Victory* (Chicago: Quadrangle Books, 1968), p. 200.

12. Naughton, "The Making of a Mayor," p. 51.

13. This poll indicated that 92 percent of the 412 persons interviewed who had voted for Locher or Celeste in the primary were planning to vote for Taft.

14. *Call and Post*, 16 September 1967.

6
Gary: The Economic,
Social, and Political Setting

Compared with other major American cities Gary, Indiana, is relatively young. The town received its incorporation shortly after the turn of the twentieth century. Geographically situated in the northwest corner of Indiana within easy driving distance of Chicago, Gary is an integral part of an enormous chain of industrial communities running along the southern shore of Lake Michigan across three states.

In a very real sense the history of Gary is the history of the expansion of the United States Steel Corporation into the Calumet Region.[1] The development of Gary grew out of the search by United States Steel officials for a site in the Calumet Region on which a large steel production facility could be established. Original plans called for the expansion of existing facilities in Chicago, but the lack of adequate space, rail facilities, and inexpensive land adjacent to Lake Michigan made such expansion infeasible. The Gary area appeared to be ideally suited to the company's needs. Located on the northwest border that separates Illinois from Indiana, it was close enough to Chicago to allow the company to take advantage of Chicago's large supply of cheap labor. Land in the area was both plentiful and moderate in cost. The bulk of this section of the Calumet Region was still largely unsettled, with Miller, Tollerston, and Clark constituting the only fully established towns.[2] These features of the Gary environment presented the steel company with a golden opportunity to buy up large tracts of land at a modest price; these extensive land acquisitions assured the company of room for immediate as well as future development. Several other factors enhanced Gary's attractiveness as the home of a major steel complex in the Calumet Region. Although sparsely populated, railroads had already begun to move in and around this portion of Indiana, sharply reducing transportation problems endemic in the large-scale manufacture of steel. The site also bordered the southern edge of Lake Michigan. Consequently, it provided easy access to crucial electrical power and to the ore vessels plowing the waters of America from east to west.

Recognizing the advantages this site held over possible alternative locations, United States Steel officials decided around 1905 to construct a new manufacturing complex in the Gary area. This decision gave birth to the idea of building a town around the mill site to service the needs of company employees and to attract new persons into the area. Thus, plans for the building of a new municipality were included in the steel company's original comprehensive design for the construction of the proposed steel manufacturing complex. Company officials exercised direct supervisory authority over the planning and development of the town. These officials viewed themselves as town fathers and guardians of the public interest, and in this capacity they sought to make Gary a model manufacturing community, not just another company town. This paternalistic attitude toward the town was translated into efforts by company officials to guide the development of the community. To accomplish this objective, the Gary Land Company was organized as an auxiliary agent of the steel company and given complete authority to coordinate the construction of the town by purchasing land adjacent to the proposed mill site, to supervise the establishment of businesses and private dwellings and, as nearly as possible, to control land speculation. Gary's origin as a company town is underscored by the company officials' decision to name the new town in honor of Judge Elbert H. Gary, chairman of United States Steel's board of directors.

Long after Gary had become a prosperous and vibrant community, steel company officials continued to exercise direct supervision over its public affairs. The central place of steel company executives in the public life of Gary during the first three decades of its history constitutes one of the most important features of its early social, economic, and political development. Much of the influence wielded by company executives in Gary's public life derived from the company's tremendous impact on the city's economy. Between 1906 and 1930, Gary was essentially a one-industry city. During this period, only two companies not owned by United States Steel were established in Gary.[3] The city's inability to develop a diverse manufacturing base over a period of nearly thirty years was due in large measure to calculated efforts by steel company officials to dissuade competing industrial concerns from moving into the area. An almost insuperable barrier to the establishment of competitive concerns was posed by the steel company's monopoly of municipal utilities. According to one respondent, although the steel company uniformly sold municipal services to the general public, it stubbornly refused to provide comparable services to potentially competitive industries. The company's desire to keep competitive enterprises out of the city was also supported by its ownership of the harbor and every foot of the city's frontage on Lake Michigan. Control of the harbor and the lake front, in effect, gave the company veto power over the launching of new manufacturing concerns requiring access to Lake Michigan. As a result of these practices the company was able to establish a near monopoly of the city's working force. This tight control of the labor market enabled United States Steel to completely dominate the economy of the city; its enormous economic influence in turn gave it important leverage in other aspects of the city's life.

Important, too, as a factor in Gary's early development was the influx into the city of large numbers of immigrants uprooted from their homes in Europe. The construction of Gary Works and its subsidiaries coincided with the period of the new immigration that brought to American shores millions of southern and eastern European immigrants. Animated by a consuming quest for economic security and a better way of life, many of these immigrants were drawn to Gary, as in the case of Cleveland, by the lure of unskilled and semiskilled employment in the steel industry. Impetus to the natural flow of immigrants into Gary was added by a high-powered publicity campaign waged by United States Steel extolling Gary as a model community and holding out the promise of exciting and profitable careers in a bustling industry. Advertisements in papers circulated through the United States and Europe recounted the Gary story. Feature articles were printed billing Gary as a major steel-producing city offering unlimited opportunities for those who wished to participate in its development.[4]

The publicity campaign waged by steel company officials to attract European immigrants into Gary had its desired effect. Although few ethnic types were among the original settlers in the city, by 1910 Gary had become a center of European immigration in the Midwest. At this time 49.1 percent of the city's total population of 16,802 was of foreign-born extraction.[5] Heavy representation of ethnics in Gary's population has remained a salient feature of the city's social structure. In 1946, Gary had one of the largest foreign-born populations per total population of any city in the United States. Since Gary was founded after the turn of the century when immigration to the United States from northern and western Europe had largely drawn to a close, the overwhelming proportion of white ethnics in Gary have come from countries in southern and eastern Europe. Among the most important nationality groups represented in Gary's population are the Italians, Bulgarians, Serbians, Poles, Romanians, Hungarians, Germans, Czechs from Bohemia and Moravia, Scotsmen and Scandinavians.[6]

Like foreign immigrants in Cleveland and other cities, European immigrants in Gary suffered from the handicaps of foreign languages and customs and low socioeconomic status. Their foreign backgrounds as well as their lack of economic resources prevented them from integrating into the northside business and residential areas inhabited by the first citizens of the city, the White-Anglo-Saxon-Protestants. Instead the vast majority of these newcomers settled in a southside district known as the Patch. Within the boundaries of the Patch each ethnic group formed its own separate community. In nearly every case, serious efforts were made by the members of these groups to reconstitute their native traditions and institutions in their new community environments. Immigrant churches catering to the spiritual and social needs of community residents became prominent features of each sector of the Patch staked out by a nationality group. Similarly, immigrant newspapers carrying news from back home and written in the native language of community residents enjoyed a considerable measure of popularity and success in the Patch. On the social side, large numbers of clubs were founded that regularly sponsored dances, picnics, parades, and many other group-oriented events.

Feelings of attachment and interdependence remain very strong among the members of the multiplicity of ethnic groups represented in Gary's population. Consequently, although much else has changed since the first decades of the city's founding, the segmentation of its ethnic units continues to be an important feature of Gary's social system. As will be shown later, the preservation of subgroups held together by common ethnic ties has had a considerable impact on the forms and substance of politics in Gary.

OVERVIEW OF THE POLITICAL SYSTEM

The first seven years of Gary's political history were characterized by a struggle for power and influence between steel company officials and a strong Democratic faction led by Thomas Knotts, first president of the town board of trustees. Company officials began their drive for power by converting extensive cash gifts or land donations for the construction of public buildings, including the YMCA and the public library, into appointments as board members to a wide variety of community institutions. Next they attempted to consolidate their power in city politics by establishing an alliance with the Republican party and using their influence to elect to key positions Republican candidates respectful of steel-company interests and prerogatives. The electoral base for this Republican–steel company coalition was the eastern European immigrant community. In the eyes of steel company managers, immigrant voters were a compliant and manipulable source of political power. The vast majority of immigrants in the city were totally without prior political experience, economically insecure, and lacking a genuine interest in public affairs. Most importantly, they were absolutely dependent upon the steel mills for their livelihood. Exploiting to the fullest the immigrants' various social, economic, and political handicaps, steel company officials regularly sent plant managers into ethnic neighborhoods to drum up electoral support for Republican candidates. Typically, plant managers made contact with representatives of major ethnic groups, emphasizing in their conversations that the job security of community residents at the mill depended vitally on their solid support at the polls for candidates endorsed by steel company executives. Frequently, ethnic clergymen were induced through financial contributions and other means to endorse from their pulpits steel-company-supported candidates. The blind faith and trust that many immigrants had in their clergymen made ethnic ministers especially effective liaison forces between the steel company and the ethnic community.

The most important obstacle to the vigorous drive by steel company officials to establish their unchallenged hegemony over the city's political system was Thomas Knotts, one of the original founders of the city. Knotts, a Democrat, viewed the political ascendancy of the steel company as a threat to popular democracy and a detriment to the economic development of the city, since steel company officials staunchly opposed the creation of a diversified industrial community. To thwart the consolidation of the company's power in the public arena, Knotts ran as a Democrat for mayor in the first community-wide election, held in 1909. He was opposed in the primary by William C. Crolius, a politician imported by steel company officials from Joliet, Illinois, to deny Knotts the Democratic nomination. Knotts and his supporters refused to participate in the regular Democratic primary with Crolius. They chose instead to hold a special nominating convention and then wage a battle in the courts for the right to display the party emblem and the title Democratic party on the general election ballot. A superior court in Hammond ruled in favor of Knotts. Shortly thereafter, Crolius threw his support behind Knotts's Republican opponent and returned to his home in Illinois.

Knotts was challenged in the general election by John A. Brennan. The general campaign was very bitter, with the Knotts forces denouncing Brennan as a "stooge" of the steel company, and Brennan's supporters countering that Knotts's hostility to the steel corporation would stifle the growth potential of the city's economy. As election day approached, animosity between the rival election factions became so severe that the governor was prompted to declare a state of emergency and put the local militia on standby alert.

Knotts won the election by a narrow margin of 71 votes, receiving a total of 1,790 votes to Brennan's 1,719. The key to Knotts's victory was the success he enjoyed in attracting the electoral support of southside ethnics. Apparently, Knotts was unusually popular in the Patch area and sought to take advantage of his ethnic appeal by helping as many immigrants as possible become eligible to vote.

The rivalry between Knotts and steel company officials that had surfaced dramatically during the campaign continued to dominate Gary politics after Knotts's election to the mayor's office. Informal control over the city council and major civic and social institutions by the managers of the steel mill served to substantially weaken the ability of the mayor to implement his administrative program. Indeed, before Knotts's four-year term expired, every imaginable step was taken by steel company officials to hamper him in the performance of his mayoral duties and discredit him in the eyes of his constituents. For example, steel company officials were the prime movers behind the mayor's arrest on fourteen separate occasions over a two-year period.[7]

Although not realizing their primary goal of removing Knotts from office before the expiration of his term, the persistent attacks by steel officials against the mayor did have the effect of so fragmentizing his electoral base that it was impossible for him to win a second term. When he began campaigning for reelection in 1913, Knotts found that his popularity in immigrant neighborhoods had sharply declined. Further, he faced opposition not only from Republicans and steel company officials, but members of his own party who had supported his bid for election during the first campaign. These dissenting political forces came together in a loose coalition operating under the banner of the Citizen party. This new organization nominated Roswell O. Johnson, a Republican, for mayor and slated two Democrats for seats on the city council.

Every person nominated on the Citizen party ticket was elected to office. Johnson defeated Knotts by 1,516 votes, obtaining the support of an overwhelming majority of the voters in the southside ethnic districts that had gone solidly for Knotts in the election of 1909. Although the election returns formally indicated a resounding victory for Johnson and his running mates, events following closely on the heels of the election made it clear that the real victors were the resident managers of the steel company.

Having finally removed their arch foe from public office, steel company officials began immediately taking over the reins of authority in the Johnson administration. William P. Gleason, a company official, was appointed by the new mayor to the park board. Pontius Heintz, chief inspector of the Gary Land Company, was named police chief. Ralph E. Rowley, another company official, was elected to the city council and became its president during his first term. Operating behind the scenes as the "shadow mayor" was Captain Norton, the man who for several years had been the steel company's chief political strategist.

The election of Roswell O. Johnson as mayor in 1913 ushered in a twenty-year period of Republican dominance in Gary politics. Steel company officials refused to support Johnson for another term because of his alleged laxity in rooting out gambling and prostitution in the city. Instead, they threw their support behind William F. Hodges, former city attorney in the Johnson administration, who had resigned in protest against the high incidence of vice in Gary. Hodges easily won the election and, as expected, showed great sympathy for the interests and desires of the steel company during his four years in office. Johnson was reelected mayor in 1921. His second term was cut short, however, by his conviction on federal charges of conspiring along with sixty-one other individuals to violate federal laws prohibiting the sale and use of intoxicating beverages. Johnson was sentenced to eighteen months in federal prison in Atlanta, Georgia, and fined $12,000. It is an interesting commentary on prevailing political ethics in Gary to note that Johnson's career in Gary politics did not end with his confinement in federal prison. Upon his release, Johnson ran again for mayor and was elected to office for a third term in 1929.

Roswell O. Johnson's election in 1929 signaled the end of an era of Republican domination of city hall. Johnson was succeeded in 1933 by Lee B. Clayton, the first Democrat to be elected to the mayor's office since the turbulent reign of Thomas Knotts. Clayton's victory represented a pivotal breakthrough in Gary politics by the Democrats. Beginning with this election, the Democratic party gradually replaced the Republican party as the controlling party organization in the city. Since 1933, Gary has had only one Republican mayor—Dr. Ernst L. Schiable—who served from 1938 to 1942. Dr. Schiable was defeated after one term in office by Joseph E. Finerty, a Democrat. From 1942 to the present the Democrats have been in continuous control of city hall. The emergence of Democratic control in Gary coincided with the arrival of the Democrats to power in Lake County generally. Resounding victories by Democratic candidates in city and county contests have led to a near total collapse of the Republican party in Lake County. In deference to the awesome power of the Democrats, Republicans have generally avoided competing in local political contests. Rather than using their limited resources to drum up support for party candidates running as sacrificial lambs, Gary Republicans have appeared to prefer to concentrate their political activities on securing patronage and other benefits from key state- and national-party officials.

Much of the impetus for the change in party power and control in Gary occurring in the 1930s was derived from the devastating blow inflicted on the city by the depression. Gary's heavy dependence on steel production rendered it as vulnerable to the disastrous economic consequences of the depression as any city in the nation. Under the pressure of the depression, the love affair between the resident managers of the steel company and working-class ethnics lost much of its fire. Roosevelt's welfare programs drew the bulk of Gary's ethnic population into a new majority coalition with blacks and labor—a coalition that was in many ways a microcosm of the national coalition underpinning the ascendancy of the Democrats in Congress and in the White House during these years. Capitalizing on their developing Democratic proclivities, Gary Democrats wooed intensively the vote of eastern European ethnics through patronage, favors, and recognition. Members of prominent ethnic groups began to receive the lion's share of welfare benefits distributed under the supervision of Democratic officials. Ethnic leaders were gradually, but systematically, absorbed into the formal structure of the local party, a process that resulted in the creation of direct links between various ethnic communities and the city organization. These measures helped to snap the final ties between ethnics and steel company bosses and facilitate the exodus en masse of ethnic voters in Gary from the Republican to the Democratic party.

Paralleling the shift in party membership by eastern European ethnics in Gary was a significant crossover into the Democratic ranks by Gary blacks. Blacks rallied behind the banner of the Democratic party for much the same reasons as their working-class white counterparts. Constituting 17 percent of the population in 1930, blacks were courted by local Democrats with assistance and promises of assistance. Roosevelt's promises of expanded opportunities for blacks in the areas of employment, education, and housing eased considerably the task by local Democrats of moving the black population significantly into their ranks. As was true of blacks elsewhere, many blacks had remained loyal to the Republican party purely out of gratitude for Lincoln's freeing of American slaves. Roosevelt's appeal to blacks on concrete economic grounds, however, substantially dimmed the importance of Lincoln's actions in the modern context. With the aid of persistent prodding from local Democratic leaders, Roosevelt's national appeal operated in Gary's black community as a catalytic force, inducing many blacks to join hands with working-class whites in a decisive retreat from the Republican to the Democratic party.

The developing strength of the Democratic party during the depression years of the 1930s was also a product of the strong political support given to Gary Democrats by organized labor. Intimate political ties between the Democratic party and labor in Gary grew mainly out of the antilabor posture of the Republicans during the struggle for unionization. Republican officials elected because of critical steel company support were compelled time and again during the 1920s to invoke measures to hamper the success of union activities. Having no other place to go, union forces naturally gravitated toward the Democratic camp. For their part, Democratic leaders welcomed the financial and electoral assistance they received from labor and showed their gratitude by integrating union members into the party's structure. Since the 1930s the romance between labor and the Democrats has seen many peaks and few valleys. High-ranking labor leaders generally sit in on crucial meetings of the county Democratic organization in which key decisions regarding the distribution of resources and the support for party candidates are made. Union leaders in turn have played vital roles in the mobilization of rank-and-file voter support for Democratic candidates.

The combination of ethnic, labor, and black political power all drawn into the same political camp laid the basis for more than thirty-five years of uninterrupted rule by the Democrats in Gary.

With these elements of the coalition that took shape during the era of the New Deal solidly unified, the power of the leadership corps that came to the fore in the Democratic party during these years was virtually invincible. By the same token, when the cohesive quality of this coalition began to disintegrate, a parallel slippage in its ability to exert a commanding, stabilizing influence over the instruments of power in the city was no doubt also inevitable.

POSTWAR CHANGES

Among the most important social developments in Gary since World War II has been the phenomenal growth in size of the city's black population. The presence of Afro-Americans in Gary's population is not a factor of recent origin, for blacks were among the first arrivals in the city. One report notes the interesting fact that at least sixty-six blacks worked in the Gary steel mill during its first year of operation.[8] It is true, however, that only a handful of blacks resided in the city prior to the close of World War I when blacks were brought in from the South by steel company managers as strike breakers. During subsequent years of the 1920s successive upswings in the economy produced a significant influx of blacks into Gary seeking job opportunities in the steel industry. At the end of this decade 17,982 blacks lived in Gary; at this point they constituted 17.8 percent of the total population. The decade of the 1930s witnessed a sharp rise in the percentage of blacks as a proportion of Gary's total population. This fact was due mainly to two parallel developments: a steady increase (except for the bleakest years of the depression) in the number of blacks migrating into Gary from the South, and substantial white out-migration from the central city to surrounding suburbs. These trends had begun to significantly affect the racial composition of Gary as early as 1944. In that year the city had a total population of 120,000 of which 24,000 or 20 percent were black. No other major northern city during this period contained a larger percentage of blacks in its population.[9] Since the end of World War II the number of whites leaving Gary to settle in the suburbs has reached near epidemic proportions. The impact this phenomenon has had on the social composition of Gary is vividly illuminated by statistics showing that from 1950 to 1960 the black population of Gary expanded nearly five times faster than the

white population.[10] No fundamental break in this pattern has occurred; to the contrary, all evidence suggests that, if anything,
it has been given impetus by the growth of black power as a
unifying force among blacks and the spread of urban racial conflict throughout northern communities. By 1967 the dual factors
of expanded black influx and ever-increasing white out-migration
had transformed a city that was once predominantly Eastern
European into one that was more than 50 percent black. Unofficial statistics in 1967 indicated that blacks were approximately
55 percent of the population, making Gary, if these figures
were accurate, one of only four American cities at the time with
an absolute black numerical majority.[11]

Blacks moving into Gary from the South were restricted by
formal and informal housing policies to the oldest and most undesirable residential areas of the city. As the number of blacks
in Gary increased after World War II, they gradually pushed
working-class white residents from the central district, known as
Midtown, to an area south of the Little Calumet River presently known as Glen Park. Northeast of downtown lies the predominantly Jewish community of Miller. Noted locally for their liberalism, Miller residents are representative of the new monied class
—individuals who have gained their wealth and social position since
the depression as a result of the twin Jewish emphasis on education and professionalism.

Since 1960 the black district has significantly expanded into
an area on the city's southwest side known as Tollerston. The
bulk of Tollerston's new black residents have been middle-income
blacks seeking residential space outside the central district ghetto.
Because of the heavy movement of middle-income blacks into the
area Tollerston has developed the highest degree of residential
integration in the city. Until recent times, discriminatory housing
policies served largely to lock black citizens out of Glen Park and
Miller.

Despite recent movement of blacks into a few formally all-
white areas, the majority of Gary's black population remains
trapped in the central city ghetto. The prevalence of ghetto life
among blacks in Gary is thrown into sharp relief by statistics
comparing their socioeconomic status with that of whites in Glen
Park and Miller. As in the case of Cleveland, housing in Gary's
black community is disproportionately substandard. In 1950,

blacks lived in 62 percent of the city's substandard dwellings while occupying only 18 percent of the acceptable housing.[12] Over the ten-year period between 1950 and 1960, the percentage of blacks living in substandard housing increased. In 1960, blacks occupied approximately 68 percent of all substandard dwellings in Gary.[13] Comparatively speaking, while 11.1 percent of the white population resided in substandard housing units, 28.1 percent of the black population occupied such dwellings.[14] Black housing in Gary is not only inferior, but also in much shorter supply than is housing in the white community. Census data firmly documents the reality of congestion as a major social problem in the black community. For example, although blacks comprised over 40 percent of the total city population in 1960, they occupied less than 33 percent of the housing units.[15] The population per household among blacks in 1960 was 4.08, as compared to 3.15 for whites.[16]

In many respects the substandard physical environment of Gary blacks is a reflection of their inability to keep abreast of their white co-citizens in the areas of education, occupation, and income. On the whole, blacks in Gary are much better educated than whites in other major cities in Lake County. But when compared with the educational experience of whites in their city, blacks in Gary clearly fall in a lower position on this socioeconomic index. In this regard we can note that in 1960 the median number of years completed in school by whites twenty-five years of age or older was 10.9 years while the median for blacks was 9.1 years.[17]

The presence of the huge United States Steel industrial complex in Gary has produced a higher level of economic prosperity than commonly found in northern cities of its size and larger. Yet when comparisons are made between the economic position of Gary blacks and Gary whites, disparities analogous to those cited above in the area of education can clearly be discerned. A combination of discrimination and rural southern background has operated to produce twice the level of unemployment in the black community as exists in the white. Thus in 1960 unemployment for whites was 2.4 percent while unemployment for blacks was 5.9 percent.[18] Moreover, far fewer blacks than whites were employed in white-collar, skilled job categories. The following statistics indicate the disparities between black and white employment in this segment of the labor market: 27.9 percent of the white labor force held white-collar jobs while only 9.1 percent of the black labor force was so employed; 18.5 percent of employed blacks were craftsmen or skilled workers as compared to 89.6 percent of employed whites; and 56.1 percent of the black labor force could be classified as semiskilled or unskilled, while 33.8 percent of the whites could be placed in these categories.[19] As could be expected, income figures for blacks and whites acutely mirror these occupational differences. In 1960 the median family income for blacks in Gary was over $2,000 less than the median family income for whites ($4,720 to $6,860). The rate of poverty among black families in Gary has consistently been more than twice as high as white families. Thus 22 percent of Gary's black population in 1960 had incomes below the poverty line of $3,000 while only 9.5 percent of whites had incomes below this figure. Poverty is in fact such a serious problem in Gary's black community that Gary blacks make up the largest proportion of those receiving public assistance from the office of the Calumet Township trustee. Indeed, the demand by blacks for relief has been so heavy that most of the welfare money spent by Lake County in recent years has been earmarked for Gary recipients.

Another important development in Gary in the postwar years has been the rise to power within the local Democratic party of an ethnic political machine. Since the early 1950s the Gary machine has been rivaled only by machines in nearby Chicago and in East Saint Louis in its ability to control the outcome of elections through the mobilization of the electorate.

Gary's ethnic machine had its genesis in the election of Peter Mandich to the position of Calumet Township trustee in 1946. Mandich was the Gary-born son of Eastern European immigrant parents. His campaign for the trustee's office in 1946 constituted the first serious effort by Eastern European ethnics to wrest civic power from the old immigrants and WASPs then in firm control of the Democratic party. The political base of the campaign was Club SAR (Social, Athletic, Recreational) founded by Mandich's good friend, George Chacharis. Club SAR's membership was composed mainly of Eastern European ethnics who shared common interests in sports and other forms of social recreation. Mandich was the club's star basketball player. When he decided to run for office he called upon other club members to work in his behalf. Virtually the entire membership of the club responded to his request and worked endless hours in his campaign. The Mandich campaign shifted the focus of Club SAR from sports to politics, creating in its wake a circle of ethnic leaders imbued with a life-long commitment to active involvement in Democratic party politics. Reflecting on the politicizing effort of this initial venture, one Gary politician commented to a researcher in 1959: "We weren't much better than hoodlums and we might have ended up worse if Pete [Mandich] and George [Chacharis] didn't get successful and get us all careers in politics."[20]

The process of machine-building began in earnest in 1951 when Peter Mandich successfully parlayed his position as township trustee and his electoral power base in the ethnic community into his election as the first Eastern European mayor of Gary. Mandich ran for a second term in 1955 and easily won reelection. During the third year of his second term, Mandich resigned from the mayor's office to run for sheriff of Lake County in the 1959 primary elections. Early retirement from the mayorship by Mandich paved the way for George Chacharis, who had served as city controller for most of Mandich's two terms in office, to succeed to the top political office in the city.[21] Chacharis's succession to the mayorship was not surprising. Chacharis had been the driving force behind the rise to power by ethnics in Gary politics from its very inception. It was Chacharis who managed Mandich's first bid for public office and who subsequently steered the course of his political career toward the mayor's office. As controller in the Mandich administration, Chacharis became the central source of power in city government, exercising in everything but name the authority of the mayor.

George Chacharis was elected mayor in his own right in 1959. The Chacharis administration was marked by extensive centralization of power in the hands of the mayor. Chacharis ruled the city with an iron fist, requiring that even the most trivial matters receive his personal approval before being acted upon by city personnel. As mayor, Chacharis also built for himself the reputation as the most generous philanthropist in the Midwest. He donated huge sums of money to charity, and almost never turned down anyone who came to him personally for financial assistance. Chacharis's propensity to live beyond his means eventually led to his political downfall. In November 1962, one year before the expiration of his mayoral term, Chacharis, along with five other

Lake County political figures,[22] were indicted by federal officials for tax fraud. Each defendant was charged with participating in the operation of a complex network of dummy and semidummy companies serving as receptacles for kickbacks exacted from individuals and corporations doing business with the city of Gary and other local agencies. Chacharis was charged specifically with requiring that subordinate city officials collect such payments and turn over a portion of this money to him. He was also accused of evading the payment of $226,686 in taxes on money derived from his participation in kickback operations in Gary. During the long and controversial trial that ensued, Gary gained a national reputation as a city whose governance lay in the hands of an administration that was corrupt from top to bottom. When it was over, Chacharis had been found guilty of the charges against him and sentenced to federal prison in Milan, Michigan. Charges against all of the other defendants were dropped.

By the time Mayor Chacharis was incarcerated in federal prison, the roots of Gary's ethnic political machine were firmly planted in the city's political system due to the planning of Mandich and Chacharis. Acting on Chacharis's advice, Mandich had begun the process of machine-building by filling the city bureaucracy with ethnic appointees. Top level positions went to members of Club SAR who played prominent roles in the civic life of their ethnic communities. As coordinator of city-hall patronage, Chacharis made sure that the preponderance of lower-level jobs were also assigned to representatives of ethnic communities. Once control by Mandich and Chacharis in city government was firmly established, they began to expand their organizational network into the bureaucratic strongholds of county government by electing members of their political family to key county positions. These county officials were expected to utilize county-level patronage resources to build up an ethnic-dominated bureaucratic structure paralleling the one established in the city. In this way, leaders of the Gary machine gradually consolidated their control over both city and county government.

At the bottom of the ethnic machine's organizational structure was the Democratic precinct organization—a grass-roots electoral apparatus for mobilizing votes in city and county elections. The key figures in this organization were precinct committeemen who maintained close contact with voters on a continuing basis and used their personal influence to turn out whopping majorities for machine candidates on election day. To fill precinct positions, machine leaders recruited persons who were immersed in the social life of their community, maintained a wide circle of friends, and enjoyed the respect of their neighbors. On election day, their effectiveness was measured by party leaders by the extent to which they were able to translate their community contacts into strong support by voters in their precinct for machine candidates.

Prodigious work by precinct committeemen in ethnic and black neighborhoods created for the Mandich-Chacharis regime an invincible electoral base. Control over the electoral process invested machine leaders with the ability to regulate the behavior of every politician of importance in the city. During the Mandich-Chacharis administrations, it was virtually impossible to get a nomination to a major public office without going through the city machine. A maverick who bucked the machine ran the risk of committing political suicide. Lacking a base within the precinct organization, he stood little chance of defeating a machine-backed candidate. If he appeared to pose a serious threat, vigorous attempts were made to buy him off, and, in all but the rarest instances, this was enough. If it was not, his defeat was assured by the entrance into the race of splinter candidates running specifically to dilute his potential base of support.[23]

The heyday of machine power in Gary extended from 1955 to 1959. Between 1960 and 1967 the organization witnessed a steady erosion of its ability to monopolize power and control elections. This decline in machine strength was due mainly to the collapse of its base of electoral power in the white community, and a number of factors contributed to this decline in influence. First, a significant rise in the socioeconomic status of whites freed a sizable proportion of the white population from dependence on the machine for critical economic resources. As whites became more economically affluent, the ability of precinct committeemen to trade favors and monetary rewards for votes in the white community substantially declined. Second, the onset of the black protest movement created enormous tension between the precinct organization and the white community. Demands by blacks for school desegregation, open housing, and other benefits were viewed by many whites as direct threats to their social and economic statuses. Consequently, whites began to question the wisdom of supporting machine candidates who consistently refused to promise that they would not give in to black demands. As this attitude spread significantly among white voters after 1960, it became extremely difficult for white precinct committeemen to work effectively in the white community. Most damaging of all to the influence of the machine in the white community was the Chacharis scandal of 1962. The revelation of rampant corruption in city hall gave Gary a black eye nationwide. White citizens felt a profound sense of betrayal since the public officials under indictment were men that they had allowed to exercise unrestricted authority over the management of municipal affairs for ten years. Chacharis's conviction represented a profound blow to their civic pride and served to significantly weaken their emotional ties to the Lake County Democratic organization.

Decreasing support for the machine by the white electorate inevitably lead to atrophy of the white precinct organization. To combat serious erosion of machine influence produced by a collapse of its organizational structure in the white community, machine leaders decided to direct a larger share of their attention and resources to their most important remaining base of electoral support—the black community. One leading figure in the regular Democratic organization candidly explained the considerations entering into the decision to focus attention of the party apparatus largely on the black community.

> You depend on your solid vote, where you know the people are for you. It's very foolish to waste all your time and effort in an area where you know you're not going to get the vote no matter what you do. So you rely on the area that's going to give you the votes. The white community and the Negro community supported the party up to the time the mayor and former mayor were involved in a scandal. The white people felt like they had been betrayed and turned on the party. Then you had to rely upon the heavy Democratic Negro precincts to carry the lead. It made sense. If you were going to break even in the white areas, you had to concentrate in Negro areas to get your majority.[24]

That the black community remained a viable base of electoral strength for the Democratic machine at the same time that the machine's strength in the white community was waning is explained in part by the fact that blacks did not share in the economic prosperity enjoyed by whites in the 1960s. The lack of significant economic progress by members of the black electorate left them heavily dependent upon the socioeconomic amenities that the machine had to offer and generally traded in return for strong electoral support. Continuing black support for the machine was based most importantly on the superior political skills and commitment of machine workers in the black community. As in East Saint Louis, machine influence in Gary's black community had been channeled through a black organization reflective of, but clearly subordinate to, its white counterpart. The activities of this black machine enabled leaders of the regular Democratic organization to rob the black community of much of its ability to undertake independent political action. Leaders of the black machine were far more effective than their white counterparts in stifling the growth of antimachine voting patterns among their black constitutents. Consequently, the base of power of the machine was more secure, stable, and enduring in the black community than in the white. Indeed, control of black political choices from the outside through the black submachine was so thoroughgoing and continuous that the analogy with colonialism at the international level is practically unavoidable. Efforts to keep alive this relationship were intensified by machine leaders once it became clear that the black and white communities could not be kept in easy alliance in the same political camp.

Key figures in the machine apparatus in the black community were black members of the Democratic precinct organization. Black precinct committeemen were key actors in the machine organization because they were far and away the most masterful grass-roots politicians in the city. Unlike white committeemen for whom politics was a part-time endeavor, many black committeemen were full-time professional politicians. Black committeemen generally worked their precincts around the clock, responding to every possible need of their constituents. Exchanging favors for votes, they were able to strictly control the outcome of elections in their precincts. Indeed, their control over politics in their precincts was so extensive that they could forecast well in advance of elections the precise vote for each candidate. Black precinct committeemen, being practical businessmen, generally sold their political influence to the highest bidder. Since no other political force could match the wealth of the city machine, this emphasis on monetary rewards invariably drew the black precinct organization into the political camp of the regular Democratic organization. In return for their support of machine candidates, black precinct committeemen could expect to receive patronage appointments in city hall as well as a host of other favors that promoted their economic interests. With greater amounts of machine largess flowing into the black community after 1962, black precinct committeemen were inspired to work even more assiduously to maintain their control over the political choices of their black constituents.

The Democratic precinct organization was only one element of the black machine operative in the black community. Other black leaders, including black elected officials, civil rights activists, and black ministers were also caught up in the web of machine influence and power. Aspiring black politicians were compelled to either become members of the machine or accept the inevitability of political defeat. Control by the machine over the black precinct organization completely ruled out the successful mobilization of the black community by a black candidate for independent political action.

> The black community had a choice of people who were competent and qualified and who ran for public office, who tried to change the system. But each time these few men were discouraged by the fact that they were defeated. They were always beaten down so the average man became discouraged to such an extent that he felt there was no need to run for public office. Those who ran, ran with the understanding that I'm going to have to get on the team, otherwise I'm going to lose.

Similarly, efforts to organize the black community through protest activity was thwarted by the co-optation of black community leadership by the machine. Leaders of organizations such as the NAACP and the Urban League were generally handpicked by white machine leaders and charged with the responsibility of keeping the struggle for civil rights within acceptable limits. Black ministers were bought off through large financial contributions to their building programs, anniversary celebrations, and other projects. In return for machine benevolence, they customarily turned their pulpits over to machine candidates and followed up their speeches with their own personal endorsements. Thus, although the white community was moving toward independence, the co-optive powers of the machine in the black community had the effect of intensifying the position of the black electorate as a manipulable source of machine power in Gary politics.

The relative position of the black and white communities in the machine's electoral coalition is clearly illuminated in the outcome of the 1963 mayoral election. Selected to run as the machine candidate in the race was A. Martin Katz, a two-term city judge with an impeccable reputation for honesty and integrity. Katz was opposed in the race by four major white candidates, including Emery Konrady, whose candidacy reflected the strong surge of reformist feelings in the white community in the wake of the Chacharis scandal. Konrady was president of a Gary oil firm and candidate for the Democratic state senatorial nomination in 1960. Over the years he had established a reputation as a militant, articulate opponent of machine politics. Katz won the 1963 primary, but only by a razor-thin margin. Although more than 55,000 votes were cast in the race, Katz managed to beat Konrady by a mere 3,095 votes (19,850 to 16,755). The crucial factor lying behind the closeness of the outcome was Katz's inability to compete with Konrady for the white vote. Konrady out-polled Katz in every white precinct in the city. Indeed, Konrady carried two of the three white districts in the city. The first district, located in Miller, was carried by Glen Vantrease, former city controller; this district happened to lie within Vantrease's home area. But for the candidacy of Vantrease, Konrady would have almost certainly scored a smashing victory over Katz in Miller—a hotbed of Jewish liberalism.[25]

In the final analysis, Katz received a modest 22 percent of the white vote. This comparatively poor showing in the white community was offset, however, by his exceptionally strong showing in the black community. Katz carried both the predominantly black fourth and fifth districts by polling more than 55 percent of the vote in each. These were the only two districts carried by Katz in the election. Overall, Katz received 51 percent of the black vote. In addition, of the total vote cast for Katz, 67 percent was black and 33 percent was white. These figures make it clear that the key to Katz's victory was the solid support he received from the black community. Essentially, Katz's black vote put him in a position to take advantage of the divisive effect of Vantrease's candidacy in the white community.

Thus as early as 1963, it was very clear to political strategists in Gary that the perpetuation of machine power in the city rested fundamentally on the continued political support of the black community. A significant erosion of the machine's electoral strength in the black community would mean a total collapse of the political dynasty founded by Mandich and Chacharis. The vulnerability of the machine engendered by its heavy reliance upon black support was not lost on leadership elements in the black community who had escaped the co-optive tenacles of the machine. Although in 1963 it was only barely recognizable, these men posed the most serious of all threats to the perpetuation of machine domination of Gary politics.

THE BLACK MOVEMENT

The critical importance of the black vote to the survival of machine power in 1963 obscured in large measure the growing discontent in the black community with the prevailing system of social, economic, and political colonialism. For many years black anger had been held in check by the conservative, legalistic approach to race relations practiced by the Gary NAACP. Racial tension had surfaced briefly in the 1940s over the question of school integration and the use of the lakefront public beach by blacks. But until the latter half of the 1950s racial flareups had been minimized by the commitment of black leaders to non-disruptive tactics in the attainment of equal opportunities and equal justice for the black community.

The struggle for black freedom in the South produced a marked shift in the character of race relations in Gary. A number of Gary blacks participated in the southern protest movement and returned home to apply their experiences to racial problems in the local community. During the opening years of the 1960s the NAACP was toppled from its preeminent place among the civil rights organizations in Gary. Into the breach stepped several local organizations lead by a corps of young blacks committed to thoroughgoing social, economic, and political reform and the use of southern-style direct-action methods, including coercive public protests, to achieve the civil rights objectives of the black community.

The first protest-oriented civil rights organization to emerge in Gary was the Gary Fair Share Organization (FSO), founded by Hilbert Bradley, a young black attorney, in 1958. Although still formally a member of the NAACP, Bradley had become greatly disturbed by the unwillingness of the local chapter to embrace an activist program. Upon losing a bid to become a justice of the peace in 1958, Bradley decided to transform his campaign organization into a community organization that would fill the vacuum in leadership created by the NAACP's moderate approach to civil rights.

In many ways the FSO was a precursor of Reverend Jesse Jackson's Operation Breadbasket movement in Chicago. The program of the organization centered around the picketing and boycotting of major commercial and industrial establishments in the city to secure for black people a "fair share" of available employment opportunities. During the height of its protest activities, the FSO scored a number of important economic breakthroughs for Gary blacks. In the downtown area the organization concentrated its attack on the Gary National Bank and the Henry C. Lytton and Company clothing store. Under pressure from FSO picketers, both institutions agreed to institute policies of merit employment that would pave the way for black employment in all areas including top management. Following the lead of these commercial and financial giants, most major downtown establishments eventually dropped racial criteria for employment. Business institutions outside the downtown area were also targets of FSO protests, which also produced encouraging results. Largely through the work of FSO, blacks were placed in every store in the Village Shopping Center. Picketing action against A & P stores resulted in the hiring of the first black manager for an A & P store in the state of Indiana. After a protracted legal battle over its right to intervene in labor disputes, FSO was able to extract promises from Kroger company officials to hire at least one black store manager and several black cashiers.

The notable exception in the FSO's history of successful protest action was its seven-month battle to alter hiring practices toward blacks at the Anderson Company. Owned and operated by John Anderson, the Anderson Company produces and distributes nationwide "Anco" automobile windshield wiper blades.

The Anderson Company was especially vulnerable to the kind of protests staged by the FSO around the city. It maintained the poorest record of black employment of any manufacturing concern in Gary. John Anderson had persistently voiced his opposition to externally induced policies that would compel him to increase the number of blacks working in his plants. Complaints against the company for its racially discriminatory hiring practices had been filed with the Gary Fair Employment Practices Commission (FEPC) as early as 1955. By 1961, the company still employed only 3 blacks out of a work force of 1,200 persons.

Extended protests by the FSO against the Anderson Company and the FEPC for its cumbersome handling of the case resulted in promises by Anderson to accept applications for employment without discrimination on the basis of race, color, religion, or nationality and to post conspicious notices when new applications for employment were being accepted. However, in a year-end address to company employees Anderson reassured his white work force that the company's policy toward the hiring of blacks had not been changed by the FSO demonstrations. He asserted that he refused to allow quarterbacking of management by the representatives of any race or nationality and vowed to protect them against malicious or other external political influences adverse to their interests and the interests of stockholders, customers, suppliers, and moneylenders.

The failure of the FSO to force the Anderson Company to adopt a policy of merit employment constituted the organization's first major defeat. In the wake of this episode, the organization began to suffer from internal dissension with charges and counter-charges hurled by both leaders and rank-and-file members over strategies and tactics used in the Anderson protests. Internal disintegration of the FSO came to a climax when in May 1962 Hilbert Bradley resigned as chairman of FSO. Bradley's resignation was followed by a substantial turnover in the leadership of the organization.

Despite a strong recommendation by Bradley that the FSO dissolve because of waning community support, the organization continued its program of community protest. However, its effectiveness as an instrument of black protest was eventually destroyed by several negative court decisions involving the right of FSO to intervene on the side of black workers in labor disputes.

In 1964 FSO was sued for damages totaling $15,000 by commercial firms from East Chicago and Michigan City, Indiana, because of losses incurred as a result of FSO picketing. When the County Circuit Court and the State Supreme Court upheld the damage claims, FSO leaders decided to make a bold step and appeal the cases to the United States Supreme Court. The FSO appeal asked the Supreme Court for a writ of certiorari opening up the rulings in the state courts for federal judicial review. FSO leaders argued in their petition to the court that the Indiana courts had gravely constrained their rights to free speech and association. The United States Supreme Court refused the requests for certiorari, thus making final the awards of $15,000 to the East Chicago and Michigan city firms.

The monetary damages placed by the courts against FSO effectively destroyed its ability to continue operating as a direct-action organization. However, the new pattern in black protest that its activities had fostered was irreversible. As the power of the FSO as a direct-action group began to falter, the central concern of the black movement in Gary shifted from equal employment opportunity to open housing. In line with this shift in direction, a new protest organization composed of liberal whites and militant blacks (many of whom had formally played key roles in FSO protests) was formed to lead the fight on the open-housing issue. The organization adopted the name Combined Citizens Committee on Open Occupancy (CCCOOO), and became commonly know as Triple C, Triple O. Under the direction of Triple C, Triple O, the struggle for open occupancy dominated the civil rights agenda of Gary from 1962 to 1963.

The bulk of Triple C, Triple O's activities centered on pressuring the Gary city council to pass a measure securing the right of open occupancy for all citizens of the city. In July 1962 an open occupancy bill drafted by Triple C, Triple O's legislative committee was introduced in the city council. Key provisions of this measure proposed to make it illegal to refuse to rent, lease, or sell real estate solely on the basis of race, national origin, or ancestry, and called for the establishment of a fair housing board comprised of seven members to enforce the ordinance. To the surprise of few, Triple C, Triple O's housing bill ran almost immediately into the determined opposition of white councilmen. When the bill came up for a vote white councilmen voted unanimously against it, defeating it on the first reading by a vote of six to three. Undaunted, Triple C, Triple O leaders campaigned for a reconsideration of the bill and succeeded in getting it placed before the council again for a vote in April 1963. This time the bill was defeated on the first reading by a slim one-vote margin. Councilman Paul Dudak, Glen Park representative, held the deciding vote since the council was deadlocked on the issue four to four. Dudak chose to abstain, thus killing further consideration of the bill for lack of majority support during the preliminary balloting.

Having failed twice to get the city council to pass an open occupancy ordinance, the leaders of Triple C, Triple O decided to try another approach. This approach involved persuading Mayor Joseph Visclosky to assist in the fair housing effort by taking a public stand in favor of open occupancy. Visclosky met with Triple C, Triple O representatives and agreed to issue a public statement indicating his support for open occupancy and open-occupancy legislation. However, when—a week later—the Mayor issued his first major announcement on the fair housing question, he reneged on his promises to Triple C, Triple O. Instead of supporting open occupancy, Visclosky criticized the housing ordinance twice defeated by the city council on the grounds that it conflicted with the Fourteenth Amendment. He charged that under the ordinance, a widow with a room to rent would be deprived of her right to choose to whom she wanted to rent.

Triple C, Triple O leaders publicly scored Visclosky for what they termed his "callous breach of good faith." Having failed again in their campaign for fair housing, it became clear to Triple C, Triple O leaders that the issue of open occupancy would begin to swiftly recede into the background and progress in this area would be stymied unless a new and dramatic protest tactic was employed. The kind of protest technique that might best capture the imagination of large numbers of citizens had been suggested several months earlier at the national level when thousands of citizens from across the country had assembled in Washington to march in support of civil rights. Following in the footsteps of the Washington march, Triple C, Triple O, in conjunction with the Gary Civil Rights Coordinating Committee, of which it was a part, announced plans for a march on Gary to protest the failure of the city council and the mayor to endorse the principle of open occupancy and to take steps to eradicate prevailing discriminatory housing practices.

The march was scheduled to begin at 10 A.M., 14 September, south of Twenty-fifth Avenue, and to move along Broadway to city hall. A program featuring speeches by both national and local leaders, including Dick Gregory and Gloster Currant, director of branches of the NAACP, was to take place in the parking lots adjacent to city hall.

By all standards, the march for open occupancy was the largest and most impressive civil rights demonstration in the history of the city. Caught up in the mood of the times, large numbers of blacks participated in this demonstration with an enthusiasm never before exhibited for a civil rights-oriented event. The march stimulated feelings of excitement and power that were— to say the least—frightening to whites who adhered to the myth of black apathy and docility. One respondent described the growing feelings of black political consciousness revealed by the 1963 fair housing march in the following manner:

> We marched down Broadway to city hall singing "We Shall Overcome." It was terrific. White people had been saying niggers can't get together. This was the first time we realized that if we can get together and march we can do anything else. We began to see people in Midtown join the march. It was quite orderly. For the white people to stand on the side and see this many Negroes together was really something—they were just amazed. This was really the beginning of a black movement in Gary.

The march on Gary was the climax of Triple C, Triple O's year-long struggle to secure the passage of fair housing legislation for blacks. Although it failed in its immediate objective, it gave invaluable assistance to other forces engaged in the difficult task of arousing the black community to a sufficient level of consciousness to make possible the commencement of actions leading to its social, economic, and political liberation. The central spot in the black movement, abandoned by Triple C, Triple O after the 1963 fair housing march, was taken over almost immediately by the Gary Civil Rights Coordinating Committee (CRCC), an umbrella organization serving as a coordinating unit for a variety of Gary organizations concerned with civil rights.[26] Leaders of this group represented both traditional civil rights groups as well as newer ones. Emergence of this group to prominence on the local scene was the result in large measure of an attempt by old-line civil rights leaders, who had been shoved aside by younger, more militant leadership elements, to regain their power and status in the black community.

In the wake of the eclipse of the fair housing issue as a focus for vigorous protest action, CRCC leaders made a tactical decision to push the housing question to the side for a time and open up the black movement on another front—de facto school segregation. Racial segregation in Gary schools had long been a source of anger and anxiety among black citizens. The black community had begun to unite around this issue in 1962 when the Gary School Board broke its promise not to further advance school segregation by building a proposed new high school inside the Midtown area. This action by the board resulted in *Bell* v. *The School City of Gary*, one of the landmark Supreme Court cases dealing with de facto public school segregation in the North.[27] CRCC broke new ground in this area when it announced in February 1964 plans to coordinate a citywide one-day boycott to protest continuing racial segregation in the Gary public schools. In announcing the boycott, CRCC spokesmen strongly criticized the Gary School Board for its failure to take action to promote integration in the schools and noted that in view of the board's intransigence on the question, the organization believed the time had arrived to take direct action. CRCC spokesmen stressed that the boycott method was being used rather than some other form of direct action because it was an economic weapon resulting in the loss to Gary schools of $1.47 for each child that remained away from school.

Despite efforts by Superintendent Lee Gilbert to head it off, the boycott took place as previously scheduled on 17 April. In terms of its immediate objectives, the boycott was a rousing success. Estimates of the number of black students who stayed away from school—out of a total of 25,000—ranged from 16,103 made by the *Post-Tribune* to 19,000 made by the leaders of CRCC. A more revealing indication of the response to the boycott was a check of schools made by the *Post-Tribune* that showed white schools had nearly normal attendance, while classrooms at the all-black schools visited by reporters averaged two to four pupils.

The dramatic school boycott staged by CRCC signaled more clearly than ever before that the black community was swiftly becoming conscious of its power and unified around common social, economic, and political objectives. It demonstrated beyond a doubt that the black community could be mobilized on a broad scale to do more than march. The overwhelming response on the part of blacks to the boycott proposal was irrefutable evidence that blacks in Gary were not asleep but aroused, aware, and angry. Although the boycott lasted only one day, the excitement and sense of accomplishment it generated were more than enough to convince black leaders interested in reversing the colonial posture of the black community to formulate concrete plans to bring about this result.

By 1965 the most important dimension of the black movement in Gary was the focus on politics and power. Between 1963 and 1965 blacks had become increasingly interested less in finding ways of making the machine responsive to their needs than in developing strategies for overthrowing the machine and instituting black control over the city political system. This transition from protest to politics was in large measure a product of the profound sense of political consciousness infused into the black community by its various experiences in social protest. By the same token, it was the result of strenuous efforts by a nucleus of committed black leaders aimed at consciously pushing the black community toward a position of political independence. These efforts, it should be noted, were taking place simultaneously with, but somewhat apart from, the array of protest activities discussed above.

The major vehicle through which these efforts at independent politics were pursued was an organization called Muigwithania. This organization grew out of plans formulated in 1960 by two black professional employees of the Lake County Criminal Court —Richard Hatcher and Huston Coleman—to bring together a group of young black men to work for the social, economic, and political advancement of the black community. The need for such an organization had become apparent in the course of extensive conversations between Hatcher and Coleman over a period of several months. Hatcher and Coleman were especially concerned about the low level of political influence exercised by the black community as a consequence of the strict control over the electoral choices of blacks exercised by the Lake County Democratic machine. They were eventually successful in persuading a number of other young professional blacks to join them in forming a black man's organization committed to community uplift. Aside from Hatcher, other original members of the organization were Dozier Allen, Tim Adams, Jon Evans, John Lawshe, and Jackie Shopshire. Once the organization was established each member was encouraged to contact at least one new person and invite him to weekly meetings. In this way the organization quickly expanded its size to about twenty active members. One of the early members of the organization explained the common concerns that drew these young men together as a cohesive force.

> At that time the black community was not together; it was controlled by the white power structure. We felt through this organization we would enable the black community to have a stronger voice in politics and the operation of the city than it had ever had before. We felt that the black community was just being exploited and that we couldn't rely upon the prevailing organizational structures to address themselves to the needs of the black community. We knew that we could not depend on the black people who then wielded some power in the city to work effectively for the black community because they were part and parcel of the white power structure.

Members of the group met for several weeks without deciding on a formal name. The task of coming up with a name was given to John Lawshe who had been elected historian. Lawshe undertook this responsibility with great diligence. His search for an appropriate name led him to an extensive examination of books on Africa. During the course of Lawshe's research, he became fascinated with the Mau Mau movement and stumbled upon the term "Muigwithania" in a book loaned to him by a sister-in-law who lived in Africa. The term, he found, was actually the name of Jomo Kenyatta's liberation newspaper during his reign as leader of the Mau Mau movement in Kenya, and it meant in Kukuyu "to come together and go forward." He felt that this perfectly reflected what the organization wanted to do: To unite black people and move them forward down the path of self-rule. He brought the name back to the group and the other members accepted it immediately. One person present at this meeting recalled of the group's reaction to Lawshe's suggestion of a name:

> We felt this name fitted us well. We were young, we were like a new independent nation trying to secure freedom from the chains of

the previous establishment. We wanted the people to know these chains could be broken if they would stick with us.

Muigwithania initially sought to foster change for Gary blacks by delivering to them badly needed welfare benefits. However, as members of Muigwithania became more and more deeply involved in community work, it became apparent that they could not deliver the social and economic goods to blacks they desired without becoming directly involved in organized political activity. Consequently, after a time politics began to assume the major place on the organization's agenda, and it gradually began to transform itself from a civic club to an active political organization.

Transformation of Muigwithania into an association concerned with promoting change through direct political involvement took place in several stages. At first it attempted to operate as an interest group, applying pressure on key political actors while attempting to remain out of the mainstream of the political arena. This approach, however, produced only limited payoffs, inspiring the organization to switch its strategy and wade into the turbulent waters of Gary politics directly and with great abandon. Before moving too far in their political endeavors, however, members of Muigwithania sought to educate themselves about the Gary political system. What impressed them the most after the decision to involve themselves in politics in an intensive way was how little most of them really knew about the nuts and bolts of Gary politics. All were political neophytes with no history of prior political experience beyond the routine task of voting. To fill in the serious gaps in their political knowledge, members of Muigwithania decided to begin a program of direct participation in the political campaigns of candidates for public office. It was felt that through these campaigns, members of the organization could gain some insight into the mechanics of conducting a political campaign and pick up pointers on how one could become an effective campaigner.

This program resulted in the quiet infiltration of Muigwithania members into the campaign organizations of a number of Lake County politicians. With some initial campaign experience under their belts, members of Muigwithania decided to run their own candidates for minor political offices. The targets of this initial foray of Muigwithania as an organized force into electoral politics were seats as delegates to the 1962 Democratic state convention. Six members of Muigwithania took the unusual step of challenging party regulars for seats in the Lake County delegation.[28] Muigwithania viewed these state-delegate contests primarily as learning experiences with no real hopes of victory. They traveled from precinct to precinct knocking on doors asking for support of their candidates—and they found to their surprise that people were responsive to the idea of having one of the neighborhood boys represent them at the state convention. When the election was over, the six Muigwithania candidates had defeated party regulars for state delegate positions.

When the Muigwithania delegates arrived at the convention, they set about purposely to expand their political education. They did not participate formally in the convention's business but just observed, talked to as many people as possible, and took copious notes. When they returned, they gave detailed reports of their experiences to the members of the group. This information coupled with the knowledge and experience gained from previous ventures convinced them that they were now ready to run a member of their group for a major city office.

After considerable discussion, Muigwithania decided to support members of the group for three seats on the city council, one at-large and two district. For the two district seats the organization endorsed Cleo Wesson, an incumbent councilman and group member, and Louis Watts. The nod to run for the at-large seat was given to Richard Hatcher, president and cofounder of Muigwithania. Hatcher's choice to run for the at-large seat was especially noteworthy since he had only been in the Gary area for three years. Hatcher had been raised in Michigan City, Indiana, and had moved to East Chicago to join a prominent black East Chicago law firm shortly after receiving his law degree from Valparaiso University in 1963. His association with Henry Walker, influential black Democrat and head of the law firm, had resulted in his appointment in 1960 as deputy Lake County prosecutor. Hatcher's selection to run as Muigwithania's candidate for the city council undoubtedly reflected the tremendous respect members of the group had acquired for his abilities as a politician and social activist since he had arrived on the Gary scene. Almost from the day of his arrival, Hatcher had immersed himself in the growing civil rights movement in the city. Eventually he became an active member of virtually every civil rights group in Gary. He became counselor for the Young Adults Branch of the NAACP; he worked actively in the Fair Share movement; he served as legal consultant for Triple C, Triple O and became a member of its advisory board; and he served on the executive committee of CRCC. Hatcher was rarely content to take a backseat in civil rights causes, but typically played a very prominent role. He was one of the lawyers in the famous 1962 Gary school desegregation case; he led a delegation of 120 persons from Gary to the march on Washington; he helped to organize the march on Gary and served as a platform orator; and he participated in the picketing of Methodist Hospital and served as a chief negotiator in the settlement of the dispute. Hatcher was encouraged in these civil rights endeavors by his Muigwithania brothers every step along the way. They had early taken note of his leadership abilities and made calculated efforts to groom him as a potential political candidate by building for him a favorable image among blacks in Gary, both through word of mouth and by pushing him out front at various affairs sponsored by the organization. Thus Hatcher was a natural choice for one of the positions on the city council eyed by the group. Consequently when he stepped forward to announce that he was seriously interested in running for an at-large seat, he encountered no difficulty obtaining the unanimous consent of the membership.

Hatcher ran for the council in the 1963 Democratic primary with the full backing of Muigwithania. When the votes had been tabulated, Hatcher had beaten all candidates in the at-large councilmanic race, pulling a surprising 12,779 votes. His closest opponent, an incumbent white councilman from Glen Park, trailed Hatcher by nearly 4,000 votes. That Hatcher ran so strongly in the councilmanic race his first time out was not due entirely to the indefatigable efforts of members of Muigwithania; for critical to his victory was the fact that he received extensive help in the race from the regular Democratic organization. Machine support for Hatcher stemmed mainly from the fact that the token incumbent black at-large councilman had been implicated in the Chacharis scandal. Wishing to whitewash its image, the machine bent over backward in 1963 to put forth a slate that was impeccably clean. Since Hatcher was a newcomer he seemed a safe choice for the at-large seat earmarked for blacks. Hatcher's strongest black rival for the position was Hilbert Bradley, long-time civil rights activist with an unsavory reputation in the white community because of his role in the protest activities of the FSO. Although an activist in civil rights too, Hatcher had not been in the city long enough to create the host of enemies in the white community Bradley had accumulated over a number of years. Given a choice between Hatcher and Bradley, leaders of the machine chose to support Hatcher. One respondent put the matter more bluntly:

> The machine slated him. You know what slates are. They just put him on the slate and said vote for a fellow named R. Gordon Hatcher. And when the *Post-Tribune* endorsed him there were no pictures of him. This meant itself 5,000 votes. It is the only white daily newspaper. He got 3,500 more votes than the top white candidate who was an incumbent and had been in office four years.[29]

No doubt central to the thinking of machine leaders in supporting Hatcher in the primary race was the view that once elected Hatcher could be easily controlled in the same way other black councilmen had traditionally been brought into line. Upon taking his seat on the council, after an easy victory over his weak Republican opponent, Hatcher quickly showed himself, however, to be a maverick of the first order. Whereas other black councilmen had generally voted as they were told, Hatcher joined an economy bloc on the council and voted frequently to curtail unnecessary spending by city hall. Other black councilmen had often been content to remain mute during council proceedings, but Hatcher used the council as a rostrum from which he could focus the attention of the city on black problems. He often admonished his fellow councilmen that their insensitivity to black needs was a major source of unrest in the black community, which, if continued, would lead to considerable bloodshed in the city streets.

These atypical actions led to Hatcher's total isolation in the council and the Democratic party. Leaders of the machine abruptly cut off his access to party patronage. Black and white councilmen joined hands in opposition to him. Despite these moves, Hatcher continued to wage one-man battles in the council in behalf of the black community.

Hatcher's councilmanic activities were not without their rewards. Whereas whites looked upon these activities with mortification, blacks looked upon them with jubilation. Hatcher's deviant behavior was vicariously enjoyed by a wide sector of the black community. Never before had there been a black politician willing to challenge so strongly the city's white power structure. As he persisted in his councilmanic efforts, a tight rapport developed between Hatcher and the black masses. There was forged a kind of dialectical relationship between his leadership and their following. They encouraged him and he led them forward.

Blacks began to demonstrate in concrete ways that they believed they had found themselves a new leader. They defended Hatcher vociferously whenever he was attacked in the white press or on radio talk shows. Blacks crowded in the council to see him perform—to watch him fight against overwhelming odds— and encourage him to "keep on keeping on." Soon the growing feelings of black nationalism and pride stimulated by the black protest movement began to converge around the heroic actions of Gary's young, dynamic city councilman. The dimensions of this process are revealed in the comments of this respondent who became over a period of months after his election to the council Hatcher's most stalwart supporter:

> We followed Mr. Hatcher in the course of his activities on the council. All of us began attending council meetings. Whites had said blacks weren't interested in problems because no blacks were in the audience. This was not true. The situation in Gary was such that we thought there was no point. This is when we began to see there was a point, and we should rally around the one person who did represent us and go forth from there.

During his first two years on the council, Hatcher successfully built for himself a reputation as a selfless politician who would not sell his people short in his dealings with the power structure. In striking contrast to the stereotyped view that blacks generally had of black politicians in Gary, Hatcher's actions on the council showed him to be more interested in securing welfare benefits for the black masses than status and material benefits for himself. Hatcher fought tirelessly for legislation to improve the social and economic positions of the black community. Basic to his political style was a willingness to speak out on controversial racial issues, even at the risk of antagonizing powerful party leaders. Hatcher also cultivated a wide circle of friends in diverse segments of the black community. Although clearly middle class, he appeared perfectly comfortable in the company of his low-income black constituents. Unlike other black politicians, he seemed interested in doing more than what was absolutely necessary to assure his reelection. He appeared genuinely committed to representing the interests of the black community in the most vital areas of power in the city. All of these factors helped to fashion for Hatcher an image as a totally different brand of black politician—one who contrasted sharply with the shallow, quiet, unimaginative, and uninspiring black political leaders who had served for years as the backbone of Gary's white-controlled political machine. The widespread belief that Hatcher was a "new breed" black politician operated to establish for him a solid power base in the black community. In 1964 this power base began to be cemented in the wake of his central role in the resurgent struggle to secure passage of an open-occupancy ordinance.

When Hatcher entered the council in 1963, the question of open occupancy was rapidly fading as a key issue in the Gary black movement. However, the issue suddenly came back to life in September 1964 when the housing committee of the council reported out a strong open-occupancy measure submitted by Mayor Katz and toughened by the chairman of the committee, Mrs. Jessie Mitchell, and committee member Richard Hatcher. Katz had embraced the open-occupancy bill as a symbolic jesture to his major electoral constituency—the black community—and had succeeded in rounding up considerable civic support for the measure. Opposition to the concept of open occupancy still cut very deeply, however, both in the general white community and in the chambers of the Gary city council. Consideration of the measure by the council on the first reading produced a surprising five to four vote in favor of its scheduling for final passage. Approval of the bill on first reading triggered substantial white resistance. The white councilman who cast the final vote in favor of the bill received death threats before he left the council chambers and had to be escorted from the meeting by armed guards. Later in the week a group of Glen Park citizens organized the Society for the Preservation of Every American's Right (SPEAR) to fight against final passage of the open-occupancy law. Leaders of the group claimed it had no membership dues and no membership meeting, but that it did have a headquarters located in the crack of the Liberty Bell.

The meeting for consideration of final passage of the bill was set for 13 November. Voting on the measure was preceded by a public hearing in which thirty-six persons were allowed to state their arguments for or against its passage. Before casting his vote, Hatcher urgently appealed for positive action on the open occupancy measure:

> The role of this council is clear. Everything fine and decent, everything sensitive and humane, all of man's infinite compassion, cries out for the passage of this ordinance. Let us not forsake our fellowman in his long history of travail. Let us dare to make a new beginning. Let us build a new city and a new man to inhabit it. Let each and everyone of us have the courage to do what we all know must be done.[30]

Hatcher's eloquence fell largely on deaf ears. The council defeated the measure by the same vote that it had passed it earlier. Hugh McLaughlin, the white councilman who had cast the deciding vote for preliminary passage, switched his vote on final passage thus assuring its defeat.

The defeat of the open-occupancy measure by the council set off a chain reaction in the black community. An emergency meeting was called by civil rights leaders, and a new organization was formed to wage the struggle to secure passage of the open-occupancy bill. This organization was named the Freedom Movement Council (FMC). Following in the path carved out in earlier years by the FSO, the FMC committed itself to a program of direct action and called for mass picketing and boycotting of downtown merchants until the Gary council made fair housing a reality for black citizens. FMC began its protest activities with an attack on the downtown Gary National Bank building and two branch offices of the bank. Gary National was singled out as a protest target because Paul Guist, a white councilman who had consistently voted against open occupancy, was manager of the Tollerston branch of the bank. FMC pickets requested that either Guist resign as manager of the bank, located in an area rapidly becoming predominantly black, or resign from the council. Guist stubbornly refused to do either; consequently the attack against the bank was escalated to a full-scale boycott. Black patrons of the bank were urged to withdraw their accounts and deposit them in the Bank of Indiana. In the face of this economic pressure against the bank, Guist resigned from the council. One person who was extensively involved in this protest action explained how Guist's resignation was secured:

> We organized our people and had them drawing their money out of the Gary National Bank. After all that money started coming out of that bank, the board of directors became concerned. Banking is their business not politics. As a result, this member of the council resigned. . . . By protesting this bank we figured that the bank official would do either one of two things: he would fall in line for the open occupancy bill or resign. So he resigned. One Saturday before he resigned black people drew $45,000 out of the bank and transferred it to another bank. Prior to that, every day some of the black people were drawing money out and moving it to another bank. This one Saturday, I guess, was all they could take. We moved them in cars and drew that $45,000 out in one day. So the following Tuesday he resigned from the council.

During December 1964 and January 1965, the FMC broadened its attack to include a massive boycott of all Gary downtown businesses. Blacks were encouraged to shop at outlying shopping centers in East Chicago and Chicago. The boycott was particularly effective during the Christmas shopping season.

> Merchants in Gary took a big beating. We caught them during the Christmas holidays. They had a lot of toys they had to put in the basement for the next year so some of them started speaking out.

Capitalizing on the mounting pressure from the black community, Hatcher maneuvered a substitute fair-housing bill drafted by the Chamber of Commerce out of the housing committee to the floor. However, once reported out, no councilman—black or white—would move for passage. Seizing on the apparent division in the ranks of black councilmen, a white councilman who opposed open occupancy motioned that the measure be tabled. Hatcher was furious with the tabling action and lashed his colleagues for abdicating their responsibility to the black community. He was, however, far from giving up the fight. Several months later, Hatcher again forced the pending omnibus civil rights bill out of the housing committee. In urging passage of the measure he warned that the bill constituted the last opportunity for the council to avoid wholesale bloodshed in the city. Once again the council ignored Hatcher's challenge and tabled a vote of the housing measure. In doing so, however, Hatcher's colleagues underestimated his stubborn, determined character, especially when aroused in behalf of a program affecting large numbers of black citizens. On 4 May 1965, Hatcher maneuvered the fair-housing bill to the floor of the Gary city council for a third time. Chances of passage of the bill on this occasion appeared somewhat brighter since Mayor Katz had appointed a Mexican American named John Armenta to replace Paul Guist. It was widely rumored that before Armenta was appointed, Katz had extracted from him a promise to vote for the housing bill if it came up again for a vote.

These views about the bill's chances proved to be correct. The Gary council voted to approve the fair-housing ordinance on preliminary passage by a vote of five to three. As expected the critical vote was cast for the bill by Armenta. One white councilman, sensing passage of the measure, stormed from the council without voting.

The final vote on the fair housing ordinance came on 18 May. Prior to the balloting, Hatcher led a successful effort to beat down four amendments proposed by councilmanic opponents of open occupancy designed to weaken the substance and impact of the fair-housing ordinance. Finally the balloting was held, and the fair-housing measure passed again by a vote of five to three. Formally designated as an omnibus civil rights bill, the ordinance in its final form created a fifteen-member human relations commission with unrestricted subpoena power, provided for open occupancy, and incorporated into the work of the commission existing city provisions relating to fair employment practices.

In retrospect, it is clear that the strong support given to the civil rights ordinance by Mayor Katz was the key element in its passage. Throughout the controversy Katz had gone to extraordinary lengths to create a climate of opinion in the white community favorable to the passage and acceptance of an open-housing ordinance. His inside political maneuvering—especially his authorization of a special commission to draft a fair-housing ordinance and the appointment to the council of a man whom he knew would change the balance of power on the open-occupancy question—was absolutely critical to the final passage of the open-housing measure by the council. However, among blacks the real hero of the hour was Richard Hatcher. They recalled his eighteen-month struggle in the council, often in the face of overwhelming odds, to get the fair-housing bill passed. They remembered his eloquent, often militant, defense of the rights of blacks to be free from the racial restrictions placed on their lives by prevailing programs and practices of the city administration. They remembered his efforts at tricky parliamentary maneuver in order to keep the fair-housing ordinance alive before the council. But most of all they remembered he stood up; that he fought with a controlled but intense passion; that he spoke in terms of their hopes, their fears, their aspirations.

Richard Hatcher's successful leadership of the campaign for open-occupancy legislation represented a significant milestone in the black movement in Gary. The struggle waged to secure the passage of positive legislation by the Gary city council in this controversial area had two important consequences. First, it reinforced and intensified gains made through previous civil rights struggles in building a sense of ethnic identity and political consciousness in the black community and moving it down the road to political independence. Second, it thrust Hatcher to the top of the leadership hierarchy in the black community and built for him a solid base of black political support. After the passage of the 1965 fair-housing law, no politician in the city, including Mayor Katz, could compete with Hatcher for the support of the black masses. This fact placed Hatcher into live contention for the mayorship in 1967, since it was generally acknowledged that the black community held the key to the outcome of the 1967 race. The big question left outstanding was whether or not Hatcher could translate his political charisma into a broad-scale mobilization of the black community, for the first time, for effective *independent* political action. Factors bearing on the question of black mobilization in the 1967 mayoral campaign in Gary are considered in the next two chapters of this study.

1. Powell A. Moore, *The Calumet Region: Indiana's Last Frontier* (Indianapolis: Indiana Historical Bureau, 1959), p. 257.

2. Ibid., p. 258.

3. These were the Gary Screw and Bolt Company (1912) and the Union Dawn and Steel Company (1917).

4. Moore, *The Calumet Region*, p. 305.

5. Ibid., pp. 305–6.

206 / Electing Black Mayors

6. James T. Jones, "Political Socialization in a Midwestern Industrial Community" (Ph.D. diss., University of Illinois, 1965), p. 65.

7. Charges against Knotts ranged from election fraud to embezzlement, perjury, and malfeasance in office.

8. Urban League, *Spotlight on Gary* (1946).

9. Ibid.

10. See Wes Scharlach, *Population Characteristics and Trends in the Gary-Hammond-East Chicago Standard Metropolitan Statistical Area* (Lake County Development Committee, 1968), p. 66.

11. The others were Washington, D.C., East Saint Louis, Illinois, and Newark, New Jersey.

12. Thomas F. Thompson, "Public Administration in the Civil City of Gary, Indiana" (Ph.D. diss., Indiana University, 1960), p. 4.

13. Gary League of Women Voters, "What Can Gary City Government Do To Insure Civil Rights for All of Its Citizens?" (Gary, Ind.: 1964), p. 3.

14. *Selected Population Characteristics, 1950-1960, Gary, Indiana* (Mishawake, Ind.: City Planning Associates, 1966), pp. 44-52.

15. Ibid., p. 71.

16. Ibid.

17. *Selected Population Characteristics, 1950-1960, Gary, Indiana*, p. 71.

18. Ibid.

19. Ibid.

20. Thompson, "Public Administration in Gary," p. 74.

21. Chacharis had been preceded in the position by Metro Holovacha, who had served for two years during Mandich's first term as mayor.

22. The others were Harold Zweig, Gary city engineer; John Diamond, manager of the Indiana License Bureau in Gary; William Chulock, a Chicago accountant who lived in Gary; Peter Mandich, Lake County sheriff; and Peter Chacharis, the mayor's brother.

23. For example, a strong Jewish maverick was likely to face at least one other Jewish candidate running with solid machine support. With two Jewish candidates appealing to fundamentally the same segment of the electorate, it became a relatively easy matter for the precinct organization to line up behind the third machine candidate and push him over the top.

24. This quotation and following unattributed quotations are derived from interviews conducted in Gary, Indiana, by the authors.

25. Vantrease's candidacy not only cost Konrady the election in Miller, but also citywide. Konrady and Vantrease appealed to roughly the same segment of the electorate. If Vantrease had dropped out of the race, most of the votes he received would probably have gone to Konrady. Those votes, when combined with Konrady's own votes, would have been more than enough to assure Konrady's victory. Recognizing the danger of Vantrease's candidacy to his election possibilities, Konrady sought to force Vantrease out of the race by accusing him of making a deal with the machine to run as a splinter candidate in return for a major appointment in the Katz administration. It is interesting to note that Vantrease did in fact eventually receive an appointment as city controller in the Katz administration.

26. Among the organizations represented by CRCC were: the Adult Women's Auxiliary; Young Adult and Youth Branches of the NAACP; Fair Share Organization; Frontiers Service Club; Combined Citizens Committee On Open Occupancy; the Calumet Chapter of the Indiana Civil Liberties Union; the Interdenominational Ministerial Alliance; the Urban League of Gary; the Unitarian Social Action Committee; Muigwithania; Semanors Civic and Social Cub; Federated Women's Club; Baptist Ministers Conference of Gary; and the United Council of Baptist Ministers of Gary and vicinity.

27. For a cogent discussion of this case, see John Kaplan, "Segregation, Litigation and the Schools—Part II: The General Northern Problem," *Northwestern University Law Review* 58, no. 2 (May-June 1963).

28. In the past these seats were only nominally competitive; the actual selection of delegates was usually left to the county chairman who fielded a slate that was never challenged in the election by other candidates.

29. Hatcher denies the charge that he was slated in the 1963 primary councilmanic race. In an intereview, he attributed his victory in the race to the ability of his supporters to capitalize on dissatisfactions stemming from revelations of rampant graft and corruption in city hall. He argued that the machine did not strongly oppose him because it had been cut down to half-strength by citizen disaffection and federal governmental surveillance in the wake of the Chacharis affair.

30. *Gary Post-Tribune,* 14 November 1964. All quotations from various editions of the *Gary Post-Tribune* are reprinted by permission of the publisher.

7

Gary: The 1967 Primary Election

THE DECISION TO RUN

Richard Gordon Hatcher's campaign for mayor of Gary was launched approximately three years before he formally announced his candidacy for the office. Imbued with strong ambitions and a natural zest for political life, Hatcher began almost immediately upon taking his seat on the city council to build for himself a broad network of support in the black community. This process began with the inauguration of a weekly house-meeting program that brought Hatcher face to face with a wide segment of his black constituency. The unstated purpose of these meetings was to establish Hatcher's reputation as a politician concerned with the needs of the little people, who was always ready to use his influence to find workable and satisfactory solutions to their problems. According to several respondents, he did an outstanding job of promoting and realizing this objective.

> At that time we didn't have lights out here, so many of our neighbors asked about street lights. A councilman was allotted so many lights. And so he must have given us a lot of his allottment because we got them on every corner within a short time. So this way he demonstrated to the people his interest in them before coming to solicit their vote. It was effective; it was a good plan. This was done three years before he announced.[1]

The house-meeting program was accompanied by steps to re-activate the RGH (Richard Gordon Hatcher) Club, a young people's group founded to assist in his councilmanic campaign. This group began holding meetings every Sunday. These meetings served both as social outlets and forums for the discussion of important political topics. One frequent topic of conversation was the variety of steps that would have to be taken to mobilize the black community behind Richard Hatcher as a candidate for mayor.

The RGH Club derives its central importance from the fact that many members of this group eventually formed the backbone of Hatcher's 1967 mayoral campaign organization. Through this group, Hatcher was able to attract a dedicated corps of young people into his political camp and to translate their youthful idealism into valuable political currency. The critical role played by the RGH Club is highlighted by the remarks of a strongly committed Hatcher supporter:

I first became involved in the RGH Club through a friend while attending Indiana University. I went to the first meeting and met Mr. Hatcher. He spoke but I was not too impressed. He was just starting in politics, did not have a gift for gab, and was very shy. I thought he just wanted money. I went to another meeting and I saw the faces of people I knew. This was a different kind of group and he was able to relate to this group better than to the larger group. He was so sincere that I said here was something for me to do rather than just sit around and be a housewife. So I started working actively in his campaign from then on.

Hatcher's search for political support was not confined to the black community. He was very much aware that if he ran for mayor he would, for example, need substantial financial backing. Fully realizing that money of this magnitude was generally not available in the black community, Hatcher turned, during 1964, to a group of liberal-to-radical Jews in Miller, cynically dubbed by the local population as the "Miller Mafia" because of their history of left-wing political involvement. Hatcher made discrete inquiries to find out whether or not the members of this group would be interested in providing some financial support should he decide to seek the mayorship. The unambiguous message that he received was that the members of the Miller group were not interested in supporting his candidacy for mayor at that time.

Many indicated that they were not completely sure where Hatcher stood on a number of issues of importance to them, particularly the Vietnam War, and thus could not give him a blanket endorsement or promise financial support until he formulated the planks in his platform.

During the early months of 1966 Hatcher continued to carefully assess his chances of capturing the mayor's office in 1967. To get as broad a perspective on this issue as possible, he consulted with blacks in Cleveland, Ohio, and Newark, New Jersey, who had participated in the political campaigns of black candidates running for mayor in those cities. The general message he received was that he ought to run—that the time was right for the election of black mayors across the country.

By the fall of 1966 Hatcher had definitely made up his mind to run. Several factors strongly influenced this decision. One important factor was the mounting frustration he felt as a city councilman with a voice and a vote but no power. Typically, the real power of all Gary councilmen was sharply circumscribed by the combined political muscle of a strong mayor and an entrenched political machine. Because Hatcher expressed points of view unsatisfactory to the white establishment, he wielded even less influence than most councilmen. Intensely driven by deep-seated political ambitions and a genuine concern for the welfare of the black community, Hatcher sincerely believed that any steps he took short of seeking the mayor's office in 1967 would be virtually meaningless. "The real power in Gary is in the mayor's office and blacks were shut out. I wanted to try to be in a position to do something really significant."[2]

Perhaps the most important factor governing Hatcher's decision to run, however, was the conclusion he reached in the fall of 1966 that his chances of winning the 1967 mayoral contest were unusually good. This conclusion was based in part on his assessment of the overall strength and viability of the Democratic political machine. An extensive scholarly examination of contemporary machine politics in Gary by Hatcher and several close associates suggested that the regular Democratic organization was so fraught with internal dissension that it was no longer capable of uniting and thus guaranteeing the defeat of a strong independent candidate.

Hatcher's conviction that he had a good chance of winning the mayoral nomination was also based on his perception of the support he was likely to receive from the black community. He harbored no illusions about the intensity of antiblack feelings among whites in Gary. After all, George Wallace had carried Gary's white precincts in the 1964 presidential primaries. Hatcher was also aware that many whites were not just antiblack but particularly anti-Hatcher since he had played a leading role in the passage of the omnibus civil rights ordinance. These facts made it plain that the overwhelming preponderance of support in his bid for the mayorship would have to come from the black community. Hatcher had become convinced by the fall of 1966 that if he ran he could in fact get substantial black support. This belief was based to some extent on his understanding of the considerable growth of black nationalism in Gary as a result of local and national civil rights struggles. He sensed among Gary blacks a general restlessness that signaled a psychological readiness to vote black, and to bloc vote, if the appropriate opportunity presented itself. Most importantly, a careful examination of the voting behavior of blacks across several recent local elections firmly indicated that Gary blacks were ready to vote not only for black machine candidates, but also for black candidates running as political independents.

Several contests involving bids by prominent black candidates for local offices were found by Hatcher to be particularly instructive on this point. One of these contests involved a bid by a black funeral director, Andrew Smith, for Calumet Township trustee in the 1962 Democratic primaries. Smith's chief opponents were Milton Bromich, running independent of the machine, and Ted Sikora, running as a machine candidate. Despite tremendous efforts by machine workers to hamper his campaign activities, Smith ran a remarkably strong race, coming in third in a field of eight candidates. An examination of the election results clearly shows that Smith was a serious candidate in the race only because he received unusually strong support in the black community. Concentrating his campaign almost exclusively in black precincts, Smith beat his major white rivals in all three of the predominantly black electoral districts. Professional politicians registered surprise at Smith's strong showing in the black community against formidable machine opposition. Some individuals who worked actively in the Smith campaign interpreted Smith's performance as a critical breakthrough for blacks, because it enabled them to realize that if they voted together they could put a black candidate into a major political office. Even George Chacharis was prompted to predict, in light of Smith's showing, that someday Gary would have a "Negro Mayor."

The race by Vivian Carter, black businesswoman and former radio personality, for city clerk in 1963 illustrated further the ability of an independent black candidate to receive black support.[3] Mrs. Carter's chief opponent was Betty Malinka, a member of the state legislature and a powerful figure in the regular Democratic organization. Although Miss Malinka was expected to coast to an easy victory because of her party connections, she won the election by a razor-thin margin of 1,579 votes (19,638 to 18,059). Significantly, although Mrs. Carter lost the citywide contest, she soundly defeated Miss Malinka in the black community, obtaining an impressive 74 percent of the black votes to Miss Malinka's 16 percent.

The impressive performance of Mrs. Carter in the black community served to affirm the significance of the movement toward black electoral independence established a year earlier in the Smith contest. Even more decisive confirmation of developing black electoral independence was provided, however, in the race by Dozier Allen, a black service-station operator, for the office of Calumet Township assessor in 1966. Allen's performance in this race was the final determining factor in Hatcher's decision to run for mayor.

Allen was one of the original members of Muigwithania and was persuaded to run for the assessor's office by members of the organization. He had previously run for the state legislature in 1964 and had narrowly missed election to one of Lake County's ten representative seats. Hatcher played a key role in Allen's 1966 campaign, working behind the scenes as his unofficial political advisor. Indeed, Hatcher's involvement in the campaign ultimately became so extensive that many persons, including members of the local press corps, began viewing Allen's candidacy as a dry run to test Hatcher's mayoral possibilities.

The field of candidates in the 1966 assessor's primary race was quite impressive. Besides Allen, major candidates included incumbent assessor Thomas Fadell, city clerk Betty Malinka running with strong support from city hall, and former Gary mayor

Joseph Visclosky. Few political observers gave Allen much of a chance of winning against such a formidable field of contenders. However, to the astonishment of practically everyone, Allen came in first in Gary and second in the overall township balloting.[4] The township race was won by the incumbent candidate Fadell; Miss Malinka ran third and Visclosky a weak fourth. Final election returns showed Fadell with 11,634, Allen 10,019, Malinka 9,202, and Visclosky 7,552 votes.

Allen's strong showing in Gary was totally unexpected and was due almost exclusively to the substantial victory he registered against the machine in the black community. Miss Malinka received only 22 percent of the black vote despite the expenditure of sizable sums of money in her behalf by the regular Democratic organization. In contrast, Allen received 60 percent of the black vote (4 other minor black candidates received a combined total of 9 percent). Of the total vote gathered by Allen, 96.8 percent was cast in black precincts and only 3.2 percent in white precincts. Thus, with three major white candidates in the race, Allen obtained nearly enough votes from the black community alone to carry the election in Gary. The Gary total was Allen 10,011, Fadell 9,690, Malinka 8,413, and Visclosky 6,777 votes. In general, the Allen race represented a tremendous outpouring of black support for a black candidate running against strong machine opposition.

The Allen election had a considerable impact on the political game plans of both Mayor Katz and Hatcher. Katz interpreted the election as establishing a new trend in voting that would have to be taken into account by every serious future candidate for public office in Gary. He noted in a prepared statement that the Allen race demonstrated conclusively that the black vote was a much stronger force in Gary politics than it had ever been before.

Hatcher interpreted the election as a breakthrough event that illustrated the weakening ties of the black community to the political machine. He believed that the Allen race proved incontrovertibly that a black candidate with a decent reputation who made a strong appeal for the black vote could get substantial black support. The Allen race removed any lingering doubt in the minds of Hatcher and his supporters that the time was right for a major black candidate to run for the mayor's office. As one prominent member of Muigwithania put it:

We felt that if we could take a man from our group with only six years experience as an organization and shake the whole Lake County Democratic party structure, and each time we shook it we got a little bit closer, which meant that we were shaking it a bit harder, then the time had definitely arrived for us to go for the mayor's race.

Having firmly established in his mind that he was going to run for mayor, Hatcher began to weld together a coalition composed of various community groups with whom he had been interacting politically over a period of several years. As an initial step in this direction he called together a black political brain trust to discuss the feasibility of his running, his chances for victory, and possible electoral strategies. In attendance at this meeting were Hatcher, Quentin Smith, James T. Jones, James Hendrick, Jesse Bell, James Holland, Henry Coleman, Robert Brown, and Fred Ford. Although expressing grave doubts about his chances of winning against the powerful Lake County machine, members of this group nonetheless encouraged Hatcher to run because they believed his candidacy would effectuate the building up of a strong opposition bloc in the black community to the continued control of the black vote by the political machine.

Hatcher consulted next with members of Muigwithania to line up the solid support of this key group. He initially received heated resistence from some Muigwithania members who believed that Dozier Allen should run for mayor since he had done such an outstanding job in the assessor's race. Resistance from this quarter faded, however, as it became clear that Hatcher rather than Allen would be the stronger, more effective, black mayoral candidate.

Once the support of Muigwithania was fully secured, Hatcher began concentrating his organizing efforts on the whites in Miller with whom he had touched base earlier. This time he was warmly received by the Miller group. The Allen race had convinced them that he had a good chance of winning, so they encouraged him to run. A formal meeting of this group, along with a few interested blacks, was held at the home of Andrew Smith, and a formal decision was made to endorse Hatcher and work with him in his campaign.

While informally working assiduously to firm up support for his candidacy, Hatcher attempted to convey the outward appearance of a reluctant candidate responding to a popular draft. Believing that he might not run, a number of opinion surveys were taken by various groups of black citizens to convince Hatcher that he was the "people's choice." Two black men, John Grigsby and Larry Turner, both of whom later played important roles in Hatcher's campaign, collected between them five thousand names on a petition encouraging Hatcher to run for mayor. Similar surveys were taken by milkmen and insurance men working in black neighborhoods. Louis Comer, a prominent black trade-union official, led a delegation of black union men to Hatcher's home to encourage him to run for mayor with their unswerving support. Initially, Hatcher's standard reply to requests that he file for the mayor's office was that he was giving the matter serious consideration. Finally, after having thoroughly established himself as the people's candidate, Hatcher made it generally known that he intended to run for mayor and was in the process of recruiting persons to work in his campaign organization.

THE CAMPAIGN ORGANIZATION

By the time Hatcher announced his candidacy for mayor in January 1967, his campaign organization had been functioning for about six months. The initial recruitment of persons into the organization was handled mainly by Hatcher and a close friend, Jesse Bell. Hatcher made numerous phone calls and personal visits around the city to individuals he felt would be willing and able to serve as chairmen of campaign committees. At the same time, Bell went about the task of recruiting workers from a cross section of the black community to perform the thousand and one small duties essential to the mounting of an effective campaign effort. After initial contacts were made with key people, membership in the Hatcher organization increased in snowball fashion, with each new recruit in turn drawing in other persons.

The campaign organization that resulted was one composed of a nucleus of sixty extremely active workers. Approximately 85 percent of these persons were black and 15 percent white. With very few exceptions everyone who participated in the Hatcher campaign did so on a volunteer basis: thus the significance of the name of the group "Volunteers for Hatcher." Everyone entered into the Hatcher organization with the clear understanding that no one would be paid and that no other commitments would be made in return for his political support. This philosophy of volunteer service underpinned the entire spirit and form of operation of the primary campaign organization.

The volunteer spirit pervading the Hatcher primary effort is also illustrated by the fact that many persons worked for Hatcher at considerable financial sacrifice. Some of the most active Hatcher supporters took off from their jobs for as long as six months (one individual took off a year and a half) in order to work full time as a Hatcher volunteer. Several took out second mortgages on their homes to get the campaign off the ground financially. One Hatcher worker drove his truck to Chicago and back for sixty days straight at his own expense to pick up campaign material. Virtually everyone paid for his own transportation and lunches while at the same time contributing out of his pocket to the campaign treasury. In some cases, sizable amounts were donated by Hatcher volunteers, no doubt the most generous contribution coming from one volunteer who gave a thousand dollars during the primary and another thousand during the general election. This aspect of the Hatcher organization was best summarized by one respondent who observed: "The only way you work for Hatcher is that it cost you money. If you wanted to work for Hatcher then you were always shelling out at every meeting. And there were people who pulled away because there was no money. We were happy to get rid of them. But if you wanted to work in the Hatcher campaign, you put out, put out of your pocket. You weren't on the take, you were on the give."

The people drawn into the Hatcher campaign organization on the volunteer basis described above were—with very few exceptions—political amateurs. Blacks participating in the organization were representative of two distinct segments of the black community. At least half of the blacks very active in the organization were low-income, grass-roots individuals with virtually no prior history of political involvement. That this sector of the black community was well represented in the organization was not fortuitous but deliberate. Hatcher campaign coordinators made a vigorous effort to identify and attract into the organization grass-roots community opinion leaders from varied walks of life—persons whom it was believed could best communicate with rank-and-file black voters. The success of the coordinators in recruiting these individuals into active campaign work was due in no small measure to Hatcher's efforts over the years to establish a close identification with the black masses through his actions as a councilman and his involvement in the civil rights movement. Every effort was made not to just give the grass-roots component of the organization symbolic status, but to make it an integral part of the organization and to encourage its involvement in every phase of campaign work. And it is central to our understanding of the 1967 mayoral primary in Gary to grasp the significant point that these representatives of the grass-roots black population were among the most dedicated, energetic, and effective of all Hatcher volunteers.

The balance of the black persons playing very active roles in the Hatcher campaign organization were middle- to low-income blacks whose previous political experience had been confined to local civil rights protests and the amateur political activities of Muigwithania and the RGH Club. These were, for the most part, Hatcher's long-time comrades in arms or young adult admirers, some of whom had been associated with him in various public endeavors since 1960 and had been instrumental in helping him to shape both the character and the direction of his political career.

Noticeably unrepresented (or underrepresented) in the Hatcher coalition were the various social groups that made up the black establishment, that is, black professional politicians, black businessmen, and other black professionals (with the noteable exception of teachers), old-line black civil rights spokesmen, and black ministers. Generally speaking, members of the black establishment believed that blacks were not prepared to support a black man for the top position in the city. Thus they disapproved of Hatcher's candidacy because they believed his campaign efforts would be futile and in the long run counterproductive. Operating on these assumptions, a group of black professional politicians, dubbing themselves the Committee of 100, sought unsuccessfully to persuade Hatcher not to run for mayor but to file for reelection to the city council.

The white component of the Hatcher organization, unlike the black, was a very homogeneous group. Whites who worked for Hatcher generally ran in the same social circles and they were drawn into the organization through the urgings of three key Hatcher political advisors belonging to this intimate social group. An examination of the socioeconomic characteristics of white Hatcher workers brings into sharp focus the homogeneous nature of this group. Their most salient common characteristics were their ethnic affiliation and economic class standing. All but one of these persons were Jewish. They were on the whole members of the upper-income bracket with a median annual income of about $25,000. All but one of them lived in Miller; the one exception lived in a community adjacent to Miller known as Aetna.[5]

Although most of these white Hatcher workers had had experience in politics, this experience did not include deep involvement in electoral politics but politics as it related to a broad range of social and political issues—a range that covered the spectrum from peace to civil rights. Their political experience then was obtained mainly through social activism. Except to campaign for a Jewish candidate for the city council—Milton Roth—in 1955 and 1959, these whites had purposely steered clear of involvement in Gary electoral politics because they believed it to be too corrupt and utterly incapable of reform. Consequently, in terms of their experience with the multifaceted, beguiling, mind-bending aspects of practical Gary politics, they too were political amateurs. True, they were not nearly as inexperienced in social organization and political movements as their black colleagues; but when pitted against an organization that had been winning elections for twenty years, their experience in these areas would mean very little.

Hatcher's primary organization then—much the same as the Stokes organization in Cleveland—was made up of amateurs with only nominal, if any, experience in traditional electoral politics. The motivations of the people who joined the organization and remained to play very active roles were complexed and varied. Some overarching motivational forces do distinctly emerge, however, from their interviews. Undoubtedly the most important stimulus for their involvement was the magnetic quality of Hatcher as a personality and a political force. Respondents cited most frequently as their reasons for joining the Hatcher organization Hatcher's personal attributes of honesty, integrity, and competence, as demonstrated by his work on the city council. The factor of honesty was particularly central to the involvement of black respondents. Many had come to view black leadership with profound cynicism and distrust and repeated time and again that they would not have worked for Hatcher—or any other black politician —unless they believed he was a man of impeccable honesty.

That they should approach political activity with a good deal of apprehension and cynicism was only natural given the history of betrayal that blacks in Gary had experienced, as the following respondent explained:

> When you take a community of people that has been bought and sold just like merchandise on a shelf, they've had their hopes built high on a member of their community and then later on they find out that he's put them on the auction block, then this kind of gives them a skeptical feeling. And they come to ask themselves the question, is there anybody that we can trust? And it only stands to reason because black people in this city have been used as a political football, tossed around by the power structure, used as they pleased.

Hatcher's integrity, demonstrated by his principled stand on issues arising in the city council, was critical to the decision by black workers to join his campaign organization. In this context one black Hatcher worker observed:

> A lot of people paid close attention to the way this man conducted himself in those council meetings and how he really fought for the issues he believed in. Not necessarily the way we thought it should have gone, but the man stuck to his convictions. A lot of time maybe I wouldn't agree that this was the way it should have been done, but what impressed me and a lot of people was that the man if he felt that he was right he stuck to it. If you take a man that's swayed by all kinds of public opinion you're not going to have a man that's worth his salt. . . . Mr. Hatcher would stand alone and fight for the things people needed in this city. I never will forget one council meeting when the people of Brunswick told him in no uncertain terms not to even run for dog catcher again in this town because he wouldn't be elected. But Mr. Hatcher still fought for open occupancy while all other Negro councilmen backed down. He was a man who stood on honesty and integrity.

Responses obtained from black Hatcher supporters—such as those quoted above—who had never participated in politics before, compels a careful reexamination of the common notion that low-income blacks do not participate in politics because they are uninterested in political affairs and have little knowledge of the political world around them. A number of Gary's black respondents asserted that they did not participate in city politics because their knowledge and understanding of the local political system convinced them that they had no reason to participate.

Prior to becoming Hatcher volunteers these respondents had exhibited considerable interest in local politics. They watched from a distance as Hatcher emerged as a dynamic force on the city council, and they admired him for the daring battles he waged as a member of that body. They admired him for his out of council activities as well.

> We protest marched at a bank out here in Tollerston because the manager of the bank was a councilman and he voted against open occupancy. Mr. Hatcher didn't sit behind a desk or something and say you should do this, he was out there. He was a councilman but he was out there. We walked all the way from Broadway West clean over to Grant Street, knocking on doors, passing out handbills, and he was with us and it was five below zero. That was impressive so far as I was concerned. He was a dedicated man; he was sincere.

Hatcher projected an image that these black citizens had never before seen in their political leaders. He was young, intelligent, a reputable lawyer, and a capable city councilman. Most importantly, he was down to earth:

> I think the key to his success is that he is a plain, ordinary Joe. The average fellow feels comfortable around him because he acts just like any ordinary fellow. You wouldn't know he was a lawyer unless somebody else told you. He'll sit and talk, and never mention it. We've been accustomed, you know how some of us are, we're a little more fortunate than others, and we want to soon project that. But he's not that kind of fellow. And that's the key to his success. He's the type of fellow that people will get out for because they have confidence in him. You can always talk to him. He's never in too big a hurry.

Hatcher's social and political activities thus convinced these blacks that he was honest, capable, and possessed an unusual amount of personal integrity. They came to believe that in Richard Hatcher they had finally found a reason to participate in politics—and they surged into action when it became clear that he was contemplating a run for the mayor's office.

Motives for white participation in the Hatcher organization substantially coincided with those of black participants. However, at some point black and white motivations sharply diverged. Whereas blacks were involved in the organization almost exclusively out of admiration for Hatcher, whites were involved for reasons that related more directly to the issue of social and political reform. Many whites joined the organization chiefly out of a desire to beat the machine, and they believed Hatcher's candidacy provided an excellent opportunity for doing so. Others were motivated chiefly by ideological concerns. These persons were primarily interested in achieving black political power that matched the numerical strength and enormous needs of the black community, and they viewed Hatcher's campaign as a vehicle through which this objective could be realized. Witness, in this context, the following exchange between one of the authors and a white Hatcher worker:

Q. What factors most strongly influenced your decision to become a member of the Hatcher campaign organization?

A. That's a rather difficult question to answer. I can say I thought America was a land of disenchanted promise. And I thought it was important for dissatisfied sectors of the country to move, that includes black people, poor whites, and campus kids. And so far as I was concerned, Hatcher's election was all about black power. I as a white man subscribe to black power. And when I say black power I don't just mean putting black men in office. I mean putting *militant* black men in office. I'm not talking about all kinds of other guys in this city who might want to run for mayor.

Q. Is this how you viewed Mr. Hatcher?

A. Yes, as a militant black cat.

Q. And is that why you supported him?

A. That's right.

Q. Any other reasons why you supported him?

A. Because I was a Jew and because six million Jews died in crematoriums. Though I will never know what it means to be black, I know a little more about what it means to be black than a non-Jew knows. Black people have had it for three hundred years and Jews have had it for three thousand years. And I dig that a little bit. I dig what it means to be burned and lynched. Not like the black man digs it, but I dig it a little bit.[6]

It was essentially this mixture of motives, some idealistic, some ideological, some pragmatic, which inspired and stimulated the various elements of the black and white communities that came together to elect Richard Hatcher as the first black mayor of Gary.

Structure and Function

Although members of the Hatcher organization often proclaimed they were practicing a form of new politics, numerous aspects of their political work were cast in the mold of traditional approaches to electoral activity. The structure and operation of the Hatcher campaign organization provides the best example of its adherence to common political norms. As in the case of practically all campaign organizations—including the Stokes organization in Cleveland—the Hatcher organization was broken down into a variety of committees assigned to carry out functions essential to the effective promotion of a political candidate for public office. Specifically, the Hatcher campaign organization was separated into fourteen committees, each having its own duties and responsibilities. These duties and responsibilities were spelled out in concise, unambiguous language in a campaign guideline authored by Jesse Bell and distributed to every Hatcher volunteer. Among the most important of these committees was the finance committee, chaired by Dr. Kessler Truelove and co-chaired by Mr. Lemuel Carter. This committee began functioning several months before the formal campaign organization was drawn together. The job of this committee was central to the success of the campaign, since a minimum level of fund-raising was absolutely necessary if the many other tasks to be performed by other components of the total organization were to be accomplished. Another key committee was the voter-registration committee. The campaign guideline succinctly emphasized the critical nature of this committee's responsibility: "without registered voters to pull the levers for our candidate he cannot win." Canvassing and registration functions were placed in the hands of John Grigsby and Larry Turner. Two other committees with overlapping responsibilities operated as fundamental components of the primary organization: the research committee and the speech-writing committee. Hatcher was quite fortunate in attracting a group of talented and dedicated scholars to serve on these committees. Research activities were supervised mainly by Charles Ross and Fred Stern, while speech-writing functions were performed by Burton Wechsler, Arthur Daronasty, and James Yeary. Although their duties were formidable, these men brought to their work intellect, skill, and determination more than equal to the challenge. Additional campaign committees, all of which played important roles in the overall effort were those of: transportation, headquarters, telephone, special assignment, signs and billboard, literature distribution, publicity and advertising, meetings, absentee ballot, new breed, labor, and celebrity and name contact.

At the apex of the campaign organization was the candidate, the campaign manager, the campaign coordinator, and the assistant campaign coordinator. Serving as campaign manager was Henry Coleman. Mr. Coleman was the only seasoned politician in the entire Hatcher camp. A veteran of thirty years in Gary politics, Mr. Coleman had managed the campaigns of numerous black candidates and was responsible for educating a whole generation of independent-minded, politically active blacks in the art of practical politics in the Gary context. His forte was anticipating the moves of the opposition and making strategical adjustments in campaign operation having the effect of confounding the most well thought-out battle plans of campaign rivals. In recent times, Mr. Coleman has become somewhat of a professional campaign manager and is an acknowledged expert in this field.

Serving as campaign coordinator was Jesse Bell. Mr. Bell, a Gary school teacher, had been a friend of Hatcher's since their association together as activists in the NAACP in the early 1960s. Possessing great respect for Bell's organizational ability, Hatcher tapped him to build the volunteer component of the campaign organization and map out its formal structure. As campaign coordinator, Bell was charged with the responsibility of handling organizational and operational problems and coordinating the activities of all working committees. Information from committees to the campaign manager and candidate was to be funneled primarily through Bell and his assistant, Claude Mayberry.

Hatcher, Coleman, and Bell operated as a kind of decisional triumvirate. From the outset it was made clear that key political decisions—for example, decisions that said whether or not the organization would strike out in one direction as opposed to another, or against one group of individuals rather than another—

were to be made strictly by these three men and could not be argued. In practice, however, such decisions were not always made by these persons alone. Instead of a fixed group of decision-makers establishing policy on key issues, in actuality, according to the circumstance and the issue, there was a rotating group of decision-makers—with Hatcher as the axis—who hammered out major policy decisions. From time to time Charles Ross, or Julian Allen (Hatcher's law partner) or Burton Wechsler, or Fred Stern, or Arthur Daronasty, or Larry Turner, in addition to and sometimes in the place of Coleman and Bell, had a hand in the formulation of key decisions.

The central core of the campaign organization was the executive board. All members of the executive board were appointed by the candidate and served at his pleasure. It consisted of the chairman and cochairman of all standing committees, plus several other persons appointed to serve by the candidate because of their expertise in certain fields. Overall, approximately thirty-six persons served on the executive board during the primary campaign.

The executive board made decisions on day-to-day, routine matters of the campaign. An elaborate system of reporting was set up whereby members of committees would report to committee chairmen, who would in turn report to the executive board. Problems of each committee were considered by the executive board in plenary sessions. Discussions of these matters took the form of wide-open debates, and "knock-down, drag-out" disputes among board members were a common occurrence. Eventually the board would agree upon certain courses of action and would then make recommendations to the candidate. We should underscore at this point the advisory nature of the executive board's function. Decisions made by the executive board did not have compulsory force but were subject to the approval of the candidate. Hatcher made it clear from the beginning—although there is evidence that some members of the executive board did not fully comprehend the implications of this—that he would retain veto power over everything the executive board did. This rule of operation was strictly enforced; on several occasions Hatcher overturned policy, operational, and procedural decisions arrived at through exhaustive actions by members of the executive board.

CAMPAIGN STRATEGY

The strategy worked out by Hatcher and his chief advisors to achieve his mayoral nomination in the 1967 primary election was influenced by a number of demographic and political considerations. Central to Hatcher's calculations for victory was the fact that he was a black man running in a city highly polarized along racial lines. Even a cursory examination of voting returns in primary elections left no doubt that white people did not vote for black people running as independent candidates for major public offices in Gary. Given this fact, it became obvious that if he was to be a serious candidate for mayor, the overwhelming proportion of his campaign effort must be directed toward the black community. Consequently, the crux of the Hatcher campaign strategy was that of mobilizing enough black electoral support to win. The central objective of this mobilization effort would be to induce every eligible black voter to register to vote and to cast his ballot on election day for Hatcher, an independent black mayoral candidate.

Another key factor entering into Hatcher's primary campaign strategy was data that showed that there were more eligible white voters in Gary than eligible black voters. As of November 1966 white registration was officially put at 52.3 percent, whereas black registration was 47.7 percent.[7] Thus though blacks constituted a majority of the total population, they were not a majority of the citizens eligible to vote in the primary election. This meant that even if Hatcher received 100 percent support in the black community—and he viewed this as a virtual impossibility—he would still need a substantial amount of white support in order to win. Yet every indication was that nothing more than nominal support for his candidacy would be forthcoming from white voters. Hatcher believed that his unpopularity among the white electorate could be realistically offset in only one way: if two or more major white candidates entered the mayoral race and split the white vote. Some key Hatcher supporters were initially extremely pessimistic about his chances for victory, because they were positive that given the threat of a black candidate in the race, the machine would unify around one candidate and use every means necessary to prevent a splinter white candidate from filing. However, this pessimism began to swiftly erode when developments within the regular Democratic organization indicated that unity might be lacking. The most important of these developments was the entrance into the mayor's race of three strong white candidates. First among the major white candidates to file for the mayor's office was the incumbent mayor A. Martin Katz. The announcement by Katz was not surprising since he had publicized his intention to run for a second term as early as April 1966.

Katz's announcement was followed shortly afterward by the entrance into the mayor's race of the Lake County treasurer, Leslie O. Pruitt, a key figure in the Lake County Democratic organization. Pruitt's candidacy for mayor was the product of a growing conviction on the part of county party officials that Katz was so unpopular in Gary's white community that he could not win re-election. These county officials argued that in contrast to Katz, Pruitt enjoyed immense personal popularity in the white community and would therefore be the party's strongest contender in a head-to-head confrontation with Hatcher.

The third major white candidate to enter the mayor's race was Bernard Konrady, Gary businessman and brother of Emery Konrady who ran unsuccessfully for mayor in 1963. In announcing his candidacy, Konrady said that he was following in the footsteps of his brother who died on the evening of his bid for reelection to the Indiana state senate. Konrady observed, "Save for his untimely death, my brother would be making this announcement in my stead."[8] He emphasized, however, that he was not campaigning on his brother's record or running in his shadow, but because surveys that he conducted indicated he had a good chance of winning.

The announcement by Konrady was welcomed news for the Hatcher camp. Hatcher had filed for mayor immediately after Pruitt entered the contest. Although the evidence of division in the ranks of the machine reflected in Pruitt's candidacy had given Hatcher some encouragement, he was still not confident that party pressure would not eventually force either Katz or Pruitt to withdraw. However, with Konrady also in the race, withdrawal by Katz or Pruitt would not be a major blow to Hatcher's election possibilities since there would remain two white candidates to split the white vote. The only other outstanding danger was the possible withdrawal by Konrady. However, this danger swiftly eroded as Konrady made it absolutely clear that he would not yield to strenuous efforts by machine officials to buy him out of the race.[9]

With assurances that at least two major white candidates would be competing for the white vote, Hatcher and his supporters reasoned that his success in the mayoral race hinged almost exclusively on their ability to turn out and deliver a large, cohesive black vote. In making this assessment, they harbored few illusions about the magnitude of the challenge. They knew, based on the previous reaction of the black community to black candidates, that one of the most intractable obstacles they would face in their mobilizing efforts was black self-doubt. They were very much aware that their conviction that Hatcher could win the mayorship was not shared by the black community as a whole. They were constantly reminded that a group of rank amateurs did not stand a chance of beating a well-oiled political machine with pratically an inexhaustible supply of political resources. These were not just superficial impressions but attitudes that had become deeply rooted in the ethos of the black community over a period of about twenty years. For Hatcher workers this suggested an indisputable fact: their biggest job would be selling to a multitude of black doubters the proposition that Hatcher could win. Until and unless this was done, the hopes of stimulating a massive black revolt of the dimensions requisite for Hatcher's election would be a lovely dream. In this context one central figure in the Hatcher organization observed: "People like to be on the winner's side, and if they don't think you can win, they don't want to waste their vote or to waste the $10.00 they might have gotten otherwise."

Intense opposition to Hatcher's candidacy from within the black community constituted another difficult hurdle that somehow had to be surmounted. Members of the black establishment had made it clear that they not only would not support Hatcher, but would work actively against him. Thus Hatcher would not only have to fight a hostile white political power structure but an unfriendly black political power structure as well. He was faced with the likelihood that at the same time his supporters were trying to sell the proposition that he could win, black ministers, black professional politicians, old-line civil rights leaders, and others would loudly proclaim that he could not win and should not win. Hatcher supporters were certain that many of these persons were deeply in debt to the machine and that every pressure would be brought to mobilize them against Hatcher and in the service of Katz. Given the inevitable opposition of this powerful segment of the black community, some means had to be devised to neutralize their strength and obliterate their effectiveness as instruments of machine power.

Even more menacing was the almost certain opposition of the black precinct organization. As pointed out in chapter six, this organization was the pivotal source of control by the machine in the black community. Hatcher knew that he could not begin to compete with the machine for the political support of black precinct committeemen. These men had made it plain that they were not committed to black power but black capitalism and that they intended to sell their services to the highest bidder. On this basis, Hatcher had no choice but to write black committeemen off as inaccessible political resources, because it was inconceivable that he could pay them the sums they could command from the opposition. Some Hatcher supporters dismissed the inevitable opposition of the black precinct organization as relatively unimportant. For example, one Hatcher worker stated:

> We learned in 1966 that the precinct organization did not command the kind of magic they claimed they did—that people could form opinions, could vote, and would vote. . . . Fred Egan, when he was running for judge in 1966, proved this. They demanded of him $3,000 per district to carry him. He said I'm not going to give you anything, and won by a landslide. They've been doing this to everybody. Yeah, we'll carry you (hand out gesture). They could always give you a fairly respectable showing by voting the ineligible names.

But this was definitely a minority opinion. Most Hatcher workers were extremely despondent over the unambiguous impressions they received in the early days of the campaign that the black precinct organization would work to bolster the power of the machine by supporting the renomination of the incumbent mayor.

> Many [black precinct committeemen] said they could not support Mr. Hatcher because as precinct committeemen they were honor bound to serve the people in power in the party at that time. But the real reason was that they owed their lives and their jobs to Katz. And also they wanted extra money. They also knew that once Mr. Hatcher won they would lose their jobs as precinct committeemen. Their refusal to work with us really shook us up because they had

quite a bit of control. We thought the black precinct committeemen were our worst enemies.

Underpinning all of the obstacles mentioned above was the important fact that the Hatcher forces were fighting a machine apparatus that not only operated in the city but whose tenacles reached far into the county as well. This broad, overarching network of power allowed the machine not only to control money, workers, and organizations but also to exercise tyrannical control over the mechanics of the electoral process. Some Hatcher people had learned from their experience in the Dozier Allen campaign that tremendous difficulties could be placed in their way by the power of county officials to alter at will the rules of the electoral game. These were the people who validated registered voters, assigned registrars and election day workers, counted the votes and controlled official public records and the dissemination of public information regarding elections. The importance of these factors to the mobilization process is suggested by the observations of this Hatcher volunteer:

The people in the county were in charge of all records and could put all kinds of pressure on people because they had the knowledge we did not have. They would change the records indiscriminately. You might go out there to see how many black people were registered and they might tell you 57 black people and 67 whites were registered, whereas in reality only 38 black people were registered. You believe this and you feel you have only a very narrow gap to cover. But if you don't believe it then you know you have to go out and get this many more. You know the records we keep many times are not the records that actually are.

To overcome these obstacles and others that would surely emerge as the campaign progressed, Hatcher and his advisors developed two strategic approaches to the black community. One involved the running of a high-pitched emotional campaign designed to stimulate an intense level of group consciousness and arouse the black masses to independent political action. This aspect of the campaign would stress over and over again the point that 1967 was not 1963 and that the time had arrived for blacks to break the control of the political machine over the black community through cohesive electoral action. The second approach involved the launching of a grass-roots effort that would take the campaign directly into the home of every black person in the city. The substantive dimensions of these campaign strategies and their relation to the mobilization process in the black community will be closely examined below.

In summary, the Hatcher primary campaign strategy was based on the central thesis that his prospects for victory hinged pivotally on the ability of his campaign organization to turn the black community on—to create the kind of excitement among black voters that would produce a massive outpouring of political support. This did not mean that the white vote was not also to be reached for when possible; but it did mean that workers should never lose sight of the fact that major possibilities for generating significant payoffs at the polls rested in the black rather than the white community. Consequently, the mobilization effort in the black community could not afford to be diluted or distracted by the quest for white votes. Hatcher believed that his chances of receiving strong support in the black community were good because he had established for himself a favorable image and because the climate of the times created a restlessness in the black community that lent itself to the mounting of independent political action. But he was very much aware that these factors would not automatically translate themselves into effective black political power. He fully realized that only through a well-organized and well-executed campaign effort could the critical conversion of resources to power be made.

MOBILIZING THE BLACK COMMUNITY

The campaign for black votes by the Hatcher organization was conducted on two distinct levels. At one level a general black community appeal was made by the candidate himself with the assistance of his campaign advisors. The central objective of this aspect of the campaign was to project and enhance Hatcher's image as a militant, articulate, committed, trustworthy politician who was eminently qualified to be mayor, and who, if elected, would work with diligence and skill to dramatically reverse the economic, social and political status of the black community. This objective was promoted through a perpetual round of house meetings and campaign rallies involving blacks from every walk of life. These meetings presented Hatcher with the opportunity to engage in a hardheaded discussion of the critical issues facing the black community, to outline his program for turning Gary around by taking its governance out of the hands of a corrupt machine and putting it into the hands of the "people," and to remind his black brothers and sisters of his record of devotion and sacrifice as a councilman and as a leader in the civil rights movement to the cause of black liberation.

Hatcher was given invaluable assistance in his campaign efforts by the members of the research committee. Considering the fact that they were all political amateurs, the members of this committee did a remarkable job of preparing background material for the campaign. Much of their success was engendered through sheer resourcefulness. They compiled a wealth of information on urban problems by simply nosing around the city and picking the brains of persons who were experts in various fields. They consulted with people on the smoke abatement board, members of the League of Women Voters, and professors and graduate students in Chicago doing books and doctoral dissertations on a variety of subjects relating to the urban scene. This information was pulled together in a thirteen-point platform that many said was one on which a candidate for national office could comfortably run. In this regard one member of the committee remarked, "I think we were trying to overcompensate for any notions of inferiority." This campaign document pulled no punches. It talked in very angry terms about poverty, discrimination, poor housing, disease, poor education, crime, and political corruption. "We saw these as priority concerns. These are the things a mayor ought to address himself to, not necessarily neglecting streets, water and air pollution—we did include air pollution and things of that kind. But these were the major social problems." Points from the platform were used as the basis for Hatcher's public presentations.

At the same time he was hammering away in his major speeches at themes emphasizing his commitment to improving the social and economic status of the black community, Hatcher was also attempting to convince black voters that he was a serious candidate—that he could indeed win provided he received sufficient black support. To give factual substance to this claim, a document prepared by the research committee called *Tell It like It Is —Hatcher Can Win*, was released for general distribution. This was probably the most important piece of material to come from the Hatcher camp during the primary. In many ways it set the tone for the entire mobilization effort. Using data worked up by Burton Wechsler on recent city, township, and county elections, this document purported to show conclusively that Katz's popularity in both the black and white communities was at such a low ebb and his position in the regular Democratic organization so tenuous, that he could not possibly win the Democratic primary for mayor. On the other hand, it cited the Dozier Allen and Vivian Carter races as evidence that Hatcher could win. The pamphlet asserted that if Hatcher received the 74 percent of the black vote received by Carter, this would give him 21,272 votes, and reminded blacks that Katz won the 1963 primary with only 19,853 votes. These figures, it was stressed, did not even take into account the white vote Hatcher was likely to receive and the projected increase in black registration for the 1967 primary. The central message this document communicated to black doubters was that they, by themselves, acting in concert, could elect their own black mayor—that they had the votes, all that was lacking was black unity around a candidate who would bring dignity to the mayoral office, and pride to every black person in America. Although it is difficult to accurately gauge the effect of this document, there is good reason to believe that it helped to push many confused, reluctant, doubting black voters firmly into the Hatcher camp.

> That pamphlet sort of launched it for us. It was given citywide publicity. The newspapers got it, people got it, and I think it really was a stimulant. After he announced, there were people saying, how can he win, why should I beat my brains out with another loser. So this pamphlet—*Tell It like It Is*—was very important.

Complementing the general community campaign waged by the candidate and top organization officials was a street-level campaign coordinated at the top and carried out by an army of volunteer workers. This second campaign centered around the implementation of a grass-roots strategy aimed at bypassing normal channels for gaining political support and carrying the campaign directly to the people. The objective of the strategy was to ignore the precinct organization, traditional civil rights organizations, and other components of the black submachine, and to use volunteer workers to perform the arduous task of solidifying rank-and-file black voters behind Hatcher's candidacy. One

Hatcher worker described the design and intent of the strategy in the following manner:

> This approach was worked out by Hatcher and [Henry] Coleman together. Ignore me as the big time preacher and go to my members. Ignore me as the ward healer and go to the man in the ward. And when the ward healer found out, the man in the ward was telling him I hear this is going on, and he found that there was something afoot that he couldn't stop. That idea came from Coleman. Ignore those guys, they're the property of the machine. There's no need of trying to buy what's Rockefeller's, you don't have that kind of money. He owns it. But if you talk to the people that don't belong to Rockefeller you'll get them. So go out into the hedges and the byways and shake them from the bushes because the bushes was where the people were hiding. That was altogether new too—that was a new approach. Because the system went to the big time preacher and the big time ward healer, all the political prostitutes. They were the leaders. They would pad their pockets and then go to their parishioners, woof, woof, woof, this is the man. But now the approach was so different they didn't know how to cope with that.

In short, the Hatcher people felt that the only way that they could beat the machine in the black community was by stealing the black vote away from all those persons who had helped maintain a vibrant, healthy submachine in the Midtown district.

Implementation of this strategy required a certain kind of political machinery. Specifically, it required the building of a volunteer organization, which operated parallel to the regular Democratic party structure, capable of placing persons committed to Hatcher in every political jurisdiction in the black community from the district all the way down to the block. Responsibility for building this street-level machinery rested primarily with Claude Mayberry, assistant campaign coordinator. Mayberry began by selecting four persons to serve as district leaders in the second, third, fourth, and fifth districts. Each district leader was obligated in turn to select area leaders who would have supervisional authority over five precincts. Within their areas, district leaders were to find persons to serve as precinct captains and block workers. The ultimate goal was to have ten persons on each block who were willing to go door to door convincing their neighbors that they should register to vote, and cast their vote for Hatcher on election day.

This organizational structure was knitted together by a set of rules and procedures defining the responsibility and authority of each Hatcher volunteer. District coordinators, for example, were expected not just to give orders, but to become actively involved in the mobilization process through the organizing of speakers bureaus, sponsoring public meetings, working along with the transportation and literature distribution committees to make sure that workers and materials were always at the right place at the right time, and so forth. Similarly, area leaders were expected to be working field supervisors, leading not watching their troops go off to battle. These persons promoted the street-level effort through various fund raising activities such as dinners and drawings, holding weekly planning sessions with precinct captains and block workers, coordinating voter registration activities, and in many other ways.[10] Workers at the block and precinct levels had perhaps the most important assignment of all: going door to door, using every technique imaginable to stimulate their friends and neighbors to disregard the advice of their party committeemen and vote for Hatcher as mayor. Each worker was supposed to report to his campaign supervisor relative to the status of his work and the problems he encountered. These reports were collected by Mayberry, who in turn presented them to Jesse Bell, who summarized them and presented this summary to the executive board for its consideration.

Because they were political amateurs, members of the street-level organization were not wedded to ancient formulas for political campaigning, so they experimented with new as well as old techniques for performing the duties of their job. For example, in order to get Hatcher campaign literature on the breakfast table of every black family, Hatcher workers placed his literature under door-to-door milk deliveries. When the cool air hit the milk bottle, moisture would develop, pasting the literature to the bottle's bottom. A Hatcher respondent described what usually happened next:

> The housewife picks the bottle up with this piece of paper or card sticking to the bottom. Now the milk will be placed on the table or in the refrigerator, but eventually the card will fall off the bottom when the family is in the kitchen. The card will fall off on the breakfast table, and there's the picture of your candidate with his name on it and they wonder how it got in the house. But the fact is the children are there and they pass the card around, let me see, let me see Mr. Hatcher. All around, and that is what you want.

Other highly successful gimmicks used to accomplish the same purpose were the passing out of balloons to youngsters who took them home and therefore familiarized their parents with Hatcher's name, and reliance upon insurance men or cleaning establishments to slip promotional cards in their customer's merchandise.

> If the people that he gives these cards to are not for Mr. Hatcher, then the cleaning man is going to risk losing business. But if he's pushing somebody that he thinks the people in this community are for, he's not going to lose business, he's going to gain business. Because that'll make them think that the cleaning man is a little closer to the mayor than I thought he was.

But no promotional gimmick could supplant face-to-face discussions by the volunteers of political issues and the attributes of their candidate with rank-and-file voters. The effort to sell blackness, to convince blacks that the time was right for black control of city government, and to convince them both that Hatcher could win and cope with the challenges of the mayor's office had perforce to be the major campaign technique of street-level volunteers. Time and again they encountered stubborn resistance to both the proposition that Hatcher could win, and that blacks were ready to govern. Note these observations by a Hatcher grassroots campaigner:

> I remember knocking on a door and the lady telling me she didn't have anything against Richard Hatcher, that in fact she thought he was a fine young man, but she couldn't vote for him because she knew once one of us got into office that things would be ruined. She felt that right now she could go down and she could talk to Mayor Katz and he would do something about her problems. She just didn't feel that once one of us got into the office this was the way it was going to be. She said she wasn't going to vote for Mr. Hatcher not because she had anything against him but because of the fact that she just didn't want a Negro in office.

To overcome these negative images of black leadership, Hatcher workers repeated over and over again his record on the council and argued that it was impossible for him to be any worse than previous mayors.

Significantly, grass-roots campaign workers found that many blacks were reluctant to cast their votes for Hatcher not because he was black, or they did not think he could win, or because they did not trust him, but because they had become accustomed to receiving cash rewards, gifts, groceries, and other benefits from their precinct committeemen for voting for machine candidates, and they feared these would be cut off if they voted for anyone else. Apparently, many black voters genuinely believed that machine politicians had accurate information about how each person voted and would use this information to punish those who did not vote as they were told. To counteract these beliefs, Hatcher volunteers initiated a whispering campaign in the black community designed to convince black voters of the confidentiality of their vote. The originator of this idea described how it operated.

I worked with the citizens in Nashville in 1960-1961. We were able to get the black people to realize that the time has come when you can't sell your vote for a drink. Then we saw there was opposition to that so we took another approach. If [X] comes to you with ten dollars for your vote, take it, because when you close the curtain nobody knows what you're going to do. We convinced the people that there was no way under God's sun that they would know how they voted. I proved it on machines to people. So if I gave you ten dollars, go ahead and vote for me. "Thank you, I'll do that." Take that ten dollars, go buy your child some shoes and then vote him out too.

This strategy enjoyed tremendous success, a fact that is heavily underscored by a personal experience the respondent quoted above had with one of his employees:

I had a lady working for me. She had been working for me for four years. I had been talking to her; she had been victimized for all these years. She had the belief that if she told a person she would vote for him, he could find out whether she did or didn't. That night—to show you how people were getting the message—in her precinct the precinct committeewoman came by passing out two dozen eggs for everyone who would vote her ticket. So Mrs. [X] took the two dozen eggs. She came to our house the next morning. She said "Mr. [X]. You know one thing. It's just recently I've gotten to the place where I can follow what you say." She said "you know this lady brought to my house these two dozen eggs and said vote my ticket." She said "I took those eggs, I had some for dinner last night and had some for breakfast this morning. But you know what? I'm not going to vote for her but I'm going to eat all her eggs." I said eat her eggs. That wave began to move over the community. Prior to that they had been fearful of doublecrossing the system. You don't doublecross the system, the system will get you. One area they came out passing five-dollar grocery certificates to shop at certain stores. They took those certificates. I said take them. Feed your family. Deceive that bastard like he's been deceiving you. Play his same game—he taught us. And we learned from him. He's been deceiving us since 1619. Deceive him —play his same game. Take everything he has to give you. Then go behind the machine and vote him out of there. They did it—and it was beautiful. Judge Kaplan said the people in Midtown were ungrateful. Took whatever there was to be given and voted against the people too. . . . I was really elated to hear that lady say that I took those eggs, ate some this morning, ate some last night. And she felt good that she was deceiving this guy who all these years had been deceiving her. A small retaliation, but it was a feeling she had never experienced before.

Hatcher volunteers were able to win over some black doubters by using a bit of homespun psychology. Essentially what they did was agree with these persons that Hatcher couldn't win. Then they went on to argue that what they really wanted to do this time was make a good showing so that even if Hatcher lost the power structure would have to recognize the effort. They told these blacks that they had everything to gain and nothing to lose by supporting Hatcher because they weren't getting anything under the incumbent administration but "crumbs from the table" anyway. The real purpose of this campaign, they were told, was to shake up the power structure by demonstrating the potential might of the black community thereby putting it on notice that if it did not become more responsive to black needs, it would be turned out when the next election period rolled around. As recalled by one respondent, the argument was phrased somewhat in these terms:

We don't think we can beat them this time. But at least we've got a spokesman in our community that the power structure's got to reckon with. So all we're saying is let's get out and give them a big showing. Let's get out and give them a big vote.

The objective of this strategy, of course, was to get black doubters to shift their attitudes from "he can't win, so I won't throw my vote away," to "he can't win but I'm going to support him just the same." Hatcher supporters knew that when they got black voters taking the latter position, his chances of actually winning would improve.

We figured if we got enough people saying that they didn't think he was going to win but they were going to vote for him, there wasn't any doubt in our mind, you know, that he would come out a winner. That's the way we did it.

If Hatcher was in fact going to win the mayoral primary, it was necessary not only that blacks already registered vote for him, but that a substantial number of additional black voters be added to the registration rolls. Voter registration therefore became one of the most critical functions of the street-level organization.[11] Before the registration of black voters could begin, the black community had to be thoroughly canvassed. For canvassing purposes leaders of the registration committee formulated a system that they hoped would allow them to locate every unregistered voter in the black community. Nightly instructions were given until every worker participating in registration knew every step in this procedure by heart. The procedure worked in the following manner. First a poll book was secured from the board of elections and canvassing cards made up for each name in the book. Block workers were then sent out into black precincts to canvass the areas according to the addresses on the cards. When a person included on the canvass card was located, his registration was verified and a record made of this fact on a note pad. Before leaving, this person would be asked to identify other persons in the building who did not live there during the last registration period or whom he knew not to be registered voters. If possible, these persons were contacted before the canvass worker left the building. In any case, a record was made of the persons identified. The worker would then move to the next house. If someone lived there other than the person listed on the canvass card, this meant that the person had moved in since the last registration. This person's name, registration status, and former place of residence were recorded on the pad. If the person who used to live there had died, the new occupant would probably know and a record was made of this fact. If he had not, an effort was made to find out where he had moved.

When a check had been made of all the addresses included on his canvass cards, the worker would have a complete record of how many people formerly lived in the area of the precinct he covered, how many people were still there, how many persons had moved to some other part of the city, how many persons were deceased, and how many possible ghost voters were in the area. Information collected by each worker was put on file in the central headquarters. When all of the canvassing information was fully analyzed it would then be possible to locate all living voters—both those who remained in their original precincts and those who had moved from say the tenth to the fifteenth precinct. Since the names of the dead were often voted in elections, it was also necessary to have accurate information on the identity and number of deceased persons. To validate data compiled by canvass workers of persons deceased, cards containing these names would be compared to records at the board of health. This comparison provided a fairly accurate estimate of the number and identity of deceased persons. If board of health records said 150 persons had passed away since the last election, then the central headquarters expected to have on file 150 cards saying deceased. This canvassing procedure allowed the registration committee to identify and locate practically every unregistered black voter, living or dead.

Identifying and locating unregistered black voters is one thing, registering them is quite another. Hatcher workers found when the formal registration period began that many black citizens were reluctant to admit that they were not registered to vote. Many were ashamed of the fact that they had been in the city all of their lives and had never registered to vote. This meant that Hatcher workers had to "figure out a way of getting them to register without insulting them." The solution they came up with was one in which the worker helped the unregistered voter to get around his embarrassment by putting himself in his place. In doing this he would make a statement similar to the following: "You know it's a funny thing, but I was [X] number of years old before I registered to vote. And when it came to my mind that I wasn't registered, I was so ashamed that I pretended for a long time that I was a voter." This would make the person loosen up and he would begin to talk. At this point the worker would ask the following question: "Say now, if the election was today (do you know the candidates running?—Yes) what choice would you pick for mayor?" If the person hesitated and said, "Well, I'd like to see Mr. Hatcher win," the worker knew he had someone that could be persuaded to register and vote for his candidate. He would then reply that the person could help Hatcher win if he followed his example and became prepared to help. "The only way you can help him is by being a registered voter. We've got transportation downstairs to take you to the registration station, will you come on down and register?" In most cases, the person agreed to come. One worker recalled that he used this technique to persuade one elderly black citizen who had been living in the city for forty-nine years to register to vote for the first time.

If an unregistered voter was not at home when a registration worker called, that card was brought back to the office to be put in a special file. Another attempt would be made a few days later to contact this person at his home. If this effort was successful and the person registered, the card would be taken out of the unregistered file and put in the registered file. If it was not, a worker would find out where he worked and what time he got off. It would then be his responsibility to be at the job site when this person got off, and to find someone to point out the unregistered voter to him when he came out. Upon locating the unregistered voter the Hatcher worker would identify himself and say "look, according to this information you live at this place or that place and you're not registered." If he agreed, he would be taken to register and then given a free ride home, or wherever else he wanted to go.

The door-to-door registration campaign was eventually broadened to include every nook and cranny of the black community. Some Hatcher workers spent hours in pool rooms and bars attempting to pick up additional registrants. Blacks in supermarkets, department stores, movie theatres, churches, virtually all public places received the same stock inquiry from Hatcher workers: "Are you registered to vote? No? Then come go with me." Black steelworkers were met at mill gates and told, "You've got to go register." Thousands of handbills were distributed informing black citizens that transportation to and from registration stations was available for those who needed it.

In general, a tremendous registration campaign was waged by Hatcher volunteers in the primary; and it enjoyed notable success. Between November 1966 and May 1967, 2,200 additional black voters were added to the registration rolls. These voters were registered, it should be noted, in spite of the concerted opposition of the Lake County Democratic machine. Machine officials used practically every possible means to discourage and hamper registration in the black community. For example, plans by the Hatcher organization to launch a roving caravan to register black voters at their homes, jobs, or on the street were sabotaged by County Clerk John Krupa who ruled that the door-to-door registration law did not permit precinct committeemen to register individuals who lived outside their precincts.[12] Additionally, Krupa denied a request by the Hatcher organization for the appointment of deputy registrars to work in black areas. Hatcher supporters forcefully argued that the need for deputy registrars in the black community was critical because of the stubborn refusal of precinct committeemen to register voters in areas where Hatcher supporters lived, but they achieved no success.

Calculated moves to obstruct registration were made by machine officials in other ways. For example, it had been customary for registration boards to be set up well in advance of the election. Threatened with possible defeat by the massive registration drive, the county organization refused to set up the boards until thirty days before the day of the election. When the boards were finally set up, their hours of operation were curtailed from what they had been in the past. In Crown Point, a slow-down procedure was instituted to discourage voters from remaining long enough to complete the registration process. Also, during the early canvassing period, efforts were made to deny Hatcher workers access to poll books to check against precinct canvasses. These obstructive methods were easily implemented since all of the people working as registrars were appointees of county Democratic officials.

At the grass-roots level, precinct committeemen intimidated welfare mothers with threats of having child support payments cut off if they registered to vote for Hatcher. Anyone having Hatcher literature in his home was subject to receive an ominous warning from his precinct committeemen.

> My precinct committeeman told me I couldn't work on the election board because my house was splattered with pictures of Mr. Hatcher. I told him just scratch my name because I would not remove his pictures out of my windows.

Hatcher volunteers surmounted these obstacles mainly through exuberance and determination. They simply refused to allow difficulties placed in their way by the machine to permanently impair their efforts to carry their campaign to the voters. Each new obstacle was thoroughly studied and strategies devised for going over or around it. As a result of the resourcefulness and determination of Hatcher workers, black voters who had never before participated in politics were reached and their voting strength registered in the primary election.

While some Hatcher workers were grappling with the black precinct organization over registration, others were contributing to the mobilization process by competing with members of the black establishment for the allegiance of rank-and-file black voters. The objective of this aspect of the campaign was to identify members of the black establishment actively involved in the Katz campaign as "Uncle Toms" who were selling out their race. One respondent explained how this was done:

> The mayor [Hatcher] never would have approved of this, but some of us would ride at night. And we knew where these guys would hang out. So we stationed certain ones at this spot, that spot, that spot, and that spot. When they came in, we'd challenge them. We pointed them out everywhere we met them. We challenged them everywhere, in crowds, in meetings, and other places we met them. We'd brand them as "Uncle Toms" who were detrimental to their own people.

These public challenges were designed to put black Katz supporters on the spot and needle them into taking actions that would diminish the luster of their image in the black community. "We got people to thinking and watching them. When we put them on the defense they started making irresponsible statements." In this way, Hatcher supporters were able to neutralize the obstructive potential of that prominent segment of the black community playing profoundly anti-Hatcher roles in the primary campaign.

This same component of the Hatcher organization also engaged in sporadic psychological and physical warfare with the entire machine appartus. It attempted to keep the opposition off balance by faking as if it was going to move in one direction and moving in another. These Hatcher workers tormented the Katz forces by reproducing literature distributed in the white community and circulating it in the black community to let blacks know how "Mayor Katz really felt about them." They blocked the distribution of Katz newspapers among blacks by picking the distributors up when they entered the black community and tailing them in cars until they left. "They knew we were from the Hatcher camp and they wouldn't dare let us catch them putting them out. So they couldn't do anything but ride." These tactics communicated to machine leaders that they would not be able to run roughshod over fearful black citizens in the same way they had done in the past.

We instilled such fear into the machine that they were afraid to bother too many of us. I'll say this. We didn't fear any mother's daughter or son. We knew we were not dealing with timid people. And an organization that sees it's losing is like a hungry man grabbing a loaf of bread. And we knew that. But we were not saints either. Mr. Hatcher didn't know that. I honestly believe he didn't know we weren't saints. We would have resorted to anything that they played; we would have played their same game. I think they knew that. They knew that this was a new black movement—that we were black and that we were not going to be cheated. They knew that we were going to resort to anything. The black man no longer fears death. Death is something the white man used to whip us with. "We'll kill you!" So what? I'm going to die here or Vietnam or some place. And that was the philosophy by which we went about our work. And I think the message was received.

In sum, Hatcher supporters believed that the machine—faced with a powerful threat from a militant black candidate—was willing to use any means necessary to win and that they should be prepared to counter provocative machine action with provocative action of their own. They also believed that in the rough and tumble world of Gary politics, this position was neither irrational nor irresponsible.

A major worry throughout the entire primary campaign was the securing of sufficient funds to support the myriad demands of effective campaigning. Successful black mobilization requires money for media space and time, literature distribution, transportation, and a thousand other small and large endeavors. Normal problems involved in raising campaign funds were compounded in Hatcher's case by his insistence that he would not make promises or commitments to anyone in return for campaign contributions. This policy, clearly set forth in campaign guidelines, severely handcuffed the finance committee in its efforts to obtain large pledges of financial support. A key member of this committee explained why this was so:

Large contributions so often depend upon promises. For a city to suddenly be asked to give without promises, a city where the average voter is not asked for money because the organizations don't need it, for the big businesses to be giving money without promises, this was a complete about-face for both the average person and for the people who had lots of money.

With large contributors unwilling to support the campaign effort, other approaches to fund raising had to be found. Since the campaign was to be one with a central grass-roots focus, an appeal was made to the community as a whole to support the campaign so that Hatcher could enter into office financially unencumbered. The idea behind this approach was a good one, but it met with limited success. "We found out that you can't get money to run a campaign by asking people to contribute nickels and dimes." The only other avenue open was that of sponsoring a variety of fund-raising affairs. Social groups such as Muigwithania were encouraged to sponsor dances and donate the proceeds to the Hatcher campaign. A group called Teachers for Enlightened Leadership, which was formed to assist in Hatcher's election, sponsored several cocktail parties to raise campaign funds. Other projects were sponsored by the campaign organization itself, including cocktail parties, and a testimonial dinner featuring Georgia State Representative Julian Bond.

Despite these efforts, campaign funds continued to fall far below what was needed to operate effectively. Toward the end of March the situation became desperate as workers in the field began to run out of bumper stickers, money for signs, and other campaign materials. An emergency meeting was called of the finance committee to consider possible strategies for raising additional funds. On the advice of Mrs. Doris Finkle, a decision was made to sponsor another cocktail party and to try to get Harry Belafonte to attend as guest of honor. Many originally thought the idea of trying to get Belafonte to come was outlandish because he was "too busy" and knew nothing about Hatcher and his campaign for mayor. Mrs. Finkle informed the group, however, that her youngest daughter attended a private school in Massachusetts with Belafonte's daughter and that she might be able to get his private telephone number from the school's headmaster. Obtaining the number from the school official, Mrs. Finkle succeeded in reaching Belafonte at his home and explained her purpose in calling. Belafonte was quite angry at first that his private number had been released; his anger soon subsided, however, and he informed Mrs. Finkle that he could not give her a definite answer to her request until he "checked" Hatcher out. Three days later Belafonte returned Mrs. Finkle's call informing her that he would not only come for the cocktail party, but would be happy to give a benefit concert afterwards.

Belafonte came, despite a trip to New York by machine representatives to encourage him not to become involved in the Gary campaign. The cocktail party was a tremendous success. Belafonte's pitch for campaign money was so strong that some persons who had intended to give $100 gave $200; almost everyone gave more than they had anticipated. More successful still was the evening concert. A sell-out crowd of four thousand persons packed Memorial Auditorium. Belafonte gave an inspired performance that lasted an hour and a half. A surprise guest of the night was heavyweight champion Muhammed Ali, who told the audience he came because he had heard that his good friend Harry Belafonte was there and because he heard that one of his black brothers was running for mayor. "So I had to come over to see what was happening." Entertainers Oscar Brown, Jr., and Jean Pace also performed during the evening.

The Belafonte concert was—from the perspective of the Hatcher movement—a pivotal turning point in the campaign. Enthusiasm by blacks for Hatcher's candidacy reached an all-time high during the Belafonte affair. Belafonte warmed the audience up with an appeal for black unity. When Hatcher walked on stage blacks shook the rafters. They cheered wildly as Belafonte assured them "he's working for your cause." Hatcher told the audience that his campaign was a people's movement, and predicted that primary election day would be remembered as the day plantation politics died in Gary, Indiana.

No longer shall we be stampeded to the polls like a bunch of cattle by a cynical, corrupt, bigoted political machine. Plantation politics is dead. The day the machine can come to us with a satchel full of stolen and extorted money and buy our vote is, thank God, over and gone.[13]

The enthusiasm stirred by the Belafonte concert continued to swell as Hatcher volunteers persisted in their grass-roots mobilizing work. A bandwagon effect began to set in as a wave of black nationalism swept across the city, centering around the man striving to become the first black mayor of a major northern city. Hatcher supporters were able to visibly observe large segments of the black community literally become politically alive for the first time, as masses of blacks, noting the enthusiasm of their brothers, began to finally realize that Hatcher did indeed have a superb chance of winning. One Hatcher worker vividly described the substantive dimensions of this transformation of the black community:

> People for the first time really began to see how important a vote was, that they could control a way of life, and that they could make or break a machine, and that they could actually control what they wanted in their own city. They could demand certain things themselves as people. I think that people never before realized this. They accepted the fact that voting time came, some people were elected, and they let it go at that. Some people had power. I think they felt there were those politicians in the area and they could go to them when problems came along and ask them to do things for their children. I think for the first time people realized if given the opportunity they didn't have to go to somebody to live as human beings, they could do it for themselves if they could possibly get an opportunity to live like everybody else.

The surge of black support for Hatcher became infectious, reaching into every quarter of the black community. Signs of a bandwagon effect were present everywhere. Pictures of Hatcher studded the windows and walls of black homes. Threats made by committeemen to have them removed began to backfire as blacks began to ask themselves: "Well, why is it they don't want me to put this man's picture in the window? Can he really do something for me? Is he really a threat?" People approached Hatcher volunteers begging to be registered and offering their services in his campaign. Indeed, so many people began to volunteer to work that this in itself became an organizational problem. Having nothing to do for many of the people who were standing around headquarters under foot, key Hatcher workers began to offer a pat reply to the question what can I do to help: "Go spread the gospel brother, go spread the gospel." And spread it they did. Katz supporters found themselves no longer able to get a hearing in the black community. Ministers who endorsed Katz from the pulpit were threatened with immediate dismissal. A person who inadvertently made a disparaging remark about

Hatcher in a bar ran the danger of getting cracked in the head with a bottle. Black political consciousness had developed full-blown in Gary, Indiana. The mood of the hour is sharply captured in these observations by a black politician who was himself running for public office at the time:

> The fever was in the air. You could feel it. If I walked from here to the alley even the average wino would ask me "where do you stand so far as Mr. Hatcher is concerned?" And I would say, I'm with Mr. Hatcher. "All right, I'll vote for you." You were either with Mr. Hatcher or against him. There was no in between. You couldn't say anything against Mr. Hatcher. If you went into an audience and made a speech for a white candidate, the audience would walk out on you. The incumbent mayor had very few people with guts enough to go into places and make a speech for him. The average black person could identify with Mr. Hatcher. The billboards all around you had pictures of Mr. Hatcher. Even the kids were taking balloons home, taking pencils home. Even my son asked me, "Dad, who do you think is going to be mayor?" I tried to out fox him. He was at the time eight years old. I said I don't know. Who do you think is going to be mayor and he said "I don't know but I hope Mr. Hatcher is." He could identify himself with the black man running for mayor. And if this was demonstrated in my household, I dare say in the household of every black man in the city of Gary, the teenagers, the minor kids were talking about voting for Mr. Hatcher, and so this had an indelible impression—it had to have had—on the parents. If they went out and voted for anyone else they would be a traitor to their race.

In summary, the Belafonte concert not only saved the Hatcher campaign financially, but gave it a tremendous psychological lift. It produced a show of solidarity and enthusiasm of such impressive proportions that even the most pessimistic blacks who wished Hatcher well became captivated by what they perceived as his greater prospects for victory. The Belafonte concert set off a wave of emotion that soared to higher and higher levels of intensity until it reached its dramatic climax on primary election day. Thus, in some sense, this event can be viewed as a triggering device setting into motion the final phases of a process of group emergence spanning over approximately a ten-year period.

Before leaving the city, Belafonte offered to give a follow-up concert for Hatcher during the general election. Hatcher wasted no time accepting his offer.

CAMPAIGN EFFORTS IN THE WHITE COMMUNITY

In striking contrast to the massive campaign effort mounted in the black community, only limited and superficial attempts were made to garner votes for Hatcher in the white community. This was due mainly to the feeling on the part of Hatcher strategists that a vigorous campaign to rally white votes in Hatcher's behalf would be a waste of time, because whites on the whole simply would not vote for a black candidate running on a strong black power platform. The statistical analysis of past elections prepared for the primary campaign by Hatcher researchers established to their satisfaction that every hour spent in the black community would yield much more rewarding results than an hour spent in the white community. Consequently, practically every aspect of the primary campaign was devoted to turning out the black vote because the black vote would unquestionably be the key to Hatcher's success in the campaign. With two white candidates in the race, it became highly probable that they would chop each other up sufficiently in the white community to nullify the possibility of either winning the election, provided the black community was mobilized sufficiently to produce a sizable and cohesive black vote behind Hatcher's candidacy.

This is not by any means to suggest that the white community was completely neglected. In fact, the Hatcher organization broke precedent with the campaign practices of black candidates running for major offices in previous elections by establishing a campaign headquarters in the first district. This facility operated under the general supervision of Arthur Lebo, a Miller resident and active member of the white group associated with the Hatcher campaign. The Miller headquarters was run almost as an independent agency in the campaign. It was established primarily as a symbolic sign to whites that Hatcher was interested in support from the total community, not just the black community and, if elected, would be not just a black mayor but a mayor for all the people. Since it was completely unreasonable to think Hatcher would get any votes at all out of Glen Park, no parallel facility was established in the sixth district.

The appeal for votes in the white community was directed almost exclusively by white members of the Hatcher campaign organization. Several house meetings for Hatcher were arranged by these persons, which allowed him to speak to from six to sixty residents of the Miller area. Literature was distributed in white neighborhoods by white campaign members with the assistance of students from the Gary branch of Indiana University. Various fund-raising drives among white citizens in Hatcher's behalf were also initiated by white Hatcher campaign workers. Three white members of the Hatcher organization put together a long and impressive campaign document entitled *Hatcher and the Progressive White Voter*, which, in addition to discussing general issues such as war, the need for federal funds, and the patronage system, offered a comparison of Katz's record as mayor with the reform platform on which Hatcher was running. The document concluded that Katz had been the best mayor in fifteen years but that his best was not enough. It argued that Hatcher on the other hand was honest, capable, supported by outstanding black citizens, and offered hopes for a new day to all Gary citizens.

These activities in the white community by white Hatcher supporters had only limited impact. In part this was due to their narrow range of effective influence in the white community. Much of their time was spent convicing their friends, many of whom had political views that would have inclined them to vote for Hatcher anyway, that Hatcher was the best of the available candidates. Virtually no efforts were made to do systematic grass-roots organizing in the white community because the motivation for such efforts was totally lacking. The impact of the electoral activities of white Hatcher supporters in the white community was also gravely blunted by intense white hostility. Scurrilous leaflets were circulated through the white community, which identified leading whites in the Hatcher campaign and labeled them communists. These whites were generally harassed with threatening phone calls, damage to their homes and other public property, hate mail, and so forth. Their children were also taunted by other children at school who often repeated remarks they had heard expressed by their parents. Similarly, students distributing literature for Hatcher in white areas were severely beaten on several occasions. The Hatcher headquarters in Miller was the target of frequent vandalism with windows being damaged by bricks and gun shots. If at one point in the campaign it became dangerous to make anti-Hatcher remarks in the black community, it was also equally dangerous to make favorable remarks about him in the white community.

Except for the Indiana Civil Liberties Union, no predominately white organization lent public support to Hatcher's campaign in the primary. Organized labor endorsed Katz and virtually all the trade union members active in the campaign—except for a small contingent of black union members—were active in Katz's behalf. A union committee headed by Louis Comer in the Hatcher organization made a concerted attempt to neutralize organized labor in the campaign but failed. The reaction of the *Post-Tribune* to Hatcher's candidacy ranged from hostility to camouflaged neutrality. Hatcher supporters complained of articles submitted to the paper being omitted or edited beyond recognition. They generally perceived coverage by the *Post-Tribune* of the campaign to be slanted, playing up violent incidents attributed to them but giving scant attention to those that could be placed at the door step of the supporters of other candidates.

Thus few inroads were made into the white community during the primary campaign. Hatcher was given only modest exposure in white neighborhoods, only a small number of general level appeals were made for the white vote, and literally no grass-roots action was mounted to rally the white electorate behind Hatcher's candidacy. There were some members of the Hatcher campaign organization who disagreed with this approach to the white community. They felt that at least a small percentage of the white vote would be needed in order to elect Hatcher and that it was not at all a certainty that Hatcher would get this white vote unless he actively campaigned for it. Some campaign workers suggested that a forceful campaign be directed toward younger whites who tended to be open-minded on racial questions and could be used to influence the voting behavior of their parents. But these views were given little consideration in light of the desperate need to channel all available campaign resources toward the mobilization of the black community.

Part of the Hatcher organization's strategic approach to the white community in the primary related to the establishment of a coalition between blacks and Latin Americans. It was felt that such a coalition would not only be important for the 1967 election but would be crucial for future elections since the Latin population was rapidly becoming a significant numerical proportion of the city's overall population. Consequently, the decision was made to make a conscious appeal for the Latin vote in the primary. The basic appeal was made by the candidate who attempted to present himself as sympathetic to the problems of all oppressed people in Gary. He made particular reference to the low socioeconomic position of Latins and contended on several occasions that they were just as much victims of economic and social discrimination as blacks. Hatcher promised when elected to provide channels of communication through which the concerns of Latins could be directly transmitted to major city officials and departments.

At the street level, Latins were encouraged to join in the door-to-door, grass-roots campaign, especially in the second and third districts where most Latins resided. The Hatcher campaign was taken directly to the Latin people through volunteer work. One enterprising volunteer rented a video tape recorder, a monitor and a camera, recruited Spanish-speaking people to perform as actors, and made a film demonstrating procedures for using voting machines. This film was then shown in about seven locations in the Latin community.

The campaign to stimulate Latin support for Hatcher in the primary was, by and large, a failure. Some Latins were recruited into the campaign organization, and they were able to make inroads into the Latin community that could not have been made by other volunteers. But generally speaking, Hatcher people were unable to establish a viable coalition between blacks and Latin Americans during the primary campaign. Several factors were probably responsible for this. First, work in the Latin community by Hatcher volunteers was greatly encumbered by the low visibility of independent Latin leadership. Latins with a citywide reputation for community involvement were, for the most part, tied in with the machine. Hatcher people were told that an independent Latin leadership corps was emerging, but they had no way of reaching it. One effort was made to cut through to this leadership corps, which took the form of a series of meetings with Latin trade union leaders, but it was basically unproductive. Second, Hatcher workers discovered during the campaign that the Latin community was badly divided between Mexicans and Puerto Ricans. Tension between these two groups arose from close residential proximity, competition for blue-collar jobs, and differences in traditions and culture. These tensions precluded the consolidation of the Latin community behind Hatcher's candidacy. Third, many Latins refused to work in the campaign on a volunteer basis. A few who demanded money were paid; but most were not because the organization could not afford to do so and because some volunteers objected to bringing Latins into the organization on a basis different from all other workers. Finally, the appeal to the Latin community was diluted by the crisis in identity faced by many Latins. This crisis stems from the fact that Latins are technically classified as caucasians, but are treated as such only when machine politicians are interested in obtaining their vote. "During election time the power structure would go to them and stress the point that they were white. And a lot of them believed it. But after they gave them their vote and they started acting white, the power structure would call their attention to it and say, what are you doing, you must think you're white?" Latins driven by a desire to be white, but frustrated because this was impossible to accomplish in fact, generally ignored Hatcher's appeal to their sense of group identity and his attempt to demonstrate a close parallel between their social situation and that of blacks.

The inability of the Hatcher organization to establish a coalition between blacks and Latin Americans was—from the point of view of Hatcher supporters—one of the most disappointing aspects of the primary campaign.

THE KATZ AND KONRADY CAMPAIGNS

Incumbent Mayor A. Martin Katz entered the 1967 primary race extremely optimistic about his chances for winning because he had expected to be involved in a one-on-one battle with Richard Hatcher. Katz figured to pick up strong support in the white community, because he would be the only rational alternative for white voters, as well as solid support in the black community, because of his reputation as a liberal on racial issues. The early announcement by Pruitt that he intended to run was the cause for initial alarm but Katz later became convinced that strong enough pressure could be brought to bear to force Pruitt's withdrawal in the interest of the party unity. Concern about his chances for winning did not emerge full-blown until Bernard Konrady filed for mayor and rebuffed all attempts to persuade him to withdraw. With Konrady and Hatcher in the race, Katz strategists calculated that he would need to poll 30 percent of the white vote and 40 percent of the black vote in order to win.

Katz anticipated that he would have difficulty obtaining a significant percentage of the white vote. Two factors laid behind this evaluation. First, he had alienated large segments of the white community by his liberal stand on issues affecting the black community. Whites were particularly distressed by Katz's strong support of the 1965 omnibus civil rights bill. Second, Bernard Konrady's brother, Emery, had run well in the white community in 1963, and it was quite likely that the same voters who voted for Emery would vote for Bernard. Further, Konrady provided disgruntled white voters dismayed by the machine's poor performance over the past four years an acceptable alternative to Katz in the mayor's race. The conclusion reached by Katz and his advisors was that they had a terrific job of rebuilding to do in the white community if they were going to get the percentage of white votes he needed to win.

On the other hand, Katz firmly believed that he would do well in the black community and identified the vote in Midtown as the central target of his campaign appeal. He believed that the very thing that made him unpopular in the white community—his record on civil rights—would garner for him from 40 to 50 percent of the black vote. Some persons interested in his election warned Katz that he should not underestimate Hatcher's tremendous popular appeal among black voters caught up in the rising tide of black nationalism across the country. One respondent recalled admonishing Katz in this regard in the following manner: "I said to him Marty, a new black man is going to be behind that voting booth, and when they are faced with the choice of supporting their own young, black, militant, aggressive leader, against a white machine politician, in view of rising anti-Semitism among blacks, who in the hell do you think they're going to vote for?" But Katz dismissed such warnings as unrealistic. He continued to insist that he would do well in the black community because he was entitled to black support. His pat response to contrary opinions, according to the respondent cited above, was "how can they [blacks] vote against me? After all, we passed the fair housing ordinance."

Katz's firm convictions that he would receive strong black support were reinforced by assurances he received from black precinct committeemen that their control over the black vote was as tight as ever, and that they would produce solid majorities for him all over the black community. They reminded Katz that they were professionals with a long history of success and suggested that it was inconceivable that a bunch of rag-tag amateurs could steal the votes of their constituents from under their noses. Similar assurances were offered by Katz's chief political advisor in the election, George Chacharis. Although many Katz supporters resented the prominent role Chacharis played in the campaign, because they felt that he was dishing out the "same old baloney" used to win elections in the past, Katz relied on Chacharis very heavily throughout the campaign. Katz considered Chacharis to be an asset in his campaign for three basic reasons: (1) he respected his political wisdom and judgment; (2) Katz controlled by himself only 40 percent of the precinct organizations, but with Chacharis behind him his control increased to 75 percent; and (3) Chacharis still wielded considerable influence with Lake County party leaders, including Leslie Pruitt, whose open support would add substantially to Katz's appeal in the white community.[14] But Chacharis was still committed to old-style machine politics and did not fully comprehend the changes that had taken place in the black community from the time he went to jail to the time he returned to the city. He advised Katz that if everything else failed, the black vote could surely be delivered by a huge expenditure of money in the black community during the week before the primary election.

Despite a strong personal appeal to black voters centering on his liberal civil rights record, and the full-fledged support of the black precinct organization, Katz's campaign never really got off the ground in the black community. Some blacks wavered between Katz and Hatcher during the early days of the campaign, but as the Hatcher movement began catching fire, support for Katz rapidly diminished. As the campaign in the black community wore on, it became more and more necessary for anyone attempting to sell Katz to black voters to proceed with extreme caution. Black committeemen found that when they visited black residences they had to go to considerable lengths to feel out the political persuasion of their constituents before mentioning Katz's name. A more direct approach only guaranteed that they would have a lot of doors slammed in their faces. Commenting on the attitude of black voters, a respondent very active in the Katz campaign remarked: "You just couldn't talk to them. 'Don't you remember he [Katz] was fighting for civil rights? He has a long history of being tolerant of the Negro.' It didn't work. Nothing worked. They were determined that one of their own would be mayor and you couldn't talk them out of it." Indeed, opposition to Katz became so intense in the black community that some black committeemen themselves took to passing out literature for Hatcher while carrying literature folders bearing the slogan "Keep Katz."

To compensate for Katz's deteriorating political position in the black community, the machine initiated a massive effort to buy the black vote. An incredible amount of money was pumped into the black community during the last few weeks of the campaign. Some respondents contended that during the last two weeks alone the machine dropped nearly $100,000 in the black community. This money was spent in various ways. Representatives of the machine invaded taverns and restaurants in the black district spreading large sums around—$500 to $1,000—imploring individuals to throw parties for Katz or undertake other kinds of political activity in his behalf. During the last five days of the campaign five women in every precinct were paid $60 apiece to make phone calls encouraging blacks to "Keep Katz." On election day black committeemen were authorized to hire twenty persons per precinct at $2 per hour to go door to door pulling out black voters and encouraging them to vote for Katz. To the amazement of top machine officials, in this election the black community took the money and still voted against Katz. One important county official who opposed plans to spend huge sums in the black community to get Katz elected commented bitterly:

They [Katz and Chacharis] overestimated the power of their money. They thought they could buy the votes in the Negro district. They couldn't. They took the money. But they took it from them the year before when they voted for Allen. He [Katz] did nothing to punish them. If they got away with it one time, they figured, well, we can do it again. They were relying on the money to do the job down there it had done in the past, but it couldn't be done because Hatcher was smart enough to know that he could raise the racial question down there and overcome the money. He [Katz] was influenced to follow this course by Chacharis who argued that you don't change something that's successful.

If Katz's political position in the black community was discouraging, it was downright dismal in the white community.

Katz originally intended to rely exclusively upon the white precinct organization to deliver the white community for him. However, a sizable proportion of that organization was committed to Pruitt in the primary. When Pruitt pulled out of the race, many of these committeemen decided to sit the primary out. Those who worked for Katz found themselves extremely handicapped by his unsavory reputation among white voters. White committeemen attempted to project the image of Katz as an honest, hard-working administrator who had improved the efficiency of essential city services, made impressive capital improvements, revitalized the various commercial centers around the city, and kept the lid on social tensions in the city. But white voters simply were not buying Katz on these terms. Many white residents refused to talk to committeemen campaigning for Katz. "You could go in peoples' homes and they would tell you get out, don't bother coming to talk to me." It was very difficult to get whites to come out to a Katz meeting. Indeed, many white voters appeared so incensed and confused that it was difficult to get them to participate in any capacity in the election. More and more Katz workers began to receive clear indications from white voters that they did not even intend to cast ballots in the primary. In this regard one Katz supporter observed:

> They [the white voters] were still angry with Katz. It was just a general feeling. When you asked them why they were angry no one could come up with any specific answer. . . . It got to the point that you knew they weren't going to come out. It wasn't the organization's fault because they worked. But you knew going through the precincts talking to people. You'd walk out and you'd say well that one is not going to vote. You just couldn't put your finger on the problem. "I'm just not going to vote." "Why?" "I just don't want to."

In the beginning when Katz workers came back with reports of white-voter hostility and apathy, they were instructed simply to go back and try harder. Once it became clear that no matter how hard they tried using the good government approach white voters could not be induced to vote for Katz, a new strategy for generating white support for Katz was employed. This strategy was designed to play upon the racial fears of whites by suggesting to them that a vote for Konrady would do no more than contribute to the election of Hatcher. Busloads of Katz workers during the final three weeks in the campaign scattered throughout the white community selling the proposition to white voters that a vote for Konrady was a wasted vote, so that if they wanted a white mayor they had no choice but to vote for Katz. They argued that Katz would receive a substantial number of black votes because of his civil rights record. Thus if white voters lined up solidly behind Katz they could assure themselves a white mayor for the next four years. The door-to-door Katz drive in the white community was supplemented by a telephone and mailing program. Ladies hired to handle the telephone operation were instructed to concentrate on the new campaign theme: a vote for Konrady is a vote for Hatcher. Small cards were mailed to practically every white home in the city. These cards cut right to the core of the new Katz appeal. They read, "Think, A vote for Konrady is a vote for Hatcher." These last minute maneuvers began to produce notable results. The white community began to come alive and to unify around Katz. Large numbers of white voters who formerly had been committed to Konrady shifted over to Katz during approximately the last ten days of the campaign when the main appeal of the Katz campaign was at its highest. But these efforts came too late to pull the election out of the fire for Katz. Some Katz supporters estimate that if the primary campaign had run just one week longer Katz could have drained enough of Konrady's white support off to win the election. Katz had been counting, however, on the black community to come through for him. By the time he realized that it was not going to do so and that he would need more white support than he originally anticipated, too much of the campaign period had elapsed for him to completely unify the white vote behind his candidacy.

Bernard Konrady entered the primary race (and remained in it) for two reasons. First, and foremost, he entered because he believed that he could win. This conviction was based on the premise that the major appeal of both Katz and Hatcher was in the black rather than the white community. This fact suggested that Katz and Hatcher would split the black vote, and each would run so poorly in the white community that he (Konrady) would have an excellent chance of polling enough of the white vote to win the election. Second, barring that outcome, Konrady believed that he could at least poll enough white votes to deny the election to Katz—this would be a secondary victory, since he was absolutely convinced that the machine had stolen the mayoral election from his brother in 1963.

Konrady based his campaign in the white community on a strong reform platform. One component of this platform involved a ringing indictment of corruption in city government and control of Gary politics by a cynical political machine. The platform also included an attack on Katz's record of performance as mayor. He accused Katz of shackling the police, thus allowing the rate of crime to soar, failing to build one public facility, increasing the tax rate while allowing city services to deteriorate, and proposing to build public housing in Glen Park and Miller for his own financial gain and that of his associates.[15] Konrady also stressed Katz's tie up with the machine, charging him with bringing into his political family "the most outrageous plunderers of public property including Gary's own Billy Sol Estes [Chacharis], who is masterminding the mayor's campaign of vice and crime and who hopes to regain the seat of trust which he so disgraced."[16] In his various campaign speeches Konrady outlined a program of reform that he contended would clean up the city physically, rid the city of ghost payrollers, check the rise in the tax rate, improve city services, halt the wasteful expenditure of city funds on projects of limited value to the city's progress and safety, and crack down on all forms of crime and vice in the city.

Konrady viewed Katz as vulnerable on all of these issues, and directed his campaign to those white voters who were most concerned about high taxes and political corruption in city government. One Konrady supporter underscored this assessment of Katz's political posture in the white community:

> I couldn't possibly see any white voters, voting for Katz. This was sin city; vice was running rampant, mothers were getting aggravated; crime was coming in all over. Anything could be bought. The police could be bought. I just couldn't see how Katz could get anywhere near the white vote he got.

Throughout most of the campaign, Konrady was clearly the frontrunner in the white community. However, Katz effectively cut the ground from under Konrady's campaign in the white community with his profoundly racial appeal for white support in the final weeks of the primary race. To Konrady's credit, he refused to counter Katz's racial appeal with one of his own. Some of his supporters advised him to accuse Katz of "trying to make Gary into a black town," but he resisted, asserting that he was confident he could maintain white support without playing that kind of racial game.

THE HATCHER CAMPAIGN ORGANIZATION ON ELECTION DAY

Election day activities of the Hatcher campaign organization centered around the production of a large voter turnout in the black community and protection of the Hatcher vote. Both of these goals were considered to be pivotal to Hatcher's primary victory. It went without saying that Hatcher could not win if a substantial percentage of the eligible black electorate did not turn out to vote. The task of turning out a heavy black vote was assigned primarily to the same street-level organization that had operated so effectively during the registration drive. It was given a powerful assist by Indiana University students and members of the Independent Voters League of Illinois. Block workers fanned out across the black community going from door to door encouraging people to vote. Transportation was provided to and from the polls, and babysitting services were made available upon request. This phase of the campaign reached near massive proportions with as many as two thousand people tagged with buttons and cards that clearly identified them as Hatcher workers beating the bushes of the black community—including pool halls and bars— and pulling out every possible black voter registered to participate in the election.

At the same time this army of volunteers was working to produce a heavy black turnout, other Hatcher people were involved in efforts to minimize the incidence of fraudulent voting. Protection of the vote on election day had become a major preoccupation of the Hatcher organization during the final weeks of the campaign as persistent rumors filtered into campaign headquarters regarding a bold attempt by the machine to steal the election. The credibility of those reports was supported by canvass statistics compiled by the Hatcher organization, which showed that in black precincts the registration poll books listed the names of 5,200 persons who were no longer precinct residents. This meant that if repeaters were paid to vote these ineligible names, Hatcher would begin the election 8,000 to 9,000 votes behind. Hatcher campaign officials, based on this information, and their experiences in the Dozier Allen campaign, were determined not to leave any bases uncovered in their effort to assure a reasonably honest vote in the primary election.

One of the crucial lessons learned by members of Muigwithania during their several forays in electoral politics was that a black independent candidate could not get a fair count on election day unless he recruited and trained an effective group of election-day poll watchers. Accordingly, two months before the primary, a program was begun to train some Hatcher volunteers to be poll watchers on election day. Responsibility for this poll-watching operation was placed in the capable hands of Mr. L. T. Allison who developed an in-service training program for persons volunteering to serve in this capacity. These poll-watcher trainees were given instructions in what to look for at polling stations, how they should proceed if they witnessed illegal voting activity, and how to circumvent pitfalls that would be placed in their way by the machine. With respect to the latter, they were given detailed instructions on the formal and informal rules of the political game.

> What does the law say you can do? Then what does the system say you can do? These are two different things. So we had to prepare them for what the law said they could and could not do, and what the system said they could and could not do. The most detrimental of them all is the system.

In addition to the poll-watching program, several other programs were instituted to safeguard the vote in black precincts. For example, some Hatcher workers were trained as voting-machine mechanics. The organization was able to get the Hatcher volunteers approved by the county as official election mechanics. Anticipating trouble, Hatcher workers surveyed the situation in black precincts the night before the election and isolated the precincts likely to have machines that would break down "automatically." Early the next morning machine mechanics working for Hatcher visited these precincts without being called in order to be on hand before the emergency occurred. Nevertheless, Hatcher headquarters still received a barrage of phone calls from angry black voters saying that they had gotten up at 6:00 A.M. to vote, had been standing in line for two hours, were running late for work, but still had not voted because the machines in their precincts were "out of order."

In order to discourage as much vote juggling by precinct committeemen as possible, a rumor was spread by some members of the Hatcher camp that the FBI would be keeping close watch over voting activities in black neighborhoods. On election day a group of Hatcher people rented several large black cars, dressed up in dark suits and large hats pulled down over their foreheads, and went from one precinct to the next in black areas standing completely silent, jotting down comments in note pads. They never identified themselves as law officers, but many election officials jumped to the immediate conclusion that they were. One person who participated in these activities recalled, "I could hear whispers of FBI, FBI, as we went along. They didn't know whether to throw us out or what. We felt that maybe this kind of thing may have stopped a few people from doing what they were going to do. And we tried to hit as many precincts as possible; we just went round and round all day long until the whole thing was over, then dragged ourselves to headquarters to find out what happened."

An effective lawyer's organization was also formed to assist in election day activities. Some of these lawyers concerned themselves with mapping out plans for legal action in case the machine succeeded in stealing the election. Others operated out of central headquarters and were on call to investigate complaints by poll watchers of illegal voting practices. Communications equipment was installed in private automobiles so that top campaign leaders or lawyers could ride by precincts and inquire about the status of things from workers on duty inside. Poll watchers had strict instructions to contact these roving vehicles, headquarters, a local radio station, and the *Post-Tribune* if they witnessed irregularities or were subjected to intimidation. A few poll watchers reported during the day being told that they could not work inside the polling place, and of being jostled around by precinct officials; but most encountered little difficulty because the Hatcher camp had made it understood well in advance of the election that it did not intend to be cheated out of this election. The nature of this understanding was best described by this respondent:

> The word had gotten around, you're not going to come in my precinct and steal. No you weren't going to do that. Now you steal over my dead body. All they had to do was get fifty votes in each area

and we were dead. You're just going to go in there and do that, and I'm going to stand there like I used to do—we weren't doing that. And we were going to resort to anything to prevent it—and we did.

One of the most important responsibilities of persons serving as poll watchers on election day was that of keeping track of the vote and periodically phoning the vote on their precinct machines in to campaign headquarters. At the end of the day they were instructed to remain inside the polling place until the machines were locked up and to make absolutely sure that they had a record of the final tally on each machine. They were then to call that tally in, before bringing it in. These precautions were considered essential because it was believed that in the past the machine had made it standard practice to tamper with machine tallies after precinct polling stations had officially closed.

We wanted to have an accurate tally so that if the machine had a certain amount of votes on it when it closed, and was locked up, if it leaves here and goes to California and back, it's supposed to have the same number of votes on it. This is what we learned in the township assessor's race: we didn't have the count on every machine.

The surveillance of the primary vote by Hatcher workers did not end with the collection of final machine tallies. Hatcher officials had been informed by a man who had taught the opposition how to steal votes that often drastic changes in the final vote were made in city hall before figures were taken to the tally room for processing. He told them that this was customarily done in one of two ways. One way was for the election inspector to drive into the city hall garage and exchange tally sheets with another person before taking the final count to the tally room. The other method involved taking the city hall elevator to the fourth floor, exchanging tally sheets with someone waiting there, and then riding back down to turn in a false sheet on the second floor. In the light of this information, the decision was made to station a Hatcher worker at every possible point where a change of tally sheets could be made. Security forces from the Hatcher camp were ready to roll the moment the voting inspector received his call to come to city hall. They trailed him all the way to the downtown destination. Other Hatcher workers were waiting to follow him into city hall and to stay with him until he deposited the tally with downtown election officials. One Hatcher worker assessed the effectiveness of this strategy for protecting the vote: "It worked in the sense that they had to find another way of stealing, they couldn't use that one on us." Respondents who worked actively for Hatcher in the primary were absolutely convinced that despite their extraordinary precautionary measures, some of the votes cast for Hatcher were still stolen. They quickly pointed out, however, that these measures were effective enough to prevent the machine from stealing the number of votes that it needed to win.

> That was our main goal. If we can keep them from stealing enough then we can win. It was just enough with the right type of enforcement to keep them from taking it. A man can steal, but if he steals too much you're going to notice it as soon as you walk in the house. So you can make everything so tight that they can't steal as much as they want without going to the penitentiary. And this was all a part of the strategy that was worked on.

THE PRIMARY RESULTS

On the day of the primary election the mayoral race was considered by most knowledgeable observers to be a toss up, with the three major candidates running within 1,000 votes of each other. This analysis during the early stages of the balloting appeared to be at least partially correct. Although Konrady failed to run as strongly as predicted, Hatcher and Katz traded the lead up to about halfway in the vote count. At that point Hatcher pulled ahead and maintained a steadily growing margin. Final election returns officially confirmed a narrow victory for Hatcher with 39 percent of the vote. Katz ran second with 35 percent, and Konrady third with 26 percent. The results of the primary election by districts are presented in table 13.

TABLE 13

GARY DEMOCRATIC MAYORAL PRIMARY ELECTION, 1967

District	Hatcher	Konrady	Katz
First	446	3,176	3,946
Second	1,260	2,847	2,809
Third	6,988	1,114	2,194
Fourth	5,496	294	2,554
Fifth	5,817	245	2,008
Sixth	265	5,455	4,399
Total	20,272	13,133	17,910

SOURCE: Board of Election voting returns.

An examination of primary election returns suggests that several factors were chiefly responsible for Hatcher's primary victory. One factor was the almost equal division of the white vote between Katz and Konrady. This division of the white vote virtually destroyed Konrady's chances of winning. Konrady had pinned his election on the polling of approximately 80 percent of the white vote; however, he fell short of reaching this objective in both the predominately white districts. He carried the sixth district, Glen Park, where white antagonism to Katz was the highest, but did so by receiving only 62 percent of the vote. In the first district, the Miller area, Konrady was defeated by Katz who polled 52 percent of the vote to his 42 percent. Overall, Konrady received 46 percent of the white vote while Katz received 47 percent.

That Katz would more than break even with Konrady in the white community was not predicted by even the most seasoned observers of Gary politics. Respondents commenting on this subject agreed that Katz picked up the bulk of his support in the white community during the last ten days of the primary campaign. This was the period when George Chacharis began to furiously pull strings in Glen Park in order to divert votes in that area from Konrady to Katz. More importantly, it was the period in which Katz sought with success to convince white voters that Konrady was a splinter candidate whose presence in the race would possibly deny them a white mayor.

A second variable greatly influencing the outcome of the primary race was Katz's inability to prevent a substantial proportion of the black community from defecting to the Hatcher camp. As we have seen, a very forceful effort was made by Katz and his machine backers to perpetuate their powerful control over the black vote. They realized too late, however, that it could not be done. That this was so is not at all surprising, because the fundamental continuous pattern coloring Katz's relationship with the black community was the tendency on the part of his administration to offer blacks too little, too late. Katz's most outstanding failing was his inability to recognize that blacks in Gary had come to the point that they would no longer be satisfied with anything less than substantial, meaningful change. He continued to harbor the mistaken notion that token appointments and the passage of symbolic social legislation would be enough to keep blacks from voting solidly for city-hall candidates. His big handicap was not that he did not try to respond to the urgent needs of the black community, but that he came too late with each of his offers. Katz began his administration by calling on blacks for advice; at that point blacks were already beyond the advice-giving stage and were seeking to share in the decision-making process. By the time Katz was ready to allow them to join in decision-making, blacks did not want that anymore, they wanted to make the total decision. Each time black aspirations and white leadership were miles apart. Consequently, although he did not realize it, Katz started the campaign behind in the black community because black aspirations had far outstripped what he was personally willing to concede at the time. Running against only white opponents, or a black opponent that did not symbolize black aspirations, as did Hatcher, there is no question but that Katz would have been unbeatable in the black community. Faced with a choice of electing one of their own, or a white incumbent who symbolized the continuance of white power and white control in a city having a black majority, many black citizens ultimately decided in favor of the former rather than the latter. Hoping to receive a minimum of 40 percent of the black vote, Katz, relying on the entire stock of machine resources including money and the ability to manipulate the rules of the electoral process, was able to poll only 24 percent of the black vote. Because of his weak political influence in other segments of the electorate, this relatively poor performance in the black community made Katz's defeat a foregone conclusion.

Katz thus emerged in the 1967 primary as a man caught in the middle between the quest by blacks for real power, and the profound resistance of whites to black social, economic, and political aspirations. The critical fact of the matter was that by 1967 racial polarization in Gary had become too severe to be adequately managed by a mayor committed to a middle course.

Most important of all in determining the outcome of the 1967 primary election was the very capable job of making the black community aware of its political potential and mobilizing it for effective political action that had been performed by the Hatcher campaign organization. Much of the success achieved by the Hatcher campaign organization in the primary is attributable to the fact that, despite its amateur and volunteer character, its electoral work was well coordinated and organized. As we have seen, committees were established to carry out the multiplicity of tasks necessary for the mounting of a successful campaign. Coordination of the work of committees was directed through the executive board, the campaign coordinator, and the assistant campaign coordinator. This coordination was carried out through general guidelines establishing a chain of command each worker was supposed to follow, and an elaborate system of reporting was instituted that provided top decision-makers with up-to-date information about the general success—or lack of it—of the campaign apparatus in achieving its objectives during each stage of the campaign.

Many problems of coordination were eliminated by the tremendous cooperative spirit of the volunteer workers. Esprit de corps among Hatcher workers was stimulated mainly by the deep commitment each volunteer brought to the cause of electing Hatcher as Gary's first black mayor. The vision of Hatcher's reign over the city's elaborate governmental structure operated to weld the primary organization into a tightly knit group and contributed to the success it enjoyed in performing the functions necessary for the political arousal of the black community.

The faulty impression should not be left, however, that the Hatcher organization at all times operated smoothly and efficiently. Members of the organization were amateurs, and they made all the mistakes of amateurs; or as one respondent put it: "Let's say we were neophytes. We made all the mistakes a successful team can make." Problems of confused scheduling, improper use of personnel, failure to check up on their assigned specific duties all wrought havoc with consistent and smooth operation. As in the case of the Stokes organization, the Hatcher organization encountered difficulties and disagreements over policies. One major dispute involving disagreements over policy and a basic clash between two key personalities nearly ripped the organization apart.

It is important to stress, however, that none of the host of organizational problems experienced substantially hampered, except for brief periods of time, the efforts by Hatcher supporters to mobilize the black community. The constant realization that they were participating in an historic event, coupled with their strong belief in the merits of their candidate, imbued Hatcher volunteers with dedication and enthusiasm that more than compensated for the mistakes and internal conflicts that arose. As one Hatcher worker succinctly put it: "The lack of smoothness was made up for by the enthusiasm of the volunteer workers, the widespread popular appeal of the candidate, and the fun of being black." No better indication of the dedication of Hatcher's volunteer group can be found than the personal statement of these workers that they spent an average of eight hours a day, aside from their regular employment, working in his campaign. A significant number claimed to have worked as many as eighteen hours a day. Most indicated that they relinquished all other outside activity to work in the campaign. Many also neglected their families, some their jobs, and a few even their health in their untiring efforts to elect Hatcher to the mayorship. The almost unbelievable enthusiasm and dedication that Hatcher's candidacy generated was described in very graphic terms by a Hatcher district leader:

> That headquarters got to be another home. People just came out and stayed. From 9 to 11, 8 to 11. Whenever this man would enter the headquarters it was just something that people felt. To me he gathers a type of feeling that can be compared to the Kennedys. You know there is a thing that goes with them. I don't know what it is, it is a thing that people built up so far as they were concerned. And to me it seems that Hatcher gathers this same type of feeling. It was just something to see. Men would work all day. They would come to headquarters to get their materials to go out and put up posters all over the city. It made no difference whether it rained. They'd stay up to 11, 12, 1, 2 o'clock in the morning, go home and go to work, and come back the next day and do the same thing. There wasn't any question of you do it, I don't want to do it; it was just something that people automatically did.

Herein lies the key to Hatcher's primary victory: his success in drawing around him a host of volunteer workers interested only in his election. These were the people who, although faced with what sometimes seemed insurmountable obstacles, continued to work endless hours, in everyway they knew how, to sell their candidate and his program to thousands of black voters. Without these devoted, industrious volunteers, Hatcher could not have been a serious candidate.

The tremendous success enjoyed by the mobilization effort in the black community is reflected both in the size and cohesiveness of the black vote in the primary election. Black turnout in the primary was an all time high. Approximately 61 percent of the eligible black electorate participated in this election. The Hatcher campaign organization was so successful in stimulating black turnout, in fact, that although white registration was higher than black registration, in excess of 3,000 more black voters cast ballots in the election than white voters. Only about 50 percent of the eligible white electorate participated in the primary election.

Blacks not only voted in heavy numbers, but they voted overwhelmingly for Hatcher. The Hatcher campaign organization beat the machine impressively in all three of the predominately black districts. Although he did not come close to carrying the mixed second district, Hatcher received an overwhelming majority of the votes in the four black precincts located in that district. In total, Hatcher received approximately 70 percent of the black vote. Given the very firm control over the black vote exercised by the machine in past mayoral primaries, the delivery of this cohesive black vote in support of Hatcher's candidacy can be properly viewed only as an incredible display of political mobilizing ability by Hatcher and his dedicated group of amateur volunteers.

1. This quotation and following unattributed quotations are derived from interviews conducted in Gary, Indiana, by the authors.

2. Interview with Richard G. Hatcher, 7 January 1969.

3. The authors wish to express their deep appreciation to Mr. Burton Wechsler, former professor of law at Valparaiso University, for making available the data on background elections discussed in this chapter.

4. The total area of the election included not only Gary but eleven white precincts in Griffith Township. As expected, few votes cast in Griffith Township were cast for Allen.

5. It is significant to note that these whites were not only homogeneous in their socioeconomic background, but also in their political and ideological leanings. When they voted, they almost always voted Democratic. However, none of them considered themselves as strong Democratic party identifiers. Rather, they viewed themselves at best as independent Democrats; some considered themselves to be radicals with no affiliation or identification with traditional political institutions. Indeed, a few had histories of radicalism dating back to the labor movement in the 1930s and the Wallace progressive movement in the late 1940s. One of them had served as the Lake County director of the Wallace campaign in 1948. During the 1960s, they were actively involved in the peace movement and draft counseling.

6. On the subject of black power as a motivation for white participation in the Hatcher campaign, another white Hatcher worker observed: "I think that Hatcher represents a form of (though not necessarily the only form) black power that is important. It seems to me that black power is an essential stage in the development of a decent America. It seems to me that the nation has not had a greater problem in its history than its relationship with the black community. No matter whatever else one may say about the democratic promise and the democratic process, it has always been compromised by the fact of slavery and segregation. . . . It seems to me incumbent on white Americans who are concerned with restructuring America to support black power movements whenever reasonable and feasible because I think it is such an important and necessary phase. And it seems to me that the Hatcher movement, less so than Hatcher himself, is one aspect of the stage—and a very important one. In a city like Gary with a majority black population, it seems not only right but absolutely necessary that when black leadership arises, as Richard certainly is, it ought to take the helm and give the black community a sense of pride and ability to govern."

7. These figures on registration are from Wechsler.

8. *Gary Post-Tribune*, 2 February 1967.

9. Evidence of machine efforts to buy Konrady out of the mayor's contest first came to light in a statement by Konrady to the *Post-Tribune* on 19 March 1967. In view of Konrady's intransigence, party leaders decided that Pruitt's candidacy would only serve to split the white vote and assure Hatcher a free ride in the black community. Consequently, they persuaded Pruitt to retire from the race in favor of Katz who stood a better chance of competing with Hatcher for the black vote.

10. For example, one area leader conducted a telephone survey, calling twenty-five people a day and asking them to support Hatcher's campaign to become mayor of Gary.

11. In Gary, any citizen 21 years old or older who meets state and precinct residence requirements (one year and three months, respectively) was eligible to register to vote in 1967. The central location for registration in the Gary area is the Lake County Board of Elections in Crown Point, about fifteen miles from downtown Gary. To reduce the inconvenience entailed in a trip to Crown Point for registration purposes, several centrally located registration stations are typically established within the corporate boundaries of the city.

12. This ruling by Krupa prevailed despite the fact that one Hatcher worker investigated the law and found that it contained no such limitation.

13. *Gary Post-Tribune*, 17 April 1967.

14. Chacharis was ultimately successful in persuading Pruitt to openly endorse Katz in the primary. However, Pruitt did not work actively for Katz.

15. See, for example, *Gary Post-Tribune*, 13 March 1967.

16. Ibid.

8

Gary: The 1967 General Election

The primary election was followed by a two-month hiatus in the work of the Hatcher campaign organization. During the summer most of those who had been key Hatcher workers in the spring found it extremely difficult to become psychologically aroused about the general election campaign. At this point practically everyone in the Hatcher camp was of the opinion that his election in the fall would be a shoo-in. Foremost in their minds was the fact that Gary was a Democratic stronghold. It had been over twenty-five years since a Republican had seriously competed in the general election for mayor. The major battle had, for as long as most could remember, been fought in the Democratic primary. When the Democratic primary decided the party's mayoral candidate, Lake County Democrats had invariably come together to administer a thorough shellacking to the sacrificial candidate nominated by a moribund local Republican party.

Expectations by Hatcher workers that he would coast to an easy victory in the fall were enhanced by their assessment of the political stature of his Republican opponent. The Republicans had nominated in the May primary Joseph Radigan, a forty-seven-year-old Gary furniture dealer. Radigan was in every sense of the word a political dilettante, having had no prior experience in electoral politics. Hatcher supporters believed that Radigan had neither the organizational support nor the flair for political campaigning capable of allowing him to seriously challenge their candidate for the mayorship. Radigan had shown himself in the primary to be a dull, and lifeless political personality. His speeches were dry, he appeared uncomfortable in large crowds, and he encountered great difficulty speaking extemporaneously. Radigan's advisors attempted to protect him from his faults as a political campaigner by holding as few large rallies as possible and by limiting his press conferences largely to prepared statements with little time for question and answers. Generally, Radigan presented an image that contrasted sharply with the charisma and dynamism projected by Hatcher. Further, although he came from a distinguished family, in political circles he was an unknown personality. One could only judge Radigan's fitness for mayorship on the basis of his reputation as a businessman, and his business experience could not be easily transferred to the qualities needed to run a multimillion-dollar city governmental operation. Hatcher had proven himself as a politician and governmental official while serving on the city council. For all of these reasons, Hatcher supporters found it irrational to imagine that Radigan, laden with all of these disadvantages, could break the three decades of uninterrupted control by the Democratic party over city government.

On the whole, an aura of confidence pervaded the Hatcher camp. This confidence was reflected in the modest and relatively uncomplicated campaign strategy worked out for the general election during the summer lull. Hatcher strategists were impressed with the solid support shown by the black community in the primary. They felt that because Hatcher was black, because he was a Democrat, and because he had proven he could win, with a moderate amount of work on the part of the volunteers, the political base in the black community could be firmly maintained. But with only one white candidate in the race, and black registration falling below white registration, 100 percent support from the black community would not be enough to win the election. Thus much of the work in the general campaign had to be directed toward making substantial inroads into the white community. It was believed that several approaches to the white community had to be taken. First, whites working in the campaign organization would use their influence to deliver a large proportion of the white vote for Hatcher in the fall. Second, Hatcher would devote a much greater share of his own campaign energies to the task of personally selling himself to whites fearful that a black mayor would not be sensitive to their needs and aspirations. Third, as the chief Democratic standard bearer, Hatcher would call upon the regular Democratic organization to bury animosities spawned during the primary and join with his volunteers in attempting to prevent a massive crossover of white voters to the Republican candidate. Token help from the regular Democratic organization in holding the white vote would be sufficient to guarantee that Hatcher would receive at the very least 30 percent of that vote, which would be more than enough for victory, assuming near unanimous support for him in the black community.

In short, expansion of Hatcher's support among white voters was viewed by Hatcher advisors as a pivotal key to his success in the general election. The shaping of the general campaign along these lines began almost immediately after the primary election. For example, in his first press conference following his mayoral nomination, Hatcher directed practically the whole of his remarks to a not too subtle appeal for the white vote. Hatcher informed the assembled newsmen that in the fall he intended to carry his campaign to every part of the city. He expressed confidence that Gary was made up of a preponderant number of decent citizens who would vote for the person they thought was best qualified to face the problems confronting the city not on the basis of race. Speaking exclusively for the benefit of suspicious whites, Hatcher made a special point to note that his administration, when assembled, would be both multiracial and multireligious.[1] Indicative, too, of the necessity of an effective appeal to the white community was the change of the campaign theme from "Progress Today, Not Promises Tomorrow," to "Let's Get Ourselves Together." The latter theme signified the need for blacks and whites to join together on a number of fronts, including politics, to build a better city.

The calm, self-assured character of the Hatcher campaign organization began to dissipate when it became apparent during the month of August that this time the political battle in the general campaign would be as rigorous as the primary in the spring. What made this general campaign significantly different from those in the recent past was the refusal on the part of the regular Democratic organization to back the Democratic mayoral nominee.

Not only was there mounting evidence that Hatcher would not receive the support of the regular organization, but it was also becoming crystal clear that a significant proportion of the regular organization was preparing to line up behind the white Republican candidate. These maneuvers meant that the worst fears of the most cynical of Hatcher's supporters were now being realized: the general election was being transformed from an interparty fight to an intraparty fight with the salient issue around which the intraparty battle would be waged being race. In other words, the regular organization was mobilizing to stir up a white backlash vote in order to defeat the party's black mayoral nominee.

This development constituted, from the perspective of the Hatcher camp, a totally unexpected turn in the campaign. When Hatcher first won the primary, party leaders gave strong indications they intended to support Hatcher in the same way they had mayoral nominees in the past. For example, on 4 May, County Chairman John Krupa scotched rumors that the regular organization would field an independent ticket in the fall election. Rather he said that he intended to get together with Hatcher to work out arrangements for the support and assistance of the party central committee in his fall campaign.[2] The political picture did not begin to change until several months later when Hatcher and Krupa failed to come to terms on the conditions under which regular organization support would be offered and accepted. As closely as it can be reconstructed, what happened at the meeting between Hatcher and Krupa was this. Hatcher asked Krupa to pledge party funds and political support to him, unincumbered by promises of regular organization influence in his administration. Krupa replied that he could only commit party funds and political instruments to Hatcher if he agreed to allow the county organization to have a hand in the selection of his major cabinet appointments and patronage workers in the city bureaucracy. Hatcher refused, saying that he would rather lose than have the members of his administration picked primarily by the county organization. "Too many people have worked too hard in this. I'm not going to abdicate my responsibilities or sell them out."[3]

Hatcher's firm rebuff of Krupa's request for guarantees of regular organization influence in his administration precipitated a groundswell of opposition to his candidacy by the leaders of the organization, and it spread in concentric fashion until it reached into every white Democratic precinct organization in Lake County. White members of the regular organization began openly expressing strong reservations about Hatcher's party loyalty. The most commonly heard opinion was that he was too independent —that he felt he did not need the party and refused to abide by well-established party policies. Others went further to suggest that his real intention was to destroy the party and turn Gary into a bastion of black power. The floodtide of party opposition to Hatcher was formally opened when County Chairman Krupa blasted Hatcher's nomination in the press as a disaster for the party and for Gary as a city because he was the captive of radical left-wingers who had worked actively in his campaign organization in the spring. Krupa hinted that these left-wingers espoused views and supported causes that were blatantly un-American. He said that in any case that he could not, as party chairman, make available to Hatcher the resources of the regular Democratic organization until he disavowed the superliberals associated with him.

Shaken by the position taken by the regular organization, Hatcher went before a meeting of Lake County Democratic party officials to plead for party help in his campaign. In his speech, he vehemently denied that anyone who supported him in the primary harbored un-American attitudes or was guilty of engaging in un-American acts. He called upon the organization to support him in the same way it would have supported Katz or Konrady if either of them had been victorious in the primary. He reiterated specifically his request for the organization's financial help, and for its political support, and warned that if these were not forthcoming everyone would know the reason would be because he was black.

> This campaign needs the political support of the regular Democratic organization, just as every other campaign has needed that support. If the support is not forthcoming everybody will know the reason for the letdown no matter what public statements are made.[4]

Hatcher concluded his speech with a plea for party unity, asserting that he was desirous of finding ways of working with the regular Democratic organization so that a joint effort involving all sincere Democrats could be undertaken to bring a better way of life for all citizens of Lake County.

It was a good performance, but totally fruitless. The die had already been cast; party officials had no intention of helping to elect a man who threatened to topple their political and financial empires. Hatcher's election would mean not only the loss of the machine's political base in the black community, but also control over the various key positions in the city administration that affected the flow of millions of dollars into the party's warchest. Hatcher's race was only of secondary importance to the regular organization's opposition. Although party leaders would have preferred to see a white man as mayor, they would have accepted a black man willing to bargain with them for control over the power resources of the city. Hatcher was black; but more importantly he was a political independent running on an avowedly reform platform. Undoubtedly the latter factor was the one that in the final analysis rendered Hatcher personna non grata to party bosses. Most of the respondents interviewed, including the candidate himself, testified to the validity of the above interpretation of regular organization officials' motives in denying Hatcher the party's financial and political support.

> There is no reason why my party should not have supported me after I won the primary. They claimed that I refused to talk to them and that's why they didn't support me. The real reason why they didn't support me was that I was black. But most of them could have eventually accommodated themselves to that fact. In the final analysis, I was not the right kind of "Negro." In me they knew they were getting not just a black man but one they couldn't control.[5]

Having made the irrevocable decision to work for Hatcher's defeat, party bosses went about the business of mobilizing Democratic support for the Republican candidate by pandering to the endemic racism of the white community. The strategy used in this regard was twofold. First, an attempt was made to paint Hatcher as a black power advocate and a left-wing extremist. The substantive content of this strategy was revealed within hours after Hatcher's speech before party officials. In reply to Hatcher's appeal for party support, County Chairman Krupa issued an ultimatum that Hatcher denounce by name alleged black power extremists Stokely Carmichael and H. Rap Brown. Hatcher refused, calling Krupa's demand irrelevant and an obvious political dodge to justify the withholding of party support. He did go on record, however, as opposing the use of violence in general to achieve social, economic, and political objectives.

Second, the machine began selling Radigan to white voters as a "white hope"—the only rational alternative to the control of city government for the next four years by a black man who was an advocate of black militancy and consorted with left-wing extremists. Fulfillment of this objective required the cooperation of the Republican and Democratic bosses. Radigan's advisors constantly reminded him that if he wanted to win he had to run as a white man, not as a Republican who happened to be white. Accordingly, at Radigan rallies in white areas, no mention was ever made of his party. Similarly, Radigan literature omitted any reference to the fact that he was running on the Republican ticket. Another essential requirement was that he remain silent most of the time. His press announcements and other matters related to communication were to be handled through his top campaign assistants. Most importantly, he was to avoid at all costs entering into a debate on the issues with Hatcher. In short, the design, as one newspaper analysis put it, prescribed that Radigan "say little and be white," while the regular Democratic organization did everything in its power to prevent Hatcher from getting the percentage of the white vote he needed to win.

The unvarnished opposition of the regular Democratic organization had two predominant impacts on the thinking of the people active in the Hatcher campaign. First, it destroyed what little faith they continued to have in the ethical character of the American political system in so far as questions of race were concerned. The comments by the following respondent are illustrative of this phenomenon:

> It [regular organization opposition] made me take a deep long thought about politics among the white people. Parties to them don't mean a thing. But most black people are loyal to the party. Had we lost, we would have supported the nominee of the Democratic party. They were using the party for their own personal benefits. Parties only mean something when the black man is not challenging the power structure. When he's challenging the power structure and defeats it, they don't mean a thing. I think that was educational to all black people in the city because it taught us one thing: the white people can have their differences of opinion but when the chips are down they're all together.[6]

Secondly, it made compulsory, if the election was not to be lost, a substantial revamping of the general campaign strategy.

We thought the hard part was over, but it was only the beginning. We began to see plays at the line, audibles being called, and we didn't expect these audibles. The formation that some of these players took when the audibles were called were disturbing because no one had ever seen it done that way before. Complete shifts were made. Swings across party lines became a popular thing—it became popular to say, "I'm not going to vote a Democratic ticket, this is the first time in my life I'm not going to vote a Democratic ticket." It became a thing of acceptance among the forces that were against us. We hadn't thought of that so we had to regroup.

The shift in strategy that occurred was more in scope than direction. That is, machine opposition required that the dimensions of the strategy be broadened far beyond what was originally anticipated. The ingredients of the strategy, however, remained basically the same. For example, Hatcher advisors still considered the black vote a critical factor in his mayoral election. However, it would no longer be sufficient to hold the line in the black community. Rather, the quest for black votes had to be redoubled through grass-roots workers that reached the six thousand black voters who voted for Katz in the primary and the thousands of blacks who were still unregistered. To accomplish this objective new campaign techniques for mobilizing the black community would have to be devised, a step that would possibly require the broadening of the campaign structure to include professional as well as amateur help. Similarly, more rigorous measures now had to be employed to counteract the mobilization of the white community by the regular Democratic organization. Inroads into Glen Park and Miller would have to be made now almost exclusively by Hatcher. It became absolutely necessary to get him as much exposure as possible in the white community of a kind permitting face-to-face discussions of issues important to the white electorate. House parties would have to be the prime vehicle for this; under the intimate circumstances of these informal gatherings, Hatcher would be able to bring his considerable verbal skills and personal charm to the task of convincing white voters that he was not an extremist, and would, as mayor, secure tangible benefits for all of Gary's citizens. One sector of the white population that could not afford to be neglected was the Latin American community. More resourceful means than those used in the primary would have to be created to identify Latin leadership so that an effective coalition between blacks and Latin Americans could finally be realized. The Latin community would have to be canvassed, and Latin citizens encouraged to register to vote. This meant that something more than token representation would have to be given to Latins within the campaign organization. Latins would have to be placed on campaign bodies from the executive board to the grass-roots block committees if any semblance of an effective campaign was to be mounted in the Latin community.

To combat the opposition of the regular Democratic organization, the general campaign would have to be elevated to a level of national importance. Democrats from all over the country would be encouraged to rally to the defense of a black Democratic candidate struggling against political obstacles placed in his way by the selfish acts of members of his own party. Political and financial help must not only be vigorously sought in Chicago and Indianapolis but also in Washington, D.C.

Perhaps the most important new requirement of all would be to construct ways and means of preventing the election from being stolen. Hatcher people interpreted the all out support of the Republican candidate by leaders of the regular Democratic organization as an act of desperation. And machine bosses had shown on several occasions that under desperate circumstances they were willing to use every resource at their command to accomplish their political objectives. Whether this would be true in this case remained to be seen. In the meantime, every precaution had to be taken, including the training of additional poll watchers and a meticulous study of election laws, to make sure that if political chicanery by the opposition did arise, they would be prepared to bring to it an appropriate response.

In sum, opposition to Hatcher by the regular organization injected an unforeseen dimension into the general election requiring a revision of original general campaign plans in a number of respects.

THE CAMPAIGN ORGANIZATION: EXPANSION AND CONFLICT

Hatcher campaign officials were of the opinion that execution of the revised general election strategy required that the base of the campaign organization be broadened. Proposals were formulated to broaden the campaign base in two major ways. One of these involved reaching out and pulling in those elements of the electoral machinery of the regular Democratic organization willing to work with them. This action was rationalized on the grounds that Hatcher was now head of the fall ticket with responsibility for the political success of all city Democratic candidates. Election of the entire ticket required that an olive branch be extended to Democratic workers and officials who had opposed Hatcher in the intraparty contest but who were now willing to work alongside the Hatcher volunteers in pursuit of a common objective. Thus a formal role was carved out in the campaign structure for the Democratic precinct organization. Campaign guidelines stressed that the volunteer organization used in the primary was not meant to "replace or infringe upon the propriety of any properly functioning precinct organization," but rather its sole purpose was that of supplementing precinct organizations "in terms of skill, hands, feet, and amateur enthusiasm."

These steps to broaden the base substantially altered the operational norms of the Hatcher campaign organization that had prevailed during the primary. Thus whereas relations among workers in the primary were generally cooperative and harmonious, relations in the general organization were strained at times almost to the breaking point. Much of the conflict in the general organization stemmed from the existence of irreconcilable differences between the precinct organization and the volunteers. Their debts paid to Katz in the primary, some members of the black precinct organization accepted Hatcher's invitation to become functional members of the general campaign organization. Not accustomed to serving in subordinate political capacities, many of these committeemen demanded, and were given, prominent positions on campaign standing committees and other organizational bodies. Many Hatcher volunteers resented the entrance of these committeemen—most of whom had fought them bitterly in the primary—into important positions in the general organization. They believed that they were now being pushed aside by people who were just simply jumping on the bandwagon in order to advance their own selfish political interests. Some volunteers were also absolutely convinced that many of the new faces now popping up in key positions were nothing more than spies paid by the opposition to infiltrate and sabotage the general campaign effort. Distrust of black precinct committeemen working in the general organization by the volunteers ran so deep that many volunteers refused to divulge their campaign plans to anyone who was not actively involved in the primary campaign organization.

It was very difficult to work in the fall because by that time we were infiltrated by a lot of other people. There was a time when you would meet, discuss your needs, map out strategy, and you knew that was as far as it would go. But speaking for myself and the opinion of quite a few others, I believe that people were sent to join us. We had three or four people who were making some peculiar moves. It was quite evident that a little money was being bounced around. So it made it difficult to go back in a huddle to call a play, expecting that the play would be radioed across the lines. We had spies, no doubt about it.

These guys were just brought in and thrust down our throat. "As of now John Doe will be a member of this committee." What, when we knew John Doe was out there killing us and I'm going to bring him into our committee? He's going to sit there and make decisions and carry it back to the same guy he's been prostituting for all these years? I can't tolerate that.

Campaign officials were very much aware of the resentment and suspicions harbored by the volunteers toward black precinct committeemen, but they believed that this was the price they had to pay for getting some aspects of the organization's work done that could only be accomplished through the cooperation of precinct committeemen. One of these officials observed in this context:

You can have a million volunteers, but when you get ready to register people you can't put their name on that form. So during the registration period we had to deal with those people who could register people. And to this extent they [volunteers] felt we were pushing them aside and it was true.

Feuding between the volunteers and the precinct organization continued throughout the campaign. This rife substantially affected the internal functioning of the general organization. Some of the most active and dedicated volunteer workers became disenchanted with the movement and either greatly curtailed their work, or dropped out of the campaign organization all together.

People stopped attending meetings. They just had no purpose. Why talk to the devil when you know the devil will strike at you. It became meaningless. So it got to the point where there was no need to participate. Myself, I stopped going to a lot of meetings. Prior to that I wouldn't miss a meeting, not only my meeting but anyone else's meeting I thought I could give some aid to.

Hatcher was careful not to be drawn into the conflict raging between these two opposing camps. Rather, he sparred with both of them, obtaining whatever support he could from one, then the other. Relying on political savvy gained through six full years of experience, Hatcher expertly hung loose from both the precinct organization and the volunteers, bouncing like a rubber ball over the controversy surrounding their ill-fated relationship.

As the campaign rolled along, other developments arose that greatly disturbed the volunteers and helped to dampen the enthusiasm they brought to their work. Some objected strongly to the official policy that everyone was expected to work not just for Hatcher but the entire Democratic ticket. These volunteers believed some of the Democratic nominees to be not only racists but traitors to the Democratic party because they were openly working with the regular organization to bring about Hatcher's defeat. Yet they were being asked to sell these men to the black community; some refused to do so; others did sell them, but with great reluctance.

Most serious was the deterioration of the power of the executive board in the general campaign. As we have seen, in the primary the board played an important role in the coordination of committee work, the thrashing out of campaign problems, and the making of recommendations to the candidate for his consideration. In the general campaign, membership on the board was expanded to include representatives of various ethnic groups (especially Latin Americans), Democratic politicians defeated in the primary, community groups, and the black precinct organization. This membership expansion made the board quite unwieldy as a decision-making body. Consequently, top officials—responding to the exigencies of the campaign and the need to make quick decisions—more frequently bypassed the board when key campaign decisions were made. Members of the board who had served during the primary became distressed over the failure of the decisional triumvirate to even bring issues before the body before they were resolved and policies made in accordance with the manner of their resolution. They contended that this left the board in the position of serving as a kind of glorified debating society, going through the motion of doing something meaningful while being denied the information needed for rational decision-making. Particularly distressing and disheartening to members of the executive board was the habitual absence of the candidate at board meetings. Hatcher's schedule in the fall was so demanding that it became impossible for him to attend board meetings more than a few times. Board members, especially those who had been active during the primary, interpreted his absence as a sign that he no longer appreciated the exhaustive volunteer service they were performing in his behalf. Additionally, his absence substantially undermined effective decision-making by the board, because many board members were afraid that Hatcher would veto proposals formulated without his direct involvement. The upshot was an erosion of the power of the executive board, and the making of major campaign decisions on a unilateral basis by Hatcher and his inner circle of political advisors. In this regard one board member observed:

> The whole board was symbolic at that point. The actual campaign was run out of an office at Sixteenth and Broadway. Most people didn't even know where it was. It was across the hall from Richard's law office with no name on the door. In fact it was empty. There was a regular secretarial staff in there and this is where the meetings were held.

In the light of these developments, the close rapport and unlimited enthusiasm characterizing the functioning of the primary organization were substantially diminished during the general election. They were replaced with a high degree of suspicion and conflict. By the same token, much of the volunteer ethos that had characterized the attitudinal disposition of primary campaign workers began to change. Workers began questioning each other's motives and thinking of where they would be in terms of their relationship to the Hatcher administration when the ballgame was over. These organizational and attitudinal changes are brought into focus by the comments of this Hatcher volunteer:

> The old philosophy of the volunteer thing changed. "I'm now seeking something because." That attitude was the result of this infiltration [by outsiders]. Questions were now being asked among the group, "What is John Doe after, what does Tom, Dick, and Harry want, what does he want, what does she want?" That wasn't asked in the

primary. At that point there were not too many successes we could put on the scoreboard but it was obvious it was changing to self. I will still say had there not been this influx of political parasites that immediately jumped off the losing wagon and jumped on this wagon and started singing real loudly—had they not come in with definite goals—I don't think that we would have had our breakdown in the whole idea of being a volunteer thing. I know people who worked (and when I say worked, I'm a hard man to work for because I demand a performance) like they were working for their livelihood, for their bread and water. And worked for nothing as though they were getting an enormous pay, who really had the volunteer spirit, they began to change. There was just not the harmony in the general election as we came nearer and nearer to the finish line. In the primary the closer we came to the finish line, the tighter it seems to me we got.

These statements are supported by numerous other respondents who stressed that the general campaign was not the same kind of crusade as the primary, and who noted a tapering off of the zeal and selfless spirit of the volunteer organization well before general election day. The point should be emphasized, however, that despite considerable internal dissension within the general campaign organization, it remained sufficiently cohesive to mount an effective mobilizing effort in the black community.

REMOBILIZING THE BLACK COMMUNITY

When the grass-roots electoral work began in the fall, there were a number of significant signs that the task of black mobilization would be considerably less difficult than in the spring. Street-level workers no longer encountered widespread self-doubt among the black masses. Blacks firmly believed that Hatcher would win because he was a Democrat—few of them remembered the Democrats ever losing in a general election. Indecision in the minds of blacks as to what candidate they ought to support—a black independent or a white incumbent machine candidate—had also substantially dissipated. Every political indicator suggested without equivocation that Radigan could expect to receive very little support in the black community—blacks were loyal Democrats, and they fully intended on election day to vote a straight Democratic ticket. These things notwithstanding, Hatcher workers knew that it would be a mistake to take the black vote for granted. There was always the possibility of a psychological letdown after becoming so highly aroused and turning out in such unprecedented numbers in the primary. The ability of the Hatcher organization to remobilize the black community for the general election would, perforce, be a key determining factor in the outcome of the general mayoral contest.

Street-level workers basically refined the techniques they had used in the primary to unite the black community and reapplied them in the general. Again they found that their most potent campaign technique was the door-to-door selling of Hatcher as a qualified, committed black candidate whose election would bring dignity to blacks across the country and good government for the first time to city hall. These workers particularly emphasized the importance of Hatcher's record on the council as an indication that he was a politician who truly believed in people and believed in change; they argued that if given an opportunity, Hatcher would make more profound changes in their daily lives than they could ever expect to occur under a white mayor. Finally, Hatcher workers repeated over and over again that this election provided blacks with a golden opportunity to elect Hatcher as the first black mayor of Gary. In the words of one worker, blacks were told:

> We have never had one [a black mayor]; we've never had an opportunity like we have now, and if we don't take the opportunity now they may annex the city before the next election comes along. It will set us back twenty to twenty-five years, and we won't be able to get a black mayor.

Workers attempting to mobilize the black community for the general election received powerful assistance from an unexpected source: County Chairman John Krupa. Respondents who worked for Hatcher in the general campaign consistently referred to Krupa as their best campaign worker in the black community. Krupa infuriated the black masses with his unsupported personal attacks against a black man whom they thought was decent, honest, qualified, a credit to his race, and who ought to be mayor. As the general campaign reached mid-course, Krupa's charges against Hatcher, from the perspective of the black community, became completely outlandish. He contended, for example, that the only difference between Hatcher and H. Rap Brown and

Stokely Carmichael was that Hatcher was quiet and "smooth" while Brown and Carmichael shouted and yelled.[7] Krupa claimed that Hatcher was using the "big lie" technique in charging that the county organization would not give him money because he was black. According to Krupa, the county organization had never given money to mayoral nominees. He said that Hatcher knew this and was claiming he was being victimized for the sole purpose of drumming up sympathy. "All America has bought Hatcher's line that he's a poor self-made man once removed from slavery and is being denied funds."[8]

Krupa coupled his charges of black power extremism with thinly veiled suggestions that Hatcher was also disloyal—maybe even a communist. Copies of the 16 September issue of the Black Muslim newspaper, *Muhammad Speaks*, were widely circulated in the white community in which Hatcher was quoted as saying that American pilots captured in North Vietnam should be tried as war criminals. However, a front-page retraction of this article a few weeks later was conveniently overlooked. At party functions throughout Lake County, Krupa questioned Hatcher's patriotism, saying that Hatcher had failed to satisfy him as to what loyalties he held dearest. He said that it was his job as county chairman to elect "red-white-and-blue Democrats" not men who would "risk our way of life for some other ism" and who thought that being an American was "nasty, old fashioned, and corny."[9] Krupa said his record of support for black candidates in the past proved he was not a racist.[10] "The only color I am against is red."[11]

Hatcher generally adopted the strategy of not dignifying Krupa's charges with an answer. However, after a time it became impossible for him to avoid responding to some of Krupa's more scurrilous comments. Hatcher's replies to Krupa were heavy with ridicule, dubbing Krupa as the modern-day version of Johnny One Note who ran the very serious risk of boring voters to death with his repetition of baseless allegations:

> I have already said that I deplore violence and that I am opposed to extremists of both the left and the right. If the County Chairman or any other person has any real evidence concerning individuals associated with me, I call upon him to bring this evidence to me and I will take the necessary steps. This has been my position in the past and will continue to be my position.[12]

Krupa's indefensible blasts against Hatcher generated reactions from both state and national party officials. State party chairman Gordon St. Angelo, worried about the effect of the rife in Gary on the party's fate in state and national elections, journeyed to Gary to persuade Krupa to support Hatcher. Krupa flatly refused to do so. St. Angelo than charged Krupa and other Lake County party leaders with practicing "McCarthyism" in denouncing Hatcher on the grounds that he was associated with left-wing leaders and refused to disavow them.[13] He called upon Krupa to immediately make peace with Hatcher or resign. A similar request was made by Indiana Governor Roger Branigin. Senator Birch Bayh also rallied to Hatcher's defense. Answering one of Krupa's charges, Bayh revealed that Hatcher was not appointed Assistant U.S. Attorney in 1962 because of his lack of experience.[14] This information was confirmed by Senator Robert Kennedy who stated that Hatcher's records in the Justice Department in Washington indicated that he was an American of the finest tradition.[15] Kennedy expressed puzzlement at Krupa's opposition and called upon party leaders to support Hatcher as they had other Democrats in the past. Hatcher received an equally strong endorsement from Vice-President Hubert Humphrey. Humphrey charged that county officials were opposed to Hatcher for superficial reasons. He stated that it was the duty of Democratic party leaders and workers to back their mayoral candidate, particularly since he was well-qualified and was the first of his race to be nominated for the mayorship of a large American city.

Krupa's crusade against Hatcher was unaffected by these actions of state and national officials. The only visible change in his approach was a broadening of his attack to encompass state and national officials whom he charged lacked the courage to challenge treasonable utterances and wanton acts of disrespect for law and order.

Krupa's unbridled attacks against Hatcher gave the black community whatever solidarity it needed to produce a massive vote for Hatcher on election day. Blacks generally interpreted Krupa's charges as an insult to the black community and a demonstration of gross unappreciation of the loyal support blacks had given white Democrats running for public office throughout the years. It is likely that Krupa vastly underestimated how strongly blacks felt about the racial issues he raised in the campaign. As one respondent put it: "I don't think the white population has any idea what men like Rap Brown, Stokely Carmichael, and Malcolm X mean to the black community." In any event, there is no question but that Krupa's attacks helped to make Hatcher in the eyes of the black masses a struggling underdog, carrying the burden of the entire race on his shoulders. Consequently, blacks who might have otherwise been apathetic rallied to protect Hatcher against the onslaughts of an insensitive white opposition. Black outrage at the unmitigated attacks by Krupa on Hatcher was expressed in a number of ways. One black minister, Dr. L. K. Jackson, pastor of Saint Paul Baptist Church, preached a sermon on Krupa in which he called his charges against Hatcher, "irresponsible," and out of line with "normality, sanity, logic, consistency, righteousness and the mainstream of American Democracy."[16] Joseph (Duke) Hill, a black precinct committeeman, fired off a telegram to Krupa insisting that he resign. A number of black organizations, including the Northern Indiana Political Alliance and the Midtown Voters League, denounced Krupa as a racist and pledged to defeat him for whatever future political office he sought. Hatcher volunteers were in the forefront of the backlash reaction against Krupa in the black community. Essentially, Hatcher workers encouraged Krupa in his personal attacks, while at the same time using them to make his name and everything he represented poison in the black community The following respondent described the work of the Hatcher organization in this regard:

> We found out in the general that we had a live issue. The issue we had was John Krupa, the county chairman. And we used him. We nettled him and made him say what we wanted him to say. He would say something and we would project it to the people. So what we did, we made him public enemy number one to the black people. We used him for our own purposes.

In short, Krupa served as an outside threat with which the black community could identify and gather the motivation it needed to come together as a cohesive unit in support of the black man who was the target of his offensive statements.

Hatcher workers in the black community were quite fortunate that County Chairman Krupa was relieving them of much of the responsibility for building black unity because, with the war chest of the regular Democratic organization closed to them, and the development of the general election into a much more serious contest than anyone imagined, a good deal of their energies had to be directed toward fund-raising. The central vehicle for fund-raising in the fall was a new campaign entitled "Dollars for Decency." Jazz Trumpeter Clark Terry came to the city to help kick off the campaign. This new fund-raising venture grew directly from Hatcher's difficulties with the regular organization. It was based on the premise that Hatcher's campaign should be funded by the community at large so that when he was elected to office he would be responsible only to the people. As Hatcher expressed it: "The cry from the people is we don't want Dick to have to give in one thing that he stands for because of the lack of finances for his campaign."[17] All Gary citizens interested in seeing a "decent," uncontrolled administration in city hall for the first time were therefore encouraged to give a dollar or more. Dr. Alfonso Holiday and Dr. Manuel Vargus were named cochairmen of the dollars-for-decency campaign.

The citizens' fund-raising effort was much better coordinated and executed than the one launched during the primary. Street-level workers canvassed the entire black community, going door to door collecting dollars for decency. Oatmeal boxes with rubber bands around them were placed in various businesses. Collection groups went around periodically to pick up these boxes and turn them in to the finance committee or to Charlotte Johnson at campaign headquarters.[18] Campaign donors were given certificates with Hatcher's picture printed in the background. These certificates were issued in different colors according to the amount contributed. Letters were sent out to churches, social and civic organizations, and unions, asking them to give whatever they could to the dollars-for-decency drive.

Response to this fund-raising drive was extremely gratifying. A multitude of black civic and social organizations used this fund-raising venture as a means of getting on the Hatcher bandwagon. Among the most outstanding contributors were the Third District Women's Auxiliary, the Shocktroops, and Unique Bronzettes (all ladies social clubs), and the Democratic Women for Better Government. Some special groups, such as the Westside Ladies for Hatcher, and Teachers for Hatcher, were formed for the sole purpose of making membership, and community door-to-door solicitations for campaign funds. The success of the Hatcher organization in generating campaign contributions from rank-and-file black citizens, as well as myriad black social, civic and religious organizations, provides a good barometer of the extent to which a traditionally fragmentized black community united solidly behind his candidacy in the general election.

Other sources were also tapped for campaign funds. A Hatcher testimonial dinner attended by more than fifteen-hundred persons at the Gary Armory raised a considerable amount. This affair was followed by a $100-a-plate dinner sponsored by the All American Alliance for Hatcher at the Sherman House in Chicago. Chief promoter of this event was Hatcher's long-time political mentor and former law partner Henry Walker of East Chicago. More than three-hundred persons attended the affair, including Hatcher's father, Mr. Carleton Hatcher, who stole the show with a lengthy dissertation on the Hatcher family. Prominent among the many guests was U.S. Steelworkers District Director Joseph Germano. Acting in behalf of his organization, Germano made a campaign contribution of $2,000. Benefit concerts were given for Hatcher by nationally known black entertainers, including the Staple Singers, a family gospel group, and Harry Belafonte. The second Belafonte concert was not nearly as successful as the first, the latter attracting only about two thousand two hundred people. It did, however, provide Hatcher with an opportunity to take a final swipe at the machine before the election. Hatcher identified his real opposition as George Chacharis, Dr. J. J. Forszt, Peter Mandich, and John Krupa. He labeled this group as the unholy quartet and asserted that Radigan was just their stooge, their puppet, their "Charlie McCarthy."[19]

One of the most outstanding achievements of the general organization was its success in tapping outside sources of political funds. Hatcher and his advisors believed reliance on outside funds to be critical; because despite the good intentions of local citizens, there was just not enough uncontrolled local money to allow him to run the kind of campaign necessary to defeat the formidable opposition he faced. Thus as his troubles with the local organization mounted, Hatcher turned to the state and to the nation as a whole for campaign funds. He received considerable help at the state level, including a $2,500 donation from the Indiana Democratic Club, which Krupa attempted to block, charging that this donation violated state statutes relating to contributions by private corporations. Trips were made to South Bend and Chicago to secure campaign funds from sympathetic outsiders. These trips resulted in a $2,000 contribution by twenty-two professors at Notre Dame and a $500 contribution by the greater Chicago Area Citizens Committee of the United Auto Workers.

At the national level a spectacular fund-raising affair was hosted for Hatcher by Vice-President Hubert Humphrey, Senators Edward and Robert Kennedy, former Senator Paul Douglas, Representative Charles Diggs, and Indiana Senators Birch Bayh and Vance Hartke. This affair was a smashing success, with several hundred persons representative of a cross section of business, economic, religious, and political establishments in Washington in attendance. Hatcher received the full endorsement of party leaders, including Vice-President Humphrey and President Johnson.

Far and away the most successful of all fund-raising strategies employed during the general campaign, however, was an ad run by the Hatcher camp simultaneously in the *Post-Tribune* and the *New York Times*. The ad was entitled "For God's Sake Let's Get Ourselves Together" and showed a white cop beating a black demonstrator over the head with a billy club. It asked Americans who said that they were for peace and unity to "put your money where your mouth is." The ad described Hatcher as a man who believed in peace and despised bigotry and ignorance and it suggested that he was running for his political life in Gary. It ended with an urgent appeal for contributions from all Americans who could afford to give any amount.

Contradicting initial reservations by some members of the executive board about the wisdom of this strategical move, the decision to run the *Times* ad turned out to be a masterstroke. Campaign contributions poured into Hatcher headquarters from all over the world. Letters containing money were received from as far away as Hong Kong. Some of the letter writers identified themselves as white Republicans who were angry at the position the local Democratic party had taken toward Hatcher. Most of these persons expressed the view that since he won the primary fair and square, his party should have supported him in the general. Several respondents contended that donations were still coming in a week after the general election was over. The size

of the contributions varied from a thousand dollars to fifty cents
sent by a poverty family in Brooklyn who expressed the wish
that "they could do more."[20]

The *New York Times* ad had the effect of not only solving the
campaign organization's financial worries, but of making Hatcher
a national figure. After the *Times* ad, attention from around the
world was spotlighted on Gary and the position the county organization was taking toward the Democratic mayoral nominee.
This national publicity put the national Democratic party on the
spot and resulted in tremendous pressure from Washington on
the county organization to settle its differences with the Hatcher
camp. In addition, the ad generated for Hatcher invaluable media
exposure. He received newspaper and television coverage that
he did not have the money to buy. Nationwide reaction to the ad
was a source of considerable heartache to the county organization. Krupa denounced Hatcher's elevation of the campaign to a
national controversy and accused him of injecting the race issue
in the campaign by including the picture of the police officer
and the protestor in the ad.

Aside from fund-raising, the major task of the street-level
organization during the general campaign was voter registration
in the black community. Two factors made a massive black-
registration drive in the general campaign critical to Hatcher's
mayoral victory: (1) the likelihood that large numbers of white
voters would split their tickets, dropping Hatcher and picking up
the Republican candidate; and (2) clear evidence that a vigorous
campaign was going to be mounted in the white community to
increase the number of eligible white voters. Given the fact that
the number of registered white voters already surpassed that of
black voters, it would be necessary to dramatically expand the
number of registered blacks just to maintain the ratio of registered black to white voters existing during the primary election.

The registration campaign in the general differed from the one
mounted in the primary in one key respect: the Hatcher organization now had the cooperation of about one-third of the black precinct organization. Involvement of the black precinct organization
facilitated the establishment of the traveling registration boards
proposed, but never employed, in the primary. Initially, campaign
leaders were again thwarted in their efforts to establish such
boards by County Clerk Krupa's ruling that committeemen could

292 / Electing Black Mayors

not register individuals who lived outside their precincts. However, this time campaign coordinator Bell asked for a ruling by state party chairman Gordon St. Angelo on this subject. St. Angelo informed Bell that Gary precinct committeemen could register people anywhere in the corporate bounds of the city. This ruling by St. Angelo made possible the establishment of traveling boards using precinct committeemen to register people on the spot. Eventually, this program of on-the-spot registration was expanded into a full-blown registration effort involving the entire campaign apparatus. This new registration drive was dubbed by campaign leaders as "Operation Saturation."

Essentially operation saturation involved the collapsing of all committee workers into the registration committee. With the help of thirteen precinct committeemen, virtually the entire campaign organization would invade a precinct, knocking on doors and bringing people out to the back of a truck or out to the sidewalk where the cooperating precinct committeemen were waiting to register them. On weekends, tables were set up on corners. Campaign workers would blanket the target neighborhood going from house to house, pulling out people and signing them up. In each district members of the indigenous population were encouraged to join in the registration effort. For example, the fourth district contained Gary's famous redlight area, where gambling and prostitution flourished. Hatcher people approached leading prostitutes and stick-up artists in the area and encouraged them to help them mobilize the people in this area. They were able to convince them to join in and play an active role by telling them they were not going to make moral judgments about their work, all they were interested in was their help in getting Hatcher elected. One Hatcher worker described precisely how they were able to get these people involved in electoral work:

We told them if you're a prositute, a stick-up man, whatever you are, if you feel yourself morally that you're right in what you're doing, then your conscience is as clear as mine. We invited them to come in our organization and play an active part. Some of them were a little reluctant because you figure here's a young lady that's been branded a prostitute, then she's coming in here to rub shoulders with people who are dead against it. You've got quite an inferiority mixup there. What we did finally, we got her to come in. We brought her in and made her feel important, like she was somebody. We put her on a committee. She worked, she was treated just like any other of our female volunteers. Our concern was political not moral. As a result, we took this one and put her to work in that particular area. When we got down there, all of the people there would see one of their colleagues calling the shots. That worked on the other ones' minds who were peeping from behind the curtains. So as a result of that another one came, and another. So we moved into the male segment of it. And the same thing happened. We had in a sense a head-quarters set up down there in a poolroom. And they would meet in there and get their instructions. They ran the whole show down there. The people who lived in there were the people who called the shots in there. Then the prostitutes starting saying, "I know Mr. Hatcher is going to cut this out, but I'm going to support him." The hustlers started saying, "well I know there'll be no more crap games, but I'm going to support him." We got them in the same frame of mind as the person who said I know he doesn't have a chance but I'm going to vote for him. But that's about what it amounts to.

A different tactic was used to reach black voters in the fifth district. This district contained an unusually large number of older black citizens. Hatcher workers found a reluctance on the part of these voters to support Hatcher, because they thought he was too young. To overcome this obstacle, teenagers were organized in the district into a young people's booster club known as the "New Breed." This group had existed during the primary but did not begin to actively function until the general campaign when its leadership and supervision were placed in the hands of Mrs. Bertha Jones, a Gary high school counselor. The idea was to reach parents in the fifth district through their children. Committees paralleling the larger campaign organization's committees were set up composed of New Breed members. They received instructions at the campaign headquarters from Mrs. Jones and her assistant, a white college senior, John Blood. When the class was over, these youngsters were experts on subjects such as registration laws, poll-watching, absentee-balloting procedure, and others. Once the teenage group was thoroughly organized and trained, the organization moved down to politically orient younger adolescents. This respondent explained the function this infant group served in the campaign:

We wanted them to tell their mothers and fathers one thing: 2d, remember 2d—that was Hatcher's number on the machine. You could hear 3 and 4 year olds, "What's Hatcher's number," they'd say "2d." We had a truck with kids riding on the back of it going through town yelling "2d, election day, 2d." Now we had little buttons and we'd tell the kids, pass this to mama. Tell mama, 2d, election day, 2d. And anywhere you'd go you'd hear little kids holering "2d, 2d."

These mobilizing activities elicited from their black targets the intended response. One Hatcher worker contends that on the first Saturday that operation saturation was employed, the organization registered some 960 people off the streets. Precinct committeemen were assigned to poll rooms to do nothing but register voters. Precinct committeemen operating out of one pool room on Seventeenth Avenue registered from that establishment alone approximately 540 people. Indeed, this operation at one point was so successful that, according to one newspaper account, 50 black people were being registered for every new white registrant. Officials in Crown Point did not want to believe that the Hatcher organization was registering that many legitimate voters. County officials charged that Hatcher people were padding the voting roster by registering vacant lots. Hatcher workers denied this allegation. "Our instructions were strictly that you register human beings. And that's what we did. Any registration that was questionable, we sent somebody to check it out before it was submitted." Overall during the fall, the Hatcher organization registered approximately 5,000 voters.

The general campaign organization received invaluable assistance in its electoral work from a number of organizations that had quietly sat out the primary election. The NAACP and the Gary League of Women Voters supplemented the Hatcher registration drive with a registration campaign of their own. During the middle of August, voter registration offices were opened by these groups, with the cooperation of Muigwithania, at 1624 Broadway. An NAACP spokesman announced in conjunction with this project that the sponsoring organizations intended to request additional voter registrars from County Democratic Chairman John Krupa. The United Viscounts, a black man's social service organization, endeavored strenuously, but without success, to arrange a debate between Radigan and Hatcher. Rejection of the idea by the Radigan camp prompted the Viscounts to ask Radigan to withdraw from the race because he was receiving his basic support from forces associated with the Democratic party and it was illegal in Indiana for two Democrats to run for the same office in a general election. Considerable help with grass-roots organizing was provided by the Gary Aid for Dependent Children (AFDC) mothers group and the Chicago chapter of the Independent Voters League of Illinois.

Hatcher volunteers continued to receive formidable resistance to their electoral work from the political machine. The preponderance of the black precinct organization refused to cooperate with the Hatcher organization in any way. A few black committeemen worked actively with the regular Democratic organization in its campaign to defeat Hatcher, joining with County Chairman Krupa in denouncing Hatcher as a black power extremist and accusing Hatcher workers of using "gestapo tactics" to coerce black voters into voting for their candidate. Most of them simply sat out the campaign, not lifting a finger to help either Hatcher or Radigan.

The major source of resistance, however, was the county organization. John Krupa continued to turn down the Hatcher organization's request for deputy registrars in the black community. In the light of Krupa's persistent denial of the Hatcher request, the Young Adults Council of the NAACP staged a march on Krupa's home to dramatize the urgency of the need for more registrars in black areas. Krupa reaffirmed his position that there was no need for more registrars in Gary. He said that he would not be swayed by demonstrations and deplored the use of young marchers by Hatcher to gain a political advantage. Krupa referred to the marchers as dupes of a left-wing plot to take over Gary. And he left no doubt whom he thought was the key figure in the plot.

> It would be the greatest thing for the city of Gary to elect a Negro mayor. But it must be a man who denounces Black Power advocates. And it must not be someone who is going to force housing integration on people. The people of Gary had better wake up. If these people are able to capture city hall, they also gain control of the police and fire departments, leaving the steel mill and industrial complex at their mercy. The leaders in Moscow and Havana must be rubbing their hands in glee over this situation.[21]

To slow down the tremendous rate of black registration, Krupa cut back on the number of affadavits for registration going to the Hatcher camp while, according to one respondent, "giving the Republicans all the affadavits they wanted." County officials initially allocated only twenty affadavits at a time to precinct committeemen working with Hatcher. These would have to be exhausted before additional registration forms could be obtained. This procedure imposed severe constraints on the registration process. A committeeman having forty people waiting in line to be registered could only register half; he would have to then request that the additional persons remain while he returned to Crown Point to pick up twenty more affadavits. The number of affadavits were raised to twenty-five and finally thirty, after a few precinct committeemen—on the urging of Hatcher volunteers —banded together to protest the limitations placed on their ability to register black voters by the prevailing policy relative to affadavit allocation. But even thirty affadavits were still far fewer than were generally required to expedite registration in the black community.

These attempts at obstruction by the county organization failed to substantially hamper the mobilization process in the black community. Blacks would stand in line for hours to register to vote. The entire black community was jumping on the Hatcher bandwagon, even elements of the black establishment that had bitterly opposed him in the spring. No one doubted, even county officials, that Hatcher's support in the black community would surpass the unprecedented vote he received in black precincts in the primary. Symptomatic of the prevailing black mood was the response Hatcher received during a campaign swing through one of the roughest, most depressed, traditionally most politically apathetic sectors of the black community. This event was described by a Hatcher worker in the following manner:

We didn't take him [Hatcher] in there until the clientele was just right—we'd been working on it. So he went down there about 3 o'clock with the intention of shaking hands. He started around Sixteenth. By 5:30 he had made two blocks. That's as far as he could get, because he had other meetings and things that he had to start going to around 6 o'clock. And you would have thought that it was some big celebrity coming to town, I mean the way people were down there. People were coming out of houses, women were coming around the corner with their babies in their arms. Everybody was trying to shake hands with him. It was a tremendous turnout. From Sixteenth to Thirteenth all the cars had to be turned around, they couldn't get through. People were all out in the street everywhere.

With the black community thoroughly remobilized, Hatcher workers were confident that if the white community produced at even a tiny fraction of its potential, Hatcher could not lose—unless, of course, the election was stolen. As we will see, this latter factor became the final, and most difficult challenge the Hatcher organization faced in its year-long quest to make Richard Hatcher the first black mayor of Gary, Indiana.

THE GENERAL CAMPAIGN IN THE WHITE COMMUNITY

Hatcher and his advisors believed that they could not afford to concede the white community to the opposition; thus a large share of the candidate's time was spent competing for the white vote. As a sign of the Hatcher organization's intention to vigorously woo the white electorate, a campaign headquarters was established in conservative Glen Park. Attempts were made to also reopen the headquarters in Miller, but the owner of the building refused to rent it to Hatcher representatives. The building remained vacant for a time, but a portion of it was eventually opened up as a "Radigan for Mayor" command post in the Miller area.

Hatcher was from time to time sharply criticized by volunteers for concentrating so much of his campaign time in the white community that it appeared he was taking the black vote for granted. These rebukes had little effect. Hatcher reasoned that it would do him no good to run extraordinarily well in the black community if he could not also poll enough white votes to win. He was relatively confident that the approximately two thousand white voters who voted for him in the primary would do so again in the general, even if he did not campaign in white areas. But with only one white candidate in the race, these votes would not be enough to guarantee his victory. Rather, his success in the general hinged pivotally on his ability to improve on the vote he received in the white community in the primary.

Most of the exposure Hatcher received in the white community in the general was provided by white campaign workers and their friends. This aspect of the campaign was again headed by Mr. Arthur Lebo. The approach to the white community at the personal level was much more systematically organized in the fall than in the primary. This time, Lebo put together a house-meetings committee composed largely of whites from Miller, with a couple of persons from the Westside, and a couple from Glen Park. Lebo's committee constructed a form that persons willing to hold house parties had to fill out, providing information relative to the time and place of the meeting and how many persons were expected to attend. A meetings schedule was set up based on the premise that Hatcher would not move from house to house, but would limit himself to two meetings a night. The standard format involved a short statement by Hatcher, in which he expressed his intention to provide the city with honest government and to use city resources to tap federal money that could be used to improve the lives of all citizens, followed by a lengthy question and answer session. This house-meetings program enjoyed outstanding success. Whites attending these meetings were favorably impressed with Hatcher's sincerity and his ability to provide articulate, well thought-out answers to their questions. Hatcher performed best in these situations; his willingness to enter into frank face-to-face discussions with persons in attendance at these meetings helped him to pick up some wavering white support. Through this meetings program Hatcher was able to score several breakthroughs. For example, although most of his house meetings were held in Miller, several well-attended house parties were also given for him in Glen Park. This was a first for a major independent black candidate. Hatcher people were pleasantly surprised by the reactions of citizens attending the meetings in Glen Park.

In addition to house meetings, Hatcher attempted to make inroads into the white community through a weekly radio broadcast and door-to-door campaign work by students from the Gary campus of Indiana University. Hatcher received help in the white community from two sources not available to him in the spring. A strong Teachers for Hatcher group was formed under the codirectorship of John Friel and Charles Brown. Black membership in this group overlapped a good deal with the Teachers for Enlightened Leadership group that had formed to help Hatcher in the spring. The Teachers for Hatcher group was much broader, however, because it contained a substantial white component. This group financed through its own resources an ad in the *Post-Tribune* containing the names of about eight hundred persons.

All of the signatures for the ad were collected outside of school because leaders of the group did not want to open themselves up to charges of participating in electioneering activities on school time.[22] Teachers for Hatcher also played an important role in providing exposure for Hatcher in the white community through the sponsoring of cocktail and house parties. In addition, some members of the teachers group served as an unofficial speakers bureau, substituting for Hatcher on occasions when he was not able to fulfill his commitments. The involvement of teachers in the Hatcher campaign was a significant accomplishment, because in the past teachers had constituted an untapped political potential. As one member of the Teachers for Hatcher group noted: "The role of the teacher in past years had been so refined, they tend to be such timid souls, that it is hard to convince them that they have not only the right but the responsibility to become active."

Another source of support in the general not available in the primary was the leadership of organized labor. Hatcher received a strong endorsement from United States Steelworkers District 31 Director Joseph A. Germano. At a rally for Hatcher held on 16 September, Germano vowed to seek support for Hatcher from "all those who have enjoyed the support of the United Steelworkers of America in the past."[23] He observed that it would be bad if steel mill workers did not support the Democratic mayoral nominee. It is important to point out, however, that Germano's strong endorsement was not sufficient to prevent his rank-and-file white constituents from crossing over in droves to vote for Hatcher's Republican opponent. The failure of union leaders to deliver for Hatcher the votes of their blue-collar constituents is an enlightening commentary on both the weak nature of union leadership in Gary, and the depth of racism among union members in general. Reflecting on his years of involvement in the Gary trade-union movement, one Hatcher supporter incisively summed up the crucial factors hampering the exercise of effective leadership by union leaders on racial questions.

On matters of race the trade-union movement in Gary has been pretty well corrupt. There is a willingness to pay lip service—every union is quite willing to have a black vice-president, but not willing to go beyond that. Even those leaders who have their hearts in the right place feel that they can't take their people with them. They're just afraid they can't carry on. They are fat and soft and don't really have a philosophy anymore except for a sort of tragic economism. "Let's get the best we can for the boys in the shop" is all it amounts to.

A significant new dimension in Hatcher's general campaign was the substantial inroads made into the Latin American community. Hatcher was much more successful in getting Latins to identify with his campaign for mayor in the general than in the primary. Several Latins held key positions on the executive board and other bodies within the general campaign organization. With the help of Latin campaign members, grass-roots electoral activity was energetically pursued in the Latin community. A number of house parties were also held in Latin areas in an effort to attract and hold the Latin vote. Each of these affairs was well attended.

Hatcher was warmly embraced by several highly influential Latin community leaders. Perhaps the most important Latin community endorsement came from Jack Azcona, president of the Mexican-American Democratic Organization. In a published statement circulated widely through the Latin community Azcona reminded Latins that the Democratic party was their traditional home, and that they had made progress under the Democrats whereas the Republicans when in power denied citizenship to them. He stated further that Latins had supported the nominees of the Democratic party in the past and nobody mentioned their nationality, race, or color.

Latin American enthusiasm for Hatcher was pushed to its highest point by the endorsement of Congressman Henry B. Gonzalez of Texas. In October Gonzalez was the featured speaker at the Gary Urban League's annual banquet. He came to Gary a day before his scheduled speech specifically to stump for Hatcher in the Latin community. During his visit, Gonzalez toured the Tricity Plaza Democratic headquarters, spending several hours there talking to Latins and encouraging them to remain true Democratics by supporting Hatcher. He pointedly endorsed Hatcher in both Spanish and English. Before boarding his plane at the airport, Gonzalez issued a final appeal for Latin unity behind Hatcher, reminding Gary's Latin citizens that in the past they had been victimized by the tactic of divide and conquer.

Despite the strenuous campaign for the white vote waged by the Hatcher organization it became increasingly evident as the campaign progressed that large segments of the white community were planning to cross over to support the white Republican candidate. The intensity of feeling against Hatcher in the white community was so great that it became difficult to work for him openly in white areas without getting verbally abused or physically attacked. One white respondent observed that in his community "every racist in the area, and by this I mean those who are usually somewhat on the fringe, were out in the open, up and down the street." Full-scale countermobilization emerged in the white community as whites became aware of the tremendous mobilization campaign being waged in the black community in Hatcher's behalf.

Countermobilization in the white community was spurred by the electoral work of the regular Democratic organization. In fact, what Hatcher faced in the white community was the united opposition of the entire Lake County machine. A majority of Democratic white precinct committeemen worked full-time for Radigan, distributing his literature and giving white voters instructions on how to split Hatcher out. Those who did not actively campaign for Radigan made only feeble efforts to discourage their white constituents from splitting their ballots in the mayor's race. The few white precinct committeemen who expressed an interest in working for Hatcher were told by party bosses this would not only be foolish but possibly suicidal. Witness, for example, these comments by a leading figure in the regular Democratic organization:

> Most party workers didn't work hard for Hatcher. I told some of them, you have to be a hypocrite or a liar if you think you can go into Miller and sell Mr. Hatcher. I said he's going to get a percentage of those votes. Some of them will be accidental, some of them will be on purpose. But they couldn't guarantee they could go in there and get X amount of votes.

With few exceptions, white Lake County politicians lined up solidly in support of the Republican candidate. Hugh McLaughlin was the only white Democratic politician at the city level to actively campaign for Hatcher's election in the general. Confining his campaign activities primarily to Glen Park, his council district, McLaughlin publicly charged Krupa with being a captive of a "strange combine" consisting of "the corrupt political machine that includes George Chacharis, Peter Mandich, the present accused robber of the poor Milton Bromich and now the GOP."[24] Hatcher received weak endorsements and no active support from either Mayor Katz or city Democratic chairman Louis Karras. Katz was in fact suspected of taking actions behind the scenes to help Radigan. For example, city-hall employees were reportedly instructed by the mayor to vote Republican in the November election.[25] One city employee (a street inspector) active in the Hatcher campaign was dismissed and told by City Sanitation Director Stanley Piet, after being sent to his office by Mayor Katz, that he would be rehired when "Radigan was elected."[26] City hall officials including Stanley Piet and Anthony Laterzo openly campaigned for Radigan without being reprimanded by Katz.[27] In what was perhaps the most glaring example of city-hall support, during fire-prevention week, Radigan himself was allowed to campaign riding a fire truck through white communities.[28]

All three white Democratic nominees to the city council campaigned independently of Hatcher in their districts. One of them, Theodore Nabhan running in the first district, worked actively to defeat him in the white community. Speaking at a first-district rally of 150 persons, Nabhan went out of his way to commend John Krupa for opposing the mayoral nominee of the Democratic party in Gary. He assured his first district constituents that he also opposed Hatcher. "I have sat on the Council for four years with him, and he is no good for Gary or any other city in the United States. He is for one man, and that is himself, and not for Gary."[29] Before the rally ended, instructions were given on a sample machine supplied by County Chairman Krupa on procedures for cutting Nabhan in while splitting Hatcher out.

Lake County Auditor Bartel Zandstra, Lake County Juvenile Court Judge Joseph Meszar, and Lake County Coroner Alexander Williams were the only county officials to pledge strong support for Hatcher in the general election. Two prominent county officials, County Clerk John Krupa and County Treasurer Leslie Pruitt, campaigned widely for Radigan in the white community. At one Glen Park Democratic rally, for example, Radigan was introduced from the stage by Pruitt. The keynote address of the night was delivered by Krupa; his speech centered on a roundhouse attack on national Democratic leaders for supporting Hatcher. Krupa told the audience of five hundred, "We cannot follow the pattern of our leaders in Washington—they lack leadership and courage. So to hell with Washington."[30] As he spoke Radigan milled through the standing patrons, shaking hands and calling for support in the November city election.

While his Democratic allies worked to destroy Hatcher's mayoral chances, Radigan campaigned throughout the white community promoting a good government, white-oriented platform. One Radigan advisor summarized the Republican campaign strategy in the following manner: "We pushed the name Joe Radigan. Very little of our literature had Republican on it; this was a part of the strategy. We wanted to lure as many Democrats as we could. . . . Almost everything was beamed at the white Democratic vote. Do you want a good honest man or do you want Hatcher?" In keeping with this strategy, Radigan promised white Democrats that his administration would oppose the bussing of school children to achieve integration and would remove constraints on the power of the police to apprehend thugs who preyed on "God-fearing citizens."

THE VOTE FRAUD PLOT

Throughout most of the general campaign Hatcher advisors worried about a possible attempt on the part of the political machine to steal the election. Beginning in late September persistent rumors floated into headquarters of various schemes, hatched out of county offices in Crown Point, to rob Hatcher of a general election victory, but no one appeared to have hard evidence to support these charges. Thus all Hatcher supporters could do was nervously scrutinize the activities of the county organization and pray that if a fraudulent vote plot materialized they would get wind of it in time enough to combat it.

We had heard rumors of the registration of nonexistent people—that registration was being carried out wholesale in some of the white areas. But there was nothing specific, just rumors. We spent hours thinking of what legal remedies we had. Were there any injunctive things? Were there any mandamus kinds of actions? What could we do? We thought about maybe going to a state court or a county court, which we felt was kind of not a very hopeful gesture with all the damned political involvements. But we were preparing legal actions of one sort or another.

This nail-biting period was brought to a dramatic halt, however, when, during the second week in October, two reporters from *Life* magazine, Bob Bradford and Declan Hahn, brought to Hatcher workers incontrovertible evidence that an elaborate plot was afoot to defeat Hatcher through massive fraudulent voting in the white community. On assignment for *Life* to cover the Gary election, Bradford and Hahn managed to strike up working relationships with key workers in both the Hatcher and Radigan camps. During one of their numerous trips to Glen Park, they were contacted by a white precinct committeewoman named Mrs. Marion Tokarski. To their amazement, Mrs. Tokarski told Bradford and Hahn of her participation in a plot emanating from Crown Point to cast 20,000 ghost votes for Radigan in the general election. Bradford and Hahn immediately turned this information over to one of their Hatcher contacts, and a meeting was arranged for Mrs. Tokarski to tell her entire story to Hatcher.

Mrs. Tokarski's revelations were too much for Hatcher to believe. "When I told him they were going to steal 15,000 to 20,000 votes, he kept saying 'That's fantastic, that's fantastic.' "[31] Hatcher's advisors urged him to use Mrs. Tokarski's information as a basis for filing a law suit charging Democratic party officials with encouraging fraudulent voting practices and asking for a postponement of the election. Hatcher balked at the suggestion. "He did not want to implicate precinct committeemen who might work for him. I told him 'Dick, if you don't go to court, you're going to lose—you're going to blow your campaign.' " While the hassle was still brewing over what to do with the Tokarski information, additional hard evidence came to light of efforts being taken by the county organization to steal the election. Eyewitnesses brought to Hatcher officials information that clerks in the county courthouse were tampering with absentee ballots. According to these reports, persons applying for absentee ballots were being urged to split Hatcher out and cast a vote for his opponent. To make sure these voters did not accidentally vote for Hatcher, they were requested not to seal their ballots before returning them to the county courthouse. Before any response could be discussed regarding these latest charges, an even more ominous development occurred: the Lake County Board of Elections, in an unprecedented move, summarily dropped over five thousand black registrants from the rolls, although Indiana law did not allow for the purge of voters until the January following a presidential election.

This audacious action by the county organization had its genesis in a series of articles by Hilbert Bradley published in *Info* relating to ghost voting in the black community. Entitled "Election Fraud —Gary Style," this series was based on several months of personal investigation by Bradley following the May primary. The purpose of the Bradley articles was to explain why Hatcher ran so poorly in some black precincts in the primary by showing how the political machine typically stole votes in the black community. Written in a humorous vein, Bradley's articles revealed that a large number of persons who voted in the May primary did so under assumed names registered from phony addresses—vacant lots, store fronts, taverns, and the like. Bradley had collected enough evidence of ghost voting by July to file a request for a hearing with the county board of elections. This request was completely ignored by county officials for four months. Then, without warning, Bradley received a letter from the election board on 14 October informing him that his request for a hearing had been approved and that the hearing date had been set for 25 October. Bradley's testimony was favorably received, and the board promised a full-scale investigation of voting irregularities in black precincts. At the very moment Bradley was testifying before the board, Republican workers were busy canvassing black precincts in search of ghost voters. On 26 October, Republican city chairman Robert Rooda, a member of the Lake County Election Board, presented the board with a list of 5,286 names of persons turned up in the Republican canvass as fraudulent registrants. Over 5,000 of the persons included on the list were black. John Krupa, Secretary to the Election Board, proceeded immediately to send out letters to all 5,286 persons on the Republican list challenging their registrations. Individuals receiving these letters were required to respond in person or by registered mail by 3 November or their names would be dropped from the registration rolls.

This was unquestionably the gloomiest period in the general campaign for the Hatcher camp. When the five thousand letters challenging black registrations came down from the county chairman, most Hatcher workers were absolutely certain that the ballgame was over—that the machine had succeeded in stealing the election from them.

They sent everybody and his uncle those letters. Some people had been living at the same address for 12 or 13 years and owned their own homes and were sent these letters. Many of them said they were not going to send this letter back because they would have to send it by registered mail which involved money. If they sent it, then they would have to come out to Crown Point and appear before the election board. So when they did this we knew we had lost. The Republicans had put on a drive for their own ghost voters. With the ghost voters they had, and the voters they took away from us, we knew we had lost at that time.

Campaign officials, however, were far from ready to throw in the towel; they had fought too hard over the past eleven months to let the whole thing slip away at the very end. But what could they do? Hatcher continued to rule out court action. An appeal to state and local officials would be fruitless. This left only one other avenue for help: the federal government. Accordingly, on the day Krupa announced his decision to nullify the registration of a large number of voters in the black community, an urgent telegram was sent to United States Attorney General Ramsey Clark. This telegram requested federal protection to insure an honest election in Gary on 7 November. The Hatcher organization informed Clark that it had indisputable proof that certain prominent Lake County election officials were engaged in massive fraudulent registrations in white areas in order to steal the election. It charged that Democratic and Republican members of the election board were in a conspiracy against Hatcher—a conspiracy that would allow more than 200 persons to go from precinct to precinct in white areas voting under assumed names. The telegram concluded that without immediate federal intervention, a fair election could not be held and the people of Gary would be robbed of their inherent constitutional rights.[32]

Hatcher people waited on a reply from the Justice Department. After several days telephone inquiries were made. The word they received back was " 'If you're going to do something you'd better do it yourself, don't count on the Justice Department for a thing.' " This response left the Hatcher organization no choice but to turn to the courts. The possibility of filing a suit in the state courts was kicked around and dismissed because it might take two or three years to get a judgment at that level and by that time the whole question would be moot. Black state senator Pat Chavis who had been sent to assist in the campaign by the state central committee suggested that they file immediately in the federal courts and that they try to get attorney William R. Ming of Chicago, the leading black constitutional lawyer in the Midwest, to handle the case. Ming agreed to handle the case, and the state central committee pledged to finance court costs incurred by the action. At that point, the legal strategy included going all the way to the Supreme Court. The suit was filed in the district court; it called for the convening of a three-judge panel to hear arguments and render a decision. A negative judgment by the panel would be immediately appealable to the United States Supreme Court.

Lawyers working on the suit were undecided whether they should go for establishing a legal basis for setting aside a fraudulent election or a postponement of the election. It was finally agreed to ask the court to do whatever was necessary to guarantee Richard Hatcher and other classes of complaintants, including all registered Democrats who had voted in the primary, and registered Democrats specifically whose registration had been nullified by the Krupa letter, a fair election. Second, the Hatcher petition asked that if the first request was not possible to grant, that the court set the election over. The Hatcher complaint alleged that defendants in the suit were involved in a scheme designed to deliberately disenfranchise large numbers of black voters, vote large numbers of nonexistent white persons allegedly registered, and defeat the candidacy of the chief complaintant Richard Hatcher. It accused Krupa of boasting to use every means to defeat Hatcher, including the disqualification of black voters, and, if necessary, willful negligence in the counting of votes cast for him in the mayoral race.[33] Named as defendants were John Krupa, Walter C. Zurbriggen, Jerome J. Reppa, Robert H. Rooda, Anthony Dobis, Jr., Louis G. Karras, Marian Evanseck, Helen Ann Repya, Bessie Manoski, Elease P. Wilson, Edward Robinson, Erma McBride, Roby Bartolomei, Meaky Metcalf, Frank Perry, Andrew Atkins, Marguerite Graves, Ortomease G. Gandeau, Issac Davis, Steven Mojanovich, Mary A. Dzacky, Martha Pruitt, John Bokash, Joseph S. Bejgrowiiz, and Dorothy Wackowski. Joining Ming as attorneys in the case were Walter K. Black (Chicago), Julian B. Allen (Gary) and Patrick E. Chavis (Indianapolis). Ming had warned his co-attorneys that the court would probably not set the election over. He said that in fact they had to be careful that the whole thing was not swept under the rug;

but it was his judgement that the suit was still worth the effort, because at the very least it would provide a basis for setting the election aside if Hatcher lost. The suit was presented to U.S. District Judge George N. Beamer who took it under advisement and shortly therafter announced the convening of a three-man federal panel to conduct a hearing on the suit on Monday 6 November one day before the scheduled general election.

Two important developments closely followed the filing of the Hatcher suit. The first was an announcement by John Krupa that he was restoring the names of the 5,286 voters removed from the registration roles. Krupa said that he was taking this step in light of advice he received from county attorneys that his action in removing the names would probably be declared illegal by the federal courts. Second was the announcement by the Justice Department—in a reversal of its previous position—that it was filing a companion suit to the Hatcher suit charging Lake County officials with inflating the number of white registrants while diminishing the number of legally registered black voters. This action constituted the first time the federal government had intervened in a local election to protect the voting rights of blacks in the North.

Despite appearances, the decision on the part of the Justice Department to enter the Gary controversy was not a precipitous move. Unknown to practically anyone was the fact that the FBI had been investigating charges of voting irregularities in Gary for six months. These FBI activities were supplemented by the work of a special team of twenty-two lawyers from the civil rights division of the Justice Department immediately after the Hatcher suit was filed in the court. When representatives of the Justice Department arrived, they found that the FBI had already meticulously photographed and sent to Washington for examination, all new registration cards and applications from the period May through October 1967. Using information supplied them by the FBI, Justice Department lawyers fanned out through white neighborhoods checking the accuracy of white registrations. Between Wednesday 1 November and Friday 3 November, when the federal suit was filed, Justice Department and FBI agents verified the existence of 300 false white registrations. They uncovered 700 additional fake names on registration rolls in white areas between Friday and Sunday. This information provided the basis for a wealth of data to support the case the federal government intended to present to the federal panel on Monday. The data included, according to one respondent, "charts and other documents." Although not inexperienced in such matters, this respondent was astounded by the ability of the federal government to amass such an assortment of information over a period of a few days. He described the investigatory capability of the Justice Department as "awesome." "I've never seen such a collection of data, such a compilation of material, which required fantastic physical effort and expertise. I would hate to have the federal government come after me the way it came in that case. It was just an absolutely incredible display of logistical ability."

On the morning of the hearing, the federal courthouse in Hammond—site of the proceedings—was jammed with press representatives and an overflow crowd of spectators. Presiding were Judges George Beamer of the Hammond Federal Court, Jesse Eschbach of the Northern District Court of Fort Wayne, and Walter Cummings of the Seventh Circuit Court of Appeals in Chicago. Before hearing testimony, the federal panel—over the strenuous objection of defense attorneys—consolidated the Hatcher and Justice Department cases.

The hearing began with the testimony of three witnesses called by the Justice Department to substantiate its allegations of fraudulent registration activities in white areas. The first witness, Mrs. Charles Luck, testified that none of the eighteen persons shown on poll books as being tenants in her apartments were living there as of 1 November, nor had they been living there for the past three months. Arthur Illyes, a second government witness, owner of lots from 4121 through 4141 on Georgia Street, which contained a used car lot but no residences, denied that a William Henderson registered at 4125 Georgia Street lived there. Mrs. Marg Fejo issued a similar denial that two persons listed as registered from her home actually lived there.

Donald H. Lotz, senior resident agent for the Gary FBI, also testified as a government witness. Lotz told the court that FBI agents had discovered 1,100 registrations in white neighborhoods that could not be verified. He said all of these false registrations had been added since Hatcher's defeat of Mayor Katz in the May primary. On cross-examination, Lotz admitted that black precincts were not as extensively canvassed as white. However, he said a thorough check had been run in the 57 predominantly black precincts and that no ficticious names were discovered on the poll books there.

John L. Howard, a black steelworker, took the stand to testify that he had received a letter from the county chairman's office challenging his registration although he had been a registered voter in Gary since 1936 and had never missed voting in a city election since that time. He said he called Anthony Dobis to complain when he received the letter, and Dobis assured him that his registration card would be put back.

Hatcher attorney William Ming called Krupa to the stand. Krupa denied that the county organization attempted to purge black voters from the rolls. He did admit, however, that he sent out letters challenging the registration of the 5,000 black voters in question, although there were no specific procedures or regulations authorizing him to take such action.

The most dramatic point in the hearing came when Mrs. Marion Tokarski took the stand to testify to widespread fraudulent registration in white areas. A description of the atmosphere of the courtroom during the time of Mrs. Tokarski offered her spectacular relevations was provided by the following respondent:

> Everything built up to Marion Tokarski. It was a packed court room. And boy when that white woman started dropping those names, everytime she dropped one there would be an audible gasp from the spectators. The tension was so thick you could cut it with a knife.

Prefacing her remarks with the declaration "I am incriminating myself in this case," Mrs. Tokarski told of her participation in the registration of fraudulent voters. She claimed to have first-hand knowledge of 107 names of persons who were either dead or had moved away who were registered to vote in her precinct in the general election. Mrs. Tokarski also testified to receiving a phone call from a Democratic district captain asking her to provide five names to be purged so her precinct could be included in a citywide purge of voters.

At the close of their arguments in the case, Hatcher attorneys asked the federal panel to put a court representative or Hatcher representative on the staff of election officials supervising voting activities in Gary's 132 precinct-polling places. They contended that this action was necessary because Hatcher could not be fairly represented by persons appointed by county chairman Krupa to serve as election judges. The only persons really committed to safeguarding the Hatcher vote, they argued, were unofficial observers who did not have the power to challenge voters or to see that proper procedures were followed.

When closing arguments had been presented, the three-judge panel recessed the court and deliberated for one and a quarter hours before returning with its decision. The court ruled in favor of the plaintiffs. In their opinion, the three judges unanimously agreed to deny the Hatcher petition to postpone the Gary election, but instead to issue a preliminary injunction against actions by the defendants that would impair the holding of a fair and non-discriminatory election. Election officials were ordered specifically not to allow the 1,100 ghost voters turned up by the FBI and Justice Department to participate in the election. County clerk Krupa and his subordinates were also ordered not to prohibit the 5,286 voters on his letter list from voting. Written records relating to the challenge of any voter in the 7 November election were to be maintained by election officials and made available to federal officials for inspection. The court noted that it was retaining jurisdiction in the case until after the election "for such further proceedings as justice may require."[34] United States marshals were ordered to post the court order along with lists of alleged fraudulent voters at all polling places, and to serve copies of the documents on all election-day workers. The three-judge panel turned down Hatcher's request that he be allowed to place his representatives at each polling place, observing that the hour was too late to change election officials and that such a step would constitute a violation of Indiana election laws.[35]

Hatcher labeled the court decision a victory. Krupa commented that the court action provided for what the county organization wanted all along—a fair election. Radigan, who had previously referred to the Hatcher suit as reckless and irresponsible said that he was confident the court decision would guarantee a fair election but would still like to see federal marshals stationed at each polling place to provide extra protection against vote stealing in black as well as white areas.

ELECTION DAY

In the wake of the multitude of charges and countercharges of vote fraud, rumors of possible racial turmoil on election day spread throughout the city during the final week of the campaign.

Taking these rumors seriously, national, state, and local officials made elaborate precautionary arrangements to firmly quash any outbreak of racial violence that might arise. Approximately five thousand national guard troops were assembled at armories in Valparaiso, Michigan City, and Hammond with orders to move into Gary the moment trouble developed. One contingent of national guard troops were ordered into South Gary near Gilroy Stadium before dawn on election day by Major General John S. Anderson of the Indiana National Guard. They were accompanied by armored personnel carriers and other riot equipment. A temporary headquarters for the state police was set up at a Valparaiso motel. Reporters counted as many as 240 state patrol cars outside the motel at one point in the day. Included among the state law officers on alert at the motel were four platoons of patrolmen specially trained in riot control. "With replacements and officers they constituted virtually the entire state police force."[36] Hundreds of state policemen joined with Gary's entire force of 248 policemen in patrolling precincts throughout the day. Federal help was provided by FBI agents and 25 United States marshals sent to Gary from several other cities. City police from nearby communities prepared to seal off Gary if rioting broke out so that "Chicago hoodlums" could not rush over to join in the violence. A central command post for law-enforcement agencies was established in Gary police headquarters. Radio transmitters were installed, putting the command post in immediate contact with police squad cars and police and national guard headquarters outside the city.

The situation in both black and white precincts on election day in Gary was extremely tense. Hatcher workers were not appointed as official precinct-observers by Krupa, but many did serve as unofficial poll-watchers, the same capacity they had held in the spring. Again an elaborate two-way communication system was set up enabling poll-watchers to immediately contact a team of lawyers operating out of central headquarters, who served as election day troubleshooters. Phones at Hatcher headquarters were ringing continuously all day. Most of the calls were from persons complaining that they were not being allowed to vote by election officials because their names were not in poll books or supplementary binders issued by the county clerk's office. One especially troublesome problem resulted from the registration of some voters in Midtown by a Mrs. Freeman who identified herself as a vice-committeewoman in the 124th precinct. However, Mrs. Freeman was never sworn in as a deputy registrar and apparently never turned in the sign-ups she recorded. Thus the names of persons she registered were all missing from poll books. A frantic search for Mrs. Freeman ensued, but nobody seemed to know anything about where she could have possibly disappeared. Hatcher headquarters also received a rash of complaints about voting machine breakdowns in midtown precincts. Mayor Katz denied that these breakdowns were deliberate but attributed the trouble to "new equipment and, in some cases, new election workers unfamiliar with the machines."[37] A few reports were received of ghost voting. William Barden, for example, told Hatcher officials that he had been informed by poll officials when he tried to vote that someone using his name had already cast his vote. He said polling officials ignored his objections and turned him away. In general, however, the incidence of vote-stealing was sharply curtailed by the close supervision by federal agents of election-day activities. This fact is underscored by the reflection of this Hatcher worker on his experiences as a poll-watcher in an all-white precinct:

I poll watched in the [X] precinct on the Eastside. The precinct committeewoman was [Y], who was named in the federal suit along with Marion Tokarski as one of the instigators of the movement to steal the election. The Democratic Sheriff was her mother. The polling place was in her garage. The Republican precinct committeeman was under her thumb. The only honest person of all the election officials both Democratic and Republican was the Republican sheriff, who was an old time Republican. He was honest, but Republican through and through. They were frightened. She [Y] was frightened especially. Around 8:00 A.M. the federal marshal came and handed everyone the injunction enjoining them from interfering with the voting procedure or attempting to steal the election. They also tacked the injunction on the door of the garage. After these documents were handed out and the marshal left, [Y] went to the polling book and crossed out another thirty or forty names which she knew about that the federal government didn't know about. It was quite obvious she was very frightened about getting caught in this. She was doing all in her power to assure Radigan's election. But she didn't want to get caught up in this suit of false people voting under someone else's name. She pointed out to me and several others that if any of these other people came in they were to be challenged.

This respondent noted that despite the cautious attitude of the Democratic precinct committeewoman, some flagrant violations did occur. The precinct inspector and Democratic judge, for example, were going behind the curtain showing people how to split Hatcher out until he called this activity to the attention of the Republican sheriff who immediately brought it to a halt. He also asserted that the police had to be called to the precinct several times because iron workers persisted in intimidating people coming in and out of the polling station. One student from Notre Dame standing around pretending to take pictures with an unloaded camera was beaten up by this group.

Not surprisingly, one of the most harassed persons in Gary on election day was Mrs. Marion Tokarski. She reported to newsmen that she had been receiving threatening telephone calls. One male caller told her "If Hatcher is elected, you'll never see him mayor."[38] When she went to vote in her precinct she was accosted outside by a man who said that she had "sold her soul for 30 pieces of silver."[39]

On balance, despite all of the rumors of racial violence, general election day was one of the calmest in recent times. There were no reports of extremely severe incidents. Again much of the prevailing peace can be attributed to the presence of federal forces, as this Hatcher supporter candidly explained:

> We were reinforced by some federal fear that was thrown around the last few days of the campaign. This was very effective. Had it not been for that the confrontation would have developed. Because they were going to steal, they've been doing it for the last twenty years so why stop now. That was going to go on. And we were determined not to allow it to go on. So the forces would have met and it would have been quite a meeting.

Election day also witnessed the heaviest turnout of voters in the city's history. At 5:00 P.M. two hours before the polls closed Mayor Katz forecast a record 80 percent turnout. Heaviest turnout was achieved in predominantly black districts. By noon more than 60 percent of the eligible black electorate had voted while about 50 percent of the white voters had turned out. At the bottom of this tremendous black turnout was the Hatcher organization. The ranks of Hatcher workers participating in the effort to turnout the black vote in the primary were swollen in the general by college students from throughout the country. A contingent of students from Notre Dame and Purdue were brought to Gary by

George Neagu, director of the South Bend Human Relations Commission. Students also came over from Northwestern, Roosevelt, University of Chicago, and other nearby schools. One delegation of one hundred students came from Illinois, Connecticut, Michigan, Ohio, New Jersey, and California. They made it clear to reporters that they were not outsiders but "mostly the children of Gary parents who have gone to school in other states."[40] Three out-of-town students indicated that they came "in response to the need for an honest election in your city."[41] Also participating in the get-out-the-vote effort were black members of a packinghouse union in Chicago, and Chicago-based black politicians State Senator Richard Newhouse, State Representative Harold Washington, Alderman William Cousins, Jr., former Alderman Robert H. Miller, and State Senator Charles Chew. Robert Lucas, director of the Chicago chapter of the Congress of Racial Equality was an additional out-of-towner on hand to lend his support to Hatcher's success in the general election. Generally, more than three thousand persons were involved in the total election-day effort to protect the vote and generate a massive turnout in the black community.

Hatcher and Radigan ran neck and neck throughout the election day balloting. At one point only 37 votes separated the two candidates. By 7 P.M. when the polls closed, both Hatcher and Radigan were declaring victory in the mayoral race. Hatcher's statement, however, conveyed an undertone of uncertainty that belied the outward image of confidence he attempted to project. He told his supporters gathered at headquarters: "I am confident we are going to be victorious tonight. This has been a campaign to try to create a different kind of city—a new Gary. I am certain right always wins over evil. I am certain we are going to win tonight."[42] In contrast to Hatcher's cautious optimism, Radigan assumed the role of a candidate who had already been declared mayor-elect. He strutted around his headquarters flashing a victory sign and declaring to his jubilant followers: "This was a hard-fought but good clean campaign. After the election I will sit down with my opposition to discuss the good of all Gary."[43] At this point preliminary returns showed Radigan polling huge majorities in Glen Park and Miller. As the night wore on, however, ecstasy turned to agony in the Radigan camp. A 10 P.M. check of the vote showed Radigan leading by 4,900 votes. Twenty minutes later, as returns from Midtown began to pour in, this lead was whittled down to 770 votes. At about this precise moment Hatcher headquarters began coming alive. By 11:00 the outcome of the election was no longer in doubt. Hatcher was leading by 2,000 votes with only 3 more precincts to be recorded. Black precincts had given Hatcher such lopsided majorities as 4 to 434, 16 to 522, and 1 to 291. The deciding vote was cast by Hatcher's home precinct, the 111th; this precinct gave Radigan 14 votes to Hatcher's 1,003. Hatcher headquarters broke out in wild rejoicing. Shouts of "Oh, no!" went up in Radigan headquarters. An organ struck up a chorus of "When Irish Eyes are Smiling," but few in Radigan headquarters were in the mood for singing.

When final totals were computed, Hatcher had won the election by the narrow margin of 1,389 votes, receiving 39,812 to Radigan's 37,947.[44] A breakdown of the vote by districts and the percentages of the vote by districts are shown in table 14. In

TABLE 14

GARY MAYORALTY ELECTION, 1967

District	Hatcher	Radigan	Percent Hatcher	Percent Radigan
First	2,012	11,636	11.7	88.3
Second	3,379	7,790	23.7	76.3
Third	11,171	2,367	82.5	17.5
Fourth	10,848	540	95.5	4.5
Fifth	10,530	366	97.5	2.5
Sixth	1,371	15,039	8.3	91.7
Total	39,812	37,947	50.9	49.1

SOURCE: Board of Election voting returns.

an exclusive postelection interview with the *Chicago Daily News*, Hatcher contended that his actual margin of victory was much higher, but that the machine managed to successfully steal between 5,000 and 7,000 votes. Asked if any fraudulent votes were cast for him, Hatcher answered, "No. I'll tell you why. The people who opposed us had control of the entire election machinery. We had control over nothing. We didn't want to do anything wrong, and even if we did we weren't in a position to do it. If any fraud went on, it went on in behalf of my opponent."[45]

An analysis of the vote indicates that several factors were most crucially responsible for the outcome of the election. First, a cursory examination of voting patterns in the election clearly shows race to be the dominant factor influencing the voting decisions of the Gary electorate. This was no doubt a natural product of the overtly racial nature of the general campaign. Both Hatcher and Radigan made valiant efforts to rise above the race issue to talk about plans for reconstructing city government and providing for the citizens of Gary a better way of life. Rational discourse on good government issues was impossible, however, in a campaign where one candidate was constantly called upon to defend himself against charges of black power advocacy and the other of being a dupe of a corrupt political machine attempting to hold on to power by any means necessary. Race inevitably overshadowed all other issues; its impact in the election was so strong that it shattered patterns of voting behavior in the white community that held sway over a period of thirty years. Leaders of the regular Democratic organization appealed to the racism endemic in Gary's white community for their own political purposes; and they succeeded in stimulating a massive defection of white voters to the Republican camp. This fact produced the single most important attribute of the 1967 mayoral election: the division of the vote along racial lines. Table 14 shows that the predominantly black third, fourth, and fifth districts went solidly for Hatcher while Miller, Glen Park, and Uptown gave overwhelming support to Radigan.

When one probes beneath the racial factor, however, one finds that a pivotal key to Hatcher's victory was his success in polling a higher percentage of the white vote than Radigan did the black vote. Given the intensity of the racial assaults leveled against him, Hatcher ran surprisingly well in the white community. He received 5,322 or about 14 percent of the white vote. Hatcher ran poorest in Eastern European precincts in Glen Park; his vote in Glen Park ranged from 4 percent in precinct 102 to 12 percent in precinct 100. Overall, he managed to capture 8.3 percent of the Glen Park vote. As could be expected, Hatcher ran much better in Miller. He received about 15 percent of the Miller vote. However, support for Hatcher significantly surpassed this average figure in wealthier Miller precincts. He polled, for example, an impressive 24 percent of the vote in the economically affluent first precinct in Miller. Hatcher made his greatest inroads in the white community among Latin American voters.

Analysis of the vote in the heavily Latin second and third districts reveals that he received approximately 60 percent of the Latin American vote.

In contrast, Radigan fell down badly in the black community. For example, in the fifth district he received a miniscule 2.5 percent of the vote. He improved on this slightly in the fourth district where he received 4.5 percent of the vote. His best performance was in the third district; there he received 17.5 percent of the vote. Most of Radigan's support in the third district came not from black precincts but from the all white thirty-fifth, thirty-sixth, and thirty-seventh precincts that have traditionally voted Republican.

Hatcher's support in the white community—though not extraordinarily large—was large enough to assure his victory. Radigan's support in the black community was too weak to offset the amount of support picked up by Hatcher in the white community. What accounts for Hatcher's white vote in an election fought mainly along racial lines? It is probable that a good percentage of the white vote Hatcher received in Glen Park came from habitual Democrats who could not bring themselves to vote for a Republican. These were persons who remembered that it was Roosevelt not Eisenhower who brought them through the depression; they had always voted straight Democratic tickets in the past, and out of habit and a sense of party loyalty continued to do so in the 1967 Gary mayoral election. Another closely related component of the Hatcher white vote was that element of the white community that initially felt cross-pressured but was inspired by Hatcher's campaign appeal to maintain their support for the entire Democratic ticket. A substantial proportion of this vote came from the Latin community. With the invaluable assistance of Latin leaders, including Congressman Gonzalez, Hatcher successfully appealed to a majority of the Latin electorate's sense of party loyalty and attachment to the group's heritage. Although persons who worked in the Hatcher campaign tended to downgrade the significance of the Latin vote, it is clear that the Latin community played the pivotal swing role in this election that the black community played in an earlier point in the city's history. Whites in Miller were more willing to judge the candidates on their merits rather than their race; this fact accounts in part for the white support Hatcher received in that area. A number of Miller residents had supported Hatcher all along even in the primary; some supported him openly, but even more kept their preference for Hatcher within the confines of their family and friendship circles. The latter point was stressed by Hatcher's campaign manager Henry Coleman in a post-election newspaper interview. Coleman contended in this article that many white voters felt compelled to support Hatcher privately because "they were afraid of their neighbors."[46] There is some evidence to support the conclusion that at least a small proportion of Hatcher's white vote came from whites who objected to the overtly racial campaign tactics employed by Hatcher's Democratic opponents. These comments by a white respondent helps to establish the basis for this conclusion:

> Defeating a Democratic nominee in this town is not easy. And the only way they [leaders of the regular Democratic organization] could defeat him was by making an overt racial appeal. But in some cases this strategy backfired. For instance in our precinct here, the fifth precinct, which consists of a large number of people up from Tennessee and Kentucky, I think the mayor [Hatcher] got about 17 votes in the primary whereas in November he got somewhere about 70 to 80 votes. Well, somebody around here who didn't want that man mayor in the primary just couldn't stomach the fact that a vote for Radigan was a purely racial vote. And I would be hard pressed to find the people. I couldn't name them, but obviously they were here.

We may note also that Hatcher's voting percentage in the white community was enhanced by the large number of ballots spoiled by whites in the attempt to vote for other Democratic candidates while splitting Hatcher out. In Glen Park and Miller 3,700 more votes were cast for councilman than for mayor. In the racially mixed second district 288 persons voting in councilmanic races did not cast a vote in the mayor's race. It is reasonable to presume that these differences were due in large measure to errors made by whites inexperienced in the practice of split-ticket voting. No such problem plagued black voters. Thus, for example, whereas large differences in the number of votes cast for Democratic council candidate Eugene Carrabine and Hatcher existed in the second district (2,406), in black precincts in this district both candidates received approximately the same number of votes. Black voters generally just went to the polls and voted a straight Democratic ticket.

Complementing Hatcher's moderate success in the white

320 / Electing Black Mayors

community was the tremendous success he enjoyed in the black community. In the final analysis the extraordinarily high mobilization of the black vote by Hatcher's campaign organization was the most important factor contributing to his general election victory. The Hatcher organization turned out a record 76 percent of the black vote; this compared to a turnout of 72 percent of the registered white electorate. Blacks voted in bloc fashion as they had done in previous general elections, but this time they did so over the opposition of Democratic party leaders. Hatcher received 96 percent of the black vote cast in the election. This combination of high turnout and cohesion by black voters—which could have only been accomplished through a mobilization effort of extensive dimensions—provided the pivotal foundation upon which the electoral coalition that catapulted a black man into the mayor's office in Gary, Indiana, in 1967 was built.

1. *Gary Post-Tribune*, 4 May 1967.
2. Ibid.
3. Quoted in *Newsweek*, 17 November 1967.
4. *Gary Post-Tribune*, 4 August 1967.
5. Interview with Mayor Richard G. Hatcher, 7 January 1969.
6. This quotation and following unattributed quotations are derived from interviews conducted in Gary, Indiana, by the authors.
7. *Gary Post-Tribune*, 21 September 1967.
8. Ibid. Actually it was true that the county organization had not officially "given" money to mayoral candidates in the past. It had, however, granted them "loans" of up to $500,000 and "inadvertently" failed to collect.
9. *Gary Post-Tribune*, 9 September 1967.
10. He was referring here to his political endorsement of Alexander Williams, Jessie Mitchell, and Jeanette Strong (former president of the Gary NAACP).
11. *Gary Post-Tribune*, 9 September 1967.
12. *Info*, 14 September 1967. All quotations from various editions of *Info* are reprinted by permission of the publisher.
13. *Gary Post-Tribune*, 12 September 1967.
14. Krupa had claimed to have evidence that Attorney General Robert Kennedy had turned Hatcher down for the position because he could not get security clearance.
15. *Gary Post-Tribune*, 1 October 1967.
16. *Info*, 12 October 1967.
17. Ibid., 17 August 1967.
18. At one point the organization had trouble with people who were not Hatcher workers going into business establishments and picking up the boxes.

Campaign Manager Henry Coleman ran several articles in the paper saying that persons authorized to pick up the boxes would be supplied with an identification card from the organization. These articles admonished merchants that campaign money was not to be turned over to anyone else.

19. *Gary Post-Tribune*, 5 November 1967.

20. *Info*, 7 September 1967.

21. *Gary Post-Tribune*, 30 September 1967.

22. A memorandum warning teachers about such practices had previously been issued by the school superintendent during the spring.

23. *Gary Post-Tribune*, 16 September 1967.

24. *Info*, 19 October 1967.

25. Ibid., 12 October 1967.

26. Ibid., 24 August 1967.

27. Ibid., 12 October 1967.

28. Ibid., 7 September 1967.

29. *Gary Post-Tribune*, 14 September 1967.

30. Ibid., 11 October 1967.

31. Quoted in the *Chicago Sun Times*, 19 November 1967.

32. *Chicago Sun Times*, 27 October 1967.

33. *Gary Post-Tribune*, 31 October 1967.

34. *New York Times*, 7 November 1967.

35. In a telegram to Krupa, Democratic state chairman Gordon St. Angelo urged Krupa to accept Hatcher appointees and an equal number chosen by Radigan as election judges. St. Angelo's statement was accompanied by a long list of senators, clergymen, party officials, and business and labor leaders endorsing the Hatcher plan.

36. *Chicago Sun Times*, 7 November 1967.

37. Ibid., 8 November 1967.

38. *Chicago Tribune*, 8 November 1967.

39. Ibid.

40. *Gary Post-Tribune*, 8 November 1967. This article had the arresting title, "Hippies Hop on Bandwagon."

41. Ibid.

42. Ibid.

43. Ibid.

44. A recanvass one week after the election however, revealed that votes on one machine in the forty-second precinct were not counted. Tabulation of these returns gave Hatcher an additional 482 votes and Radigan 6. This boosted Hatcher's margin of victory to 1,865 votes, the total votes for each candidate being: Hatcher, 39,812, and Radigan, 37,947.

45. *Chicago Daily News*, 11 November 1967.

46. *Chicago Tribune*, 9 November 1967.

9

A Summary View of Political Mobilization

INTRODUCTION

Throughout the post-World War II period, millions of black Americans migrated into large northern cities, and millions of whites moved from the central cities to surrounding suburbs. These simultaneous migratory patterns created (and are still creating) a demographic context that substantially increased the possibility that blacks would attempt to elect members of their own ethnic group to the mayorship of cities because of its symbolic and substantive importance. In the preceding chapters we have attempted to demonstrate that such an accomplishment is by no means an automatic process. We have argued that a large numerical concentration of blacks within a governmental jurisdiction is at best only a potential political resource in the quest for electoral black power. Numerical concentration is a resource that must be supplemented by other political resources, including a heightened political consciousness, independent leadership, organization, and group cohesion, if black electoral success is to be achieved. In this chapter our objective is to review and summarize the factors that contribute to political mobilization in black communities and the additional factors that influence whether or not a black candidate will be elected mayor of a large city.

THE INGREDIENTS OF POLITICAL MOBILIZATION

The early stirrings of the mobilization process in both Cleveland and Gary began with the emergence of the civil rights movement in the early 1960s. Civil rights action on the national level was, of course, an important stimulant in this process, but local civil rights activities were even more significant. Numerous demonstrations and other activities performed the double function of involving in direct political action thousands of blacks who had previously been politically inactive and exposing the stubborn racism of the white establishment. The combination of these two factors contributed to several developments: it encouraged a growing number of blacks to engage in politics; it shattered the notion that blacks were experiencing normal progress and thus were satisfied with their lot; it reinforced the idea that blacks had to act in unison, not as individuals, if they wanted to improve their socioeconomic-political condition; it provided blacks with a growing sense of group consciousness and cohesion; and it identified the incumbent white administration as the common enemy of virtually all black people. In a word, the civil rights movement served to mobilize black resistance to the prevailing system of domestic colonialism.

Out of this process of political awakening and growing group solidarity emerged a new set of black leaders distinguished by their identification with the aspirations of the black masses. Both Hatcher and Stokes and the people surrounding them provided ample evidence to the black community that they were not sell-out risks to the white establishment. Unlike numerous traditional black leaders, these new leaders projected the image of selfless people whose major concern was not the promotion of their own personal interest but the overall interest of the black community. This factor, for example, contributed more than anything else to Hatcher's widespread popularity in Gary. First as a civil rights activist and later as a member of the Gary city council, Hatcher had demonstrated to the black masses that he was dedicated to the advancement of the total black community and could not be induced to sell out black interests through promises of money or threats of political or physical retaliation. In this respect he presented a public image that contrasted markedly with that of traditional black leaders who had on innumerable occasions compromised the interests of the black community for personal rewards. This ability to overcome the distrust the black masses had of orthodox leadership can be viewed as a pivotal ingredient of the political mobilization process. Testimony to the critical nature of trust and confidence in the mobilization process was provided by a number of respondents. Witness, for instance, these words of advice offered by one black respondent to blacks in other cities wishing to follow in the footpath of Gary blacks.

> I hope if we didn't do but one thing, our movement here will inspire black people in other places to look around in their community and find a candidate. I am willing to go and help some other people look around in their community and find a candidate. I don't want to pick one of those cities with just a sprinkling few whites. I want to pick one of those cities like Chicago. It would be a pleasure for me to go into Chicago, help those people find a candidate and prove to them that the Daley machine can be beat. But here's the thing. Now you're not going to do this with one of those stiff collars. The people are not going to buy him. He's got to be identified with the grass-roots people, the ordinary John Doe, as a man who stood up, stood alone, spoke out for what he thought was wrong regardless of the consequences. That is the kind of man it's going to take in Chicago to bust Daley. Whenever I find that the people have chosen themselves a candidate who can identify with the grass roots, whether it be Chicago or some place else, I will be more than willing to offer my services for free.[1]

Emergence in the black community of a leadership corps and a candidate enjoying the trust and confidence of the black masses made possible the formation of a grass-roots campaign organization composed of volunteer workers.[2] The formation and development of such a campaign structure is critical to the mobilization of the black electorate for several reasons. First, given the unlikely possibility that any black mayoral candidate around whom the mobilization process would focus will have at his disposal a sizeable campaign war chest, the creation of such an organization serves to substitute volunteer citizen activity for extensive economic resources. This fact takes on immense importance in circumstances such as those faced by Hatcher and Stokes who had to confront powerful and entrenched Democratic organizations and wealthy Republican organizations. Second, members of the organization provide an indispensable link between the candidate and the black electorate. Both Stokes and Hatcher found that the individuals in the best position to sell them to rank-and-file black voters and thus compete with professional black politicians for the loyalty of the black masses were the volunteer representatives of the grass-roots black community. In effect, the campaign volunteers became parallel precinct committee people and successfuly challenged the traditional precinct workers. With hundreds of volunteer workers —many of whom were grass-roots individuals with no previous experience in political campaigning—using every possible means to deliver the vote of every eligible black voter on their behalf, Stokes and Hatcher were able to bypass the traditional political structures that had historically delivered the black vote to white mayoralty candidates. Third, such a campaign organization created a band-wagon effect within the black community, which made it very difficult for any segment of the community to withhold support. A crusade-like atmosphere, charged with high emotionalism, prevailed and encouraged blacks from varied walks of life to participate in a historic event.

Thus one of the keys to black electoral mobilization is the involvement of large numbers of citizens at the grass-roots level who are emotionally involved in the struggle to elect a committed black politician to a major elective office and who in fact view the battle that must be waged to accomplish this objective as a crusade. It should be stressed, however, that this emotional zeal and the political energy it produces must be channeled by effective organization and capable leadership. Without a substantial degree of organization and leadership support, the grass-roots movement in the election will collapse in the midst of chaos and confusion. Certain elemental things must be done if the galvanizing of massive black participation and intense cohesion in the election is to be realized. Among the more important tasks that must be accomplished by those serving in the upper ranks of the campaign organization is fund-raising and research. A multiplicity of ways must be tested for raising necessary monies to operate the campaign. Except in unusual circumstances, such as those which lead to the *New York Times* advertisement placed by the Hatcher organization and the contributions of some wealthy individuals to the Stokes effort, the most effective method for raising funds will generally center around small contributions by rank-and-file citizens and moderate contributions from liberal whites and established black organizations. Funds from regular party organizations and labor union sources are most likely to be cut off from an independent black candidate. It is also unlikely that donations will emanate from business sources that are open to retaliation from regulatory city hall departments. Consequently, the bulk of campaign funds are most likely to be derived from rank-and-file sources within the black community, although white liberals and special events, such as the Harry Belafonte concert in Gary, will also be important.

In addition to fund-raising, the upper echelons of the campaign organization must expend considerable energy in conducting research on the social, economic, and governmental issues of the city so that the literature distributed to the public and the major policy statements made by the candidate are well documented and carefully prepared. This requires the combined efforts of an effective team of volunteer researchers and literature writers who can collect and prepare a multitude of information for dissemination. Such an accomplishment provides the candidate with an opportunity to demonstrate to voters that he is exceptionally well informed and prepared to assume the mayorship, and that he is a candidate that black people can be proud of.

Fund-raising and research are obviously important; however, central to the mobilization effort is the work performed by the street-level organization. As previously indicated, the members of this organization are assigned the critical task of selling the candidate to their friends and neighbors. In doing so they must overcome the obstacles of black self-doubt—the feeling that blacks cannot elect a member of their race to a major public office—and the myth of black inferiority—the belief that a black man is not as capable of performing effectively in a key public office as a white man. To sell their candidate to the black masses in the light of these obstacles, street-level campaign workers must use personal-contact techniques with rank-and-file voters to convince them that the candidate is eminently qualified to hold high public office, that he has a very good chance of winning if the black community unites behind him, and that if he is elected he will fulfill the goals of the civil rights movement by opening up to blacks expanded opportunities for social, economic, and political mobility.

If the campaigns run by both the upper-level campaign members and street-level campaign members are successful, the results will be, as noted earlier, a bandwagon effect generating a massive outpouring of public support for the candidate. The emergence of this bandwagon effect denotes the epitome of group cohesion and electoral political consciousness, which culminates on election day with unprecedented mobilization in the black community. During this period, grass-roots campaign activity is intensified, with thousands of workers pounding the streets seeking to reach every eligible black voter and performing other specific tasks. On election day the focus of the grass-roots as well as the high-level campaign organizations centers on the performance of three critical tasks: (1) organizing a last minute canvass of every black neighborhood; (2) making sure that every black voter gets to the polls and votes for the candidate; and (3) devising mechanisms to protect the candidate from massive vote stealing by the opposition. Around the performance of each task carefully planned grass-roots organization must be developed. Persons active in the street-level organization must join forces with other interested parties such as college students, members of good-government groups and experienced civil rights workers, in a door-to-door drive to insure that every eligible black voter gets to the polls. These workers plus others stationed at polling places should supply all voters with sample ballots and other materials that will help them cast a legitimate vote for the candidate.

While these segments of the organization concentrate on turning out black voters, other segments must center their attention on making sure that each vote cast in the election is fairly counted. The key to this effort is to have persons trained as election day poll-watchers. These persons act as the eyes and ears of the campaign organization inside the precinct polling place, and they should be instructed to immediately report to central headquarters any activities that appear to violate city or state election laws. Calls concerning illegal efforts to tamper with the vote or interfere with the electoral process should be relayed to teams of lawyers working out of central headquarters, who investigate such complaints and decide upon appropriate responses to them.

The culmination of the mobilization process is indicated by an unprecedented black voter turnout and cohesive vote in the election. Both the high turnout and the high cohesion are the necessary requirements for the establishment of a solid base of black support for the candidate. This base of support is indispensable to the election of an independent black candidate to the mayorship of a major American city. Whether or not this base is sufficient for electoral victory is dependent on additional factors, which are discussed below.

THE REQUIREMENTS FOR SUCCESS

We want to underscore the fact that black mobilization does not necessarily mean black victory. Only where blacks are 51 percent or more of the voting electorate would successful mobilization of the black vote be sufficient for victory. In most cases, however, the black electoral base for black mayoral candidates will not be so extensive. Consequently, black candidates must include the white as well as the black community in their strategy for victory.[3]

Several factors have a crucial bearing on the extent to which a black mayoral candidate running on solid black support will be able to garner enough white votes to win. One factor relates to the strength and cohesiveness of the dominant white political organization. If the dominant white organization in the city is both strong and highly cohesive, it will be extraordinarily difficult for the black candidate to obtain significant electoral support in the white community. Under such circumstances the dominant white organization can in all probability hold the white community together by settling on one white candidate to run in a head-to-head contest with the black candidate, such as was the case in East Saint Louis. Given the choice of a white or black candidate, the overwhelming majority of whites will unquestionably cast their votes for the candidate of their own race. On the other hand, if the white-dominated organization is weak or divided, it might not be in a position to prevent several major white candidates from getting in the race. This situation tends to favor the black candidate because with a splintering of the white vote among two or more candidates, the number of white votes he needs to win the election is measurably reduced. As we have seen in previous chapters, it was precisely such fragmentation within the white organizations in Cleveland and Gary that facilitated the election of Stokes and Hatcher.

A second factor affecting the ability of a black mayoral candidate to obtain the necessary votes for victory in the white community is the socioeconomic characteristics of the white electorate. The presence in the white electorate of a large number of middle- and upper-income Jewish voters may provide a black candidate with a sympathetic base of support in the white community due to the tendency toward liberalism evidenced in Jewish voting behavior. If Jewish citizens are not eligible to vote in the election because of their residence in the suburbs (as was the case in Cleveland), some are likely to provide financial or organizational assistance. On the other hand, if the electorate is disproportionately composed of blue-collar ethnics with a history of competition with blacks for jobs, schools, homes, and many other city facilities and resources, the chances of receiving more than a modicum of support from the white community will be slim.

As a rule of thumb, we can say that the larger the degree of white support a black mayoral candidate will need to win and the smaller the number of whites sympathetic to his mayoral aspirations, the more he will find it necessary to stress the notion that he intends to be mayor for all the people of the city.[4] In addition, he must project the image that he is sincerely committed to being both progressive and honest. This commitment will have to embrace a program of institutional reform and an aggressive attack on the social and economic problems of the community. In either case, the most effective vehicle for selling himself to white voters will be small house parties, which provide opportunities for interpersonal contact and meticulous appraisal of his personality as well as his programs by inquisitive and curious white citizens. These house parties must be arranged primarily by whites active in the campaign organization, although other white organizations mobilized during the campaign—such as teachers groups—might prove useful in this respect.

In all but very unusual circumstances, elections involving a bid by an independent black candidate running with solid black support to become mayor of a large American city will be decided by a small number of votes. Given this fact, it will be necessary for black mayors, in addition to appealing to the general white community, to seek viable coalitions with other

Third World groups. Indeed, as another rule of thumb, we can say that the closer the possible outcome of the election, the greater the need for the black candidate to make an effective appeal for the votes of other nonblack minorities. This proposition is supported by our analysis of the 1967 Gary mayoral election. In the primary when the white vote was split and it seemed reasonable that if Hatcher received solid support from the black community he could win, only modest steps were taken to involve Latins in an effective way in the campaign. However, in the general election when virtually the entire white community was threatening to cross over to the Republican camp, extensive efforts were made by Hatcher workers to draw Latins into the campaign organizations and to encourage them to play key roles in the mobilization of the Latin vote.

In sum, successful mobilization of the black community alone will probably not be enough in the immediate future to elect a black candidate to the mayorship of major American cities. Supplementing the primary base of support in the black community must be a major effort to penetrate the walls of the white community and the seeking of alliances among other nonwhite minorities.

CONCLUSION

In this study we have attempted to demonstrate that the post-World War II substantial increase in the percentage of blacks as a proportion of the central-city population will not automatically produce black control of city government. Rather, if blacks are to translate the potential resources of numbers and concentration into actual political power, they must overcome the historical constraints that have stifled the development of independent black political action, and engage in a successful process of political mobilization. Such mobilization does not occur overnight but is a multistaged process beginning with black involvement in civil rights protest activity and culminating in the election of a black candidate to the top public office of the city. The key to this mobilization process is the development of a high degree of political consciousness among the black masses, and the utilization of the factor of race as a unifying force that arouses the political interest of every sector of the black community and creates incentives for black solidarity in the electoral arena. Central to the success of the mobilization strategy is leadership and organization. Low-income blacks whose socioeconomic conditions have constituted formidable barriers to their effective involvement in politics must be convinced that black political leaders and candidates will not sell out once invested with powers and responsibilities of public office but will in fact deliver meaningful benefits. Black political leadership of this sort will enhance the political efficacy of low-income blacks by instilling within them a sense of trust, and making available to them channels of decision-making unprecedented in the history of black America. In doing so they will help to lay the crucial psychological framework for black rebellion against domestic colonialism through the political process. Ties forged between black political leaders and the black masses must be reinforced through organization. Effective black organizations serve as the crucial institutional link that holds the black community together as an effective political force on a continuous basis. They also perform administrative functions essential to the transformation of black political consciousness into unified political activity in the electoral process.

In recent years, political mobilization efforts by blacks in the cities have mainly been directed toward the election of black mayors. The extent to which winning the mayorship of a city eventuates in a substantive improvement of the quality of life among rank-and-file blacks is the question we turn to in part three. As we shall see, a black mayor encounters numerous obstacles in pursuing the objectives of his program and black liberation in general.

1. This unattributed quotation is derived from interviews conducted by the authors in Gary, Indiana.

2. It is important to note that this new political energy must be focused on one black candidate. If the new momentum is dissipated by the involvement of several completing black candidates, it will be impossible to build unity in the black community, and the result is most likely to be the continuation of a white-controlled city hall.

3. The significance of this point is underscored in a recent study published by the Joint Center for Political Studies, which shows that most medium- and large-size cities with black mayors do not have a majority black voting-age

population. Indeed, in half of the cities studied, the black voting age population was less than 30 percent of the total. See Herrington J. Bryce, "Black Mayors of Medium and Large Cities: How Much Statutory Power Do They Have?" *Focus*, vol. 2, no. 10, August 1974. The point should also be stressed that even if the black base was 51 percent or more, the inclination to run campaigns exclusively in the black community must be tempered by the realization that a black mayor would still have to govern a city in which whites were a sizable and influential segment of the population.

4. Thus, this kind of political stance was more crucial to the election of Thomas Bradley as mayor of Los Angeles, California, where blacks are 17 percent of the population than of Kenneth Gibson as mayor of Newark, New Jersey, where blacks are 54 percent of the population.

PART III

The Problem of Governance

10
Black Mayors: The Dilemmas of Power

What difference has the election of a black mayor made in the lives of citizens in your city? This is one of the key questions asked of respondents in Cleveland and Gary in our research on the performance of the Stokes and Hatcher administrations.

Inquiries regarding the performance of black mayors take on enormous importance in view of the frequently voiced claim that political empowerment of the black community can best be achieved through the ballot box.[1] Relying on the process of mobilization, blacks can, according to this analysis, gain control over instruments of power in cities and use these instruments to deliver crucial benefits to masses of black citizens. The election of Stokes and Hatcher in 1967 provided the first opportunity to test this theory of black political empowerment.

Implicit in the emphasis on electoral politics as a solution to the multifaceted problems of urban blacks is the assumption that blacks will enjoy as much success as earlier ethnics in translating their control over cities into important instrumental benefits. Our data from Cleveland and Gary, however, do not support this assumption. To the contrary, they suggest firmly that black mayoral administrations will face much more severe constraints than those encountered by other ethnic administrations on their ability to respond effectively to the pressing needs of the black community.

It is important to note that these limits on black mayoral power will exist irrespective of the quality of leadership exhibited by the individual mayor. Social, economic, and political constraints that limit his ability to deliver meaningful benefits are rooted into the environment in which he operates. These constraints inevitably produce for the black mayor dilemmas of power that place the goal of thoroughgoing urban reform far beyond the competence of his administration.

Black mayors share with white mayors a range of problems that sharply restrict their ability to engage in effective policy-making. Few contemporary mayors have sufficient power to effectively manipulate the forces of their environments. Rather, the hard reality of the situation is that due to the accumulation of urban problems over many years, the task of running a major American city has become a nearly impossible one. Indeed, these problems have become so immense that often the best a mayor can hope to do is hold the line against urban decay and social conflict. As Ford Foundation urbanist Paul Ylvisaker has observed, "Under present rules of the game, no mayor of any central city can win."[2] Among the most vexing problems adversely affecting the leadership capabilities of big city mayors are the following: (1) a declining tax base spawned by reliance on the property tax and the dispersal of large sectors of the white community —both citizen and business—into surrounding suburbs; (2) the influx into central cities of high-cost citizens—especially poor blacks —in desperate need of governmental assistance for survival; (3) racial conflict generated by competition between blacks and whites for dwindling job opportunities and access to decent schools, homes, and recreational facilities in the central cities; (4) the emergence of a city bureaucracy protected by civil service, "which has become increasingly autonomous and has taken on an increasingly large role in the governing of the city";[3] (5) decentralization of power from strong party organizations over which the mayor exercised control, to a plethora of governmental agencies and competing interest groups over which he has little effective control; (6) the impact on the social, economic, and political life of cities of policies made by corporate elites in private sanctuaries beyond the effective scrutiny and influence of any public official, including mayors; and (7) insensitivity to central city needs by important state and national officials.

The problems delienated above are accentuated in the case of black mayors by the additional factor of race. If the political and economic resource base needed to adequately cope with expanding urban problems is weak for white mayors, it is even weaker for black mayors. The special demographic and political conditions in a major city that contribute to the election of a black man as mayor also create numerous constraints on his effective action and therefore more rigidly constrict his capacity to govern. What this means is that the black mayor—more so than the white mayor—is likely to be powerless (or power poor) under circumstances that demand that he command and sagaciously exercise enormous power. Lacking sufficient power, his programs of urban reform will not produce the instrumental benefits so passionately desired and urgently needed by his black constituents. This gap between needs and performance vividly illuminates the crucial dilemmas that the absence of power produces for black mayors.

Before proceeding further, it is necessary that we spell out the unique constraints that impose such extraordinary limits on the effective political power of black mayors. First, it is undoubtedly true that in the foreseeable future most black mayors will be elected in dead or dying cities whose accumulated maladies are swiftly moving toward the point of no return. These cities will bear only a modest resemblance to the financially secure governmental structures captured by white ethnics. The election of black mayors signals instead the onset of black takeover of bankrupt cities consumed by social conflict, physical decay, and enormous financial problems. Black majorities in cities reflect the salient trend of white exodus to the suburbs and the concomitant build-up of high-cost black citizens in the central cities. White settlement in the suburbs places the most valuable taxable assets in the metropolitan area beyond the jurisdiction of central-city officials. However, increased demands for services coupled with years of neglect make the fiscal needs of central cities more pressing than ever before. When a black man is elected mayor, these trends are accelerated as middle-class whites, engulfed by racial fears, flee in unprecedented numbers to suburbia, and poverty-stricken blacks, fired with visions of unlimited opportunities, settle in large numbers in the central city. In sum, black mayors will inherit monumental problems but will lack the basic fiscal resources to adequately cope with these problems. Consequently, unless extraordinary remedies are found for the declining income base of central cities, black city administrations will operate under circumstances that offer little hope for success.

Second, given the weak fiscal resources of central cities, black mayors will have no choice but to seek supplementary revenue from outside sources. One such possible source is the state government. But black mayors are likely to find that state officials will not be very responsive to their pleas for fiscal assistance. Suspicion and tension between local and state officials are deep-seated and long-standing. The election of a black man to the top political position in the city will most assuredly not mend the fractured relationship between city government and state government. In a period when state governments are hard pressed to marshal sufficient resources to adequately meet the needs of politically active and influential white citizens, it is unlikely that state officials will respond in a serious way to the request by black mayors for greater shares of state fiscal resources.[4] To the contrary, given the present complexion of state politics—often involving an alliance between suburbs and rural areas against central cities—it is quite probable that state officials will continue to place the interests of affluent suburbanites over the interests of disadvantaged central city residents when decisions concerning the allocation of state funds are made. Thus, at the crucial point when black city administrations will be struggling for fiscal survival, state governments are more likely to be a part of the problem than a solution to it.

More hopeful as a source of external funding for black mayoral administrations is the federal government. As a consequence primarily of important political linkages between local and federal officials, the federal government has tended to be fairly sensitive to the fiscal problems of city governments. However, for black mayors federal funds are both a bane and a blessing. Although these funds have been crucial in helping city governments satisfy citizen demands, they have also served to tighten federal control over city decision-making. In many instances federal intrusion in local affairs of this sort is highly undesirable.[5] Recent decisions by the Nixon and Ford administrations to sharply cutback funds for urban poverty programs further illuminates the excruciating dilemmas surrounding the role of contemporary black mayors. Compelled to pin their hopes for funds on outside help, they are constantly threatened with being abandoned at sea by changes in political winds completely beyond their control. Under such circumstances, it is easy to understand why even the most able black mayor will often watch helplessly as his plans for urban reconstruction are mutilated by a host of inimical political forces.

Third, black mayors must cope with the opposition they will face from other actors in the power structure of city government who will be hostile to their programs of social and economic improvement for low-income citizens and black political empowerment. In this regard, it can be noted that black mayors will inherit entrenched city bureaucracies staffed by white workers with maintenance needs and incentive systems that clash markedly with their own. Many of these persons will be the mayor's natural political enemies, having opposed him vigorously in the campaign, and will engage in overt and covert forms of political sabotage at every opportunity. However, because they are protected by civil service, he will have no choice but to accept their insubordination as an administrative handicap that cannot be easily corrected.

Defiance and opposition from the city bureaucracy will likely be matched by open resistance to the mayor's program by other white-dominated city agencies such as the council and the police department. Operating in most instances with an inexperienced staff, the black mayor will be in no position to compete with the leaders of these agencies for support from the local press, the business community, labor, and other crucial political interests. His difficulties in this respect will be magnified by his position as an outcast in the local party structure. Elected over the intense opposition of regular party leaders, the black mayor can expect little assistance from the local party in his continuing struggle to amass sufficient power to govern the city. More likely, local party officials will be among his most aggravating political adversaries. Of all the political forces arrayed against the black mayor, party politicians will assume they have the most to lose if his administration succeeds. Consequently, on programmatic as well as racial grounds they must usually wage a continuous campaign of opposition, isolation, and sabotage.

Finally, the election of a black man as mayor of a major American city builds up extraordinarily high expectations from his black constituents that cannot be satisfied. As we have seen, the waging of emotionally stimulating campaigns is a key ingredient in the mobilization effort in the black community that must be made to elect a black man to the mayorship. However, one of the unintended consequences of this mobilization process is the generation in the minds of black constitutents of exaggerated notions of the mayor's power to dramatically reverse the priorities of local government. Many black citizens are unaware of the myriad constraints that limit the leadership potentials of black mayors. The price the mayor must usually pay for overestimations of his real power is widespread citizen disappointment in his performance. Consequently, many black citizens who staunchly supported the black mayor in the election will become disillusioned and withdraw their political support from his administration.

In light of the dilemmas of power discussed above, the job of big city mayor—especially when the position is held by a reform-oriented black politician—emerges as one of the toughest and most challenging public offices in America. The remaining sections of this chapter examine the success and failures of Stokes and Hatcher in meeting the challenges of the mayor's office, and assess the meaning of the Cleveland and Gary experiences for the future of black politics in America.

CONFRONTING THE CITY BUREAUCRACY

Carl Stokes and Richard Hatcher entered the mayor's offices of Cleveland and Gary deeply committed to fulfilling the social and economic aspirations of their black constituents. They were not in office very long, however, before they discovered that the political environment of city government substantially mitigated against a shift of policy priorities in the direction of the black community. One of the most important impediments they faced in this respect was intense and persistent opposition from the city bureaucracy.

Hatcher's problems with the city bureaucracy in Gary were multidimensional. Although he was generally expected to transform the Gary city government into a marvel of efficiency and productivity, Hatcher found that he was saddled with a city bureaucracy that was, in terms of its organizational structure, patently obsolete. Even a cursory examination of the structure of city government revealed a city bureaucracy with no clearly established lines of authority for departments and no well-established chain of command—nor was there very much coordination of functions and responsibilities. Each department operated in effect as a separate entity; the only common link between them was the requirement that each of thirty department heads report directly to the mayor. Few rules governing the conduct of employees were set forth; those that did exist were generally ignored. Under such circumstances, bureaucratic efficiency was an irrational expectation.

The city bureaucracy was not only inefficient but entrenched. It was virtually impossible to fire experienced city employees —even those not covered by civil service—without creating the kind of political difficulties Hatcher wanted most to avoid. Consequently, whereas implementation of the administration's program required competency and honesty, the bureaucracy continued to be incompetent and corrupt. This defect was compounded by the stubborn defiance of the mayor's orders by holdovers from the previous administration. These individuals did not attempt to hide their dislike both for the mayor and the social, economic, and political priorities of his administration. Several publicly proclaimed that their allegiance was not to Hatcher but to the county organization—and they boldly challenged Hatcher to fire them because of their attitudes and their political loyalties.

The first five months of the Hatcher administration were characterized by continuous conflict between Hatcher and members of the city-hall work force, including several members of his cabinet who charged the mayor with failing to sufficiently delegate authority.[6] In June 1968 Hatcher finally began taking steps to gain control over the city bureaucracy. The first of these steps involved seeking outside help. Major universities in the Gary area were called upon to make available to Hatcher urban specialists to advise him on administrative matters. Private research and philanthropic agencies such as the Ford Foundation, the Potomac Institute, and the Urban Coalition were also approached for funds and technical assistance. Through these sources a corps of expert talent was assembled to evaluate priorities and suggest possible avenues of administrative reform. In addition to these part-time consultants, the Ford Foundation

342 / Electing Black Mayors

awarded Hatcher a grant to hire three full-time special assistants (or super executives) to work in critical areas of his administration. With this money, Hatcher established the posts of special assistant for personnel and finance, special assistant for housing and community development, and special assistant for public safety.

Hatcher's next step was the convening of a three-day conference involving fourteen members of his cabinet for the purpose of engaging in wide-ranging, straight-forward discussions on administrative reform. Out of this conference came a series of proposals for wholesale administrative reform of the municipal bureaucracy. The most important recommendation put forth by the conference was one proposing a substantial decentralization of administrative authority. A chain of command was established within departments, and department and division heads were delegated considerable authority to run their operations without constantly checking with the mayor. Conference participants also agreed that Hatcher would have to get tough with those elements of the city bureaucracy who persisted in flaunting his authority.

Stokes also faced considerable hostility from members of the city bureaucracy in Cleveland. Like city workers in Gary, members of the Cleveland bureaucracy were—for the most part— protected by civil service and therefore beyond the effective administrative control of the mayor. Stokes attempted to solve the problem of bureaucratic resistance by promising pay raises and better working conditions to city workers.[7] Although these incentives helped to reduce tension between city workers and the mayor's office, they did not totally erase the hostility Cleveland's predominantly white municipal work force felt toward a city administration headed by a black man.[8]

Stokes's administrative problems were compounded by conflicts between the mayor and members of his executive staff. These conflicts centered primarily around disputes between Stokes and his major administrative appointees over the extent to which decision-making authority should be centralized in the mayor's office. Sharp disagreements on this issue and a range of specific policy matters resulted in a rash of resignations and dismissals among key members of the Stokes administration.

The first major city officials to leave the Stokes administration were Paul D. White, law director, and Dr. Kenneth Clement, special consultant to the mayor. White was a prominent black lawyer and former municipal-court judge. As law director, he served as acting mayor in Stokes's absence and was first in line of succession if the office of mayor became vacant. White resigned after only four months in office. His resignation was prompted by what he viewed as Stokes's unwillingness to consult with him on important matters falling within his area of responsibility.[9] White was succeeded in the position of law director by black Cleveland attorney, Clarence James.

Dr. Clement, who served as Stokes's campaign manager in 1967, took the position as special consultant to the mayor at an annual salary of $1.00. In addition to advising the mayor on a range of subjects, Clement was given the responsibility of coordinating city-hall patronage. Clement terminated his position with city hall after five months. During his brief affiliation with the Stokes administration, Clement had been embroiled in frequent policy and personality conflicts with the mayor. His ultimate departure from the Stokes administration was sparked by what he described as Stokes's insufferably low tolerance for honest criticism.

Turmoil and conflict within the Stokes administration led to the resignation or removal of other city officials. In September 1968 Stokes fired Police Prosecutor James S. Carnes because Carnes publicly criticized a committee to investigate police procedure established by law director James. For several months prior to his dismissal, Carnes had been feuding with the mayor over the issue of salary increases for assistant city prosecutors. In October 1968 Stokes fired Police Chief Michael J. (Iron Mike) Blackwell because he refused to obey the orders of the safety director and resisted efforts by Stokes to reform the police department. Blackwell was replaced by Deputy Inspector Patrick L. Gerity. Gerity's career as police chief was just as tumultuous as Blackwell's. The new chief took over the reigns of the police department in the midst of heated attacks by the council on the Stokes administration for failing to halt a sharp upturn in crime and a parallel dispute between the police department and the mayor's office. Gerity was the proverbial man in the middle. He was lashed by the city council for failing to put enough men on the streets to insure citizen safety. Council President Stanton called for the resignation of both Gerity and Safety Director Joseph McManamon, charging them with failing to provide leadership. "The Police Department has never been worse. It lacks leadership. There is need for revision."[10]

Gerity was also the object of attacks from the Cleveland Police Patrolman's Association, which repeatedly accused him of attempting to defend the mayor's office against legitimate police complaints by harrassing and intimidating its members. In September 1969 the association filed suit in U.S. District Court asking for a permanent restraining order barring Gerity from interrogating patrolmen concerning their membership in the association, and threatening or suggesting disciplinary action against patrolmen who were association members.[11] Finally, Gerity began openly feuding with Mayor Stokes and Safety Director McManamon. The most serious incident was Gerity's criticism of the administration's decision to appoint 60 policemen to the force over his objection that department evaluation of the men had found them to be unqualified for police work. Gerity boycotted swearing-in ceremonies for 209 new policemen because of his objection to the appointment of 60 of them. Stokes was bitterly stung by Gerity's criticisms and began immediately looking around for a new police chief. When word spread that Stokes was considering several outsiders as his replacement, Gerity called his men together for a pep talk to ask them to stick together and vigorously oppose an outside choice.

On 26 January 1970, Stokes announced the appointment of his third police chief in two years. The man chosen by Stokes to succeed Gerity as chief was William P. Ellenburg, a twenty-six-year veteran of the Detroit police force. Ellenburg was greeted with a cool reception by Cleveland police, who resented the appointment of an out-of-towner. Ellenburg left no doubt, however, that he intended to be a strong chief and began immediately to shape the Cleveland force in his own image. William Ellenburg's career as Cleveland police chief turned out to be one of the shortest, and most controversial, in the city's history. One week after his appointment, Cleveland was jarred by charges made by Lawrence A. Burns, former Mafia attorney and fixer, that he had made monthly payments to Ellenburg to protect an abortion racket in Detroit from 1959 to 1963. Ellenburg vehemently denied the charges, and Stokes went on Cleveland television to ask citizens not to leap to conclusions until the chief's guilt or innocence had been firmly established. The seriousness of the charges against Ellenburg was heightened by the fact that Burns had submitted to a lie detector test in Detroit and passed with flying colors. Ellenburg, on the other hand, flatly refused to take a lie detector test. Stokes's image was so impaired by the Ellenburg affair that he personally lead a team of investigators to Detroit to look into the charges. Arriving in Detroit, Stokes told newsmen:

> This is important to me. Maybe you don't understand how important it is to me. The problem of a police chief is the biggest problem I have as mayor. It is the biggest problem any mayor can have today. I picked my man and I am responsible for picking him. Certain charges have been leveled against him and I have decided to come to Detroit—to the source—and investigate those charges. No one else could investigate them as I can. And when I am through, I will go back to the people of Cleveland and report what I have found.[12]

The investigation conducted by Stokes in Detroit neither confirmed nor denied the charges leveled against Ellenburg. Seeing no apparent relief from the cloud of suspicion the charges against him had established, Ellenburg voluntarily submitted his resignation as chief to Stokes after only ten days in office. Stokes immediately appointed veteran Cleveland police inspector Lewis W. Coffey as the new chief.

The shock of the Ellenburg resignation was eclipsed in impact six months later by the resignation of Benjamin O. Davis, Jr., as Cleveland safety director. Davis had been appointed safety director after Stokes's first safety director Joseph McManamon resigned in December 1969. McManamon was generally despised by rank-and-file police. He had been at the center of numerous disputes between the Stokes administration and the police, and was viewed by officers in the ranks as Stokes's hatchet man. Cleveland policemen were especially disturbed by the way McManamon handled the 1968 Glenville uprising in which three policemen were killed by black nationalists.[13] Davis's appointment as a replacement for McManamon was enthusiastically applauded by Cleveland police. They were most impressed by his military credentials and his reputation as a sound administrator. At the time of his retirement, Davis was the top-ranking black person in the United States military, holding the rank of lieutenant general. In 1954 he became the first black person to be named a general in the Air Force.

During his service as safety director, Davis was an invaluable asset to the Stokes administration in the white community. Complaints by whites about Cleveland's high crime rate sharply diminished as Davis quickly established his reputation as a strong advocate of law and order. Under Davis's command, relations between the Stokes administration and the police department markedly improved. Cleveland police believed that Davis was on their side and would back them up in their frequent clashes with nationalist groups in the black community.

The favorable opinion of Davis held by whites was not shared by blacks. A number of incidents occurring over a period of several months convinced many blacks that Davis was the wrong man for the job of Cleveland safety director. Blacks accused Davis of discriminatory law enforcement, taking a hard line against black nationalists (such as the Black Panthers) but failing to aggressively pursue whites who regularly attacked blacks in white neighborhoods. Davis's reputation declined to such a low ebb in the black community that he was subjected to blistering attacks by the *Call and Post*, a black newspaper that had been uniformly supportive of policies of the Stokes administration.

Davis's resignation was prompted by conflicts between the mayor and the safety director over police policies toward the black community. Friction between Stokes and Davis first developed in April 1970 when Stokes turned down a Davis requisition for dumdum bullets (soft-core bullets that expand on impact) for Cleveland police. The split between Stokes and Davis widened when Stokes refused to take action against persons in the black community who criticized Davis's approach to law enforcement. Davis identified these persons as his enemies and therefore the enemies of law enforcement. Stokes disagreed, saying he could not take action against these individuals as long as they had not violated any specific laws.

In his letter of resignation Davis cited two reasons for his decision to leave the Stokes administration: (1) that he was not receiving from Stokes the support his programs required; and (2) the continued support and comfort Stokes gave to the enemies of law enforcement. Upon receiving Davis's letter, Stokes insisted that he name the specific enemies of law enforcement he had in mind; when Davis refused to do so, Stokes released the names of seven individuals and institutions that the general had labeled in previous conversations as his enemies.[14] Stokes told newsmen that Davis wanted him to silence each of these persons and organizations by cutting off city money and firing them from city jobs.

The charges contained in Davis's letter constituted the worst political blow visited upon the Stokes administration since his election in 1967. Commenting on the impact of the Davis resignation, one close Stokes associate stated: "If all the deepest thinkers in a 50 mile radius had gotten together to decide how they could most hurt the mayor, they could not have decided upon anything more damaging than this."[15] For three years Stokes had been valiantly struggling to reverse the widespread notion in the white community that he was soft on black criminality. Davis's charges had the effect of undoing much of what had been done in establishing the credibility of the Stokes administration on the sensitive issue of law and order.

Periodic scandals in the Stokes administration also resulted in the resignation or dismissal of a number of other key city officials. In the early months of his administration Stokes fired one of his top black assistants—Geraldine Williams—after a Cleveland newspaper published a story accusing her of being part owner of a cheat spot—a liquor establishment selling liquor on Sunday and after hours in violation of city codes. Another Stokes assistant—William Stein—was fired after being shot in the home of one of his married female clients. Stokes was forced to ask for the resignation of his public relations assistant, William Silverman, in the wake of revelations that Silverman's services were being financed by a $72,000 grant from the Greater Cleveland Associated Foundation, a tax-exempt institution. Undoubtedly, the most damaging scandal of all, however, was the civil service scandal resulting in the resignation of two Stokes's appointees —Charles L. Butts, and Jay B. White—from the Civil Service Commission. Butts and White were later convicted of destroying 940 answer sheets and 940 identification sheets of a 1968 promotional examination administered to members of the police department. Charges that both men had committed perjury in testimony before the county grand jury investigation of the police scandal were dropped.

The above discussion embraces only a partial list of key individuals who left the Stokes administration at various points. Overall, between December 1967 and July 1970, more than twenty major officials resigned or were fired from the Stokes administration.[16] Indeed, departures from Cleveland city government under Stokes took place at such a devastating pace that it appeared at times the administration was entrapped in a perpetual game of musical chairs.

The problems of mayors Stokes and Hatcher with the city bureaucracy were not limited to the work force in city hall. Like other big city mayors, they were called upon to respond to demands for high salaries and other prerequisites by aggressive and politically conscious organized groups of city workers. The tactic most frequently employed by the organized city bureaucracy in Cleveland and Gary has been the strike. On several occasions, strikes by city workers during the Stokes and Hatcher administrations produced crises of major proportions. A strike by Gary firemen in 1967 for higher wages, for example, sparked a serious confrontation between the Hatcher administration and the fire department. On the first night of the strike, a four-alarm fire broke out at the Broadway Lumber Company. Only three members of the Gary Fire Department actively fought the blaze—Fire Chief Alonzo Holiday and two assistant fire chiefs. Assistance from Civil Defense volunteers and firemen from surrounding towns was impeded by striking firemen who threw bricks, cut water hoses, and engaged in other acts of sabotage. Fire trucks from Hammond and East Chicago were turned back at the scene of the blaze by Gary firemen who jumped on trucks and pulled out hoses. In the midst of the confusion, the Broadway Lumber Company burned to the ground. Damages were estimated to range in the millions of dollars. Before the firefighters dispute was settled, 59 firemen were suspended and contempt of court proceedings were initiated by the city against the firefighter's union.

In Cleveland a transit strike in 1970 brought public transportation to a halt, and created massive traffic jams in the downtown area. The strike also had a catastrophic impact on downtown business, with some major department stores reporting an initial drop in sales of as much as 30 percent. Before significant headway could be made on a settlement of the transit strike, Cleveland was hit by a garbage strike. With strikes by two major service units occurring simultaneously, the city of Cleveland was practically paralyzed; garbage piled up on the streets, and health and safety problems mounted in the absence of dependable public transportation. City officials attempted to ease the garbage problem by instituting a system of "do-it-yourself" pickups, but the plan fizzled out after being in effect less than an hour.

Stokes was able to bring the 1970 service crisis to a halt only by agreeing to wage demands that would cost city taxpayers over twenty million dollars in excess of original budgetary projections. To meet these added expenses, Stokes had to violate his promise not to ask for a tax increase. In doing so he created a storm of political protest from city councilmen and rank-and-file taxpayers. Thus, the political revolt of Cleveland's organized bureaucracy in 1970 placed Stokes in a no-win position. Whatever decision he made regarding the demands of the city's labor force would produce more political liabilities than assets.

The most difficult problems Stokes and Hatcher faced relative to the organized city bureaucracy centered around their relationship with the police. White policemen tend to naturally resent the election of a black mayor and frequently attempt to use every means possible to defy his authority. Friction between Hatcher and the police surfaced within weeks of his election when more than a third of the force walked off the job in protest over low wages. Although an early settlement of the strike was reached, a sizable dissident element of the department never fully accommodated itself to the reality that a black man was in command of the mayor's office. When Hatcher ordered policemen to remove American flag shoulder patches from their uniforms because blacks considered them symbols of white racism, smoldering resentments by white police rushed emotionally to the surface. Gary policemen protested the order, claiming that the flag was a symbol of American patriotism and insinuating that the mayor's attitudes raised serious questions concerning his status as a loyal American. In the wake of stubborn police defiance of his order, Hatcher capitulated, defusing for a time tension between his administration and rank-and-file white policemen.

Stokes's problems with the police were far more serious. Conflict between Stokes and the police stemmed in part from his insistence on sweeping reforms in the police system. Stokes's reform program was aimed at making the police department not only more efficient but also more responsive to the black community. Cleveland policemen fought the mayor on the issue of reform at every turn; they regarded the mayor's plans as too radical, and resented mayoral interference in the internal affairs of the department. The most fundamental factor underlying friction between Stokes and the police, however, was Stokes's handling of the 1968 Glenville rebellion. This incident involved three nights and two days of violence in Cleveland that left ten people dead, including three policemen, scores of injuries, and millions of dollars in property damage. The wave of violence was triggered when police were allegedly lured into the Glenville section of Cleveland and ambushed by a group of black nationalists. Fred (Ahmed) Evans, a well-known Cleveland black nationalist, was arrested and charged with leading the attack.[17] Word of the gun battle between black nationalists and the police quickly spread, crowds of community residents formed, and a full-scale urban riot precipitiously developed.

Mayor Stokes was informed of the crisis about one hour after the violence in Glenville erupted. Stokes immediately conferred with police officials and set up a command post at city hall. The mayor then worked through the night to bring the violence under control. Early the next morning Stokes met with more than one hundred black leaders to discuss strategies for preventing a further outbreak of violence. No concensus was reached. Later that afternoon, Stokes met with black leaders again and approved a plan to defuse tensions by withdrawing white policemen and national guardsmen from the riot area and replacing them with about five hundred black citizens and policemen. In making this decision, Stokes was aware that he ran the risk of alienating white policemen infuriated by the death of their comrades. But at the time the decision was made, he was concerned primarily with avoiding further lost of life and was persuaded by arguments by black leaders that the black community should be given a chance to solve its own problems. The strategy agreed upon was implemented on the second night of the disorder. Only black persons with appropriate placards and armbands were allowed into the interior of the riot area. Black mayoral representatives walked the streets, breaking up crowds, cooling tempers, and keeping the peace. The mayor's strategy was a qualified success; although occasional lootings and burnings were reported, no further violent clashes took place. Stokes had gambled, and apparently won. On the next night black emotions had sufficently subsided to permit the imposition of a curfew and a return to patrols by white police and national guardsmen.

Stokes's bold action in removing white guardsmen and policemen from the riot area was warmly appluaded by the local press and the black community. At the same time, the decision was roundly condemned by white ghetto merchants whose stores were looted, some members of the city council, and rank-and-file policemen. White policemen angered by the previous days' events were anxious to move into the black community and take retaliatory action against militants of every description. In the heat of the first night's violence, some white policemen had already been reported involved in the shooting up of a black militant club house, and a nearby ghetto apartment building,[18] and the beating and tear-gassing of black patrons in a ghetto tavern. The restraining order issued by the mayor inflammed the passions of white policemen beyond the boiling point. Police radio messages bristled with obscene and derogatory comments directed toward the mayor and his committee. When the police dispatch broadcasted for a car to answer an emergency in the black community, an anonymous voice replied "Get the hell off the air." A request for cars to respond to a fire call produced the reply, "Let Mayor Stokes go piss on it." Other calls elicited responses such as "Let 'em burn the damn place down," and "To hell with the mayor."

In the weeks following the Glenville rebellion, Stokes's relations with the police steadily deteriorated. One Cleveland police officer resigned in protest against the mayor's handling of the Glenville incident; another sixteen-year police veteran traveled to Columbus in an attempt to persuade Governor Rhodes to remove Stokes for "willingfully neglecting to enforce the law, gross neglect of duty, malfeasance, misfeasance, and non-feasance in office."[19] The Cleveland FOP issued a strong denunciation of the Stokes administration and called for the resignation of Safety Director McManamon. Posters showing Stokes and McManamon together with the caption "Wanted to answer questions for the murder of three policemen," began appearing on the bulletin boards of police stations throughout the white community.[20] These incidents were clear signs that the breach between Stokes and the police was so wide that it could never be healed.

In succeeding months, Stokes attempted desperately to mollify the police by approving their requests for more equipment, higher salaries, more personnel, training in guerrilla-warfare tactics, the creation of a special backup unit to deal with dangerous felons, and special fringe benefits such as time-and-a-half pay for over- time and the payment of tuition fees for policemen who com- pleted college courses. These measures had little visible impact on the attitudes of Cleveland policemen toward their black mayor. Indeed, white policemen were so irredeemably hostile to the Stokes administration, that they felt compelled to actively cam- paign against him in the 1969 general election. To circumvent state restrictions against police involvement in politics, members of the FOP secured petitions to act as election day judges to challenge the registration of citizens voting on Issue 1 concerning the extension of the right to vote to nineteen year olds. On elec- tion day, the FOP concentrated its efforts in black precincts; some of the policemen involved refused to remove their fire- arms at polling places. The effect of FOP election day activities was to give a powerful boost to the candidacy of Ralph J. Perk, Stokes's Republican rival, by driving blacks away from the polls through harassment and intimidation. Stokes won the election despite police opposition; however, during his four years in of- fice, he was never able to win the support and cooperation of a significant portion of Cleveland's predominantly white police force.

CONFLICT WITH THE CITY COUNCIL

Political opposition to the policies of the Stokes and Hatcher administrations was by no means confined to the city bureau- cracy. Both black mayors also faced serious and substained re- sistance to their programs of urban reform from their respective city councils. Given Hatcher's background as a former city coun- cilman and the presence of four blacks and one Mexican-Ameri- can on the nine-man Gary council in 1967, many political observ- ers predicted that his relations with the council would be extraordinarily productive. This assessment, however, proved to be almost totally inaccurate. Hatcher's first term as mayor was characterized by an uninterrupted series of confrontations with the city council. Only two councilmen, one black and one white, consistently voted to support the mayor on major policy issues. John Armenta, the Mexican-American who was expected to hold the balance of power in favor of the administration, turned out to be one of Hatcher's most vociferous and persistent critics.

In retrospect, it is clear that many members of the council viewed the election of a black mayor under controversial circumstances as a golden opportunity to reassert the council's authority as a coequal branch of city government. To fulfill this objective they went to extraordinary lengths to embarrass, rebuff, and antagonize the mayor—all for the purpose of whittling his perogatives and authority down to managable size. For example, one of the first actions taken by the council after Hatcher's election was to revert to the procedure of requiring a three-fourths vote to pass a measure returned to the council from the city planning commission. This action effectively killed efforts by the commission to rezone certain areas of the city to facilitate the construction of new public housing units; it also sent a firm message to city hall that the council did not intend to rubber stamp administration proposals. Upon formally declaring its independence from city hall, the council quickly proceeded to turn back one measure after another transmitted for its consideration by the mayor.[21]

The climate of conflict surrounding Hatcher's relationship with the city council resulted in the imposition of huge revisions by the council in the mayor's annual budgetary requests. Thus in 1970 the council trimmed nearly one million dollars from the administration's proposed public-employee salary schedule. Hatcher's request for $1,000 across the board raises for firemen was reduced by the council to $600, an act of economy precipitating the disastrous firemen's strike discussed earlier. Additional council cuts eliminated the entire staff of the Gary Youth Commission. And in an action clearly designed to humiliate the mayor, the council voted to reduce the salary of human relations commission director Charles King from $14,000 to $13,000. King had consistently been one of the council's most vocal critics and one of Hatcher's strongest supporters.

Hatcher's most serious conflict with the council centered around the attempt by the council in 1969 to dilute the formal powers of the office of mayor. This action took the form of a proposal by councilman John Armenta to reduce the number of Hatcher's appointees to the fifteen-man human relations commission (HRC) by nine and distribute them equally among the members of the council. Armenta argued that such a redistribution would result in broader community representation on the commission. The Armenta proposal was headed for certain passage when two hundred members of black youth gangs crowded into the council and persuaded several councilmen to change their vote. One of the youthful spokesmen addressed the members of the council in the following emphatic terms: "What you want us to have? Nothing? You're crawling with us and we're tired. The game is over. If you mess with the mayor you'll have to talk to us about it. That's not a threat, that's a promise."[22]

When asked why they consistently failed to support Mayor Hatcher's policies, most Gary councilmen were inclined to reply that Hatcher was not a practical politician—that he rarely attended council meetings and did not make them privy to his plans in advance. In an interview with one of the authors, Hatcher rejected these charges, asserting that he was readily available for councilmanic consultation. Hatcher expressed the belief that the reasons for the council's opposition to his legislative program were almost purely racial.

Stokes also encountered considerable resistance to his policies from members of the Cleveland city council. For a city of its size, the Cleveland city council is unusually large. The council is composed of thirty-three councilmen, all elected from wards. Throughout most of the Stokes era, blacks held twelve council seats; the balance—twenty-one—were held by whites. Early in the Stokes administration a deep split developed in the council along racial lines. White councilmen, seeking to protect the interests of their white constituents, lined up solidly in opposition to Stokes.[23] Black councilmen—with several notable exceptions[24] generally supported the major legislative programs of the Stokes administration. Opposition to Stokes by the dominant white councilmanic faction rendered Stokes largely ineffective in his political relations with the council. Lacking a voting majority, Stokes had to rely upon the veto or threat of a veto as his primary political weapon.[25] Although his veto power provided some bargaining leverage, it was far from enough to give Stokes the kind of influence with the council he needed to transform his dreams of municipal reform into public policy.

Stokes's first serious clash with the council came in February 1968 when he proposed an increase in the city income tax from

.5 percent to a full 1 percent. Council leaders strongly opposed the tax increase on the grounds that such an increase lacked popular support and had not been satisfactorily justified by the administration. In the wake of stiff council opposition, Stokes decided to take the political offensive. His first step was to engage in a round of political speeches designed to mobilize support for the tax increase from important community organizations. Next, Stokes took out full-page ads in both Cleveland daily newspapers urging citizens to pressure councilmen to support the tax proposal. This tactical maneuver enraged Stokes's councilmanic opponents. Councilman Anthony Garofoli accused Stokes of attempting to blackjack the council and vowed not to be intimidated. Council President Stanton observed that he had never been subjected to such pressure in all his years on the council, and added: "I'm not impressed by the newspaper camapign to stampede this council without proper documentation."[26]

Stokes's campaign to secure a tax increase was given a substantial boost by the passage of a referendum proposal that decreed that Cleveland policemen and firemen be paid salaries 3 percent higher than those paid to policemen and firemen in any major city in Ohio. The passage of this proposal produced immediate demands by other city workers for higher wages. In light of these developments, the council voted to approve Stokes's request for a tax increase.

The skirmish over the 1968 tax increase marked the beginning of a period of continuous conflict between the council and the Stokes administration. Like their counterparts in Gary, white Cleveland councilmen took advantage of the special political problems faced by the city's black mayor to assert their independence from the city administration. Operating as a cohesive unit, the council majority subjected the administration to a number of political defeats. For example, a vigorous campaign by Stokes to get a tough gun-control law established was defeated in the council by a two-to-one vote. Despite the tradition of pro forma council approval of mayoral appointments, two key Stokes appointments—one to the Transit Board and one to the City Planning Commission—were rejected by the council. In 1969, the council took the unprecedented step of withdrawing $7 million from Stokes's prepared budget and placing it in a reserve account that could not be tapped without prior council approval. The intent of this action was to diminish the independent administrative authority of the mayor.

The most serious setback suffered by Stokes at the hands of the council was his failure to induce council action on the Lee-Seville public-housing project. This project involved plans by Stokes to build 277 units of public housing in a middle-class black neighborhood called Lee-Seville at a cost of $4.5 million. The Lee-Seville housing proposal ran into strong opposition in the city council. Leading council opposition to the Stokes proposal was Lee-Seville councilman Clarence Thompson, who objected to the housing project on the grounds that it would lead to the overcrowding of schools and recreational facilities and impose a severe strain on existing sewer lines. In view of Thompson's objections, the chairmen of council committees considering various aspects of the Lee-Seville proposal agreed to invoke the principle of councilmanic courtesy and pigeonhole the legislation until differences between the mayor and Thompson were ironed out.

Beginning as a minor dispute, the Lee-Seville issue mushroomed into a major political battle between Stokes and the city council. Stokes denounced Thompson's position as a subterfuge to hide the class prejudice of Lee-Seville residents toward low-income blacks. He called upon the council to allow the people to decide the issue by holding public hearings on the Lee-Seville project. Thompson remained adamant, arguing that he was not against the construction of public housing for the poor but was concerned about the deleterious physical effects of such housing on his neighborhood.

Charges and countercharges generated by the Lee-Seville controversy locked Stokes in the most intense political battle of his administration. Stokes took his campaign for public housing to the public, exhorting community leaders to organize mass rallies to pressure the council to begin public hearings on Lee-Seville legislation. In doing so, he clashed sharply with Lee-Seville residents who assailed him for making their neighborhood a laboratory for his experimental housing program. They also roundly condemned Stokes for insinuating that their resistance stemmed from class bigotry rather than honest concern for the physical well-being of their neighborhood.

The battle over Lee-Seville raged for more than a year. A vote in the council to reactivate Lee-Seville legislation on 17 June 1969 set the stage for the demise of Lee-Seville as a major public issue. Consistent with its previous stand, the council voted twenty to thirteen to keep Lee-Seville legislation pigeonholed in committee. Viewing the council action as the end of the road, Stokes announced that he was abandoning his campaign to establish public housing in Lee-Seville.

> Ladies and gentlemen of the Council, from this point on, the issue of public housing in Lee-Seville is entirely up to you. My responsibility as mayor has been fulfilled.[27]

Underlying Stokes's monumental defeat on the Lee-Seville project was the unflagging political opposition of the council president James Stanton to the programs of the Stokes administration. Conflict between Stokes and Stanton dated back to 1968 when rumors began to spread that Stokes was maneuvering to oust Stanton as council president by defeating his councilmanic allies in the 1969 city elections. Stanton—who was known to be politically ambitious—had maintained tight reigns on the council through his power as president to make committee assignments. If Stokes succeeded in removing him as council president, Stanton stood not only to lose his power, but would also be robbed of his chances for higher political office.

Seeking to protect his political interests, Stanton became one of Stokes's most persistent and vociferous opponents. It was Stanton who first raised the issue of the foundation grant to William Silverman and led the charge to force Stokes to fire Silverman. Stanton also played a crucial role in the Lee-Seville controversy, backing Councilman Thompson fully, and holding a majority of the council in line against pressure by Stokes to force Lee-Seville legislation out of committee. On the floor of the council, Stanton played Brutus to Stokes's Caesar, taking advantage of every opportunity to project potshots at the Stokes administration. The tug of war between Stanton and Stokes reached its apex in the 1969 city elections with both men fielding opposing slates of candidates for the city council. This contest proved to be a standoff, with Stokes as well as Stanton picking up new seats and losing old ones. Failing to substantially break Stanton's grip on the council in the election, Stokes joined a dump Stanton bid in the postelection reorganization of the council. With strong support from county party leaders, Stanton was able to easily defeat his opponent—twenty-first-ward councilman Edward Katalinas—in the party caucus, and retain his position and power as council president. Although a virtual shoo-in for Congress in 1970, Stanton continued to vigorously oppose Stokes. His unceasing opposition so crippled Stokes's legislative program that Stokes was prompted to accuse Stanton of stopping the wheels of city government single-handedly: "In my 20 years in public life, I have never seen government brought to a halt by one man, such as Council President Stanton has done."[28]

Thus, both Stokes and Hatcher faced deep-seated and enduring opposition from the Cleveland and Gary city councils. The consequences of this opposition were far-reaching, affecting significantly their ability to implement programs of social reform.

COMMUNITY CONFLICT

Policies of the Stokes and Hatcher administrations were also strongly influenced by conflict and tension in the black and white communities of Gary and Cleveland. One of the most important sources of conflict in the black community was the inability of both black mayors to immediately fulfill the social and economic aspirations of their black constituents. Apparently, promises by Stokes and Hatcher during the mayoral campaign established in the minds of many black citizens unrealistic expectations of the extent to which their administrations would be able to solve pressing problems in the black community. In Gary, for example, many blacks viewed Hatcher as a miracle worker who would solve over night community problems that had been ignored for decades. This perception of Hatcher's powers was an inevitable by-product of the high-pitched, emotional campaign waged in the black community to achieve his election to the mayor's office. As one respondent explained:

Dick [Hatcher] tried to be everything to everybody. That poor fellow in the street felt that things were going to be different once Hatcher took office. Everybody who wore a button or carried a placard felt "I'm going to get something out of it. Everything is going to change." Not that Dick said these things were going to happen, but this was the feeling—that Dick was going to be a cure-all for all the ills of the ghetto. Dick was going to be a cure-all for all the problems of the community.

Neither Stokes nor Hatcher could satisfactorily explain to rank-and-file blacks the constraints on their power that prevented them from living up to their campaign promises. The upshot was a tremendous sense of disillusionment by many of their most ardent black supporters. Having placed total faith in the election of a black mayor as the answer to their problems, these citizens began to suspect that they had become victims of yet another act of political betrayal—that the black man they had put in the mayor's seat was selling them out. Consequently, within weeks of their election, Stokes and Hatcher were faced with the immense problem of growing hostility toward their administrations in the black community

To cope with this problem, both Stokes and Hatcher sought to establish programs that would demonstrate beyond the shadow of a doubt that they were sensitive to the needs of the black community. Thus, one of Hatcher's first formal acts as mayor was the announcement that his administration would give priority attention to problems in the areas of housing and employment. This announcement was designed as an unmistakable signal to the black community that Hatcher intended to live up to his campaign promises that he would use the office of mayor to reverse the cycle of poverty and dependence among low-income black citizens.

Hatcher fully recognized that he could not successfully tackle social and economic problems in the black community without obtaining outside funds—especially funds from the federal government. Consequently, much of his time—and that of his staff —was devoted to identifying and vigorously pursuing outside funding sources. These efforts enjoyed remarkable success. By the end of his first year in office, Hatcher had successfully obtained federal commitments to Gary in excess of $30 million.[29] This achievement earned him the title of master of the art of "grantsmanship" from local officials across the country. By June 1970, the total amount of federal assistance to Gary had climbed to $86 million, with $10 million from HUD still to be released. Federal funds secured by Hatcher were supplemented by substantial donations from private foundations, businesses, and local civic associations. Most of the funds raised by Hatcher from public and private sources were used to establish housing and employment programs in the black community.

Stokes also launched an aggressive campaign to secure public and private funds to underwrite social and economic programs for low-income black citizens. In March 1968, he traveled to Washington and returned with a pledge of $12 million in federal funds to reactivate the University-Euclid urban-renewal project. Federal money for this program had previously been held up because of deficiencies in Cleveland's renewal efforts under the Locher administration. Stokes successfully argued that in the few months he had been mayor, substantial progress had been made in improving the city's ability to establish and maintain a workable renewal program. Another request for federal funds by Stokes resulted in a $1.5 million grant from OEO to the Hough Area Development Corporation to promote and develop small business enterprises in the black community. Stokes was also able to secure a pledge of $1.5 million from the New York Life Insurance Company to improve the quantity and quality of housing in the Hough area.

By far Stokes's most impressive fund-raising venture, however, was a program labeled by Stokes's publicity assistants as Cleveland Now. This program, established in May 1968, involved a vigorous effort to raise $177 million over a period of eighteen months to attack problems in housing, jobs, and health. Specifically, the money would be channeled into six separate programs in the areas of employment, youth resources, health and welfare, neighborhood rehabilitation, economic revitalization, and planning. The bulk of the funds for the program—about $142 million—would come from the federal government. About $23 million would be provided by state and city governments. The balance of the funds —some $11 million—would be raised through solicitations from business and industry and private citizens. To facilitate the collection of private funds, Stokes assigned the Greater Cleveland Growth Association the task of raising $10 million from the business community. At the same time, a special organization called Group 66 was established to raise $1.5 million from private citizens.

In its totality, Cleveland Now represented the largest most ambitious program of urban reconstruction in the history of the country. In announcing the program, Stokes stressed its importance as an avenue through which citizens from every walk of life could participate in the redevelopment and revitalization of their city.

Response to the mayor's plea for communitywide support of Cleveland Now was instantaneous and overwhelming. John

Sherwin, cochairman of the business fund-raising effort announced on 2 May that $350,000 had already been pledged from industry and foundations to support a $750,000 summer-activities program. Numerous other contributions from business and industry quickly followed. The campaign for public contributions was given a spectacular start by a $1 million donation from Dr. Leland Schubert, a retired college professor and resident of the Cleveland suburb of Bratenahl Place. Gifts of all sizes soon began pouring into Cleveland Now offices from across the city. Cleveland Now containers were placed in shopping centers and schools; special projects were developed by youngsters, civic clubs, and other groups to raise money in support of the mayor's community development program.

During the first phase of the Cleveland Now campaign more than $5,678,000 was raised. This money in turn earned over $188,000 in interest, for total receipts of over $5,860,000. The overwhelming proportion of these funds were spent on projects designed to revitalize and rehabilitate the black community. Thus a report published in November 1969 showed that more than $1 million was spent on improving the quality of ghetto housing; $205,000 on job development in the black community; $557,000 to promote small-business development in the black community; and more than $1 million on black youth-services activities.[30] In sum, Cleveland Now represented a tremendous effort on the part of the Stokes administration to provide viable solutions to the social and economic problems of Cleveland's black citizens.

The vigorous pursuit by Stokes and Hatcher of public and private monies to tackle pressing problems in the black community removed much of the doubt from the minds of rank-and-file citizens in Cleveland and Gary regarding their sensitivity to the needs of the black community. These programs constituted indisputable proof that the priorities of city government had changed drastically under the leadership of a black mayor. The political payoffs to Stokes and Hatcher of this perception of their administrations by blacks were inestimable. Essentially, both mayors were able to effectively reverse the trend of waning support for their administrations established during their first months in office. By the end of their first year as mayor, both Stokes and Hatcher were riding new crests of popularity in the black community.[31]

This is by no means to suggest that Stokes and Hatcher were

able to mobilize support for their administrations by all sectors of the black community. To the contrary, long after their programs of social and economic reconstruction had begun to show significant results, they continued to receive substantial opposition to their administrations from some important elements of the black population. For example, blacks associated with organized crime in Gary continued to be dissatisfied with the Hatcher administration, because Hatcher sought to follow through on his campaign pledge to crack down on syndicate operations, including numbers and prostitution rackets in the black community. Legitimate black businessmen were also at odds with the policies of the Hatcher administration. Many of these individuals had been accustomed to receiving special funds through the Lake County political machine in return for their political support. Hatcher refused to honor this hoary tradition, thus depriving these black businessmen of thousands of dollars in patronage benefits.

The most serious opposition Hatcher had to face in the black community, however, came from members of his campaign organization who believed that he was not faithfully executing the objectives of the campaign. Specifically, complaints by Hatcher volunteers centered around the following issues First, many were bitter because they were not consulted on initial appointments to Hatcher's administration. Some of these persons had expected to receive appointments to positions in the Hatcher administration themselves but were bypassed; others merely wished to have a say in major appointments and were dismayed when persons they did not support were given key positions in the new administration without their consent. Second, many volunteers were disturbed by the fact that Hatcher did not take significant steps to remove his enemies from the city bureaucracy and replace them with his political allies. Third, and most important, many volunteers sharply criticized Hatcher for not using the office of mayor to build a power base in the black community. On this issue volunteers observed that Hatcher had neither established an ongoing political organization of his own nor attempted to destroy the machine organization in the black community. Volunteer members had hoped that the campaign organization would be transformed into a permanent political force working on a continuous basis to expand the influence of the black community in the political process. Hatcher and his advisers, however, vetoed the maintenance of the campaign organization as an instrument of power after the election. They contended that the organization was tired from the grueling campaign and needed a rest and that they were compelled by the rush of events to shift gears from electoral politics to administrative politics. Quizzed on this point a Hatcher aide told one of the authors:

> We don't have time to give the organization right now. We're struggling for our lives down here and if we don't produce, we won't need an organization. It would not be in our best interest to start right now. There are certain dynamics that have to be worked out. We've talked about this and we're waiting until the next election to get people involved again.[32]

Few of the black volunteers agreed with this approach. Most of them felt as if they had been used to place Hatcher in office and then arbitrarily cast aside.

The upshot of the decision to disband the campaign organization was to drive a substantial political wedge between Hatcher and many of his closest political allies. Dejected and disenchanted, a number of the volunteers vowed not to work in another campaign; others suggested that if they worked, they would do so only after extracting definite commitments from Hatcher in advance. The decision to disband the campaign organization in the black community left no effective political organization in the black community to challenge the influence of the black precinct organization. Consequently, the roots of the machine's power in the black community remained intact, making it nearly impossible for independent black candidates—even those with the support of the mayor—to successfully compete for major public offices.[33]

Lingering opposition to Stokes in the black community emanated fundamentally from two sources. Cleveland black nationalists continued to be a major thorn in the side of the Stokes administration. The chief complaint of the nationalists was that Stokes did not project the image of a relevant and committed black politician—that he was too much wedded to the system. As evidence, they cited the disproportionate number of white moderates and black conservatives appointed to key positions in the Stokes administration. They also pointed to the law and order orientation of the police department, and Stokes's own public attacks against hoodlumism in the black community. Tension between the Stokes administration and the black nationalists became very severe in the wake of Stokes's dismissal of Geraldine Williams as one of his administrative assistants. Many nationalists considered Miss Williams their only link to city hall.

Criticism of his administration by black nationalists was not a matter of small concern to Stokes; he was very cognizant of the fact that his credibility among this element of the black community might very well mean the difference between tranquillity and violent social unrest. To strenthen his rapport with black nationalist groups, Stokes agreed to participate in a nationalist-sponsored parade celebrating the anniversary of the Hough riots. Although the image of the mayor of Cleveland marching in a parade with black nationalists carrying rifles (which turned out to be fake) was shocking to many Clevelanders, this gesture by Stokes went a long way toward salvaging his reputation in the eyes of radical blacks who had tremendous influence in the black community. This bow in the direction of black nationalism was followed up with the allocation of Cleveland Now funds to black nationalist groups for community service programs, the appointment of Baxter Hill, a leading Black nationalist spokesman, to the community relations board, and the close monitoring and control of police action against black nationalist groups. These steps by Stokes eventually reaped huge benefits. After the assassination of Martin Luther King, Stokes was able to keep the lid on violence in Cleveland by calling on black nationalists to serve as agents of peace in the black community. Similarly, during the Glenville disorders black nationalists were among the most effective of the black leaders dispatched to the black community by Stokes to quell further violent upheavel. By the end of his first term, relations between Stokes and black nationalists had improved to the point that many nationalists were motivated to actively campaign for his reelection. Indeed, a number of nationalists by that time had become convinced that Stokes was not only a relevant and committed black leader but their best insurance against massive assaults against them by the police. Asked by an interviewer in 1969 what would happen if Stokes lost, one nationalist leader morbidly replied: "The police will open war on us. We'll catch hell."[34]

The other major source of opposition to the policies of the Stokes administration in the black community was middle-class blacks. One issue of tremendous concern to middle-class blacks was law and order. Many middle-class blacks frequently complained to Stokes about the ineffective protection they were receiving from the police department against black hoodlums who roamed the streets beating up people and breaking into their homes in the name of black nationalism. Councilman Leo Jackson was so enraged by the wave of black-on-black crime in his district that he led several demonstrations to city hall to demand that the police department upgrade its law enforcement activities in the black community.

The most intense criticism of the Stokes administration registered by the black middle-class, however, came from the citizens of Lee-Seville over the issue of public housing. As we have seen, despite a determined effort by Stokes to convince them that they had an obligation to open the doors of their community to low-income blacks, the overwhelming majority of Lee-Seville citizens remained adamantly opposed to Stokes's plan to locate a major public-housing development in their neighborhood.

Opposition in the white community also presented a host of political problems for the Stokes and Hatcher administrations. The election of a black mayor tends to inspire automatic hostility and resistance in the white community. This reaction by whites stems in part from the fact that the election of a black mayor means the reduction in white control over city government. Former mayors in Cleveland and Gary customarily catered to the special needs of white groups, giving to whites reassurance that city government was being run in their interest. The election of Stokes and Hatcher changed all of this. To their chagrin, white citizens who had always been first in line when benefits were distributed were now forced to stand back and watch the priorities of city government shift toward the black community. This shift in priorities, coupled with the natural inclination of whites to find the idea of a black mayor repulsive, served to make white opposition to the policies of the Stokes and Hatcher administrations virtually unavoidable.

Gary whites viewed Hatcher with an unusual degree of cynicism and suspicion because of his reputation as a black militant. Hatcher's ringing defense of black power in numerous speeches around the nation led many white citizens of Gary to the conclusion that he was the worst kind of black official—one who was supersensitive to the needs of blacks, to the detriment of whites. In this context it is interesting to note that a number of our white respondents in Gary suggested that they would readily accept a more moderate black as mayor, but were unalterably opposed to Hatcher because he had gone overboard in his advocacy of black causes. As evidence of the rampant bias of the Hatcher administration they pointed to the fact that nearly all the federal programs were established for the black community. At the same time, they charged that services by the city administration to the white community had declined to an all-time low. Specifically, they complained that under Hatcher, garbage collection in the white community had become erratic, streets and curbs had deteriorated, and fire protection had become substantially ineffective. White citizens also blamed the Hatcher administration for a sharp rise in street crime. They contended that the presence of a black man in the mayor's office had given blacks the impression they could do whatever they wished and get away with it. Letters to the *Post Tribune* frequently accused Hatcher of handcuffing the police and coddling black gang members through federally sponsored programs.

Unlike his relationship with the black community, Hatcher's relationship with the white community did not improve. To the contrary, the longer Hatcher remained in office, the more intolerable he became to a sizable proportion of the white electorate. By the end of his first year in office, Hatcher's relationship with the white community had reached such a low point that a serious campaign was underway to disannex predominantly white Glen Park from the rest of the city. The campaign for disannexation centered around the issues of law and order, improved services, a moderate tax rate, and protection of neighborhoods, jobs, and schools from black encroachment. Spearheading the drive was Gary Councilman Eugene Kirkland and state Senator Bernard Konrady, both of whom perceived the annexation issue as an excellent device for promoting their political careers at Hatcher's expense.[35]

Serious opposition to the Hatcher administration was exhibited not only by Gary's white citizens, but also by its white-dominated institutions. For example, Hatcher was at war with the white press in Gary from the day he stepped into office. The *Post-Tribune*, Gary's only daily newspaper, was extraordinarily harsh in its coverage of the Hatcher administration, playing up mistakes and underplaying important accomplishments. Hatcher did not find the response by the *Post-Tribune* to his administration either surprising or difficult to explain. In his view, the paper represented the very personification of a racist institution that refuses to accommodate itself to the reality of black mayoral leadership:

> Behind its [*Post-Tribune's*] criticism of me is the notion that a black man could not possibly be capable of running the city better than white men have been able to do. So they criticize me for being an incompetent administrator. . . . In any other city, if the mayor went to Washington and brought back millions of dollars in federal funds, he would be greeted at the airport with a brass band. Yet when I come home I am criticized by the local press for being out of the city too much, or for going around the country making black power speeches.[36]

Another major white institution that refused to reconcile itself to Hatcher's control over the mayor's office was the Lake County Democratic machine. Hatcher's tenure as mayor was marked by intense conflict between his administration and the regular Democratic organization. Hatcher was able to beat but not destroy the county machine. The survival of the black precinct organization in the black community after 1967 left the machine in an excellent position to continue to compete with Hatcher for black political support. In the 1970 Democratic primary, control over the black precinct organization in Gary by the machine resulted in the defeat of every candidate endorsed by Hatcher. Hatcher's political influence was successfully challenged by the machine again in 1971 when Dozier Allen defeated him in an intraparty contest for the chairmanship of the Gary Democratic organization. Allen ran for the party chairmanship with the solid backing of the county machine.

The Allen victory was a prelude to an all-out attempt by the machine to beat Hatcher in the 1971 mayoral primary. Tapped to run as the machine candidate in the 1971 primary was Dr. Alexander Williams, black county coroner and long-time member of the regular Democratic organization. The results of the 1971 mayoral primary were surprising given the substantial inroads the machine had previously made—or appeared to have made—into Hatcher's base of power in the black community. Hatcher won the 1971 primary by a comfortable margin of 13,908 votes. It is important to point out that Hatcher's victory in 1971 did not rest on an organized mobilization effort as in 1967 but upon his continuing personal popularity with rank-and-file black voters.[37] Apparently, leaders of the machine grossly overestimated the extent to which Hatcher's rapport with the black community had been damaged by his frequent clashes with his 1967 campaign volunteers and sundry other elements of the black political power structure. The overwhelming support for Hatcher by blacks in the 1971 mayoral primary (Hatcher received 90 percent of the black vote) clearly demonstrated the resiliency of his image in the black community as a strong, honest, progressive, and effective black administrator.

Contributing also in important ways to Hatcher's 1971 victory was the weak popular appeal of Dr. Alexander Williams in the black community. Running with the full force of the Lake County machine behind him, Williams was able to poll less than 9 percent of the black vote. Central to Williams's poor performance in the black community was his image as a racial moderate and a puppet of the white-controlled Lake County machine. Despite constant denial that he was a machine candidate, Williams could not exorcise from black minds the conviction that white machine bosses were calling the shots in his campaign and would exercise commanding influence in city government if he became mayor.[38]

During the first six months of his administration, Stokes's relationship with the white community—in comparison with Hatcher's—was fairly good. Stokes did not present as militant an image as Hatcher and thus was not viewed to be as much of a threat by rank-and-file white citizens. Moreover, a higher percentage of Stokes's cabinet was white, moderating to a large degree the impression of a black takeover. Stokes also went to greater lengths than Hatcher to win over large segments of the white community. He employed the concept of the town-hall meeting to move his entire cabinet into white neighborhoods for a series of face-to-face encounters with white citizens. These meetings served Stokes extremely well. Drawing on his famous wit and charm, Stokes was able to transform hostile white citizens into responsive admirers who competed with each other for handshakes with the mayor at the end of the evening. Stokes was able also to prove his courage by dueling with hecklers planted in the audience. Invariably the overriding impression that he created was one of fairness and genuine concern for the problems of all Cleveland citizens. As a result, he was able to significantly diminish the fears many whites had that a black mayor would be insensitive to the needs of the white community.

Stokes's relationship to the white community was strengthened considerably by the strong support he received from the white business establishment. Leaders of the Greater Cleveland Growth Association were among Stokes's closest advisers and political allies. Stokes relied upon these business leaders to not only spearhead major civic programs like Cleveland Now but to also intervene politically in his behalf to enhance his ability to compete with other important city and county institutions.[39]

Cleveland newspapers also helped to promote Stokes's acceptance in the white community. Both the *Plain Dealer* and the *Cleveland Press* were "cautiously supportive" of the Stokes administration. Although their treatment of some issues—such as the fight over public housing—was extremely damaging, the white Cleveland papers generally sought to defend Stokes against attacks from some of his most abrasive white critics. Both papers displayed considerable pride in the fact that Cleveland was governed by a black mayor, and consistently emphasized how well Stokes was managing to cope with the "handicap" of his blackness.

Stokes's relationship with the white community took a decisive turn for the worse after the July 1968 Glenville rebellion. Many whites had looked upon Stokes as a safety valve against unrest in the ghetto. Although not blaming Stokes directly for the Glenville uprising, few whites could hide their disappointment that a black mayor could not keep the black community under control. Feelings of disappointment turned to hostility when it was revealed that $10,000 in Cleveland Now funds had been awarded to Ahmed Evans to conduct a summer youth program and that part of these funds had been used to buy the weapons that had killed the three white policemen slain in the Glenville disturbance. After Glenville, Stokes was the object of bitter denunciation by white Cleveland policemen. These attacks were played up in banner headlines by the *Plain Dealer*. White extremists began coming out of the woodwork, espousing doctrines of racial hatred. One faction of George Wallace's American Independent Party started an abortive move to disannex the Westside from the rest of Cleveland. Many white Clevelanders began making plans to move to the suburbs; others who stayed in the central city remained profoundly suspicious of Stokes's cozy relationship to militant elements in the black community. These white attitudes dictated that Stokes make an all-out effort to sell himself again to the white community in the 1969 mayoral elections.[40]

Stokes's most serious political problems in the white community centered around his poor relations with the Cuyahoga County Democratic party organization. Relations between Stokes and county officials were strained to the breaking point by the 1967 mayoral primary. Rivalry between Stokes and party officials continued after the 1967 election, with the party chairman Porter seeking to combat what he viewed as efforts by Stokes to consolidate all power in the mayor's office. When Stokes announced for reelection in 1969 Porter first opposed him, and finally reluctantly acceded to county party endorsement of Stokes in the primary. As soon as the official party endorsement of Stokes was validated, Porter announced his resignation as party chairman. Dr. Samuel R. Geber succeeded Porter as acting county chairman. Reversing Porter's stand, Geber pressured county party officials and rank-and-file workers to campaign actively for all endorsed candidates, including Stokes.

The truce established between Stokes and the county party organization was short-lived. Reelected mayor by a comfortable margin, Stokes made the decision early in his second term to begin to vigorously press for representation and power for the black community in all major areas of Cuyahoga County politics. Stokes was particularly concerned about increasing black influence within the structure of the county Democratic organization, since blacks had been one of the prime contributors to party success, but had never received benefits commensurate with their contributions. To facilitate a concerted drive to wring concessions from party officials, Stokes joined with a number of prominent Cleveland black politicians to form the Twenty-first District Democratic Caucus. The caucus would serve as an independent force to mobilize black political resources with the view toward enhancing the bargaining power of the black community within the Democratic party. Congressman Louis Stokes, brother of Carl Stokes, was elected chairman of the caucus.

The caucus launched its first assault against the power structure of the county organization at the May 1970 county convention. Seeking to establish a firm foothold in the leadership hierarchy of the county organization, the caucus recommended the selection of the black Cleveland councilman George Forbes as vice-chairman of the County Central Committee. Forbes's selection was vigorously contested by the Cleveland city council president James Stanton who accused Forbes of maintaining unswerving loyalty to Mayor Stokes. As an alternative to Forbes, Stanton recommended Dr. Kenneth Clement, former Stokes campaign manager, who had become an arch foe of the Stokes administration. When the county convention met, Clement was elected vice-chairman. Stokes issued an immediate denunciation of the convention proceedings as a farce and an affront to the mayor of Cleveland because he was not consulted in the selection of party officials. Declaring his independence from the county organization, Stokes described himself as a "national Democrat" and said that in the future he would endorse candidates for public office as mayor of Cleveland not as a party official.

Following Stokes's lead, the Twenty-first District Caucus announced its formal withdrawal from the Cuyahoga County Democratic party. At a meeting held on 23 May, the caucus voted to forbid its members from holding any office in the Democratic party organization or accepting membership in its executive leadership. Further, the caucus pledged to enter its own slate of candidates for the November election. Announcement of the caucus slate in September sent shock waves through Cuyahoga County politics. Viewed previously as a satellite of the county party, the caucus struck a crucial blow for independence by endorsing ten Republicans along with a number of Democrats. To underscore the fact of independence, the caucus also announced that it was dropping the word "Democratic" from its name. County party officials were enraged by the endorsement of Republicans by the caucus and vowed to take revenge against Stokes, whom they held responsible for the action. Responding heatedly to the caucus action State Representative Anthony Russo declared: "I don't see how there can ever be a reconciliation with the party. I don't think Mayor Stokes wants to run for reelection next year with the party endorsement."[41] The most drastic reaction to the caucus came from Cleveland Congressman Charles A. Vanik, who announced that he was withdrawing his offer to recommend Louis Stokes to the powerful House Appropriations Committee because Stokes had lost his credentials as a Democrat in view of caucus endorsement of Republicans. Vanik's action had the effect of making the split between the caucus and the county organization permanent. Mayor Stokes announced that in light of Vanik's decision, he was closing off all discussions with party officials relative to the return of the Twenty-first District Caucus back to the Democratic party. In a strongly worded statement, the caucus echoed Stokes's position, declaring Vanik's actions as contemptible, and asserting that it would not be blackmailed into deserting its principles, organization, and unity. "The 21st District Caucus reaffirms its independence and rejects Mr. Vanik's conditions."[42]

Stokes's troubles with the county organization served to reinforce the growing feeling he had that he should not run for reelection in 1971. His revolt from the party organization virtually guaranteed that his reelection would be an uphill battle. As in 1967 and 1969, his election in 1971 would depend heavily on his ability to mobilize substantial support in the white community. However, this time, unlike 1969, there would be no major push by party officials to open the doors of ward clubs in the white community. Indeed, party regulations prohibited campaign activities at party meetings by nonendorsed candidates. Without substantial party support in the white community, Stokes's ability to pull enough votes out of the white community to win reelection was a major question mark.

Beyond electoral considerations was the larger question of whether or not the rewards of the mayorship in terms of concrete achievements were worth the efforts that would have to be summoned to win reelection. During his second term, Stokes found himself at war with practically every major political organization in city government, including the press, the city council, and disparate elements in the black community. And a number of searing battles still lay ahead. Rejection of a proposed tax increase by the voters had left the city in such desperate straits that a sizable proportion of the city bureaucracy would have to be laid off. Stokes did not relish the storm around the mayor's office that these necessary economies would produce.

These considerations weighed heavily on Stokes's mind as he contemplated his political future in the spring of 1971. His ultimate decision came as a shock to his friends and enemies alike. In April 1971 Stokes announced that he had decided not to run for reelection. The official reason given by Stokes for retiring was his desire to expand his political influence to the national level. Behind this public position stood the stark reality that Stokes had come to the conclusion, after months of soul-searching, that he had gone as far as he could as mayor of Cleveland. Having labored diligently for four years to bring about major reforms in city government, Stokes was discouraged by the results. Rather than endure the mental anguish, personal sacrifice, and physical dangers of mayor for two more years, without a reasonable prospect for making major improvements, Stokes decided to bow out.

It would have been highly uncharacteristic of Stokes to retire from politics altogether. Having stepped out of the 1971 race, Stokes assumed the role of back-stage manipulator. In the primary, he supported James M. Carney, who defeated the city council president Anthony J. Garofoli in the mayoral race. The general election witnessed the entrance of Arnold Pinkney, black school-board member, as an independent candidate for mayor running with the support of the Twenty-first District Caucus. Stokes made the interesting move of shifting his support in the general election from Carney to Pinkney. In a magazine article, Stokes explained the factors underlying this shift in his political support:

> I felt the city was entering a period when there could be no more change or movement; the need was for someone to hold what we had won until the mood changed and someone else came along to build on it. I wanted it to be a Black man. I sought out Arnold Pinkney, my former administrative assistant, who was then president of the School Board, and asked him to run.[43]

Despite an all-out effort in the black community, Stokes was not able to transfer his political prestige and popularity to Pinkney. To the surprise of many political observers, the 1971 mayoral election was won by the Republican candidate Ralph Perk. The key to Perk's victory was the overwhelming support he received

374 / Electing Black Mayors

374 / Electing Black Mayors

374 / Electing Black Mayors

in the white community. While whites were voting en bloc for Perk, blacks were splitting their votes between Pinkney and Carney. In contrast to Stokes's massive sweep of the black community, Pinkney was able to poll only 75 percent of the black vote. The other 25 percent was cast for Carney.

Pinkney's inglorious defeat in 1971 marked the end of Carl Stokes's career in Cleveland politics. Immediately after the election, Stokes hit the speaking circuit, seeking to develop a national constituency. His quest for national stature culminated at the 1972 National Black Political Convention, where furious efforts were made by Cleveland delegates to obtain convention endorsement of Stokes for president. This move was quickly deflected by a resolution passed by the convention not to endorse a candidate for president prior to the Democratic and Republican conventions.

The reelection of Richard Nixon as president in 1972 represented the final event in Stokes's political career. With all viable options in politics closed to him, Stokes decided to accept an offer to become anchor man of a local television news program in New York City. At the time Stokes departed for New York City, the political future of blacks in Cleveland appeared nearly as dim as in 1965, when Stokes suddenly emerged to shake the foundations of American urban politics.

EVALUATION OF THE STOKES AND HATCHER ADMINISTRATIONS

The trials and triumphs of the Stokes and Hatcher administrations discussed above point to both the possibilities and the limitations of the electoral process as an instrument of power for the black community. That the election of black mayors in Cleveland and Gary has made a difference in the lives of black citizens in these cities is beyond dispute. Reforms in the city bureaucracy introduced by Stokes and Hatcher produced substantial improvements in the housekeeping functions of city government. These improvements resulted in savings totaling millions of dollars in public funds.[44] Reforms of this sort laid the basis for a significant reordering of the priorities of city government. Stokes and Hatcher attempted more vigorously than had any previous mayors to harness available resources and direct them toward the alleviation of poverty and hopelessness in the black community.

In Cleveland, under Mayor Stokes, this vigorous search for resources resulted in the construction of an unprecedented number of public-housing units for the black poor, the establishment of day-care centers and health clinics in the black community, the generation of seed money to establish businesses owned and operated by blacks, and many other important benefits. Similarly, in Gary, under Mayor Hatcher, the first public housing was built since the Korean war; programs to attack problems in the areas of employment, drug abuse, and health were launched; and poverty funds previously centralized in the county were transferred into the economy of the central city. In both cities blacks were hired in significant numbers for the first time in supervisory and skilled jobs in city government. The entrance of blacks into the city bureaucracy in professional capacities resulted in the generation of millions of dollars in additional revenue for the black community. For example, before Stokes took office in Cleveland, few blacks were employed by the city government. Those who were on the city payroll usually held menial, low-paying positions. When Stokes took office, he made the establishment of an effective affirmative-action program to recruit talented minorities into city employment one of the priority goals of his administration. Over a period of four years he was able to dramatically reverse the pattern of black exclusion. During this period more than 270 minority individuals—most of them black —were hired in high-level, professional positions. The annual aggregate income of these new city employees was more than $3 million.[45] Similar programs were adopted in both cities to facilitate competitive bidding by black firms for city contracts. The resulting increase in the profits of black businesses had an appreciable affect on the social and economic condition of many blacks in Cleveland and Gary. In general, the economic benefits that Stokes and Hatcher were able to transfer to the black community had the effect of lifting many blacks into the middle class, and paving the way for the forging of new career opportunities for blacks with training, skill, and initiative.

Perhaps as important as the tangible benefits were the psychological rewards. The aggressive attempt by Stokes and Hatcher to root out the underlying causes of black poverty had the latent consequence of diminishing black distrust of city government. These efforts stood out as incontrovertible proof that a black mayor could be trusted not to forsake his race once he assumed office. Moreover, they provided impressive evidence that the black community could expect to receive greater sympathetic understanding from a black mayor than from a white mayor, irrespective of his ideological inclinations.

Stokes and Hatcher were also important symbols of black pride and achievement. Their political exploits were vicariously shared by masses of blacks who looked upon them as the quintessence of the successful and effective community leader. Feelings of racial pride produced by the election of black mayors tend to be especially strong among black youth. Commenting on this phenomenon one black respondent in Gary observed:

> Mayor Hatcher's election has taught black youngsters one important thing: the only thing standing between my being mayor or fire chief or city engineer or city attorney is education. If I can get the education I can get the job. The proof of the pudding is in the tasting. I don't believe my son can be president until I see a black president. I can't encourage my son to be [President] Johnson because Johnson is white. But I can encourage him to be Richard Hatcher because Hatcher is black—and we tried to get the blackest one we could find so white folks couldn't claim him.

Although the accomplishments of the Stokes and Hatcher administrations are undeniably important, they have not been enough to ignite the process of decolonization in the black community. One crucial aspect of such a process would be black control over major public and private institutions in the city and county, and the utilization of the resources of these institutions to place the management of social, economic, and political matters affecting the black community in black hands. No such change in the power position of the black community in Cleveland and Gary has begun to emerge. Nearly a decade after the first successful mass mobilization of blacks in the electoral process, the power structure of both cities remains overwhelmingly white. Few blacks own major businesses in the downtown area or play major roles in the operation of such establishments. Banks, department stores, automobile agencies, insurance companies, indeed all moneymaking institutions of great significance, are still managed and controlled by white suburbanites. In Gary, U.S. Steel stands as a corporate giant, absorbing the labor of the black community, despoiling the environment, and causing irreparable injury to health, yet beyond the effective economic and political control of the black city administration.[46] Consequently, blacks remain concentrated in semiskilled positions in the corporation, and major corporate profits flow out of Gary into the accounts of company officials in Pittsburgh and stockholders across America. The Cleveland Browns football team constitutes another corporate enterprise heavily dependent upon black labor. Yet black interest in the team is almost purely athletic not financial. Black participation in corporate profit-sharing—as in the case of U.S. Steel in Gary—is minuscule. Colonial economic relations remain fixed. Stokes did much to assist the development of small businesses in Cleveland; however, the larger imperative of black expansion into the corporate structure represented the kind of political issue that lay far beyond the competence of his administration.

In no area where substantial power to influence the distribution of resources in Cleveland and Gary resides are blacks adequately represented. Blacks in both cities are most heavily represented in city governments; but even in this area it is clear that black visibility greatly surpasses black power.[47]

Outside the central city, black representation and influence have not been significantly broadened by the election of black mayors in Cleveland and Gary. County government remains a sacred white preserve, and blacks continue to have only token representation (and practically no influence) at the state level. The impact of black power in the city has therefore been substantially diluted by countervailing powers exercised by whites in control of important state and county agencies.

Underlying the absence of adequate black representation and influence has been the failure of Stokes and Hatcher to institutionalize black power by building permanent bases of black political strength in the black community. Hatcher had a golden opportunity after the 1967 election to weld the black community into a cohesive political machine that could control elections and make demands on party officials for significant representation at all levels of the party structure. A calculated decision was made not to move in this direction; as a consequence, the black community remained unorganized for political purposes in the interim between elections.

The push by Stokes to consolidate power in the black community after the 1969 election is precisely the kind of effort that must be made if progress toward the institutionalization of black power is to be achieved. The Stokes experience serves to highlight the fact that this process will be fraught with tension and frustration. Party officials will not readily accede to demands by independent black political organizations like the Twenty-first District Caucus for representation and influence. The struggle for power is likely to be quite protracted, requiring a high degree of discipline and commitment on the part of black leaders and their constituents. It has been the absence of such sustained discipline and commitment that has rendered the Twenty-first District Caucus in Cleveland largely ineffective as an instrument of power in recent times, much of its potential diluted by internal feuding among the top leadership. It is hoped that future generations of black politicians will be able to avoid the pitfalls that have so shattered the black political movements begun so auspiciously in Cleveland and Gary in 1967.

1. This position is most often voiced by whites as an argument against extralegal black protest. Moderate and conservative black leaders have also warmly embraced the thesis of the primacy of electoral politics. Perhaps the most articulate moderate black spokesman on this point is Bayard Rustin who, in a widely read article published in 1965, called for the mobilization of the black vote in the following terms: "The urban Negro vote will grow in importance in the coming years. If there is anything positive in the spread of the ghetto, it is the potential political power bases thus created, and to realize this potential is one of the most challenging and urgent tasks before the civil rights movement. If the movement can wrest leadership of the ghetto vote from machines, it will have acquired an organized constitutency such as other major groups in our society now have." Bayard Rustin, "From Protest to Politics: The Future of Civil Rights Movement," in *Black Liberation Politics: A Reader*, ed. Edward Greer (Boston: Allyn and Bacon, Inc., 1971), p. 250. Black nationalists also generally include success at the ballot box as a crucial element in their program for community control and institutional reform. See, for example, Stokely Carmichael and Charles V. Hamilton, *Black Power* (New York: Vintage Books, 1967), chap. 2.

2. Quoted in *Newsweek*, 3 August 1970.

3. Raymond S. Franklin and Solomon Resnik, *The Political Economy of Racism* (New York: Holt, Rinehart and Winston, Inc., 1973), p. 211.

4. Ibid., p. 215.

5. For example, the political base established through the numerical concentration of blacks in central cities is now being seriously threatened by federal pressure for metropolitan government.

6. This issue eventually lead to the resignation of Hilbert Bradley, long-time civil rights activist, as Hatcher's city attorney.

7. *Cleveland Press*, 23 May 1968.

8. One solution to the problem of bureaucratic resistance, of course, is the substitution of black workers for white. In both Cleveland and Gary, however, changes in the racial composition of the city bureaucracy were stifled by civil service regulations as well as political considerations. Given the anxieties aroused in the white community by the 1967 mayoral elections, neither Stokes nor Hatcher believed he could afford to further alienate whites by attempting to remove white workers en masse from the city bureaucracy. Given the exclusion of blacks from the city bureaucracy in the past, a massive substitution of whites by blacks would have also meant a substantial reduction in the quality of city services until such time as blacks gained the necessary experience to perform their job assignments efficiently and effectively.

9. Specifically, White complained that he was not consulted until the last minute about legal aspects of a proposed utilities building on Lakeside Avenue. Further, he expressed dismay that he was not consulted on the appointment of a chief counsel nor informed of legal details surrounding a multimillion dollar agreement with the airlines for improving Cleveland Hopkins Airport.

10. *Cleveland Press*, 6 May 1969.

11. *Cleveland Plain Dealer*, 12 September 1969.

12. *Cleveland Press*, 3 February 1970.

13. In August 1968, six hundred members of the Cleveland Fraternal Order of Police passed a resolution calling for McManamon's resignation because of what they viewed as his mishandling of the Glenville incident.

14. The seven individuals and institutions on Stokes's list were: The Cleveland Council of Churches; the *Cleveland Call and Post*; the Friendly Inn Settlement House; Harllel Jones (leader of Afro-Set); Rev. Baxter Hill (director of Pride, Inc.); the Rev. Arthur Lemon (director, Cleveland Community Relations Board); and the United Committee to Combat Fascism.

15. *Cleveland Plain Dealer*, 29 July 1970.

16. For a complete listing of these officials and a brief description of the factors surrounding their departures, see the *Cleveland Plain Dealer*, 29 July 1970.

17. After a long and controversial trial, Evans was convicted and sentenced to death.

18. A black janitor in the building was later found dead.

19. *Cleveland Press*, 14 August 1968.

20. Louis H. Masotti and Jerome R. Corsi, *Shoot-Out in Cleveland* (New York, Frederick A. Praeger, 1969), p. 108.

21. As a case in point, in March 1969, the council vetoed administration legislation that would have greatly improved Gary's housing crisis by permitting private developers to build 590 low-cost housing units in the Miller area.

22. Marshal Frady, "Gary, Indiana," *Harper's*, August 1969, p. 39.

23. The solidarity of the white bloc was broken to some extent in 1970 when two white councilmen joined with eight blacks to form a rebel Democratic caucus within the council.

24. One of Stokes most vocal critics was black councilman Leo Jackson, representing Ward 24. Jackson frequently complained of the rising crime rate in the black community and chided Stokes for his tolerant attitude toward black militants.

25. To override a mayoral veto by two-thirds majority, white majority councilmen had to receive the assistance of members of the black minority. Under ordinary circumstances black councilmen were unwilling to join with the dominant white faction to override a Stokes veto. On the importance of Stokes's veto power, see Kenneth R. Greene, "Overt Issue Conflict on the Cleveland City Council: 1970-1971" (paper delivered at the annual meeting of the American Political Science Association, New Orleans, Louisiana, 1973), p. 12.

26. *Cleveland Press*, 14 May 1968.

27. Ibid., 17 June 1969.

28. *Cleveland Plain Dealer*, 26 June 1970.

29. Among the federal grants received by Hatcher in 1968 were $4 million to complete Gary's Midtown West urban renewal project, $4.8 million for the initiation of a renewal program in Gary's Small Farms area, and $1.3 million to establish a comprehensive model cities program.

30. See *Cleveland Press*, 27 November 1969.

31. This point is established firmly in our formal interviews and private conversations with blacks in Cleveland and Gary. For an assessment of Hatcher's popularity in the black community, see Sheldon Stryker, "The Urban Scene: Observations from Recent Research," address to the College of Arts and Sciences, Alumni Institute, Indiana University, 6 June 1969.

32. This unattributed quotation is derived from interviews conducted in Gary, Indiana, by the authors.

33. For a detailed discussion of the postelection breach between Hatcher and his campaign volunteers, see William E. Nelson, Jr., *Black Politics in Gary: Problems and Prospects* (Washington, D.C.: Joint Center for Political Studies, 1972).

34. Samuel Lubell, "Negroes are Proud of Stokes' Record," *Cleveland Press*, 17 October 1969.

35. The reaction of blacks to the Glen Park disannexation movement was mixed. Some responded angrily, considering it an insult that when a black mayor takes over whites make plans to separate from the city. Hatcher denounced the movement as a new "apartheid" and accused its leaders of "murdering" the city. Other blacks, however, took the position that if whites wanted to leave, blacks should let them—that Hatcher should not occupy himself attempting to pacify bigots wearing track shoes. Some even wryly suggested that if Glen Park separated, the city of Gary should disconnect the sewers at the border line and charge toll fees for Glen Park whites who would have to drive through the heart of the city to get to their jobs at U.S. Steel.

36. Interview with Mayor Richard G. Hatcher, 7 January 1969.

37. See Nelson, *Black Politics in Gary*, pp. 30-31.

38. This impression was greatly magnified by a rumor that spread through the black community that Williams had tried to withdraw from the race but was slapped and forbidden to do so by machine boss George Chacharis. Although the truth of the rumor was highly questionable, many blacks apparently believed it. Hatcher sought to capitalize on the rumor by promoting the campaign theme "unbought, unbossed, and unslapped."

39. Stokes in fact came to expect that the Growth Association would perform this function automatically. Thus when the Growth Association failed to become actively involved in his fight to establish public housing on Cleveland's Westside, Stokes wrote its president a letter upbraiding the organization for refusing to

"come to grips with the gut issues of the central city." See the *Cleveland Plain Dealer*, 28 July 1970.

40. Stokes was able to generate sufficient support in the white community to turn back strong challenges from "law and order" white candidates in the 1969 primary and general elections. A close analysis of the 1969 campaign clearly reveals, however, that much of Stokes's success in the white community was attributable to the official endorsement he received from the Cuyahoga County Democratic party.

41. *Cleveland Plain Dealer*, 29 September 1970.

42. *Cleveland Press*, 16 December 1970.

43. "Why Carl Stokes Quit Cleveland," *Ebony*, November 1973, p. 134.

44. For example, one newspaper account in 1970 suggested that reforms in bidding practices before the Gary Board of Works made by Hatcher had resulted in revenue savings of approximately $600,000 a year. See *Gary Post-Tribune*, 29 August 1970.

45. For a listing of these individuals, their job titles, and salaries, see the document published by the Stokes administration entitled, *Meaningful Minority Employment* (Cleveland: Office of the Mayor, 1971).

46. An interesting account of the autonomous position occupied by U.S. Steel in Gary is Edward Greer, "Limits of Black Mayoral Reform in Gary: Air Pollution and Corporate Power," paper delivered at the annual meeting of the American Political Science Association, New Orleans, Louisiana, 1973.

47. In Cleveland, the election of a conservative white mayor in 1971 has substantially reduced even the symbolic presence of blacks in major administrative positions in city government.

11
Conclusions and Lessons

The crucial lesson to be learned from the Cleveland and Gary experiences is that the election of a black mayor does not automatically mean that the colonized position of the black community will be significantly changed. Constraints placed on the administrative authority of black mayors by a host of economic, political, social, and psychological factors make it impossible for their administrations to effectively satisfy the quest for black liberation. That is, black mayors simply do not have the political power to insure that black people can attain well-paying and meaningful jobs, effective health care, decent shelter and food, liberating educational opportunities, cultural activities, and all the other dimensions of a life-style that would encourage the development rather than the oppression of black people. Consequently, strategies and the accompanying tactics for liberation must look beyond the election of black mayors.

Indeed, one of the significant findings of this study is that the election of black mayors and the subsequent increase of black administrators is a double-edged sword. On the one hand, the increase of black urban officials does have symbolic and substantive payoffs for ordinary black people. In some cases (but not all), it may help to have a black person who understands and can relate to black people administering urban services—particularly police services. In several cities black policemen, for example, have formed separate organizations to challenge the racism of the local police department. On the other hand, however, the increase of such black officials suggests that the general relationship of black communities to the larger society will shift from a colonial to neocolonial relationship. That is, that the historic relationships of economic, political, and sociocultural domination between white society and black society will continue, but the administrators of this fundamentally exploitative and oppressive association will change from whites to blacks.[1]

When Carl Stokes, for example, was confronted by a just rebellion in the black community of Cleveland he may have agonized more about how to handle the situation than former mayor Locher would have; but since the white community, the downtown business interests, the media, and the state and national governments expected him to control the rebellion, that is exactly what he did. His method was less repressive, but the basic point is that he did not support the rebellion of his people; he opposed it by using his position as mayor to restore law and order in Cleveland's black ghetto. Likewise, he used his mayoralty resources to end a strike by sanitation workers (who were mostly black workers) fighting for a decent wage during a period of runaway inflation because his institutional role was essentially that of a neocolonial administrator. Black mayors, urban renewal and housing officials, policemen, teachers, and social welfare workers may well include numerous sincere people who are vigorously attempting to serve the needs of the black community; however, it is apparent to us that the changing of personnel skin color in an unaltered value system and exploitative institutional structure can at best achieve only marginal changes. If basic changes concerning the life opportunities and quality of life for masses of black people are to be accomplished, then basic systemic changes must occur. The evidence of this study and everything else we have learned about American politics compels us to conclude that black liberation requires fundamental structural changes in the society as a whole.

A brief look at some of the economic constraints placed on Stokes and Hatcher can illustrate the point. From the perspective of the black community, both men were certainly vast improvements over the mayors they replaced. Yet, as we have seen, neither of them, despite incredible hard work and innovation, could significantly affect the level of unemployment and underemployment among blacks in Cleveland and Gary. They could not because the economic base of both communities continued to be controlled and influenced by national corporate elites who make their decisions on worldwide profit-making possibilities, not on what is good for the people of Cleveland and Gary. The large economic interests in Cleveland and Gary focused their attention on how to make more money in the future; they did not base their decisions on how to organize resources and technology to meet the material and social needs of all people in the community. As we have seen, within this framework of a profit-making economic system controlled by multimillionaires, black people have always been used (and continue to be used) as a source of cheap labor for, at first, southern plantation owners, and more recently, northern "plantation" (factory) owners. In both cases, blacks were and continue to be used as a means for wealthy people to increase their wealth—and as a means for pitting black workers against white workers; thus driving wages down, increasing competition for the available jobs, and stimulating racism between people. Historically, and at the present, black people have been at the bottom of this economic system, and, according to all the evidence we have, will remain there as long as the American economic system and the social system that accompanies it is based on profit-making rather than on meeting human needs. This conclusion has been reached in light of the fact that the less than one percent of the American population that controls the economy (and thus the lifeblood of every major urban center) has accumulated billions of dollars in profits from this colonial relationship with black communities and has historically proven itself unwilling to provide black people with full employment. The only time blacks have approached full-employment conditions in the history of this system has been during times of war when blacks have been expected to give their lives so that American economic elites may protect their international access to cheap labor, raw materials, and markets.[2] Indeed, as this is written (Winter, 1976), the national unemployment rate hovers around 8.5 percent (in reality it is higher),[3] and thousands of white workers at all levels of skill and formal education have joined the multitude of black unemployed and underemployed. This economy, as it is presently based, is simply not geared to provide black workers (and many white workers) with a job that can support a decent standard of living nor that can stimulate the creative capacities within people.[4] It is this fundamental fact that both Stokes and Hatcher were unable to overcome. They were forced to conduct their electoral campaigns and subsequent administrations in the existing political and economic framework and were unable in their own communities to successfully challenge the ownership and control of production and resources by the economic elites and their political allies.

This inability to attack the fundamental character of the economy and the political order was related to their reluctance to use the mayor's office and resources in an effective attack on white racism. Both Stokes and Hatcher took the position that they saw themselves as mayor for all people in their cities not just the mayor for black people. Their strategy for playing this role, however, did little to actually educate white people about their racism and thus to lay the basis for the elimination of social and economic inequality in American society. They both sought to resolve the common problems confronting black and white people in their cities by turning to the federal government to fund various kinds of urban reform programs. By pursuing this strategy they tended to reinforce the notion among both blacks and whites that their problems could be resolved within the present socioeconomic system by relying on the federal government as well as to continue the competition between the races for the limited urban reform resources that were available. They did not attempt to educate their constituents to the basic facts concerning the socioeconomic system nor to challenge white racism as a main foundation of that system. Instead of attempting to show white people how they are also oppressed by a socioeconomic system that dehumanizes people and why they should join black people in a common struggle against this system, Stokes and Hatcher fell into the trap of promising whites that their problems could also be solved by more federal programs. Because they lacked a correct perspective on the root causes of urban problems plaguing Cleveland and Gary, Stokes and Hatcher basically had no effective means for combating the white racism they encountered. Many white people in the city bureaucracy, the media, on the city council, in the Democratic and Republican parties, and in the neighborhoods did all they could to obstruct the efforts of the newly elected black mayors instead of supporting their leadership.

These people were no doubt attempting to protest the rather marginal material and psychological benefits they had carved out within the status quo and were determined to thwart what they perceived as a black power take over that would eliminate them from their positions to be replaced by blacks. To some extent this was the case. Given the fact that the economy in these cities was not expanding, the availability of jobs and thus money for housing, education, medical care, food, and so forth was on the decline, and thus competition between the races was intensified, it is not difficult to understand why whites would be threatened by the ascension of blacks to positions of power in the political system. Thus, instead of joining blacks in a common attack against the controllers of the economy, the whites in Cleveland and Gary acted in a way that most whites have acted historically in this country. That is, they sought to secure and protect their own economic slots regardless of the human cost to others and to blame people of color for their problems. Stokes and Hatcher did little to shift white people's focus from this outlook to an outlook that would challenge white racism and thus erode one of the main barriers that divides people. Because of this fact, the racial situation in both cities did not improve.

Our basic conclusion from this analysis, therefore, is that the effort for black liberation cannot be achieved within a societal framework that is based on economic exploitation and the racism that accompanies it. In our opinion, black people must devise a strategy and set of tactics that will move them in the direction of alternative economic and political arrangements in which they and all working people will *own* and *control* the economic and political resources in their communities and through them control the political and sociocultural dimensions of life.

The organizational manner in which these goals may be realized is currently a wide-open question deserving much debate and practical experience. Robert Allen, for example, has suggested that an independent black political party be established as a vanguard social, economic, and political institution in the ongoing struggle for black liberation. Such a party, according to Allen, "must devise a mixture of tactics to fit a variety of contingencies. . . . Tactical innovation should be the order of the day, and anything workable goes—depending on specific conditions and the relation of forces—from legal struggle, to electoral politics, to direct action campaigns, to force."[5]

Earl Ofari has cautioned that there can be no shortcut to fundamental change for blacks in this country. He calls for "patient organizing—away from the ruler's media—and class struggle" on the part of black people as a means for developing a "mass-based working class consciousness united against capitalism."[6] In order to develop such consciousness, Ofari suggests three consciousness-raising tactics that could be utilized in the present context:

> . . . the running of independent candidates in local elections to agitate for working class needs and spread radical ideas to a broader base of people; founding of unemployment councils to fight layoffs for jobs, increased social security, welfare, and workmen's compensation benefits; and a working class united front around inflation, layoffs, the wage-price freeze and other related issues.[7]

He suggests that within the united front, black workers should be in the position of leadership to counter middle-class domination and that "where white workers are involved, the obvious way to beat down racism is for black workers to educate through leadership and practice while keeping paramount a class perspective."[8]

The people who have given the most penetrating and careful thought to providing theoretical direction to the black struggle are James and Grace Boggs.[9] They have pointed out that black people must go far beyond spontaneous rebellion to achieve fundamental change. Their analysis of the world revolutionary process and the development of the black struggle within the United States makes clear that a key factor in a successful liberation struggle is the leadership of a revolutionary party. Such a party would help to mobilize masses of people around their own grievances, project a vision of a new social order that would solve their grievances, develop a cadre of leaders with whom people can identify, and devise programs "that will take the masses stage by stage to ever higher levels of political struggle, political consciousness, and actual control of power." The creation and development of such a party is a primary responsibility of black leaders, according to the Boggses.

Many writers on the black liberation struggle have included a consideration of local electoral politics as a tactic within the liberation process. Consequently, we believe that it is important to specify what we think are the key lessons of this study and other historical experiences as they relate to the issue of electoral politics as an instrument of change. Perhaps the first point that should be made is that there should not be any confusion concerning *electoral politics as a strategy for liberation versus electoral politics as a possible tactic among many tactics for liberation.* We feel that it is a basic mistake to view electoral politics as the main *strategy* for black liberation (strategy here meaning the key instrument or form of struggle for gaining political power to resolve the social problems confronting black people). In other words, we maintain that if all of the cities in the nation with a substantial black population had a black mayor, and that approximately 20 percent of all other local, state, and national elected offices were held by black people, life opportunities would be better for blacks, but they would still be in an oppressed neocolonial position in this society. We say this because the formula that argues for political equality within a capitalist-racist framework as the main route to black liberation ignores three crucial factors: (1) the historic and continued tension between the black middle class (those most likely to run for elected posts) and the black working and under class; (2) the continuing role of deep-seated racism in this society, which can not be overcome by voting; and (3) the high correlation between economic power and political power. Those with unusual wealth have enormous power within the American political system and can make extremely important decisions concerning the quality of life within any community without the consent of those who live and work there.[10] Our understanding of these three factors forces us to conclude that getting a "fair share representation" (which might include more than 20 percent for historical compensatory purposes) is not sufficient to insure that black people will gain community control over their own economic, political, and sociocultural environment.

Additionally, we think that it is important to be clear on the point that electoral politics cannot bring social, economic and political equality to black America. The fundamental difference between capitalism and socialism is that under capitalism a relatively small percentage of the population own and control the means for producing human amenities and through such economic control exercise inordinate political and social influence. Under democratic socialism (as we define it), the means of production would be communally owned; the social surplus would not go to profit-making individuals but into community services (schools, hospitals, housing, food stuffs, cultural events, and so forth); and people would be organized in real democratic structures so that they could participate in making such allocation decisions and all the other basic decisions which affect their life situation.

There is no historical evidence to suggest that such fundamental changes can be made through the voting process. We doubt that the owners of General Motors, ITT, Standard Oil, Chase-Manhattan, and so forth, would allow their wealth to be appropriated through popular elections without resorting to expanded police-state measures to forestall such change. In fact, the evidence points to the conclusion that American corporate elites and the people who work for them will do all in their power to protect their current status, including calling off elections at anytime or violently over-throwing duly elected governments. A few examples should suffice to support this point. During the "red scare" of the early 1920s, several socialists in the New York state legislature were expelled for not having supported World War I;[11] in 1955–56 the U.S. government under Eisenhower prevented elections in Viet Nam when it became apparent that Ho Chi Minh would gather about 80 percent of the vote; in the early 1960s, Julian Bond was denied his seat in the Georgia Legislature because of his color and politics; in Chile a duly elected government has been overthrown by a military coup supported by American corporations and the U.S. government. In recent years, thousands of Chileans have been killed, tortured, and imprisoned for supporting the administration of Salvadore Allende who was attempting to radically change the social, economic, and political system of Chile via the parlimentary system. In short, we feel that black people cannot afford to trust the rulers of this country to relinquish their control on the basis of elections. They are more likely to change "the rules of the game" than face defeat. Using electoral politics as the main strategy for liberation is a losing strategy and one that could be very costly in black lives.

What about local electoral politics as a tactic? We feel that this is a more knotty problem. As we understand the situation in early 1976, it is clear that both the government (Watergate) and corporations (the energy crisis and economic depression) are losing their grip on legitimacy in the eyes of many Americans. With the addition of these issues to the long list of crises that emerged in the 1960s, the very foundation of the American political economy and social life is in a state of decline. As this decline continues and political struggles intensify in this country, we expect that the past pattern of using black people as scapegoats and as targets of repression will increase. Support for this view can be drawn from the fact, for example, that in recent times the Black Panther Party in Oakland, California, has been raided by the police and eleven Panthers have been arrested for no apparent reason. Across the bay in San Francisco, the police were stopping young black males between 5'7" and 6'2" on the street, questioning them concerning the so-called Zebra murder cases, and issuing them pass-cards as though San Francisco were South Africa. In Boston thousands of whites have demonstrated and engaged in mob action against bussed black students. In Quincy, Massachusetts, the police have adopted the use of machine guns in unmarked cars; and in Seattle, the police have been issued dum-dum bullets, despite the united opposition of the entire Third World community to such action. We suspect that the political situation in America could become more reactionary as those in power attempt to retain their privileges and that the bulk of police-state tactics are most likely to be used against blacks and other Third World people. Although the election of a black mayor and other black officials is no guarantee against police repression, it is possible that black officeholders could help curb such developments. As we have indicated, black mayors do not have the power and resources to liberate black people; however, their presence in city hall could be used as a means for providing some protection and assistance for blacks using other means to move toward liberation.

With this basic advantage in mind, we would still like to call attention to the main shortcomings of using electoral politics as a tactic. We do not think that these shortcomings dictate that electoral politics should never be used. To the contrary, given the resources that reside in public positions that can only be obtained through electoral office, we believe that it would be unwise for black people not to attempt to place as many representatives of the black community as possible in these positions. Further, we recognize that the black vote can be a vital resource for influencing the decisions of public officials and turning public policy in the direction of the satisfaction of basic socioeconomic problems in the black community. Finally, the involvement of the black masses in electoral campaigns can serve as a pivotal mechanism for the forging of group unity and the arousal of political consciousness. These benefits notwithstanding, it is nevertheless essential that the following shortcomings of electoral politics as a tactic also be clearly recognized. First, utilizing a great deal of political energy to put a black person in the mayor's seat has the tendency to reinforce the erroneous notion that someone in a high governmental office will free black people instead of each person taking the responsibility for freeing him or herself and also making a contribution to total community freedom. Many black people in Cleveland and Gary made this psychological error and then were deeply disappointed when Hatcher and Stokes were unable to significantly improve the situation. The danger is that this kind of thinking could lead to political apathy (nothing works) instead of encouraging careful appraisal of the advantages and disadvantages of a particular tactic. As Boggs has noted, each person must be involved in the liberation process; to rely on a few leaders in high places would be to fail to take advantage of the tremendous desire and talent of all black people. In the struggle for liberation, we must look to each other, not to someone above us. The second shortcoming is that electoral politics includes the tendency of mobilizing people and their skills into a campaign organization that functions around election time but then usually falls into a dormant state thereafter. People who have learned to work together and have increased their skills through cooperative experience find that after the election there is little or no opportunity for them to continue their work; thus there is an inclination for the organization to fall apart. Since the struggle for liberation is a continuous process, organizational forms and operations should reflect that fact. If campaign organizations are to be built, then thought should be given to how they relate to on-going community organizations. Third, there is the consideration that the type of campaigns required are all-consuming. That is, if a serious effort is to be made to elect a black mayor, that effort will require virtually the total energy of the key participants. If people are deeply involved in an election campaign they will have little time left over for engaging in other kinds of organizing. Finally, an election campaign tends to focus the struggle around what happens in the voting booth rather than in the community and work places, thus reinforcing the establishment point of view that change can be brought about within the system instead of in the streets.

The history of black struggles in this country points to the opposite conclusion; to the extent that black people have made progress, that progress has been won in direct community and work-place action that went beyond the "legal" constraints of the political system as it is structured. In fact, such direct action makes an election effort possible by creating a more aroused and united community. It is doubtful that Stokes and Hatcher would have experienced the success that they did had it not been for the civil rights action and rebellions that occurred prior to their elections. In short, we feel that if local elections are to be used as a tactic, caution should be exercised in relying too heavily on electoral politics and the relation between electoral tactics and other tactics should be deeply investigated.

In considering other kinds of tactics it is important to take into account the characteristics of the opponent. According to our analysis, the main barriers to black liberation are white racism, the exploitative economic system of the United States, and the political and social features that accompany these two factors. Racism and economic exploitation not only relegate black people to a colonial position here but have similar consequences for other Third World people in Asia, Africa, and Latin America. Accordingly, it is to the advantage of black people in this country to forge linkages with and learn from the experiences of other people in the world who are struggling to win their freedom. In this sense, the resurgence of Pan-Africanism as an important philosophical and political issue in the black community may significantly enhance the prospects that meaningful alliances will be formed between blacks in the United States and blacks on the African continent. It is important for American black people to encourage alliances between progressive people throughout the world and those within the United States because they can lead to a many-sided front against the common enemy.

Similarly, we believe that the black liberation struggle in this country will strengthen its prospects of victory by forming linkages with other Third World communities within the United States and progressive white people who are struggling to overcome economic exploitation and racism and to build viable alternatives. If black (and white) liberation is to become a reality in the United States, it must be understood and fought for by millions of Americans, it cannot be won by a minority of the population, although a minority can play a key educational and leadership role. As Boggs has pointed out: "It has always been blacks who pioneered in rebelling against the system, now it is blacks who will pioneer in creating a new system."[12] And in this pioneering effort to build a more humanistic way of life, white people would do well to reexamine their own position in this society. Despite all the talk about "white ethnic" power in cities, most ordinary white workers have very little political power to control their lives and are economically marginal in the work world.[13] It is true that they are one step above most Third World people on the economic ladder, but that one step is much smaller than the numerous steps between most white workers and the multimillionaires who control the economy and government. It is in the interest of white people to unite with black people rather than allowing their historic racism to be used by the rulers of this country to divide the masses of people. Rather than oppose progressive black leadership in the cities, working-class white people must come to the understanding that they could learn much from black leadership. There can be no humane future for this country unless racism is overcome, and white people have the primary responsibility in eliminating this social disease.

The issues raised above are by no means exhaustive. Specific events will no doubt occur that will shape the struggles ahead, and black people will be called upon to utilize a wide variety of tactics to secure freedom and build a new social order for all human beings in this country.

Whatever form the struggle takes, it is important that lessons be drawn from past experience and much reflection be given to the current situation in the United States as the economy plunges into a deeper depression and the liberation struggles of people throughout the world gain strength. The second half of the 1970s and the 1980s promises to be a period of major upheaval within the United States and the world. Those who seek to provide leadership for the social changes pending must project ideas that will stimulate people to struggle for a more humane future, provide a workable program to guide the struggle, and build the necessary people's organizations that can lead these struggles. In all of these efforts the relationship between theory and practice is a never-ending process, and the election of black mayors is a "lesson-pregnant" development in this unfolding process.

1. For a more detailed development of this theme, see Robert Allen, *Black Awakening in Capitalist America* (Garden City, N.Y.: Doubleday, 1969).

2. For an incisive discussion of American imperialism, see Harry Mugdoff, *Imperialism* (New York: Monthly Review Press, 1969).

3. Federal unemployment statistics underestimate the number of unemployed people because they do not count workers who have been jobless for so long that they have stopped looking for work.

4. On the issue of alienated labor in capitalism, see Erich Fromm, *Marx's Concept of Man* (New York: F. Ungar Publishing Company, 1961).

5. Robert Allen, *Black Awakening in Capitalist America.*

6. Earl Ofari, "Marxism-Leninism: The Key to Black Liberation," *The Black Scholar* 4, no. 1, September 1972.

7. Ibid.

8. Ibid.

9. See particularly, James Boggs and Grace Boggs, *Revolution and Evolution in the Twentieth Century*; James Boggs, "Blacks in the Cities: Agenda for the Seventies," *The Black Scholar*, November-December, 1972; and James Boggs, *Racism and the Class Struggle* (New York: Monthly Review Press, 1970).

10. On this latter point, see Ralph Miliband, *The State in Capitalist Society* (New York: Basic Books, 1969); Michael Tanzer, *The Sick Society* (Chicago: Holt, Rinehart, and Winston, 1971); and Gabriel Kolko, *Wealth and Power in America* (New York: Praeger Publishing Co., 1962).

11. Sidney Lens, *Radicalism in America* (New York: Crowell Publishing Co., 1966).

12. James Boggs, "Blacks in the Cities: Agenda for the Seventies," *The Black Scholar*, November-December 1972, pp. 57–58.

13. For documentation of the economic marginality of white workers, see the essay by John Howard, "Public Policy and the Working Class," in *The Use and Abuse of Social Science*, ed. I. Horowitz (Brunswick, N.J.: Transaction Books, 1971).

Index